TIME

IN OUR TIME

TIME

*Memoir
of a Revolution*

SUSAN
BROWNMILLER

AURUM
PRESS

First published in Great Britain
2000 by Aurum Press Ltd
25 Bedford Avenue, London WC1B 3AT

All rights reserved. Published by arrangement with The Dial Press, an imprint of
The Bantam Dell Publishing Group, a division of Random House, Inc.

Design by Helene Berinsky

A catalogue record for this book is available from the British Library.

ISBN 1 85410 700 3

1 3 5 7 9 10 8 6 4 2
2000 2002 2004 2003 2001

Printed and bound in Great Britain by
MPG Books Ltd, Bodmin

Contents

IN OUR TIME

PROLOGUE

I WAS NOT THERE at the beginning. Few people were. And although I can speak with confidence of a beginning, of certain documented rebellions sparked by a handful of visionaries with stubborn courage, there were antecedents to those rebellions, and antecedents to the antecedents. This is how things happen in movements for social change, in revolutions. They start small and curiously, an unexpected flutter that is not without precedence, a barely observable ripple that heralds a return to the unfinished business of prior generations. If conditions are right, if the anger of enough people has reached the boiling point, the exploding passion can ignite a societal transformation. So it was with the Women's Liberation Movement in the latter half of the twentieth century.

As I said, I arrived a bit late. On a Thursday evening in September 1968, I walked with my friend Jan Goodman to a decrepit office building on Broadway and East Eleventh Street, in Manhattan, and took the creaking elevator to Room 412, a tiny suite that belonged during the day to the Southern Conference Education Fund.

Jan had been telling me, "They're talking about women," but I hadn't wanted to believe her, hoping that my activist days were behind me. In the four years since the two of us had gone to Mississippi to join the civil rights movement as summer volunteers, I'd redirected my energy into building my career. I was thirty-three, a reporter for *The*

Village Voice, a freelance contributor to the best glossy magazines, and a full-time network newswriter at ABC-TV, where I grappled in quiet frustration with my outsider status. I was militantly against the war in Vietnam, an unpopular stance in broadcast news, where journalists in those years seldom questioned their government's actions, but my political opinions weren't the problem. I was a woman in a defiantly male preserve of clacking typewriters and cranking moviolas, and some of my colleagues had made it plain from the outset that they didn't think I belonged there. In an antediluvian age before the routine deployment of female anchors and foreign correspondents, there was an abiding feeling that women didn't have a feel for hard news and breaking stories. They couldn't be trusted to handle a stopwatch or make a cool judgment. I was stealing the bread off the table of some decent, deserving guy trying to support his wife and kids. Not all my coworkers shared these prejudiced views, but even the friendly ones liked to remind me how lucky I was to be holding "a man's job."

Caroline Bird had coined a phrase for women like me that year in *Born Female: The High Cost of Keeping Women Down*. She called us "loophole women," the few exceptions in any field that men let in to prove they weren't barring everyone else. Loophole women inhabited a lonely niche and usually felt like oddballs. Even if we resisted the Freudian dictum that our career aspirations were unfeminine and unnatural, we bowed to the general assumption that the impulse to succeed at "a man's job" was a peculiar quirk in our individual psyches.

Imagine a world—or summon it back into memory—in which the Help Wanted columns were divided into Male for the jobs with a future, and Female for the dead-end positions; in which young, pretty, unmarried women with a taste for adventure were aggressively recruited to put on a uniform and trundle a meal cart down the aisle of an airplane ("Fly Me! I'm Carol!") but weren't allowed to train as pilots (or bus drivers, or railway conductors, or mechanics, or firefighters); in which a male-only admissions policy or infinitesimal quotas excluded the brightest and most talented female students from the finest law, medical, engineering, architecture, and veterinary schools in the nation; and where a teaching certificate or a nursing degree was "something to fall back on" if, heaven forfend, you didn't get married and have children. Imagine a time—or summon it back into memory—when a husband was required to countersign a wife's application for a credit card, a bank loan, or automobile insurance, when psychiatrists routinely located the cause of an unsatisfactory sex life in the frigid, castrating, ballbreaking female partner, when abortion was an illegal, back-alley procedure, when rape was the woman's fault, when nobody dared talk about the battery that went on behind closed doors, or could file a complaint about sexual harassment. And remember the hostile humor that reinforced the times: the endless supply of mother-in-law jokes, the farmer's daughter, the little old lady in tennis shoes, the bored receptionist filing her nails, the dumb blond stenographer perched on her boss's lap, the lecherous tycoon chasing his buxom secretary around the desk.

A revolution was brewing, but it took a visionary to notice. Betty Friedan had published *The Feminine Mystique* in 1963, defining the "problem that has no name." I'd read it in paperback a year later, around the time I went to Mississippi, and although Friedan had defined the problem largely in terms of bored, depressed, middle-class suburban housewives who downed too many pills and weren't making use of their excellent educations, I'd seen myself on every page. *The Feminine Mystique* changed my life.

A book by itself does not make a movement, as Friedan, an old warrior in progressive causes, knew full well. Demonstrating what we all came to respect as her uncanny prescience, Friedan founded the National Organization for Women in 1966. My Greenwich Village neighbor Jane Jacobs, author of *The Death and Life of Great American Cities*, a book of tremendous import, was on the list of prominent women she hoped to snare as charter members. Jacobs was involved with other concerns that season, but she showed her invitation to Jan and me. We immediately wrote to Friedan, proudly detailing our civil rights credentials and asking to join, but even prescience has blind spots. Her reply informed us that NOW was not soliciting general members; NOW was to be a select committee of professional women who would lobby Congress.

A year or so later NOW was ready to open its doors to a general dues-paying membership and local chapters. My colleague Marlene

Sanders, ABC's sole woman correspondent, was an early NOW recruit though a quiet one, muffled by the objectivity that newspeople are supposed to live by. She tried several times to enlist me, dropping flyers on my desk, but Friedan's earlier rebuff and my radical leanings made me think that NOW would be too clubwomanish for my taste.

Crisp and efficient, Marlene had worked her way up from local radio to anchor a five-minute broadcast at noon. *News with the Woman's Touch*, sponsored by Sweetheart Soap, was considered the pinnacle of success for a female. If Marlene were a man, the men used to joke, she'd be running the news division. I longed to be a correspondent, but "we already had a woman"—Marlene. I seethed in silence. So did others. The young men in the office, the ones holding entry-level jobs, had begun to let their hair grow long. One day a copy assistant came into work carrying a Dylan album and a bag of pot. Another lent me his dog-eared copy of *Peoples War, Peoples Army* by the North Vietnamese general Vo Nguyen Giap. A third young man wriggled out of the draft and moved in with me. I wore a "GENE MCCARTHY FOR PRESIDENT" button on my coat, journalist's neutrality be damned, and marched down Fifth Avenue against the war.

Still, I believed I could make a go of it as an upwardly mobile female middle-class striver. Sensing the winds of change, the fashion trendsetters from Courrèges to Carnaby Street were making it easier to be a woman. Lipstick color had lightened to a mere touch of gloss. Thanks to the wonders of Lycra, pantyhose and a bra slip had replaced wires, garters, and girdles, allowing me to breathe normally for the first time since high school. Wobbly heels, the bane of my existence, were "out" and flats were "in." Nails were permitted to be short and unpolished, hair didn't need to be teased and lacquered, the pantsuit had come into vogue, and skirts were completing their startling climb from below the knee to mid-thigh. I Pucci'd and Gucci'd and hung on the words of Eugenia Sheppard, the *Herald Tribune* fashion columnist intelligent women read daily for guidance, and kept hoping the camouflage would let me fit in.

With this background, and that wardrobe, I walked into Room 412, where a clutch of civil rights veterans and antiwar activists were talking about the universal oppression of women. The name of the group was

New York Radical Women. Two weeks earlier they'd staged the Miss America Protest, their first national action, unfurling a banner inside Convention Hall at Atlantic City that read WOMEN'S LIBERATION.

My old daybed had preceded me into the office suite. The year before I'd passed it on to Carol Hanisch, a young civil rights worker I'd gotten to know when she'd relocated to the city. When the women's talkfest had grown to the astonishing number of thirty, Carol had dragged the rickety Swedish modern sofa from her apartment to Room 412, where it gave me an instant sense of belonging as I entered the sea of blue jeans, long hair, and lipstick-free faces. Slightly put off by my careerist incarnation, Carol hadn't been sure that I'd get the idea of women's oppression. I got it smack in the face that very first night. Perhaps the revelation was not as great as the vision that struck Saul of Tarsus on the road to Damascus, but it was close.

It happened without warning. From a centrally located chair, a young woman whose name, I later learned, was Kathie Amatniek asked a simple question. The question, it turned out, was one of her favorites, a key to the process called consciousness-raising, a group exercise designed to unlock the door to collective truths unmediated by the opinions of men.

"When you think about having a child," Kathie asked, "do you want a boy or a girl?"

Oh brother, I thought, *this is naive.*

One by one, the assembled young women "went around the room." I got the impression that more than a few resented the topic or had exhausted their interest in it at previous meetings. In any event, a woman named Peggy Dobbins abruptly exclaimed, "I've already had a baby, Kathie. I gave birth while I was in college, because I didn't know how to get an abortion. I had a perfect little boy, and I had to give him away."

In the sudden hush, the next speaker picked up the theme. "I had a legal abortion in a city hospital. My parents paid two board-certified hospital psychiatrists to testify that I was too mentally unstable to bear a child. I wasn't mentally unstable, I just didn't want a baby, but all my life I'm going to carry that stigma."

A third woman told of her Mafia-protected abortion, a blindfolded trip by car to an unknown destination, a huge payment in cash, and a fee to the go-between; no questions, no names.

My turn was coming. *One* abortion? These young women barely out of college are talking about *one* abortion?

"I've had three illegal abortions, one in Cuba and two in Puerto Rico. The last one was a year ago. Jan, you're my best friend but I never told you. I wasn't sure what you'd think. What I want to say now is, I guess I'm lucky to be alive."

And with that, my eyes filled with tears. I could not go on. I was in no shape to mention that in my second unwanted pregnancy my luck almost ran out, how the Park Avenue gynecologist looked at me helplessly and said, "You're a resourceful person, ask around, you'll connect with someone," how in the month before I connected with the clinic in San Juan for a safe, surgical D & C, I'd been led on a wild-goose chase to Harlem, where a woman offered to do "a packing," your basic wire hanger procedure, how I'd taken a bus to Baltimore, where a nervous doctor in the basement of a row house waited till midnight before shooting me up with sodium pentathol (a truth serum, to flush out a possible police agent), had me sign three blank sheets of paper (he could fill in a statement or confession later if something went wrong), and then said he wanted to try a saline injection (he must have known it could kill me at under three months), how I'd fled from Baltimore still pregnant, running on survival instincts and running out of time, how I arrived in San Juan with a name on a scrap of paper, how I found Dr. Pardo, who showed me his trembling, arthritic hand, how I screamed that I wasn't going back to New York without an abortion, how he gave me directions to the San Turce clinic for poor women, how Dr. Manuel Otero Roque said brusquely, "Come back tonight with six hundred dollars," how I showed him my three hundred in traveler's checks, how he spat out, "Cash them," and how he saved my life.

That was my second abortion. By comparison the first and the third were a snap. The Park Avenue gynecologist had been right: I was a resourceful person. Driven by desperation, I'd been canny enough, and sufficiently solvent, to flee from dangerous back-alley procedures, and I'd been secretive after the fact. For instance, there was the employment application I'd needed to fill out for the personnel department after I'd been hired into the newsroom at ABC. Part of one page was divided down the middle, with one side labeled Male and the other Female. On the Male side there were questions about the applicant's draft status. On the Female side I read the following: "Date of last period? Have you ever had an illegal operation?" People find this intrusive line of questioning on an employment application hard to believe today, but given my record of illegality it is burned into my memory. Naturally I lied.

Saying "I've had three illegal abortions" aloud was my feminist baptism, my swift immersion in the power of sisterhood. A medical procedure I'd been forced to secure alone, shrouded in silence, was not "a personal problem" any more than the matter of my gender in the newsroom was "a personal problem." My solitary efforts to forge my own destiny were fragments of women's shared, hidden history, links to past and future generations, pieces of the puzzle called sexual oppression. The simple technique of consciousness-raising had brought my submerged truths to the surface, where I learned that I wasn't alone.

New York Radical Women in the fall of 1968 was filled with such stories. Women were reinventing themselves, a movement was being born. Before the year was out I had quit the safety net of my TV job for the marginal life of a feminist soldier. Diving into the swift current headfirst was a rash decision that I've never regretted. As Women's Liberation careened forward during the next decade, its clamorous demands and bold new thinking profoundly altered the contract between the sexes, not only in the United States, where the grievances and political theories first erupted, but in the farthest reaches of the world.

At its inception the women's movement appeared to have two distinct wings—the reformers of NOW and the radicals of Women's Liberation. NOW was a dues-paying membership organization that welcomed the participation of men; its organizational structure, with an elected national board and state divisions, was determinedly hierarchical. Women's Liberation, in name and spirit, sprang from the radical ferment of the civil rights, antiwar, and counterculture movements. Decentralized and antihierarchical, it functioned and flourished within an amorphous framework of small, ostensibly leaderless, usually short-lived groups (such as New York Radical Women) in which a male presence was unthinkable. NOW's commitment to equal opportunity in employment was its strong suit. The fast-beating heart of Women's Liberation was analysis and theory. As a general rule, NOW preferred to rely on traditional forms of protest: committees and picket lines, lawsuits and lobbying, while Women's Liberation broke new ground through theoretical papers, imaginative confrontations, and inventive direct action. The explosive creation of the antiviolence issues—rape, battery, incest and child molestation, sexual harassment—and later on, the controversial development of antipornography theory, belonged to the domain of Women's Liberation, as did the early surge of lesbian feminism and the rise of a vital, alternative feminist press.

Having offered this neatly compartmentalized overview, I must amend it to say that in the early seventies the formation of a NOW chapter in a small southern or midwestern city was a radical act, while in New York some of the era's most colorful, catalytic figures, Kate Millett, Ti-Grace Atkinson, Florynce Kennedy, Rita Mae Brown, and Shere Hite, started their feminist journeys as NOW volunteers. Moreover, the entire movement, radicals and reformers alike, was known generally as Women's Liberation or, slightingly, Women's Lib.

Thinking, organizing, speaking, writing, litigating, and raising money are among the components that propel a movement forward. By 1970 the women's movement had attracted a cadre of smart, knowing young lawyers and a legion of inventive law students, the first to be admitted to the great male academies. There was never a shortage of thinkers, organizers, speakers, and writers in Women's Liberation, but money was elusive, to say the least. Our movement steamed into the popular consciousness without a dime. In the late sixties its first manifestations, awkward, original, and totally surprising, were ignored by the media or treated with uncomprehending hostility and humor. Yet only a few years later the story of Women's Liberation had become *the* unfolding news event of the decade, the dissemination of feminist ideas through newspapers, magazines, books, and TV talk shows a political phenomenon unprecedented in history.

Our ideas of equality had gained popular acceptance. Heated arguments were erupting in the bedroom and on the street, at dinner parties, on tennis courts, and in public bars and bowling alleys. Liberation battles were being fought on the home front of people's private lives, at the workplace, on the college campus, inside the legal system up to the Supreme Court, and within the major political parties, labor unions, professional associations, and social clubs.

All these stories were reported as news, adding to the momentum, but paradoxically, as the movement grew in size and strength its diversity and healthy decentralization were slighted. The media's habitual use of a single individual to define or symbolize a political issue led to the increasing identification of feminism with a mere handful of visible authors and journalists, chiefly Friedan, Kate Millett, Germaine Greer, and Gloria Steinem, whose careers were inextricably entwined with the cause. These talented communicators, plus a few others—like Shere Hite, Marilyn French, and me—who broke into the public consciousness during the seventies by means of our books, were on average a generation older than the typical twenty-something activists whose radical impulses and bold perceptions were the revolution's driving force. Although it was seldom commented upon at the time, the age advantage, with its acquired skills and worldly savvy, that the feminist "stars" brought to the movement was one of its sources of tension, which is to say, feminism made its public figures as much as its public figures helped to make feminism, but recognition flowed solely in one direction. By 1972, Gloria Steinem had emerged as feminism's most articulate, effective spokesperson and leading iconographic figure, while *Ms.* magazine, the semi-mainstream publication she founded, assumed the role of feminism's popular voice.

As for myself, I had cast my lot early with the radical wing because I found it intellectually thrilling to be on the cutting edge of new thought and action, and also because radical activism suited my temperament. When *Against Our Will*, my book on rape, was published in 1975, I was anointed with my own portion of media fame, but I wasn't cut out for, and soon grew to dislike, its awesome demands, the peripatetic life of airports, speeches, sound bites, and public receptions. By then many of the original radical visionaries I had known, respected, and clashed with earlier in the decade were dispirited and inactive, and most had already lost what little name recognition they'd had, while a second generation of visionaries, building on the initial breakthrough, was pioneering issues undreamed of by the movement's founders. I continued to bridge the disparate worlds of movement organizer and author into the 1980s, the decade that marked radical feminism's decline.

All movements eventually wane and nobody likes to be reminded of past injustices when conditions improve. It is also true that the pell-mell rush of events that got us from there to here, a better place indeed, was poorly understood in its time, if only because it is nearly impossible to gain perspective on great social transformations while they are happening. I set out to write this memoir with a sense of urgency because I could see that much of the movement's story had already been lost or distorted. To fill the gaps in my own knowledge, I reached out to activists I'd known and worked with, and to many others I'd known of only by their reputations. It appeared that they all had been waiting for a historian's call and the chance to illuminate the record. Their voices are as important as mine; I treasure the role they played in Women's Liberation and am grateful for their memories and reflections.

The pages that follow, written from the partisan vantage point of a participant-observer, are my attempt to recapture a vivid piece of radical history that changed the world.

THE FOUNDERS

OF THE THOUSAND or so white volunteers who joined the southern civil rights struggle during the mid-sixties, at least half, including myself, were women. Many of us went on to found—or to play a major role in—the Women's Liberation Movement a few years later. History seldom offers parallels this tidy, but as it happened, many of the female abolitionists of the nineteenth century had gone on to organize for women's suffrage. These two vivid epochs were separated by more than a century, yet nearly identical forces applied. After fighting alongside men in a radical movement to correct a grievous wrong, the women then woke up and wondered, "What about us?"

Political organizers understand that the important thing about action is reaction. There you are, taking a stand, struggling to express a new idea, and the response is so powerful—positive or negative—that it reverberates into new responses and reactions, especially in you.

Lucretia Mott and Elizabeth Cady Stanton were part of the American delegation that traveled to London in 1840 for a World Anti-Slavery Convention. As the high-minded congress got under way, the male abolitionists voted not to accredit and seat the women. For ten days Mott and Stanton watched the proceedings from the visitors' gallery, where in mortification and anger they hatched the idea for a women's rights congress that became the historic Seneca Falls Convention of 1848.

White women in the civil rights movement during the 1960s were also consumed by a vision of equality, one that seemed important enough to risk our lives for. (And one white woman, Viola Liuzzo, did in fact lose her life to a sniper on the Selma-to-Montgomery March.) Although Martin Luther King, Jr., came to embody the stoic heroism of those hopeful years, to kids on the college campuses, and to many older radicals like me, SNCC, the Student Nonviolent Coordinating Committee, was the true cutting edge of the movement.

SNCC had been formed after the lunch-counter sit-ins in February 1960. And it was SNCC that sent out the call for an army of northern volunteers to help register black voters in Mississippi during the summer of 1964, the call to which so many white women responded. SNCC was cast in the image of a young, fearless black male, a concept that may have been necessary for its time, but its corollary was that women of both races were expected to occupy a lesser role.

Jan Goodman and I were in the second batch of volunteers for Mississippi Freedom Summer. No longer part of the student community from which SNCC drew most of its volunteers, I was by then a researcher at *Newsweek*, stuck in a dead-end job, and Jan was directing inner-city programs for the Girl Scouts. During our orientation session in Memphis, we were told that Meridian needed emergency workers. Michael Schwerner, the project director, James Chaney, a local organizer, and Andrew Goodman, a summer volunteer who hadn't had time to unpack his duffel, had just been murdered in nearby Neshoba County, although their bodies would not be found for another forty days. When no one else at the Memphis orientation session volunteered for Meridian, Jan and I accepted the assignment. Between us, we had a good ten years of organizing experience, hers in Democratic primaries and presidential campaigns, mine in CORE, the Congress of Racial Equality, and both of us together in voter registration drives in East Harlem. The night we arrived in Meridian, a field secretary called a meeting, asking to see the new volunteers. Proudly we raised our hands.

"Shit!" he exploded. "I asked for volunteers and they sent me white women."

On other projects in other Mississippi towns that summer, white women were reminded of their second-class status as movement workers through a variety of slights. Because of the southern white male's phobia about mixing the races, our presence in the volunteer army of integrationists was construed as an added danger to the movement's black men. I do not wish to underestimate this danger, but there will always be a germ of a reason, sound or unsound, behind the perpetuation of sexist practice. When antiwar activism got under way a year or so after Mississippi Freedom Summer, there was also a logical reason why women in that movement were relegated to second-class status: the draft for the war in Vietnam directly affected young men.

Women the world over are required to modify their behavior because of things that men fear and do.

SNCC was a "beloved community" to Mary King and Casey Hayden, an encompassing lifestyle dedicated to the perfection of moral virtue. They were among the first white women to have staff jobs in the Atlanta headquarters. Mary was the product of six generations of Virginia ministers on her father's side. Casey, from East Texas, entered student politics through the Christian ecumenical movement and helped to found Students for a Democratic Society (SDS), the primary force on the white New Left. She had married Tom Hayden but they were living apart.

The two women studied the French existentialists in their evening hours to broaden their understanding of theory and practice. When they'd exhausted Camus, they turned to Simone de Beauvoir. Certain passages in *The Second Sex* spoke to them so directly that they began pressing the book on others. Some people in the movement started grumbling that Mary and Casey were undisciplined sentimentalists "on a Freedom high."

In the fall of 1964, Mary and Casey wrote a position paper on women in SNCC that owed its inspiration partly to Beauvoir and partly to their experience in their movement work. "The average white person doesn't realize that he assumes he is superior," they wrote. "So too the average SNCC worker finds it difficult to discuss the woman problem because of the assumption of male superiority.

Assumptions of male superiority are as widespread and deep-rooted and as crippling to the woman as the assumptions of white supremacy are to the Negro."

Expecting ridicule, the two white women did not sign the paper they passed around that November at a staff retreat on the Mississippi coast. Thirty-seven manifestos and proposals had been prepared for the retreat at Waveland, and most were being ignored. A wrenching split within the organization was consuming everyone's energy.

One evening Stokely Carmichael and a few others took a welcome break down at the dock. Camping it up, he joked, "What is the position of women in SNCC? The position of women in SNCC is prone."

Alas for Stokely, his riff became nearly as famous as his later calls for Black Power. While language purists wondered if Carmichael had really meant "supine," his jest came to symbolize the collection of slights suffered by women in SNCC.

One year later Mary King and Casey Hayden gathered the courage to sign their names to an expanded version of their paper and mailed it to forty women activists against the Vietnam War. The second broadside recounted a list of movement grievances—who gets named project director? who sweeps the office floor? who takes the minutes? who speaks to the press?—before it concluded "Objectively, the chances seem nil that we could start a movement based on anything as distant to general American thought as a sex-caste system. Therefore, most of us will probably want to work full-time on problems such as war, poverty, race." King and Hayden titled their paper "A Kind of Memo."

Another year passed and "A Kind of Memo" found its way to a national SDS conference that convened at the University of Illinois in Champaign-Urbana two days after Christmas in 1966. Fifty women, a lot for that time, caucused in the school cafeteria to discuss it.

"Heather Booth and I were there," recalls Marilyn Webb, who would play a significant role in the founding of Women's Liberation in Washington D.C. "When the SNCC letter from Mary and Casey was read aloud, it precipitated a three-day marathon discussion about women in SDS. We'd been dealing with civil rights, with the Vietnam War, we'd been urging resistance to the draft with slogans like 'Women Say Yes to Men Who Say No'— that had been our mentality. This was one of the first conversations where we talked about what was happening with *us*. We ended up talking about everything, including our sexuality."

Community organizers trained by Saul Alinsky, who ran workshops and wrote primers on the principles of activism, Marilyn Webb and Heather Booth were soon to marry New Left leaders. They were to try as well to marry the new women's thinking to SDS. The political union, however, was not to be.

The following April, "A Kind of Memo" surfaced yet again, this time in *Liberation*, a leftist-pacifist magazine. Having served as catalysts, Mary King and Casey Hayden then retired from the fray. SNCC, their beloved community, no longer welcomed white participation. They had lost their political moorings. It would be characteristic of the emerging feminist movement that various women would surface for brief moments in leadership roles and then, exhausted by the effort, depart from the scene.

•   •   •

Nineteen sixty-seven was a panicky year. There were riots in the northern ghettos, calls for Black Power, falling bombs in Hanoi and Haiphong, a lottery for the draft, demos at local induction centers, and a gigantic March on Washington to End the War Now. China was in the throes of its Cultural Revolution, Che Guevara was dead in Bolivia, and the sudden explosion of dope, hard rock, longhaired hippies, and flower children seemed to catch everyone by surprise. Women on the left, affected by all these phenomena and more, were gathering in small, informal "rap" groups, study groups, and workshops to simply talk with one another.

In New York, Robin Morgan, a poet and a former child actress—she had played Dagmar in the early TV show *Mama*—heard Judith Duffett, a community activist, defend "A Kind of Memo" in a debate on radio station WBAI. She got on the telephone, trying to locate the rap group Duffett said was afloat in the city.

"I must confess," says Morgan, "that I went to Judith Duffett's Tuesday night discussion group with a double agenda. The subconscious agenda was *Oh my God, I need this*. The conscious agenda was *I'm a good leftist revolutionary woman; I'm going to give these women some real politics because they obviously don't know their Marxism and they don't have an economic take on their problems*. So I went to a meeting. And with what I now realize was extraordinarily touching bravery, we talked about our lives."

"Liberation" was in the air: Black Liberation, Third World Liberation. Vietnam and the draft dominated the national SDS convention in Ann Arbor that June, but standing out conspicuously among the scores of workshops was one called Women's Liberation, the earliest use on record of those soon-to-be-famous words. Elizabeth Sutherland, an editor in book publishing and a fundraiser for SNCC, and Jane Adams of the SDS staff helped get it going. Focusing on SDS, where men made policy and speeches while women stuffed envelopes and cooked dinner, they composed a resolution demanding "full participation in all aspects of movement work." To soften the blow for the women's male comrades, husbands, and lovers, Sutherland and Adams ended their exhortation—"Freedom Now!" with a conciliatory appeal: "We love you!"

Hoots and catcalls greeted the resolution when it was read to the full convention. *New Left Notes*, the SDS newsletter, mocked the women's rebellion in its next report with a cartoon of a leggy doll in polka-dot bloomers waving a placard that read WE WANT OUR RIGHTS & WE WANT THEM NOW!

Another nasty rebuke to the women occurred in Chicago over the Labor Day weekend, one that would push the new movement forward dramatically. Two thousand leftists had convened the National Conference for New Politics to discuss a third-party campaign for the 1968 elections. (Martin Luther King, Jr., and Benjamin Spock were bruited about as ideal running mates.) The National Conference for New Politics, an amalgam of the Old Left and the New, was bedeviled by chaos. A black minority forced through a resolution giving them 50 percent of the votes. Debates grew violent over Zionist imperialism and the Palestinian question. At a women's workshop chaired by Madlyn Murray O'Hair, the successful litigant in the Supreme Court's decision banning prayer in the public schools, the proposed topic for discussion was how women could organize other women more effectively against the war.

Antiwar work was not why Jo Freeman had come to the conference. Steeped in a family heritage of Democratic Party politics in Alabama, Freeman had been radicalized by the Berkeley Free Speech Movement in 1964. After working for Martin Luther King's Southern Christian Leadership Conference in Atlanta, she had transferred to SCLC's Chicago office, but that phase of her life was behind her. Like her namesake in *Little Women*, Jo was a stubborn, coltish, no-nonsense doer. She believed that the time was right for a feminist movement.

So did Shulamith Firestone, who was fed up with the galloping male egos in her left-wing Jewish youth group. The young woman called Shulie had shrugged off the Orthodox Judaism of her family back in St. Louis a few years before and was now studying painting at the Art Institute of Chicago. At five feet one inch tall, she gazed at all comers through owlish glasses, tossing the mane of dark hair that cascaded below her shoulders. Somewhere along the line, the studious, nearsighted yeshiva girl had transformed herself into a fearless dynamo—abrupt, impatient, grandiosely self-important, consumed by a feminist vision. She was twenty-two years old.

Neither Jo nor the other women at the Chicago conference could remember having seen Firestone at political gatherings before. She was an unidentified comet. Working together, Jo and Shulie turned O'Hair's workshop on its heels, ramming through a resolution to give women delegates 51 percent of the convention votes, to reflect the percentage of women in the general population.

The two insurrectionists headed for the mimeo room, where they commandeered a typewriter and stencils and worked through the night, adding and refining paragraphs: condemning the media for portraying women as stereotypic sex objects, calling for the overhaul of marriage, divorce, and property laws, demanding easy access to birth control information and the right to abortion.

Back at the main session, Jo ran down the aisles handing out copies of the resolution while Shulie charged to the podium. "Cool down, little girl," the session chairman told her. "We have more important things to talk about than women's problems."

"And *then*," says Jo Freeman, "a guy grabs the mike and says, Ladies and gentlemen, I'd like to speak to you about the most oppressed group in America today, the American Indian.'" So much for the resolution on women.

Days after the snub at the National Conference for New Politics, Jo Freeman hosted a meeting of angry women at her apartment. Shulie Firestone brought her kid sister Laya. Naomi Weisstein, Heather Booth, Amy Kesselman, and Fran Rominski, all from SDS, filled out the room. Soon more SDS women, Sue Munaker, Evie Goldfield, Vivian Rothstein, came aboard. They called themselves the West Side group because Jo Freeman lived on the West Side of Chicago. They were probably the first Women's Liberation group in the nation.

"We talked incessantly," Naomi Weisstein recalls. "We talked about our pain, we discovered our righteous anger. We talked about our orgasms, and then we felt guilty for talking about our orgasms. Shouldn't we be doing actions? After all, the New Left was about action. We talked about the contempt and hostility that we felt from the males on the New Left, and we talked about our inability to speak in public. Why had this happened? All of us had once been such feisty little suckers. But mostly we were exhilarated. We were ecstatic. We were ready to turn the world upside down."

Under Jo Freeman's editorship, the Chicagoans put out seven issues of a mimeographed national newsletter filled with short essays and reports on actions that was grandly titled *Voice of the Women's Liberation Movement*. Before its demise early in 1969, the *Voice of the Women's Liberation Movement* had eight hundred subscribers around the country.

"Other groups in Chicago were spinning off," Freeman recalls. "Rogers Park, which is north of Chicago, and Hyde Park, the university district. The word went out exceedingly fast in the New Left network. I give Heather Booth the credit. She had the connections, and she had the commitment."

Visiting friends at the University of Chicago that fall, Pam Allen had no idea that women were holding their own meetings until Sue Munaker, one of the West Siders, blurted it out in her presence. "I'm interested," Pam heard herself saying. "I can organize in New York."

A southerner from a churchgoing Republican family, Pam had worked for SNCC at Holly Springs during the Mississippi Freedom Summer. The following year she'd moved to New York and married Robert Allen, a black intellectual and writer. As the white half of an activist interracial couple, Pam was afraid she was losing her political compass. She felt unwelcome and useless in the growing black power movement that attracted her husband, and she was out of her element in the predominantly white antiwar movement focusing on the draft. She saw Women's Liberation in its small-group manifestation as crucial "free space" where she and other radical women could withdraw for a while and gain a perspective on their oppression.

Shulie Firestone was moving to New York as well, to paint and to organize. The Chicago women sent her off with a list of SDS contacts. Pam Allen had her own list and began making phone calls. At a regional SDS meeting on the Princeton campus, she recruited Bev Grant, a folksinger from Portland Oregon, and Anne Koedt, an artist and set designer who identified herself as an idealistic socialist and was a ten-year veteran of the left. Anne Koedt would soon write one of the germinal papers of the new movement.

"Nothing—*nothing*—could have stopped me," Koedt recalls. "I was already on fire with feelings that went deeper than any political feelings I had ever known before. But when I had tried to talk about women's oppression with my other political friends, they thought I was crazy. Some man actually had said to me, when I'd made a mild argument by today's standards, "Boy, somebody must have kicked you in the head when you were little!' There wasn't even a minimum language to begin a discussion in those days. But I knew what I wanted: a women's movement."

Reserved and contained—some called her aloof—Koedt was from Denmark. Her parents had been in the Resistance during the Second

World War, harboring Jews in their basement until the refugees could be ferried to Sweden. Her father, a photographer, had made fake passports for the Resistance leaders. Unlike most of the founders of Women's Liberation, Anne never developed a taste for open conflict.

New York's first Women's Liberation meeting was held at Pam Allen's Lower East Side apartment in November 1967 with Shulie and Pam, Anne Koedt, Bev Grant the folksinger and songwriter, Cathy Barrett from New Orleans, who did guerrilla street theater, and Minda Bikman, a nonpolitical friend of Shulie's from Chicago. "Somebody else was there, too, but I don't remember her name," laughs Pam Allen. "She spent the entire evening telling us why we shouldn't be meeting."

New York's preeminence as a movement hub would solidify a few weeks later when two civil rights veterans, Kathie Amatniek and Carol Hanisch, appeared. They had been introduced to Shulie by Bill Price, a *National Guardian* reporter who'd covered the National Conference for New Politics and taken note of the spitfire who hadn't gotten the floor. Amatniek and Hanisch would join Firestone and Koedt to become the leading visionaries and stubborn defenders of the radical feminist faith.

Amatniek was a Red Diaper Baby who had been taught that there was something called male chauvinism. "As a result I'd always been battling it individually, I'd been a feminist since the age of twelve. At fourteen I'd read Beauvoir—it was my mother's book, I'd thought it was about sex." At Radcliffe, Kathie had been one of the few women on the *Harvard Crimson*. During Mississippi Freedom Summer, she had "battled the housework issue" in SNCC's Batesville project. Kathie had close-cropped, honey-colored hair and a voice that was small and tenacious. Her propensity to do battle would reach legendary proportions inside the women's movement, where she would assume the nom de guerre of Kathie Sarachild the following year.

Carol Hanisch, an Iowa farmer's daughter, red-haired and freckled, had quit her job as a wire service reporter in Des Moines to join the church-sponsored Delta Ministry in Mississippi the year after Freedom Summer. Impressed by her heartland values, the

Southern Conference Education Fund asked her to manage their New York office. SCEF was an Old Left organization founded by Carl and Anne Braden of Louisville, Kentucky, who never dreamed that their young Iowa protégée would strike out on her own in a feminist direction.

"Kathie and I had been discussing a lot of personal stuff," says Hanisch, "like how men treated us. Basically, we wanted them to shape up. We'd reached the point of saying we needed a movement, but we hadn't reached the point of saying we were going to organize one. Then Shulie invited us to a meeting."

"It was at Anne Koedt's apartment," continues Amatniek. "I remember feeling—this is me, characteristically me—that I disagreed with practically everything that was getting said, but I was so grateful to them all for being there."

Another grateful recruit was Anne Forer, a pot-smoking Red Diaper Baby with a contagious giggle who taught kindergarten in Chelsea. "I vaguely knew that women were meeting, and then Bev Grant gave me Anne Koedt's address, so I showed up one Thursday evening. Up to that point my big problem with women was that I saw them as competition. I walked into that meeting and witnessed something different. Women were seeing their interests as one. It was the most wonderful thing that ever, ever happened."

Forer was to give a name to the women's process of "going around the room and rapping."

"In the Old Left," she explains, "they used to say that the workers don't know they're oppressed so we have to raise their consciousness. One night at a meeting I said, 'Would everybody please give me an example from their own life on how they experienced oppression as a woman? I need to hear it to raise my own consciousness.' Kathie was sitting behind me and the words rang in her mind. From then on she sort of made it an institution and called it consciousness-raising."

By January the New Yorkers, who'd named their group New York Radical Women, were plowing into their first action. The venue they chose was a march on Washington against the Vietnam War called by Women Strike for Peace. Founded in 1961 in response to nuclear testing, WSP was the largest, most important women's peace group in the country. Its middle-class members, liberals and leftists, wore hats and gloves, and fur coats if they had them, when they went out to picket, and stressed their roles as wives and mothers when they lobbyied their legislators.

On January 15, 1968, the opening day of Congress, five thousand women, named the Jeannette Rankin Brigade in honor of the congresswoman who had voted against both World Wars, marched around the Capitol with their antiwar banners. A rump group of thirty New York Radical Women led by Firestone, Koedt, and Amatniek marched with their own float, a papier-mâché coffin draped with a big streamer proclaiming THE DEATH OF TRADITIONAL WOMANHOOD. A second banner proclaimed DON'T CRY! RESIST!

The peace activists were appalled. So were several members of Chicago's West Side group. Stopping the Vietnam War was still the chief priority, wasn't it? New York's action, they howled, was petty, disloyal, divisive.

New York was deliberately upping the ante. They were telling the women of the left that if they were going to organize *as women*, they should talk about women's issues. It was time to end the pretense that they were some sort of ladies' auxiliary composed of wives, widows, girlfriends, and mothers.

Some women got it. Marching with friends, Rosalyn Baxandall, a rangy blond community activist with a ready grin, saw the streamer-bedecked coffin and the offbeat slogans, and fell into step behind the funeral cortege.

"What are you doing next?" she asked Amatniek.

Next was a confrontation at the Women Strike for Peace post-rally meeting. The New Yorkers walked in with their coffin, and Kathie spoke about women organizing as women as chairs scraped and some of the WSPs left the room.

"Sisterhood is powerful!" Amatniek cried.

"People were shocked," Carol Hanisch remembers.

On the train ride home Amatniek bumped into Gerda Lerner, who had been on the Jeannette Rankin Brigade march. The Austrian-born leftist historian had recently published *The Grimke Sisters from South*

Carolina, a biography of two abolitionist women. "You're making the same mistake as the nineteenth-century feminists," Lerner scolded. "You must not separate yourselves from the rest of the movement."

"Gerda Lerner got it," Amatniek says. "She understood exactly what we were doing, and she didn't like it one bit."

"I was very upset," Lerner admits. "Their disruption had seemed to me quite incomprehensible." She broke off her argument with Amatniek and moved down the aisle to engage the softspoken Anne Koedt. Koedt was also "incomprehensible," she recalls, but Lerner continued to probe and prod in her disputatious manner. "By the time I got off the train I was already quite impressed," she says, "and I was to learn how to work with these women."

Back in New York, Ros Baxandall volunteered her St. Marks Place apartment for a new round of meetings. "So we met at my apartment for maybe a month and a half before Carol Hanisch got us the SCEF office," Baxandall relates. "Maybe twenty or thirty people would come once a week. We even had an early split at my house. Several little splits. Joan Lester and Marilyn Lowen wanted to do something about cooperative child care. They didn't care about consciousness-raising, so they went off and did child care. And then Peggy Dobbins and some others wanted to talk about witches and matriarchy, that's what they wanted to explore. I was into everything. More and more meetings."

· · ·

A series of shuddering events in the first half of 1968 rocked the nation. January: The Tet Offensive in South Vietnam defied the predictions of General William Westmoreland. March: President Lyndon Baines Johnson, the focal point of antiwar rage, said he would not seek re-election. April: An assassin's bullet struck Martin Luther King, Jr., on the balcony of a Memphis motel; the black ghettos exploded. Days later, SDS students at Columbia barricaded themselves in the president's office while black students occupied a separate building. May: Leftist students went on strike, tearing up the cobblestones of Paris. June: Moments after his victory in the California primary, Robert Kennedy was murdered in the kitchen of a hotel in Los Angeles. Believers in Armageddon might think it had arrived.

Most women on the left were still focusing their activism on the Vietnam War, Black Power, and the November presidential elections. Some hurled themselves into the primaries on behalf of Senator Eugene McCarthy. Those who'd become implacable enemies of "the System" were to join in the plans, later termed the Chicago Conspiracy, to disrupt the Democratic National Convention.

Against this background of turmoil, and partially in response to it, the small groups of Women's Liberation were proliferating around the country and gaining momentum. The flash point had been their second-class status inside the New Left, but meeting in private without the intimidating presence of men had opened the floodgates to a host of larger dissatisfactions that none of them had dared to articulate before. Unaccustomed personal confessions led to intimate, searchingly honest discussions. The first generation of women to embrace the Pill, they were having more sex, and having it earlier, than any previous generation of American women, yet the mythic freedoms of sexual liberation were proving elusive. The Pill did not solve the problem of an unsatisfactory sex life, a thoughtless or promiscuous husband, an insensitive or clueless lover. Sexual liberation did not address the nuts-and-bolts reality of housework, pregnancy, abortion, child care. There were many issues to be resolved. Beyond the heady discourse at the weekly meetings, the rush of unaccustomed sisterhood, the thrill of newfound articulation, there was little agreement on how to proceed.

In Chicago, Heather Booth, Evie Goldfield, and Sue Munaker of the West Side group drafted a statement from a leftist perspective. Men were not the enemy, they insisted. Social institutions and conventional expectations constrained both sexes. The West Siders urged the new groups to leaflet women factory workers on Vietnam and women's low wages, to form consumer co-ops and child-care centers, to wage antiwar guerrilla theater in shopping malls, to canvass door-to-door and talk "to the wives of working-class men about the war, racism, and the presidential election." These actions, they said, would assuredly be liberating.

Not everyone agreed. Naomi Weisstein wanted to storm singles' bars to talk about sex roles, but on the night of her proposed action, Shulie Firestone's sister Laya was the only other West Sider who showed up. Vivian Rothstein, who had traveled to Hanoi in 1967 with Tom Hayden and a select delegation of SDS-ers, made sketches for a radical women's costume, a tunic, simple and cheap to make, that "would not be co-opted by the fashion industry." The idea didn't fly. Increasingly at odds with the male identified leftist faction, Jo Freeman continued to type mailing labels and cut stencils for the *Voice of Women's Liberation*. "The women in that early group," Freeman says, "were not only New Left, they were mostly the wives and girlfriends of New Left leaders. They weren't ready to break with men."

New York, however, continued to up the ante. In February, Anne Koedt, unaccustomed to speaking in public, summoned her nerve to challenge a citywide meeting of women on the left. The large room at the Free University on West Fourteenth Street was packed with ideologically warring "heavies" from various SDS factions whose rage had turned against the capitalist system. "It is not enough," Koedt said with quiet clarity, her eyes glued to her written speech, "to speak in terms of 'the System.' We must expose and eliminate the causes of *our* oppression."

Women's oppression was primary, Koedt insisted. It went deeper than economics and reached wider than the self-doubt and subordination they were experiencing in the male revolutionary movements. "We've never confronted men," she said. "We've never demanded that unless they give up their domination over us, we will not fight for their revolution. We've never fought the primary cause."

"What about Jackie Kennedy?" the leftists catcalled. "Is Jackie Kennedy oppressed?"

The following month Shulie Firestone addressed a small rally in support of the peripatetic abortion crusader Bill Baird, a messiah of birth control whose confrontations with the law were getting him arrested up and down the East Coast. "Let's not kid ourselves," she taunted the crowd. "It's not a distant aunt who faced this problem. We do, ourselves. And if by some accident any of you women have avoided it, you can count yourselves lucky or bless the Pill. Let's face it. Woman is scared shitless. She's been told to shut up and stop talking a million times. If she dares to have an opinion, she is called shrewish and opinionated. Even I—after months of work in Women's Liberation—had my fears about speaking openly for free abortion today. *God, what would my father think?*"

But the days of fear and cowardice were over, Shulie predicted. "Women are angry at last. So angry, Bill Baird, that we no longer need you to fight our fight."

Prodded by Firestone, New York Radical Women spent the spring of 1968 putting together its first collection of writings. Mimeographed and stapled, it bore the ambitious but accurate title *Notes from the First Year*. Nearly half of *Notes*, which sold for fifty cents to women and one dollar to men, consisted of transcribed material from consciousness-raising sessions and speeches. Shulie contributed an analysis of the nineteenth-century suffrage movement, its successes and failures, that ended with her exhortation "Put your own interests first, then proceed to make alliances with other oppressed groups."

Anne Koedt provided the dynamite and the fuse for *Notes* in an essay that took up one single-spaced page. She called her paper "The Myth of the Vaginal Orgasm."

In this landmark essay Koedt struck at the heart of young women's disappointments in the midst of a media-celebrated sexual revolution. The dread charge "frigidity" that psychoanalysts had thundered from the Freudian pulpit in the forties and fifties had destroyed the potential for sexual happiness of their mothers' generation, sending countless healthy, normal women to the analyst's couch. Determined not to suffer the same fate, the daughters had thrown themselves joyfully into sexual activity, claiming new freedoms promised by the Pill. But the Freudian dictum that "a mature climax" was achieved only through vaginal intercourse still ruled the day. Cowed by male authority as their mothers had been, the daughters had viewed their failure to reach vaginal orgasm as their own sorry fault. Even worse, they'd accepted the judgment that clitoral orgasms were "immature."

And here was Anne Koedt, synthesizing the newest scientific information in simple language, claiming there was only one kind of orgasm no matter how it was achieved, taking apart the old myths within a political framework of male sexual exploitation and female oppression. " 'Myth' threw people into a tizzy," Koedt recalls. "It never occurred to me that would happen. At the time I thought that sex was a less important concern than getting the left off our backs so we could have some space to do our own thinking."

Notes from the First Year was ready for distribution in June. Cindy Cisler designed the cover. Shulie rode herd on the job because she was leaving for Paris and wanted to take a copy to Simone de Beauvoir. The hoped-for meeting did not take place. Beauvoir had left Paris for *her* summer vacation, Anne Koedt recalls—"But she sent us a nice note later."

(*Notes from the First Year* would be followed by *Notes from the Second Year*, a thick, substantial newsprint edition. The third year's *Notes* was the last of the ambitious, historic project. By then a sea-swell of movement theorists had contracts with commercial publishers, and many of the *Notes* contributors were working on full-length books.)

• • •

A few days before Bobby Kennedy's assassination, an unstable hanger-on in Andy Warhol's circle had barged into the pop artist's New York loft and shot him in the stomach, claiming he had reneged on his promise to make her an underground star. Warhol was hospitalized in intensive care while the gunwoman, Valerie Solanas, was trundled to Bellevue for psychiatric observation.

A would-be writer and artist, Solanas had chosen extreme means to fulfill Warhol's assertion that everybody should have fifteen minutes of fame. Prior to the shooting she had been a familiar figure on downtown street corners, peddling a manifesto for her one-woman organization, the Society for Cutting Up Men. The SCUM Manifesto was the fulmination of a sadly disturbed woman who had somehow arrived at the truth that men held all of society's power. Solanas had written with chilling insanity, "A small handful of SCUM can take over the country within a year by systematically fucking up the system, selectively destroying property, and murder."

Solanas was represented at her pretrial hearing by Florynce

Kennedy, an irrepressible, eccentric, black activist lawyer who handled the Billie Holiday estate and lent herself freely to a rainbow of causes, from Betty Shabazz, the widow of Malcolm X, to NOW. Flo Kennedy was not the only NOW member to latch on to Solanas as a vivid symbol of woman's oppression. Ti-Grace Atkinson, Betty Friedan's slim and elegant choice for president of the New York chapter, summarily announced to the press that she would monitor the Solanas trial on NOW's behalf. NOW's membership immediately voted that she retract her statement.

Several months later Atkinson would cause another ruckus when she demanded that NOW revise its by-laws to have rotating leaders chosen by lot.

"She wanted chaos," explodes Dolores Alexander, who had quit her job as a reporter for *Newsday* to become NOW's first executive secretary.

"I was torn," admits Jacqui Ceballos, a Friedan loyalist who had left her husband after reading *The Feminine Mystique*. "I told Ti-Grace I'd vote for her resolution, but I would not leave NOW if she lost."

She lost. Atkinson walked out of NOW and announced she was forming a new organization.

•   •   •

Roxanne Dunbar, a doctoral student at UCLA, was among those who were very taken with Valerie Solanas. She was honeymooning in Mexico City when a small squib, "Superwoman Power Advocate Shoots Andy Warhol," appeared in an English-language paper. "I took it as a sign," Dunbar reminisces, "a mystical symbol that women were rising up in the United States."

Named Roxie by her father, a truck driver and tenant farmer, Dunbar had fled the rural poverty of western Oklahoma and settled in California with her husband and daughter. By 1968 she and her husband were divorced and he had remarried, taking custody of their child. "Those were confusing, volatile times," she relates. "The war was driving me crazy, the Panthers were getting killed in Berkeley, people were talking about Free Love. Now that sounded like a man's idea!" On impulse Dunbar had driven to Mexico with her current lover, found a justice of the peace to marry them, and was making plans for a honeymoon in Cuba.

"It was May," she recalls. "Students were rioting in Paris, and Mexico City was afire with demonstrators protesting the Olympics. Then, after a few weeks, comes this little story about Solanas. I imagined I had an obligation to start a movement for women. Boston had been a center for abolitionists and suffragists in the nineteenth century, so the idea came over me, 'I will go to Boston.'"

A stranger to the city and completely alone (her new husband had been left behind), Dunbar placed an ad for a women-only meeting in *Resist*, a publication of the New England draft resistance and sanctuary movement. It drew one response. Dana Densmore had been searching for like-minded souls.

Densmore, a volunteer draft counselor, was a second-generation radical. Her mother was the indomitable Donna Allen, a founder of Women Strike for Peace. "That January, I'd gotten a phone call from my mother," Densmore relates. "She'd uttered the magical words 'Women's Liberation. For us! It's begun.' In her usual enthusiasm Donna was skipping over the hard part, but the powerful conjuration just sizzled." Donna Allen and Dana Densmore were the first of several mother-daughter pairs to cast their lot with the new movement.

Roxanne and Dana composed a second ad and placed it in the *Avatar*, a countercultural paper run by Mel Lyman, a local guru with a large following in Boston. "Women!" the copy read. "Come and join us if you need to breathe."

Betsy Marple Mahoney, a white working-class mother from the South End, answered the call. Betsy had quit high school at seventeen to get married and have a child. Seven years later, when her husband began beating her, she'd gotten a divorce. The shy, stubborn, introspective young woman hung out at a leftist bookstore, reading whatever she could get her hands on, and flirted briefly with the Communist Party. "I was always analyzing things in my own head," she says, "and I didn't trust the left's attitude toward women. So I joined this new group, and we called ourselves the Female Liberation Front. Our second name, Cell 16, came later. We knew we were flying in the face of all leftist conventions, committing blasphemy of the first order." When Roxanne Dunbar proposed that their little group start putting their thoughts down on paper, Betsy named herself Betsy Luthuli, in honor of the famed African chieftan, for her first piece of writing. But quite soon she renamed herself Betsy Warrior, and Warrior she has remained ever since.

•   •   •

Although the war in Vietnam was still uppermost in her mind, Marilyn Webb in Washington, D.C., was afire with a vision of an autonomous women's movement within the New Left. "I saw it as coalition-building," she says. "I felt we could build a women's movement that would work together with the antiwar and civil rights movements. Coalitions had already been built, mainly around the war, for the marches on Washington, and I saw women as yet another constituency, *my* constituency. At that point I did not see the need for a completely separate movement because I believed that the men I knew would be supportive of coalition-building, especially if you organized your other constituency to help with a range of broad-based issues. You know, "We have our issues, but we also have other issues."

Webb riffled through her Rolodex for the phone numbers of activist women, putting out feelers for a national conference that would address the new constituency's concerns. Would key women in several cities like to convene in the Washington vicinity for an August weekend? With Dee Ann Pappas, who'd begun a women's group in Baltimore, she booked a Friends meetinghouse and school in Sandy Springs, Maryland, a pastoral suburb of D.C. with a Quaker history.

"Hi all," Webb's cheery last-minute instructions began. "This meeting should not be seen as one which comes out with a set program or structure. Hopefully we can come away with an idea of where we're at and where we have to begin moving towards."

Two key SDS women declined her invitation. One was Bernardine Dohrn, a law school graduate in Chicago, soon to be the interorganizational secretary of SDS, and later a founder of Weatherman. Famous for her leather miniskirts and plunging necklines, Dohrn had tried her hand at a women's strategy paper, "The Look Is You," after a mocking article on the fledgling movement appeared in *Ramparts*, the slick leftist magazine. But the siren of SDS wasn't interested in leaving what she believed to be the main arena. Another no came from Cathy Wilkerson in Washington, an SDS-er from an upper-class background (her father owned radio stations) whose favorite putdown was "How bourgeois can you get?" Dohrn and Wilkerson were careening on another course, one that would ultimately wreck SDS in the name of violence.

Last-minute confirmations for Sandy Springs came from some women who weren't on Marilyn Webb's list but who had heard about it on the movement grapevine. Roxanne Dunbar called to say that she and Dana Densmore would be coming from Boston. Sara Evans of SDS was coming from Duke University in North Carolina. Judith Brown and Beverly Jones from the University of Florida in Gainesville were preparing a strategy paper, and they were bringing an eighteen-year-old student, Carol Giardina. Toronto would be represented, and so would Detroit and Pittsburgh. Two, possibly three, groups with ideological differences were coming from New York. Baltimore and Washington promised to bring food for the weekend. San Francisco and Los Angeles struck out. Chicago's West Siders pooled their money to send Sue Munaker and Fran Rominski; Jo Freeman hitchhiked east on her own.

Ultimately only twenty conferees attended the Sandy Springs conference, but their volubility lasted all weekend. Agreement was harder to come by. Some women quoted Beauvoir, some quoted Friedan; others expounded on Vietnam and the Black Panthers. On Saturday morning the Gainesville theorists, Judith Brown and Beverly Jones, respected activists in the southern organizing branch of SDS, presented their paper, "Toward a Female Liberation Movement." They asserted that the enemy "at this time" was man, not capitalism, and urged that women put women's issues first. The heretical argument found few allies besides Carol Hanisch and Kathie Amatniek of New York. "It felt like us against the world," Hanisch recalls.

Marilyn Webb shuddered when Roxanne Dunbar, in a miniskirt and combat boots, read portions of The SCUM Manifesto aloud. "I'd never heard of Valerie Solanas. I thought the stuff was completely off the wall. Roxanne said, 'I'm not advocating you should go out and shoot men, but you must see that metaphorically she was standing up for herself as a woman.' People started picking up on it. And I was thinking, *This is a complete disaster*."

Sunday's anguished session on how to attract black women to a bigger, more comprehensive meeting in November was mired in frustration. Everyone in the room felt the absence of black women keenly, but the realists argued that aggressive recruitment was doomed.

On a reel-to-reel tape of the meeting, which has been preserved, one can hear loud cries of racism, humble apologies, painful explanations. Someone suggested trying to contact Kathleen Cleaver, wife of the Black Panthers' Minister of Information. Someone else replied that the Panther women would not take a step without their men.

"It's absolutely essential," insisted a speaker, "that we have a militant Black Power woman in on the formation of our ideology. It's for our own good that we need it."

"Black militant women are into very different things now," someone retorted. "I don't understand how if you're women and your concentration is on women, why you are just picking black militant women as opposed to all kinds of women with different ideologies. Why don't we have Women Strike for Peace, the NOW women, Vietnamese, Cubans . . . ?"

"Black women hold the cards on oppression, they hold the cards on being shot down in every single way, and they let white women know that. I don't want to go to another conference just to hear a black militant woman tell me she is more oppressed than I am and what am I going to do about it."

"This group could expand and expand and be essentially all white, that is a real possibility."

"If that happens, our ideology will be wrong."

"The Panther women won't come. Panthers don't speak to whites on policy matters, they negotiate with whites only on very strategic situations. The women would be killed if they came to our conference."

Roxanne Dunbar suggested trying to get in touch with Flo Kennedy, the New York lawyer in NOW who'd been drawn to the case of Valerie Solanas.

It is fashionable today to criticize the women's movement for being white and middle class from its inception, yet no movement agonized more, or flailed itself harder, over its failure to attract vast numbers of women of color. As early as January 1968, just before she left New York to resettle in San Francisco, Pam Allen had circulated her "Memo to My White Sisters," a plea and a warning that unless the new movement reached beyond itself "to make alliances among poor black women," and with underprivileged women everywhere, "we will lose our chance of finding our humanity."

Belief in human perfectibility was the chief driving force among the Women's Liberation founders. Horrified by the specter of an all-white movement, multicause utopians like Pam Allen would criticize, exhort, and berate, and eventually become disaffected. Feminist visionaries like Shulie Firestone and Kathie Amatniek, Carol Hanisch and Anne Koedt, would forge a new path, acting on the necessity to wrench free from this paralyzing, no-win debate.

"There were so few of us then who even wanted to call ourselves feminists," remembers Anne Koedt. "I realize now how badly it could have gone if we hadn't broken loose. That was the thrilling thing about Kathie and Shulie—they were so cleanly feminist. I include myself in this small group as well. We didn't feel we had to apologize all the time when the leftists talked about Vietnamese women or black women or poor women. Of course we cared about all of those women, but we wanted to care in the context of feminism."

During the life of the movement, the flagellation that took place at Sandy Springs would repeat itself periodically. It was reinforced by the belief, born of feminine insecurity, that middle-class white women had no right to make any demands for themselves, or to achieve something of political importance on their own. Black women did come into the movement singly, and sometimes, although rarely, they came in groups. Burdened by two distinct forms of oppression—three, when the voices of black lesbian feminists began to be heard—they never forgot their divided loyalties, and how could they?

Criticism is easy; working for specific goals in an imperfect, complicated world is hard. The failure to attract poor black women, or poor Hispanic women, or "ghetto women," or "welfare women," would be used as a club against Women's Liberation by its critics with numbing consistency for the next thirty years. Yet no other movement in our lifetime achieved such broad-based societal changes that cut across so many class and racial lines.

AN INDEPENDENT MOVEMENT

ON THE RIDE HOME from Sandy Springs, Carol Hanisch presented her idea to Kathie Amatniek and Cindy Cisler. The leftist women had called them self-indulgent for sitting around doing consciousness-raising while people were dying in the ghettos and getting killed in Vietnam. She knew their chief task was to develop an analysis of women's oppression, but it was time for an action, something brave and audacious to put Women's Liberation on the map. She'd been thinking about the Miss America Pageant in Atlantic City.

"I'd always watched the contest as a child," Hanisch reminisces. "With new feminist eyes it suddenly clicked that Miss America was a very oppressive thing—all those women parading around in bathing suits, being judged for their beauty. So we took it back to the group in New York. The biggest resistance was the fear that some people wouldn't take it seriously; they might think that protesting Miss America was a silly women's action. But then we started doing consciousness-raising, and everybody turned out to have strong feelings—maybe not about Miss America specifically, but certainly about standards of beauty. So we sort of threw ourselves into it."

No one threw herself into it harder than Robin Morgan, who had begun to attend meetings of New York Radical Women. A poet married to a poet, the flamboyant, bisexual Kenneth Pitchford, Morgan thrived on the theatrical confrontations pioneered by the Yippies, the

New Left pranksters led by Abbie Hoffman and Jerry Rubin. She was a savvy organizer who could fire up the troops, run off the flyers, get the police permits, order the buses, and alert the press.

"Atlantic City and Chicago happened within one week," Morgan recalls in movement shorthand.

Atlantic City was the Miss America protest of September 7, 1968. Chicago was the assault on Mayor Daley's city by ten thousand radicals during the Democratic National Convention, August 25–30. Robin told the Yippie steering committee she would not be available for Chicago.

"They looked at me like I landed from nowhere, not even Mars, and said, 'You've got to be kidding, the revolution is going to start in Chicago.' And I said, 'No, the revolution is going to start in Atlantic City.'" Then she pulled together the women she was close to, Peggy Dobbins, Judith Duffett, Barbara Kaminsky, Lynn Laredo, Florika Romatien, Naomi Jaffe, Adite Kroll, and went into high gear.

"Miss America was perfect for us lefty Women's Liberationists," Morgan explains. "Made to order. She touched capitalism, militarism, racism, and sexism, all in one fell swoop. Capitalism because they used her to sell the sponsors' products, militarism because she went off to entertain the troops, racism because there had never been a black Miss America at that point, and clearly she was objectified as a woman."

Lindsy Van Gelder was a cub reporter at the *New York Post* when the city editor tossed Morgan's "No More Miss America" press release on her desk.

"It said 'women reporters only,'" Van Gelder recalls. "The city desk thought this could be a funny story. I was writing a lot of funny stories as well as general news at the time. This is very difficult to explain to my daughters, and to younger women who are my friends, but in those days we didn't have a context to think about Miss America. We weren't even using the word 'feminism' yet. Miss America was a sacred cow, the kind of thing that women were supposed to aspire to. It made perfect sense that anybody who would be protesting Miss America had to be a kook. So I set off to interview Robin Morgan."

Midway through the interview, Van Gelder revised her assumptions. "The original press release was strident and rhetoric-filled, the way that many things were in that era, but Robin in person exuded an intelligence that was literary. She was very good at making links with other political movements, with the antiracist and antiwar struggles. I also recognized her from *Mama*, but I thought it wouldn't be cool to bring that up till the end of our conversation. So I came back to the *Post* with what I thought was a serious political story about a serious new movement, but the city desk still wanted 'funny.' So I complied. This was how the term 'bra burner' got coined."

Robin had mused about a Freedom Bonfire, in which the oppressive paraphernalia of femininity—girdles, bras, eyelash curlers, and copies of *Playboy* and the *Ladies' Home Journal*—would be consigned to flames on the famous old boardwalk. Brightening her first-paragraph lead, Van Gelder composed the fateful words "Lighting a match to a draft card has become a standard gambit of protest groups in recent years, but something new is due to go up in flames this Saturday. Would you believe a bra burning?"

The *Post* story, "Bra Burners & Miss America," ran the next day. "Robin was not listed in the phone book," Van Gelder relates, "so there I was, sitting at the city desk, getting inundated with calls from all over the universe from people who wanted to talk to Robin Morgan."

"Lindsy thought she was doing us a favor," Morgan explains. "What happened was that before we even hit the boardwalk, our permit was revoked. I had split my ass to get the damned permit. So I went back to the police and said, 'We're *not* going to have fires, we're going to have a Freedom Trash Can. We're going to *throw* bras into it. Nobody talked about a fire—where did this idea come from? We're not burning anything.' But that's where it got started, before the demonstration."

"And in fact," Van Gelder says, "they never burned their bras because of the fire laws in Atlantic City. But the term became history. I shudder to think that will be my epitaph—*She invented bra burning*."

"But we got a good press turnout," says Morgan, "because of Lindsy Van Gelder's piece in the *Post*."

"It was a gorgeous day," recalls Jacqui Ceballos, a divorced mother with four children who was one of the mainstays in New York NOW. "Sunny, perfect. Sometimes you don't forget the weather. At 9 A.M. the buses were lined up in Union Square. I think I was the only NOW member to get onboard. They handed out these song sheets, so we sang all the way: 'Ain't she sweet, making profits off her meat. Beauty sells she's told so she's out pluggin' it. Ain't she sweet?'"

"I wrote those lyrics!" exclaims folksinger Bev Grant. "I also was there to shoot the demo for Newsreel and Liberation News Service."

"Martin, my husband, drove a bunch of us down," says Alix Kates Shulman, then a thirty-six-year-old housewife and mother. "I never told Martin, but we needed to buy a block of tickets so a group could get inside Convention Hall. I took the money from our joint checking account."

By 1 P.M., more than one hundred demonstrators were parading around a cordoned-off section of the boardwalk. Eighteen-year-old Carol Giardina had come up from Florida. Kathie Amatniek had brought her grandmother. Resplendent in a white pantsuit, the lawyer Flo Kennedy led a chorus of "Ain't She Sweet?" with Helen Kritzler, who playfully hooked a wired brassiere over her dress. They were cheered on by an ebullient Kate Millett, the downtown artist and up-town scholar who was a presence in NOW and Radical Women; her landmark book *Sexual Politics* was two years in the future. Clara DeMiha, age sixty-eight, a stalwart from Women Strike for Peace, moved to the front of line, waving two huge posters: GIRLS CROWNED, BOYS KILLED and END THE WAR IN VIETNAM NOW. Leah Fritz, poet, housewife, and mother of two, took a stack of flyers and worked the crowd.

"I came up from D.C. with Marilyn Webb and Donna Allen," Char-lotte Bunch, a cofounder of Women's Liberation in that city, recollects. "We had our own flyer with softer language and a more leftist analysis of what Miss America was about, but the New York organizers would not let us pass it out because it didn't follow their precise line."

But it was hard to discern any "precise line" in the midst of the protest's freewheeling antics. Someone had rented a live sheep. In high hilarity, the animal was crowned Miss America with a blue rosette and yellow ribbons. Carol Hanisch and Lynn Laredo escorted it around the boardwalk. More demonstrators arrived, scrawling new posters with fresh Magic Markers: NO MORE MISS AMERICA. THE REAL MISS AMERICA

LIVES IN HARLEM. CAN MAKEUP COVER THE WOUNDS OF OUR OPPRES-
SION? IF YOU WANT MEAT, GO TO A BUTCHER. I AM NOT SOMEBODY'S
PET, TOY, OR MASCOT.

Dressed in a miniskirt and tank top, the artist Florika chained herself to an eight-foot, star-spangled Miss America puppet while Peggy
Dobbins, playing a Wall Street financier in her husband's suit, conducted a mock auction: "Step right up, gentlemen, get your late-model
woman right here! She can push your product, push your ego, push
your war!"

"People on the sidelines were yelling at us," says Alix Shulman.
"They were shouting, 'Go back to Russia, you ugly, lezzie, commie
whores.'"

"They were alternating 'Hey, good-lookin'—whatcha doing
tonight?' with 'Boy, get a load of that one—what a dog!'" Leah Fritz
remembers. "The men acted as if we were conducting a beauty contest.
I'd never felt such humiliation. The experience was worth a hundred
consciousness-raising sessions."

"After a while some of us stopped demonstrating and began talking
to them, person to person," recalls Jacqui Ceballos. "We said,
'Wouldn't you like your daughter to aspire to something else besides
Miss America?' We really reached them. Some of the men agreed, but
some women just clung to their men—they were afraid of us."

"To their credit, some of our husbands also stood behind the barriers," says Robin Morgan. "Kenneth Pitchford, Steve Kroll, Hank
Kaminsky. They were very careful not to be protective."

A Freedom Trash Can became the site of a joyous, incantatory
purging of feminine trappings.

"No more girdles, no more pain! No more trying to hold the fat in vain!"
A ribbed corset sailed into the can.

"High heels mean low status!" With a whoop Judith Duffett bade
farewell to a pair of spikes.

A nervous Pam Kearon ran up and tossed in a long-line support bra.

Leah Fritz slam-dunked a set of falsies.

Eyelash curlers, fake lashes, tweezers, and tubes of mascara went
into the trash.

Pirouetting on the boardwalk, her ponytail knotted in red chiffon,

Alix Kates Shulman had an inspiration: She would write about a fictional heroine whose life was governed by male standards of feminine beauty. Three years and many revisions later, she broke into print with *Memoirs of an Ex-Prom Queen*, the first feminist novel of the new generation.

That evening a score of demonstrators with tickets took their seats in the front row of the balcony at Convention Hall. As the outgoing Miss America, Debra Barnes, gave her farewell speech, Amatniek and Hanisch unfurled their banner. It read WOMEN'S LIBERATION.

Security officers grabbed Naomi Jaffe as the others fled. Down on the convention floor, Bev Grant and Miriam Bokser took advantage of the confusion to release two stink bombs. Sprinting toward the stage, Peggy Dobbins popped the cap and squeezed hard on a third plastic vial.

"Miriam accidentally sprayed me," Bev Grant remembers. "It was more Keystone Kops than anything else."

"Bev and Miriam got away and I got busted," laughs Dobbins. "They took me straight to the Atlantic City jail."

Afterward the women would say that the noxious fumes were from the setting lotion of Toni Home Permanent, a pageant sponsor. "This was pure stinky stuff," reports Hanisch, wrinkling her nose a quarter century later at the memory of the smell.

Network television cameras broadcasting the pageant live to an audience of millions resolutely avoided the banner hanging from the balcony, but viewers at home (I was one) could detect a commotion, some faint shouts and cries, as the last of the disrupters were hustled from the hall.

Setting a pattern for future Women's Liberation events, the organizers had insisted that they would speak only to women of the press. Charlotte Curtis, the acerbic society reporter for *The New York Times* and the epitome of chic in her little black dress and double strand of pearls, had hitched a ride on the demonstrators' bus. Her coverage in the Sunday paper was colorful and sympathetic.

"Charlotte was extraordinary," says Robin Morgan. "God love her, she made us look reasonable and nice."

Although "bra burners," the dread appellation, was immediately af-
fixed to the movement, the boardwalk hijinks and civil disobedience of
the Miss America protest had global ripples as both national and foreign
journalists seized on the story. Shana Alexander, for one, opined in her
Life magazine column that she wished the protestors had "gone farther."

• • •

Deep mistrust, serious divisions, emotional charges and countercharges always characterize the inner life of a movement for social
change, and Women's Liberation was no exception. The ripples inside
the movement from its first national protest were profound. Unhappy
rumblings, internal grievances, theoretical disagreements, personality
conflicts, and jealousies among the founders gnawed on the fragile
concept of sisterhood.

Robin Morgan had gotten too much personal publicity, some people griped—Miss America was supposed to have been a collective action, without leaders and spokespeople. In a written critique, Carol
Hanisch excoriated the protest's individualistic "hippy-yippee-campy"
aspects. Placards like UP AGAINST THE WALL, MISS AMERICA and MISS
AMERICA IS A BIG FALSIE had come across as antiwoman, she maintained, and some demonstrators had been needlessly disruptive. (Because of Peggy Dobbins's court case, she refrained from mentioning
the stink bombs.)

The bottom line was control: Who had a right to speak for the
movement? Whose strategy and tactics, whose worldview, would triumph? A deep division of style and substance separated the stubborn
visionaries, Amatniek and Hanisch, Firestone and Koedt, who were
groping toward an independent feminist position, from "the politicos,"
led in New York by Robin Morgan, who were determined not to break
with the left.

Scores of new adherents joined New York Radical Women after the
Miss America protest. Attendance at the Thursday meetings jumped
from thirty to fifty, then to one hundred and upward, and continued to
grow. Latecomers stood pressed against each other in the tiny ante-
room of the fourth-floor SCEF office. At times the meetings took on
the flavor of a tent camp revival, a hallelujah chorus.

This was the moment when I wandered in and had my own instant conversion.

I set my eyes on the memory channel and "image" the room:

Wherever Kathie Amatniek sits is a locus of power. She is an apprentice film editor, but her heart is in political theory and writing. Kathie claims that we have no leaders, adding, "My leader hasn't arrived yet—when she appears I will follow her." Yet it seems to me that Kathie is making a bid for leadership every time she opens her mouth. Her insistence that we "go around the room" at each meeting so every woman "can speak from her own experience" can be irksome and controlling. Kathie speaks all the time, while some women never get to open their mouth. One day Kathie tells me her dream: to find the perfect revolutionary man and walk with him through life into the revolutionary sunset. Kathie reminds me of Amelia Earhart.

It is harder to track Shulie Firestone's vaporizing trail. She waitresses in a Village coffeehouse and lives on the Lower East Side, where she paints big abstracts in swirling colors, although lately she has turned to writing. Shulie grouses about the lack of men in her life and exclaims in the next breath that it must be an omen that Simone de Beauvoir is also a Capricorn. She is going to be the American Beauvoir, she says. It is only a matter of time; it's already too late for Susan Sontag.

The prim evangelist working the phone, her titian hair secured in a bun, is Lucinda Cisler, the abortion activist. Cindy is in NOW, Cindy is in New Yorkers for Abortion Law Repeal, Cindy is a devotee of Bill Baird's, a messiah of birth control whose confrontations with the law get him arrested up and down the East Coast. Cindy is usually with James Clapp, her partner in activism, but Clapp is not allowed into these all-women meetings.

Cindy is on the telephone now, trying to reach Gloria Steinem, who writes a political column for *New York* magazine. "Gloria Steinem should be here to cover this meeting," Cindy says into the phone. "This is important. I'm calling from Women's Liberation." Cindy is a trained architect. She writes letters and compiles lists in the distinctive block print that architects learn in school. But Cindy doesn't work as an architect; she lives hand to mouth and works on abortion.

Here comes Kate Millett, fresh-faced, her long hair in a braid, bounding in late. Kate is one of those universal joiners, like Cindy and Jacqui Ceballos, who stand out in a group. A midwesterner from St. Paul, raised Catholic, Kate went to Oxford for her graduate studies before she returned to the States and ran into a wall of academic rejections. Finally she found a teaching fellowship at Barnard. Kate joined New York NOW at its first or second meeting while she was writing her doctoral dissertation, a feminist reevaluation of four male icons of liberated sexuality: D.H. Lawrence, Henry Miller, Jean Genet, and Norman Mailer. Kate has many irons in the fire and she's tending to all of them, but her true love is art. She is an avant-garde sculptor married to Fumio Yoshimura, a Japanese immigrant who is also an avant-garde sculptor. An editor at Doubleday wants to publish Kate's unfinished doctoral thesis, provisionally titled "Sexual Politics," so Kate has something to groan about over coffee after the meeting. How is she going to turn her academic dissertation into a book?

I, too, wonder about Kate's book. "But it's obvious—women are equal! What's to write about?" I mutter. Little did I know that Millett was inventing a whole new field called feminist literary criticism between her appearances at the meetings.

Like me, Ellen Willis starts coming to New York Radical Women after the Miss America protest, but unlike me, she hurls herself into the center of things and becomes an insider. Her posture is tense, her hair is frizzy. Ellen's father is a New York anomaly, a liberal Jewish cop with a left-wing past. She is *The New Yorker*'s rock critic. Ellen sits on the floor, hugging her knees to her chest, spinning original theory that brings down the house.

Ellen does not like to be crossed, I learn one evening when I top her rhetoric with a wiseacre remark. She is doing a riff on women's unpaid labor and crescendoing to a climax—"We'll go into the suburbs, we'll invade every nuclear family, we'll organize a union of housewives—"

"Nah," I cut in, dragging on a cigarette. "The shops are too small."

I get a big laugh from the room and a startled glare from Ellen, who is not used to being interrupted. But I mean what I said. Union organizing requires a sizable group of workers at the target site. The house-wives' "shops" were too small.

"You'd better watch it if you want to stay in this movement," Judith Duffett warns me. Judith is a Wellesley graduate in an unhappy marriage who does secretarial work at *Modern Bride*.

So I got off on the wrong foot with Ellen Willis. Over the years Ellen and I would disagree on other substantive issues, like the Jane Alpert case, antiviolence work, and pornography, but I want to give credit where credit is due. Ellen was a dazzler in New York Radical Women. Among her other achievements, she popularized the words "sexism" and "sexist" in her mainstream writings.

The one with the big soulful eyes and gritty wit is Irene Peslikis, a painter, proud of her Greek heritage and immigrant parents. Irene is not from the left, but she walked in the door one Thursday evening and thought, *Oddball women, rebels! Just like me!* Irene quickly converted to the movement look—no makeup, blue jeans, work boots—and helped to create the style of confessional discourse that lies at the heart of consciousness-raising.

Several struggling young artists are in New York Radical Women. Wanting to be a painter, like wanting to act or write, is a common ambition in the counterculture. The artists in Radical Women get sucked into the vortex, they become the vortex, adapting readily to consciousness-raising and producing some of the best early papers, the groundbreaking essays that are laboriously typed on stencils, mimeographed, and sold for ten cents through the mail. In an era of technological leaps, Women's Liberation is the last major American movement to spread the word via a mimeo machine.

Artist Pat Mainardi's paper is called "The Politics of Housework." In it she examines every weaseling excuse that men put forward to avoid sharing the household duties, culminating, of course, with "Housework is too trivial to even talk about." Mainardi's paper is a knockout. It gives political importance to a formerly private and personal female complaint. In a household where both partners work, why are *we* the sex that does the unpaid, repetitive, boring, time-and-energy-consuming tasks? Where is it written in the book of law that *we're* supposed to do the laundry, dust the table, wash the dishes? After I read

Pat Mainardi's paper, I no longer think of housework as my private battle with the man in my life. It's part of the universal male-female problem.

New thinking that flows from a reexamination of women's daily lives is what this new movement is all about. As Pat Mainardi insists, "Participatory democracy begins at home." As Carol Hanisch writes in her paper on consciousness-raising and action, "The personal is political."

The personal is political! Housework is political. Abortion is political. Standards of feminine beauty are political. Women's oppression is political. Sexual satisfaction is political. A reevaluation of male-female relations is political. What else are we on the verge of discovering? What other so-called trivial issues and private battles consigned to the "personal" will we bring to light and redefine as political?

In Ruth Hershberger and Elizabeth Fisher, New York Radical Women have a connecting link to an earlier generation of feminists who fought the good fight in the 1940s and were stifled a decade later. Hershberger's 1948 classic, *Adam's Rib*, prefigured many issues we had yet to rediscover. She even had a chapter on rape. During the early seventies *Adam's Rib* was republished and gained a new audience, but it didn't help Ruth's bank account. She did proofreading to earn a living. Ruth was fun to hang out with. She'd seen the feminist uprising come, go, and come again. Elizabeth Fisher, cranky and difficult, was to found *Aphra*, the first feminist literary magazine, in 1969.

Most astonishing are the new people without any prior political involvement who leaped right in and became radicalized overnight, like Barbara Mehrhof and Sheila Cronan, two caseworkers for the Bureau of Child Welfare, who would produce exciting, germinal papers for the movement in the years ahead.

Mehrhof and Cronan had wandered over to NOW's weeklong demonstration in front of the Colgate-Palmolive building on an impulse one day after work. The NOW women were protesting the soap company's refusal to put women in management positions even though women bought most of its products. Kate Millett was there with one of her avant-garde art pieces, a giant toilet bowl with feet, to make the point that Colgate flushed women's aspirations down the toilet.

Cindy Cisler told them on the picket line about another group called Women's Liberation, although some people called it New York Radical Women. Mehrhof and Cronan decided to check out Room 412. Barbara had grown up in a working-class neighborhood in Brooklyn; her father repaired television sets. Sheila's father managed a gas station in Southern California. What propelled these two bright young women from nonpolitical Catholic families to make the leap into radical activism besides a vague yearning to make something more of their lives?

To this day, Barbara Mehrhof cannot explain it, but she remembers that she and Sheila came to the meeting wearing dresses: "I'd never seen so many women in dungarees, T-shirts, and no makeup—at least not that many in one place. Kathie Amatniek stood up to start the meeting, and I heard her say, 'Men oppress women.' She said it real casually, like it was something they all knew. My reaction was, *Yes, that's what it's all about!* We were hooked."

Pam Kearon completes the fierce triumverate of working-class Catholics who come into New York Radical Women and have an instant conversion. She gravitates naturally to Barbara and Sheila. Pam was a brilliant student at St. John's, with a degree in mathematics. She hasn't a clue about clothes, she trembles in social encounters, and she is painfully naive about the way the world functions. On the subway after a demonstration one day, Pam summons her nerve to ask me a question. She wants to know if I sleep with the editors of the magazines I write for to get my articles published. Gently I tell her that things aren't as bad as all that. But there's a lot more to Pam than first meets the eye. One of her papers, called "Man-Hating," is circulated in mimeographed form. "Man-Hating" is smart, tough, and funny, a self-assured rebuke to the leftists who tell us that capitalism is the enemy we should hate.

•   •   •

Then there were the anti-imperialist women, as they were called, a hostile, inimical presence at the meetings they chose to grace, bristling to defend their worldview that capitalism was the root of all evil. Their enemy was personified by anyone who uttered the F-word, or looked

like she might. The F-word was "feminism," an anathema, an impre-
cation, a dangerous right-wing deviation concocted by misguided
members of the bourgeoisie, as Lenin so famously informed the German communist Clara Zetkin in 1920 in his *Conversations on the Woman
Question*. In 1968 it was impossible to hold a women's meeting in radical circles without a representative of the anti-imperialist clique on
hand to proclaim, "Let's make this clear once and for all—we aren't
feminists, we are radical women."

Kathy Boudin, daughter of the revered left-wing lawyer Leonard
Boudin, came by the night I was struggling to analyze sexual harassment on the street—this was before we had the phrase "sexual harassment."

"Construction workers who whistle and catcall," I floundered,
searching for words, "are telling us that we may think we're middle
class but we have no class status at all if our men aren't around to protect us. By whistling they're proving that they can easily declass us."

Boudin, sacked out on the floor, stolid and groggy in boots, jeans,
and workshirt, opened one eye. "You're full of shit," she muttered, and
went back to sleep.

One year later Boudin was a helmeted, street-fighting Weatherwoman, clashing with the police in Chicago and Pittsburgh, acting on
her creed that women would prove their equality with men in side-by-
side armed struggle. In March 1970 she fled from the rubble of a townhouse explosion on West Eleventh Street in Greenwich Village, a
bomb factory gone awry, to pursue her commitment to violence with
the Weather Underground. Convicted in 1983 for armed robbery and
murder, she is in the state correctional facility for women at Bedford
Hills today.

By the time I got to the meetings of New York Radical Women,
SCEF was already grumbling about the strange goings-on in their New
York office on Thursday nights. Politically incorrect! A bourgeois tendency that needs redirection! One evening we are visited by Jane Mc-
Manus, a friend of SCEF and the widow of a founder of the leftist
weekly *The National Guardian*. On this trip to New York from Cuba to
see old friends, Jane McManus makes us her political mission.

"You girls have it all wrong, sitting around talking about your sex lives and your orgasms," she scolds. "Why don't you organize around the high cost of food in the supermarket? That's a real women's issue."

Jane McManus is so hopelessly out of step with the times that even the anti-imperialist women cannot suppress a snicker.

We tumble out of the meeting at midnight, to go home or to extend the talkfest over coffee at the Yum Yum or Ratner's. It is always at that moment that a tiny figure shrills, "Sisters, sisters, we didn't resolve the question of structure!"

Judy Gabree, or Judy Thibeau, since she wishes to reclaim her pre-marriage name, seizes the moment to hand out her flow chart with squares, circles, and arrows. She distributes her structure proposal at the close of every meeting, but few of the Radical Women share her interest in orderly process. What is alive in this room, what is new, what is exciting, has been conjured into being in the absence of structure.

As the SCEF office empties, Carol Hanisch, armed with a broom and a dustpan, dutifully lingers behind, dumping ashtrays, sweeping up the debris.

So that's what it was like in New York in the fall of 1968, and that's what it was like, given the differences in locale and personalities, in five or six or eight other cities that season, that year, in Chicago, Washington, Boston, Seattle, Gainesville, Toronto. Each city quickly developed its own stamp, its original theorists, its acknowledged or unacknowledged leaders, its stars, cliques, rifts, and internal splits. The initial explosion was close to spontaneous combustion, but no movement for social change is ever a truly spontaneous occurrence. The grievances and dissatisfactions had been simmering for a number of years, among all strata of women. If not, they couldn't have boiled over so quickly.

I have to admit that after my first flush of enthusiasm, my attendance at New York Radical Women was sporadic. In truth, the early meetings weren't feminist enough for me. I wasn't convinced in 1968 that this group, or this movement, would ever get beyond the interminable debate over whether the enemy was man or capitalism. I was wrong.

So, for other reasons, was Betty Friedan. I remember the night the author of *The Feminine Mystique* and the founder of NOW arrived in her trademark long skirt and high-heeled boots to brave the generation gap and take notes on this scruffy, unladylike phenomenon called Women's Liberation. As the voluble drama swirled around her, she scribbled page after page in a spiral notebook, alternating her labors with vigorous shakes of her head: No, No, No!

• • •

Bored with consciousness-raising and eager for action, that fall some of the politicos—Robin Morgan, Florika, Judith Duffett, Peggy Dobbins—had melded their small discussion groups into WITCH. The useful acronym stood for Women's International Terrorist Conspiracy from Hell, but it could also mean Women Inspired to Tell their Collective History, Women Interested in Toppling Consumer Holidays, and a host of imaginative variations. Proclaiming that witches were the original female rebels, hounded, persecuted, and burned at the stake because they had knowledge that men wanted suppressed, WITCH devoted itself to hit-and-run guerrilla theater, called "zaps."

"I didn't relate to the witches-as-matriarchy part," says Rosalyn Baxandall, "but I liked the theatrical actions." So did some other regulars in New York Radical Women. There was always fluidity between the two groups.

For Halloween 1968 the WITCH women donned rags and fright makeup to invade a branch of the Chase Manhattan Bank and "put a hex" on Wall Steet. Robin still swears that the Dow-Jones index took a steep dive the next day. The strangely compelling, artistic Florika, vague about her Romanian ancestry, up-front about her bouts with prostitution and drugs, excelled at choosing WITCH targets. She liked to zap a bastion of capitalism and a symbol of the Vietnam War in one blow.

"Florika did these interesting collages," Baxandall reminisces, "like putting Vietnamese women in an ad for Chanel No. 5. She also led an action against Revlon's corporate headquarters, called Revlon Napalm."

"There were spin-offs, covens, in other cities. Chicago WITCH, Washington WITCH," recollects Morgan. "WITCH may not have known much about the real history of witches, but WITCH had joie de vivre."

The short, colorful life of WITCH lasted approximately six months, going out in a blaze of confusion at a bridal industry fair at Madison Square Garden. If you believed that capitalism was the root of women's oppression, it made sense to zap an industry that profited from women's romantic hopes and dreams. It was okay to raise the slogan "Confront the Whoremongers," but everyone agreed that releasing a cage of white mice on the convention floor hadn't been cool.

•   •   •

Theory was taking precedence over action in other cities. Roxanne Dunbar and Dana Densmore, the two Solanas champions in Boston, had been inspired by the passions at Sandy Springs to try their skills at writing. At breakneck speed their small collective put together a journal of poetry and polemics in October 1968 that was a handsome step up from the movement's usual mimeographed tracts. The art nouveau cover, a voluptuous nude adorned with curly pubic and underarm hair to complement her Medusa tresses, was designed by Dana's sister Indra, and the text was composed on an IBM typesetting machine borrowed from a local merchant over a long weekend.

It had not occurred to the Boston women to date their journal or give it a title, although future issues would bear the name *No More Fun and Games*. "We were a strange, manic crew," Dana Densmore reflects. "We didn't see an orderly future which would in turn become history and require documentation. We saw ourselves on the verge of a great upheaval."

The most talked-about piece in the debut issue was Densmore's "On Celibacy," a provocative call, in the age of so-called sexual freedom, "for an acceptance of celibacy as an honorable alternative . . . to the degradation of most male-female sexual relationships."

"Doesn't screwing in an atmosphere devoid of respect get pretty grim?" Densmore wrote. "Why bother? You don't need it. Erotic energy is just life energy and is quickly worked off if you are doing interesting things. Love and affection and recognition can easily be found in comrades . . . who love you for yourself and not for how docile and cute and sexy and ego-building you are. Until we say, 'I control my own body and don't need any insolent male with an overbearing presumptuous prick to come and clean out my pipes,' they will always have over us the devastating threat of withdrawing their sexual attentions."

"There was never a point when we all went celibate," Dunbar explains. "Dana had a husband. Actually we all had relationships. Celibacy was not meant to be a requirement but a positive choice, a breathing space for however long a woman desired it without thinking she was a barren old hag. A lot of people misunderstood Dana's position."

Meanwhile in Chicago, Naomi Weisstein was also grappling with sexually subversive ideas. A Phi Beta Kappa from Wellesley with a Ph.D. from Harvard, ranking first in her class, Naomi had wound up in the tiny psychology department at Loyola after a humiliating round of job interviews punctuated by "Who did your research?" and "How can a little girl like you teach a great big class of men?" Loyola was a job, at least, even if it wasn't as prestigious as the University of Chicago, where her husband, Jesse Lemisch, was in the history department. Naomi was an experimental psychologist who specialized in the neural basis of visual perception; she needed sophisticated computers that were beyond the budget of Loyola's underequipped labs. Worried that she was falling behind in her field, she worked out her rage in the West Side group, and in the speeches about Women's Liberation she was being invited to make. On her feet she could be smart, fierce, and compassionate. She could make people laugh.

Invited to give a paper at the University of California at Davis in the fall of 1968, she presented "*Kinder, Küche, Kirche* as Scientific Law, or Psychology Constructs the Female." Straying from her field of visual perception, she lambasted current Freudian psychology and two of its principal adherents, Erik Erikson and Bruno Bettelheim. Erikson's popular theory held that women possessed an empty "inner space" that could be filled only by motherhood; Bettelheim insisted that even women who wanted to be scientists wanted "first and foremost to be womanly companions of men."

"Psychology has nothing to say about what women are really like," Weisstein thundered from the platform, "because psychology *does not know*."

After she'd finished reading her paper, there was a frightening moment of silence, and then the audience of academics stood up and cheered. *I have become a powerful orator*, she thought. *The women's movement has given me my voice.* Requests for copies of *"Kinder, Küche, Kirche"* poured in; it was anthologized widely.

• • •

Marilyn Webb's plans for a national Women's Liberation conference in Chicago were proceeding apace. In her mind the conference was to be an updated replay of the historic Seneca Falls Convention of 1848. In line with her politics, it would also include reports on the current status of women in revolutionary Vietnam and Cuba. With seed money from the Institute of Policy Studies, a leftist think tank, she paid four organizers twenty-five dollars a week to get the ball rolling. Helen Kritzler, of New York Radical Women, went to Boston to solicit a contribution from Abby Rockefeller, a friend of the antiwar movement. Nervous about meeting the daughter of David, chairman of the Chase-Manhattan Bank, Kritzler invited Roxanne Dunbar to come along. The encounter turned into a boon for the Boston women.

"Abby had graduated the year before from the New England Conservatory of Music," Dunbar remembers. "Studying the cello. And she'd gotten involved with draft resistance. She had this eighteen-year-old roommate, Jayne West, a scholarship student from Ohio, also a cellist, who had just gotten into tae kwon do. Both of them were depressed and overweight, pasty-faced, but then they joined our group and came alive. Jayne began teaching all of us tae kwon do, and the first thing Abby did was write a check for the Chicago conference. Neither she nor I actually went to the conference, but she paid for the facilities at the YWCA camp and for the report that was written up afterward."

Less than a month after Richard Nixon's election, 150 radical women representing twenty cities in the United States and Canada—and perhaps fifty assorted shades of opinion on the left-to-feminist spectrum—convened over the Thanksgiving 1968 weekend at Camp Hastings, a YWCA retreat in Lake Villa outside Chicago. Some women carpooled, other arrived by plane. Anne Koedt made the journey by car with Shulie Firestone and Ti-Grace Atkinson. Irene Peslikis had her plane ticket paid for by Kathie Amatniek. "Kathie insisted that I had to be there, she said it was us against the world," recalls Peslikis.

"Cold. Bitterly cold" is what Jacqui Ceballos of NOW remembers. "Snowing. They were waiting for us at the airport with signs, and then we had a long, long trip to that camp. I was assigned to an upper bunk bed. There was no politeness or thoughtfulness that this was an older woman who maybe should have the lower bed. I had a feeling of hostility all around me. And the food, the hot dogs, ran out before the weekend was over."

"Twice as many people showed up than we expected," says Charlotte Bunch, one of the organizers. "We were frantically trying to find them places to sleep."

"Charlotte was walking around with a lanyard and a whistle, like a YWCA counselor," says Rosalyn Baxandall. "She didn't want us to smoke—I guess she was way ahead of her time."

"Once again Sheila Cronan and I were the only ones in dresses," laughs Barbara Mehrhof. "We were still wearing dresses. Judith Brown was there from Gainesville, Dana Densmore was there from Boston, Dolores Bargowski was there from Detroit, and Anne Koedt's sister, Bonnie Kreps, was there from Toronto. At the sex workshop I heard them speaking in Danish."

"I came from Boston with two friends from SDS," says Nancy Hawley. "I had one kid at home and I was pregnant with my daughter."

"Some women brought their children," recalls Baxandall, "but I left Finny at home with Lee. I had just stopped breast-feeding. Marilyn Lowen had her kid there, and we all breast-fed her kid."

"Naomi Weisstein brought copies of *"Kinder, Küche, Kirche"*" says Mehrhof. "It was the first time we'd seen it."

"Ti-Grace Atkinson gave an eloquent speech," says Marilyn Webb. "I don't remember what she said but I remember feeling that she and the others were the most brilliant women I had ever met. I believed a real historic event had happened. The potential of a mass movement was so great. I had no sense at all that we couldn't continue working together."

"There was a lot of heavy, hard debate," says Carol Hanisch. "Fights about consciousness-raising, and how important it was. Fights about how independent the women's movement should be, and what its relationship to the left should be. Fights about the establishment press, and what our relationship to it should be. Fights about whether we should copyright things or just throw them out there for anybody to use."

"I was shocked at how strongly people denounced each other," recalls Charlotte Bunch, who identified closely with the anti-imperialist women. "The polarization was so physically and emotionally exhausting that afterwards I couldn't drive home."

Choosing this occasion to adopt the movement name of Kathie Sarachild, in honor of her mother, Kathie Amatniek gave a workshop on consciousness-raising, but it was poorly attended.

"Everyone went to the sex workshop," recalls Carol Hanisch. In that no-holds-barred session, Anne Koedt presented an expanded version of "The Myth of the Vaginal Orgasm." Dana Densmore shook up the proceedings by suggesting a respite of celibacy. Shulie Firestone drew outraged cries when she insisted that technology must offer an alternative to childbearing in the womb.

"I was doing a lot of listening," says Nancy Hawley, who liked bearing children. (Soon after she gave birth to her daughter, Hawley would initiate the Boston Women's Health Book Collective, the amazing array of young mothers who created *Our Bodies, Ourselves.*)

Unlike their more decorous sisters in NOW, the radical theorists who'd gathered at Lake Villa were temperamentally unsuited to hierarchical order. Neither could they agree on how to proceed. "There was a lot of distrust that weekend," Jo Freeman sums up. "Nobody was willing to cede leadership to anyone, except to their friends."

Although Marilyn Webb was reluctant to see it, the left-feminist split was irreconcilable. Lake Villa was the first and last time that a national conference of radical women would convene.

Cross-fertilization of ideas continued to take place, however, through intense personal correspondence, mimeographed papers and movement journals, and eventually mainstream magazine articles and popular books. But the radical, creative wing of the women's movement would remain decentralized, localized in small groups from city to city, for the duration of its vivid existence. Ultimately New York, the media capital of the nation, would triumph as the theoretical base of the pure feminist position, idiosyncratic Boston would continue to provoke and challenge, and the Washington-Chicago left alliance would cease being a force in the ideological wars.

• • •

A raucous antiwar rally in Washington early in January 1969 gave the feminists their final proof that the left was not ready to embrace Women's Liberation. The unhappy target on this occasion was none other than Marilyn Webb, the woman who had not wavered in her belief that everyone could work together.

MOBE, the National Mobilization to End the War in Vietnam, had selected the weekend of Richard Nixon's swearing-in to hold a Counter-Inaugural rally. Through her impeccable SDS connections, Marilyn had been given the go-ahead to speak on behalf of Women's Liberation. Generously she agreed to share her time with Shulie Firestone, so that New York's stronger feminist position would get an airing.

A newcomer to New York Radical Women named Margaret Polatnik had come up with a wild idea on the drive home from Lake Villa. If the MOBE men were going to burn their draft cards after the rally, as they usually did, the women should burn their voter registration cards to dramatize that electoral politics had failed to secure equal rights.

"Everybody thought that was a great idea," remembers Barbara Mehrhof. "So we decided to work on this action of giving back the vote. We met a lot at Irene Peslikis's loft, making sashes that said 'Feminism Lives.' One night someone got the bright idea to call Alice Paul, the last living suffragist in Washington, to ask her to join us."

Octogenarian Alice Paul had led the radical wing of the suffrage movement during the Wilson era. She had chained herself to the White House gate, imperiled her health with a hunger strike, and gone to jail for the vote. "She told us," says Mehrhof, "she did not think giving it back was a good idea."

Kathie Amatniek Sarachild did not think giving back the vote was a good idea, either. Neither did Anne Koedt. And when WITCH heard that New York Radical Women was going to raise the slogan "Feminism Lives" at the Counter-Inaugural rally, they were enraged. They threatened to wear sashes with the counter-slogan "Feminism Sucks."

"Thank God, or Goddess, we did not do that," says Robin Morgan, "But we came *this* close. I still thought of 'feminism' as a dirty word."

The day before the Counter-Inaugural, women from New York, Boston, and D.C. met at Marilyn Webb's apartment to review Marilyn's and Shulie's speeches. "The general feeling," says Webb, "was that mine wasn't militant enough and that Shulie shouldn't attack movement men at a public rally."

"Marilyn was very good about taking suggestions," says Rosalyn Baxandall, "but Shulie said we could take it or leave it."

"Shulie said her speech was like a poem, and if she couldn't read it the way she wrote it, she'd leave the movement," Webb recalls.

"After the meeting, Shulie and I went to visit Alice Paul," says Barbara Mehrhof. "We still wanted her to join us. She lived in a very old house near the Capitol with a plaque on the front, THE WOMAN'S PARTY. The first thing she asked was, 'Are you the women who called from New York?' We said, 'Oh, no, absolutely no.' So she let us in. I remember the house was dark, and the long dining table was stacked with leaflets for the Equal Rights Amendment. She took us upstairs and there were all these paintings, portraits of women, on the wall. She asked if we recognized the women, these nineteenth-century and early-twentieth-century suffragists, and we didn't. She was a little contemptuous of us; she didn't see us as the new generation ready to carry the torch. I think she knew that we were the women who'd called from New York."

It was drizzling on Sunday, so the Counter-Inaugural rally was held in a large circus tent on the Washington Mall. "I believe," says Marilyn Webb, "that twenty thousand people were there."

"Dave Dellinger announced the speakers," relates Mehrhof, "the speaker for the Chicago Seven, the speaker for the Fort Hood Three, the speaker for the veterans, the speaker for the blacks. And he forgot us. Somebody called up, 'What about the women?' and he said, 'Oh, yes, we're gonna hear from the girls.'"

"Women, you schmuck," shouted Ellen Willis.

The grounds were muddy and the rickety platform was swaying by the time the final speakers, Marilyn and Shulie, were called. The women's plans to burn real voter cards had been scuttled, so Sheila Cronan and a few others carried big mock-ups instead. Down below, the crowd had grown restive.

"Dellinger set us up very badly," says Webb. "He said, 'Now the women are going to speak and they've asked all the men to clear the stage.' I don't know where that came from. Not in my memory did anyone ask that. There was this paralyzed GI in a wheelchair—they had to lift up his wheelchair and hand him down from the stage. Shulie was standing next to me, telling me to hurry. They're handing down the GI in the wheelchair, and I'm trying not to read the speech but just say it."

"Women must take control of our bodies," Webb chanted into the mike. "We must define our own issues. We will take the struggle to our homes, to our jobs, to the streets."

And then it happened. From somewhere in the restive crowd came a yell.

"Take her off the stage and fuck her!"

"Take off your clothes!"

"I'll go to the streets with you. Down an alley!"

"The men went completely nuts," recalls Ellen Willis. "From our point of view this was the mild, conciliatory speech. And they were going berserk."

"Screams and fistfights were breaking out in front of me. Screams and fistfights," says Webb. "Men were hitting each other. Beating each other up. And Dave was getting hysterical, like a riot was going to happen."

"Dellinger was trying to get us to leave," Willis remembers. "He was saying, 'Cut it short for your own good.'"

"Shulie was afraid she wouldn't get to speak," says Webb. "She grabbed the microphone before I had finished."

"By that time," says Mehrhof, "you could barely hear her. The rally was over."

That evening the women were holding a postmortem at Marilyn Webb's apartment when the telephone rang. A voice Marilyn believed might have been Cathy Wilkerson's, from SDS, bellowed, "If you ever give a speech like that again, we'll beat the shit out of you." Then the connection went dead.

For Marilyn Webb, who'd worked so hard for a left coalition, "that was the moment when it all broke up. That was the moment when I suddenly knew that Women's Liberation was going to be an independent movement."

WHICH WAY IS UTOPIA?

VISIONARIES BY NATURE are difficult, impatient people. In 1968 no one besides Betty Friedan and a handful of radicals could imagine a mass feminist movement. One year later the prophetic author was already complaining that people, issues, and events were spinning out of control. So it goes when passions are released, the overlooked find their voices, and new ideas float into the culture.

Collectively and individually, the movement was mining new thoughts, and finding a receptive audience, on a daily basis. As ideas built on ideas in voluble profusion, an avalanche of poetry, essays, and theoretical papers poured from the typewriters of the young activists in Women's Liberation who suddenly and vividly had something important to say. The restless founders of Women's Liberation reckoned it might take five years to transform the future. In the meantime their movement was going to be the perfect social model of things to come. Unaccustomed to working together, awash in ideological disagreements, and sharing the New Left's distrust of leaders, they gravitated to small, non-hierarchical groups where, in principle, everyone got a chance to speak and be heard. The small groups, however, did not turn out to be leaderless. Strong personalities with forceful opinions inevitably emerged.

Few of the emerging leaders cared to admit that they were, or wanted to be, in command, even as they pushed for the ascendance of their beliefs or were singled out for media attention. Others protested

that if everyone could not be equal inside the movement, how could
the movement transform the world? Resentments with some logical
basis were compounded by the competitive emotions of jealousy and
envy.

Group pressure becomes a powerful weapon inside movements for
social change as people fall under the obligation to surrender a portion
of their independence in order to work toward common goals. During
the late sixties and early seventies, the group pressure exerted inside
the Women's Liberation Movement was particularly intense. The Cultural Revolution raging in China had captured the imagination of
many American radicals. In addition, the battle against male privilege
had made the Liberationists wary of advantage, success, and achievement, especially in the women they'd bravely begun to call their sisters.
Those at the bottom of the undefined hierarchy invented a special vo-
cabulary of accusations to put a brake on standout figures in the name
of a utopian collective ideal.

Getting your name in the paper was "personal publicity" that made
you a a "star," guilty of the sin of personal ambition. Verbal fluency
and confidence were defined as the "advantages of class privilege."
Writing for a mainstream publication, even putting your full name on
your work in a countercultural paper, was castigated as "ripping off
the movement's ideas." Often an activist had only to distinguish
herself by a talent for public speaking or a forceful ability to get things
done in order to be tagged a "star," an "elitist," or a "male-identified
woman."

Flo Kennedy defined the phenomenon of ganging up on an individual as "horizontal hostility," misdirected anger that rightly should
be focused on the external causes of oppression. As a frequent target of
collective antagonism, I privately dubbed it "the herd mentality." Most
people simply called it "trashing." In Chicago, New York, Washington,
Boston, and elsewhere, trashing had a pernicious effect on the movement's inner life.

• • •

Jo Freeman was the odd woman out in Chicago's West Side group. It
perplexed her to see a friendship network develop among the other

West Siders from which she was excluded. Wounded by a string of machinations—meetings she wasn't told about where important votes were taken, a coup that took *Voice of the Women's Liberation Movement* out of her hands—Freeman quit the Chicago movement late in 1969, although she continued to write theoretical pieces under her movement name of Joreen. In two critical essays, "The Tyranny of Structurelessness" and "Trashing," she tried to pin down the unexpressed group dynamic that had worked against her.

Naomi Weisstein believed that Jo's isolation had been brought about by her blunt, peremptory manner and her tendency to sulk when things didn't go her way. Yet Naomi, agreeable and well liked, was to learn that even she was not exempt from group criticism and pressure.

Urged on by Vivian Rothstein, the West Siders had organized the Chicago Women's Liberation Union as a citywide umbrella group to promote their socialist/feminist/anti-imperialist ideals. Their tiny office on West Cermak gave way to larger space on West Belmont. Jane, the underground abortion service with the codelike name, was affiliated with the Union but avoided its hot and heavy ideological debates. A graphics collective produced some of the era's most striking, sought-after posters, none signed. (WOMEN WORKING, a twist on the ubiquitous construction-site sign, still hangs in my office.)

Naomi and Vivian set up a hugely popular speakers' bureau to handle an average of twenty-five requests a month from colleges and community groups in the Midwest. To demonstrate the movement's leaderless nature and to encourage the confidence of timid, inexperienced women, the bureau sent out its speakers in pairs. Naomi, a dynamic speaker unafraid of crowds, conducted training sessions for the neophytes with sample scenarios, videotapes, and group critiques.

Ellen DuBois, the historian, who joined the Union while a graduate student at Northwestern, remembers the egalitarian policy of the speakers' bureau as a crucial part of her feminist empowerment when she was "just a student, a kid." Naomi Weisstein, one of its principal architects, looks back on the policy with deep regret. Because Naomi far and away overshadowed the less adept speakers, the bureau asked

her to refrain from public speaking altogether. She began to feel
that the movement that had given her her voice was now taking it
away.

"The motivation was not to stop Naomi," Ellen DuBois insists.
"The whole point of the speakers' bureau was to teach others how to
do it."

A zealous believer in the collective process, Naomi bowed to the
group's will.

"We were all desperately ambitions," Weisstein reflects, "but people didn't want to recognize that there were enormous differences in
individual talents, abilities, gifts. I spent years trying to appease other
women in the movement, trying to be less powerful, so they wouldn't
hate me."

•   •   •

Boston was seething with small liberation groups in 1969, all going
their own way. The most visible and adventurous was the
Dunbar/Densmore/Warrior group, Cell 16 of Female Liberation,
named for 16 Lexington Avenue, Cambridge, where Abby Rockefeller
had turned her basement into the group's office. Buoyed by the success
of *No More Fun and Games* the previous October, the women put out a
second issue in February. Nearly half of the 128-page journal was written by Dana Densmore, expounding on sex roles, liberals, sisterhood,
and "The Temptation to Be a Beautiful Object." The editors proposed
that the movement adopt the newly coined word "sexism," which had
popped up in a southern newsletter, in place of the Old Left's "male
chauvinism" and "male supremacy." They explained, "A sexist, then, is
a person who promotes sexism."

In May, Roxanne Dunbar joined with Nancy Hawley, who'd attended the stormy Lake Villa conference outside Chicago, to organize
a New England regional meeting on Women's Liberation. Six hundred
women flocked to Emmanuel College, a Catholic girls' school in
downtown Boston, over the Mother's Day weekend. Reporters were
barred, but a few sneaked in and wrote mocking accounts of Cell 16's
karate demonstration.

The Emmanuel College conference was a signal event for the

Boston movement. It inspired the formation of the socialist-feminist Bread and Roses, led by Meredith Tax and Linda Gordon, and it brought together, at Nancy Hawley's Saturday afternoon workshop, the nucleus of a group of young mothers who went on to make history as the authors and editors of *Our Bodies, Ourselves*.

But that year it was Cell 16 that represented "Boston" to the national movement. Invited to address the first Congress to Unite Women held in New York in November, Cell 16 treated the assembly to a Chinese revolutionary drama. They strode on stage and proceeded to cut off their long hair to cries of "No, no! Don't do it!"

"Mine was matted and stringy but Martha Atkins had beautiful auburn tresses," chuckles Dunbar, who lectured the audience on how long hair "belongs" to men.

"Men like my breasts—should I cut them off too?" Anselma Dell' Olio of NOW called out.

"Hair grows back," Dunbar retorted.

Ivy Bottini, the president of New York NOW, was transfixed: "People were sobbing and crying. This was pure performance art, but who ever saw performance art affect an audience like that?"

Bottini grew alarmed when she saw a camerman filming the sequence. Marlene Sanders of ABC, the movement's only ally in television, and a member of NOW, was doing a documentary on Women's Liberation, but Bottini thought the haircutting drama was too intimate for public consumption. Seizing her opportunity later that evening, she diverted the crew's attention while a relative newcomer named Rita Mae Brown poked into the unattended ABC film bag. A full magazine of conference footage was removed and destroyed. "I wasn't trying to hurt Marlene," Bottini insists. "This was for us. We needed to digest it before it went out to the world."

Sanders and her crew discovered the film was missing when they packed up to leave. "The theft didn't lend the movement any credibility in the ABC newsroom," she wrote years later. She believed it reflected the split in the movement between those who wanted to work through the system and those who wanted to undermine establishment institutions.

Roxanne Dunbar still wishes the film had survived.

Soon after the haircutting incident, Dunbar's autocratic charisma began to pose problems for the other visionary theorists in Cell 16.

"To her credit, Roxanne wasn't afraid to work with strong women," Dana Densmore reflects. "But a leader needs followers, and we weren't followers. We all had our own opinions, and too often our sense of what we needed to do did not coincide with hers. In those days Roxanne was a great admirer of the Chinese revolution. If any of us disagreed with her, she thought we should have a criticism/self-criticism session and hash it out until we saw the error of our ways."

One evening Dunbar threw Cell 16 into turmoil by declaring that it was counterrevolutionary to keep pets.

"Abby Rockefeller had two dogs and some cats, and one of the cats had had kittens," Densmore relates. "We'd sit on the floor in Abby's basement with puppies and kittens crawling around. I don't see where it had any influence on our activism, but Roxanne came in late that night and said that she'd had a dream. She was in China and she saw an inscription on a wall. Someone translated it for her and the mysterious inscription said 'Too many yip-yips.' She understood this to be a message that there were too many little animals around, so she wanted Abby to take her dogs and cats to the animal shelter." Abby stood firm, however.

Most of the group was relieved when Roxanne left Boston in December 1969 to pursue her radical vision in New Orleans. Dunbar's role as a catalytic feminist founder and thinker had run its course. The rest of Cell 16 fought a takeover attempt by the Socialist Workers Party and stayed together until 1973, when the sixth and final issue of *No More Fun and Games* was published.

•   •   •

New York had the reputation of a sea of barracudas to movement women in the rest of the country. Although New York represented the roiling center of pure feminist theory (in opposition to Chicago and Washington's socialist/feminist/anti-imperialist vision), inside the city the divisions between the leftist "politicos" and the pure feminists ran deep.

New York Radical Women had grown so large and unwieldy that

each time a newcomer walked in the door, the interminable debate, "Is the enemy man or capitalism?" cranked up anew. The January 1969 Counter-Inaugural fiasco in Washington had been the last straw for Shulamith Firestone and Ellen Willis. They announced they were forming a new group whose key principles would be "feminist" and "action." Firestone came up with the name.

"You know how women intellectuals used to be called Bluestockings?" Shulie said one evening to the group at Irene Peslikis's loft. "We're radical women intellectuals, so we should call ourselves Redstockings."

The appealing name would resonate in movement history, not always, alas, for comfortable reasons. Redstockings acquired instant cachet when, for their first action, the women disrupted a New York State hearing on abortion law reform. Five weeks later their public speak-out, "Abortion: Tell It Like It Is," would mark a turning point in the national campaign to legalize abortion.

After that powerful beginning, fights over equality began to sap the group's cohesion. As Barbara Mehrhof saw it, Kathie Amatniek, Shulie Firestone, and Ellen Willis functioned as a leadership clique, and everyone else's ideas were disregarded. Sheila Cronan proposed that Redstockings hang a banner from the Statue of Liberty, and she and Barbara spent many nights sewing the words. "Free Abortion on Demand" on a huge cotton sheet at Irene Peslikis's loft. They were hurt and bewildered when the leaders scuttled Sheila's plan. As a result the outsiders started meeting separately on another night of the week. Calling themselves the Class Workshop, they began to explore their family histories.

"We got together out of a feeling that no one was paying any attention to us," says Cronan, "and we came up with the idea that it was because of our working-class backgrounds. A lot of the Jewish women had grown up in radical families and had gone to expensive colleges where they'd been involved with radical groups. They were used to speaking out and being listened to, at least to some extent. We didn't have that confidence. We felt that the Jewish women thought the Catholic women were intellectually inferior or kind of stupid because we didn't speak their political language."

For a while Redstockings rented a storefront on Avenue A and East Eleventh Street where new women were processed through monthly orientation sessions.

"Kathie was very nervous about the new people," says Irene Peslikis. "She kept saying, 'Who are they? How can they call themselves Redstockings? We don't know their level of consciousness.'"

"Shulie would never work on ordinary stuff," says Mehrhof. "She said she could only work on creative things."

After covering Woodstock, the rock concert of the century, for *The New Yorker*, Ellen Willis took off for Colorado with the man she lived with to organize for the antiwar G.I. Coffee House movement. Irene Peslikis felt betrayed.

"Sending literature through the mail became our big contribution," she sighs. "I was the only one with a car, so I went to the far reaches of Queens and Brooklyn carrying bulk literature and delivering it to outposts, to organize new groups. I'd get up in the morning, make a list, and think *movement, movement, movement*. It seemed endless."

When Ti-Grace Atkinson had departed from NOW, she formed the October 17th Movement, which had died aborning. She revived it as THE FEMINISTS, with capital letters. Cofounder Anne Koedt recalls, "At first it was a very good little group, a place where you could hear yourself think without the din from the politicos." But when Koedt returned from a short vacation in the summer, she was handed a new and rigid set of membership rules. She bowed out quickly.

In Koedt's absence four women from the Class Workshop, Mehrhof, Cronan, Pam Kearon, and Linda Feldman, had switched their allegiance from Redstockings to Ti-Grace. Atkinson, raised in a wealthy, conservative Louisiana family, yearned for an army of disciples. Mehrhof, Cronan, and Kearon possessed inventive feminist minds and poorly developed egos. Linda Feldman, the only Jewish woman in the group, was equally insecure.

"Ti-Grace's philosophy was that we were all supposed to be equal," says Sheila Cronan. "We were supposed to share power and not have any hierarchy. She really believed in that philosophy, and probably still does, but her personality made it difficult for her to follow through."

THE FEMINISTS set up a mailing address on Liberty Street and met twice a week, usually at Cronan's Upper West Side apartment. "That's where we put the mimeo," Barbara Mehrhof remembers. "Ti-Grace said every revolution needs a mimeo machine."

In this self-styled vanguard of egalitarian activist-thinkers, missing a meeting became grounds for expulsion, and no more than 30 percent of the members could be married. Eventually THE FEMINISTS banned all women living with men from their ranks. As a vanguard collective, THE FEMINISTS was a curious experiment in churchlike discipline and ultrademocracy. One of their tasks was to figure out how to counter the domineering tendencies of Ti-Grace, a bundle of nerves in constant motion who talked nonstop at their meetings and snagged all the media attention because she was already a "movement star." THE FEMINISTS devised a random lot system for their political work. Ti-Grace took her turn cutting stencils, running the mimeo, and stapling the group's theoretical papers, the humdrum chores they labeled "shitwork," while Linda, who was easily flustered, was sent out to do the Barry Gray radio program. Feldman's performance, they had to admit, was poor.

Pam Kearon found a way for the timid ones to gain practice in public speaking. They scoured *The Village Voice* every week for notices of other people's political meetings. "If we couldn't find something to do with women," Cronan relates, "we'd go anyway and stand up and make statements during the question period. I remember a meeting of the Gandhi Society where we stood up and denounced him. The people running these meetings must have been bewildered, but we found the exercise very helpful."

Ti-Grace abandoned her philosophy studies at Columbia to earn her living on the lecture circuit. The other FEMINISTS conceded that they had no right to stop her—Atkinson's love affair with the media brought in speaking engagements and fees. Barbara, Sheila, and Pam applied themselves to writing, which they loved. Separately and together, they composed position papers on marriage (a form of slavery), prostitution (it separated women into the bad and the good), Amazon women (true feminist heroines), and the biological origins of women's oppression. Pam tried her hand at movie criticism. Ti-Grace worked up a broadside on the oppressive nature of love. All THE FEMINISTS' papers were sold through the mail for ten cents a copy, yet something was still out of balance. Even though each FEMINIST put her name on her own theoretical work, to the public the only FEMINIST was Ti-Grace.

"Sometimes she came up with cockamamie ideas," Mehrhof laughs, "like when she said we shouldn't appear with men in public. Linda Feldman was devastated—she asked if the ban included her father. And then Ti-Grace returned from an out-of-town speech and told us about the famous man she slept with."

The group was also having trouble with their leader's talking jags and constant motion, and her irate mood when they didn't apply themselves as hard as she did.

"We weren't fledglings anymore," says Mehrhof. "By then we knew that we could fly on our own."

In April 1970, THE FEMINISTS passed a resolution directed at Ti-Grace: all future media interviews would be determined by lot. Atkinson resigned two days later. During the next decade she would pursue a stormy course in feminism without being part of a group.

•   •   •

Rosalyn Baxandall remembers 1969 in New York as the year of the truth squads. Nine or ten women would burst in unannounced on somebody's husband and confront him with a list of grievances. Baxandall says the name was borrowed from the State Department's "truth squads" that descended on a college campus after an antiwar teach-in. Irene Peslikis believes the tactic came straight out of *Fanshen*, William Hinton's account of a liberated Chinese village, circa 1949, where timid peasants learned to "speak bitterness" and "struggle against" their landlord oppressors.

Ros's husband and Marilyn Lowen's husband were confronted by the truth squads for their womanizing. Lee Baxandall sat through his struggle session so penitently that Rosalyn began to feel sorry for him. Marilyn Lowen's husband went into a rage at the group's intrusion. "It was scary," remembers Peslikis.

Robin Morgan joined the truth squad that confronted Judy Gabree's husband at *Penthouse* to demand that he quit his job at the porn magazine. Porn boss Bob Guccione took the women on, defending his empire in the name of sexual liberation. Robin, sitting on the floor, began nursing her six-month-old son, Blake.

She relates, "I said to Guccione, 'Do you see? This is a breast and this is a baby. This breast has a real functioning purpose. It feeds a child. This is what a breast is made for, not for your ogling.' And then, *quite* unintentionally, a stream of milk hit him in the eye. It was one of my best moments."

Robin, whose small group had remained intact after WITCH fell apart, was the best known "politico" in the city. After the episode with Guccione she came up with a new idea: "We were becoming bursitis-ridden, literally, from carrying around these goddamned mimeographed papers in shopping bags when we'd go to some college for a weekend of organizing. So I said, "This is ridiculous. Wouldn't it be wonderful if we could publish all of the papers in a book, a publicly available source, so the word can really get out.' And some people said, 'Yeah, that would be amazing.'"

Those were expansive days in publishing, when sympathetic editors were racing to offer contracts to New Left activists like Tom Hayden, Abbie Hoffman, Jerry Rubin, and the Soledad Brother George Jackson. Pressing her connections, Robin approached John Simon at Random House. "He said," she remembers, "that I had to get the material in fast because six months down the line there might not be any interest. So, bright-eyed and bushy-tailed, I went back to the group, thinking we'd do the anthology as a collective. And all hell broke loose."

Robin ran into the kind of opposition that would become all too familiar inside the movement. How would they divide the money? Maybe they weren't ready to go public! Would the publisher or their collective have final editorial control? Finally the women accused her of being on a personal star trip.

"After two or three meetings in which we continued to struggle with these things, something in me snapped," Robin says. "To my shock, I heard myself saying, 'Well, sisters, if the group won't do it, *I will.*'"

•   •   •

Nineteen sixty-nine had dawned hellishly for Betty Friedan. Her stormy marriage was coming apart. The insiders in NOW compared notes on her drinking and the knock-down-drag-out fights she had with Carl that left her with shiners on several occasions. NOW's sit-in/press conference at the male-only Oak Room of the Plaza in February was a great success, but Dolores Alexander, who'd left a job in journalism to be NOW's executive director, had to stall the press until Betty arrived. That morning Friedan had telephoned Dolores to say she couldn't show up—Carl had hit her the night before and she had a black eye. In a panic, Dolores phoned Jean Faust, a former president of the New York chapter, who rushed to Betty's Dakota apartment to see if she could do something with makeup. When Friedan finally swept in to the Plaza to face the press, she had on a mink coat and dark glasses. "I asked her to take off the dark glasses so I could have a look," Dolores recalls. "Jean had done a fabulous job. She looked fine."

Friedan got a Mexican divorce in May, but the dissolution of her twenty-two-year troth did not improve her famous temper. She yelled at the volunteers, reducing them to tears. In the thick of their battles Carl used to taunt that her beloved NOW was a a bunch of man-hating dykes. Betty began to pick up on the theme, muttering darkly about infiltratration. One day she turned on Dolores, warning some board members that their executive director was involved in a lesbian conspiracy to take over NOW. Dolores was dumbstruck. She was still involved with men, and the possibility of being a lesbian had not yet occurred to her. Of course there were lesbians in NOW, solid, hardworking activists like Toni Carabillo, who didn't bother to hide it, and Ivy Bottini, a mother of two who was just beginning to discover her lesbian identity. But NOW's lesbians had considered their sexual orientation to be a private matter until Rita Mae Brown had walked in the door.

By her own account, Rita Mae Brown was born in rural Pennsylvania, her father unknown, and adopted by relatives who ran a butcher shop in York. After spending her teen years in Fort Lauderdale, she attended the University of Florida before coming to New York to take her degree at NYU. Writing and filmmaking were her ambitions; stirring the pot was her pleasure. If Ti-Grace Atkinson, the sleekly coiffed blonde-turned-Amazon-warrior, had given Friedan some sleepless nights, Rita Mae Brown, a lesbian Huck Finn with curly short hair and intense dark eyes, was Friedan's nightmare come true.

"The first time I saw Rita Mae," recalls Jacqui Ceballos, "she looked like a little doll, a real southern belle. I was so proud to have her in the group. I thought, *Oh, we are finally getting the college women.*"

"Rita Mae was a true original," laughs Dolores Alexander. "Funny, witty, a wonderful speaker, and very evangelistic. She had this crusade to seduce every straight woman she knew."

Ivy Bottini was smitten. "I'll never forget the first meeting she came to," Bottini reminisces. "She was wearing a short skirt and a ruffled white blouse and she said, 'As your token lesbian in this room . . .' *Lesbian*! She'd uttered the word. You could have heard a pin drop, it was that quiet. I loved her for it. Dolores and I made her head of the newsletter committee."

Friedan was apoplectic. A survivor of the fifties, when union people and progressives were red-baited and hounded, she had a premonition that the same thing would happen to the women's movement, with dyke-baiting as the inquisitors' tactic. Friedan took stock of the new loose cannon and started muttering about the Lavender Menace.

For all Rita Mae's hands-on success in gaining converts, she felt the straights in NOW didn't want her, and after a few tumultuous months she quit. Believing the downtown radicals might be closer to her style, she exchanged her blouses and skirts for a secondhand military coat with epaulets and gold buttons and started coming around to the Redstockings meetings.

"The Redstockings didn't think of lesbians as a Lavender Menace or run for the door when I raised the issue," she remembered years later. "They simply weren't interested."

"Yes, Rita Mae was with us for a while," muses Kathie Amatniek Sarachild. "But it's funny, I always tend to forget that."

"There was such an assumption of heterosexuality at the beginning of the women's movement," says Ellen Willis, shaking her head.

•   •   •

Martha Shelley, a lesbian poet in Daughters of Bilitis, was showing Greenwich Village to some visitors from the Philadelphia chapter on a hot summer evening in June 1969 when they walked past Christopher Street and witnessed—she learned the next day—the first night of the Stonewall riots. "Oh, that's nothing, we have riots in New York every night of the week," she remembers telling her guests.

The truculent City College graduate, from a working-class Ortho-dox Jewish home, had read *The Feminine Mystique* "very early." At twenty-five she was writing poetry and working as a secretary at Barnard—"a nest of dykes, but what did I know?"—and going to Daughters of Bilitis meetings, "because I was a dyke but I wasn't a cute, WASPy, blond dyke, and I didn't do well in the Mafia-controlled bars."

D.O.B., the nation's first lesbian organization, had been founded in San Francisco in 1955, with a deliberately obscure name, by Del Mar-tin and Phyllis Lyon. The New York chapter, which rented space in a dingy warehouse, could count on ten members for its monthly meet-ings, and maybe thirty for a dance, but it suited Martha better than NOW, where, after some tentative forays, she had sensed that "a lot of the straight women felt uncomfortable around me." Still, it annoyed her that the D.O.B women were as conservative and square, in their own way, as the NOW women.

"In those days I was dropping acid, smoking dope, and also going to antiwar marches," she recounts. "I thought D.O.B. was nuts to try to prove to straight America that we were just like them only gay."

Stonewall changed everything. A month after the police bust of the drag queen bar and the unexpected street-kid resistance, the gay men of the Mattachine Society and the Daughters of Bilitis placed an ad in *The Village Voice* calling for a protest rally in Washington Square Park and a march to Sheridan Square. Several hundred people turned out for the unprecedented action. For the first time in history there were shouts of "Gay Power!"

"I jumped up and made a speech," Martha remembers. "I said, 'We'll be back.'"

Gay militance was rising and Martha was in the thick of it. That summer she helped form a new group with Jim Fouratt, the instigator of the Central Park Be-In and other whimsical Yippie happenings, and shop owner Bob Kohler, a befriender of street queens. Meeting at Alternate U., a radical lecture center on West Fourteenth Street, the militants attracted many previously closeted gays from the New and Old Left. "Our politics were left, feminist, gay, radical," Martha joyfully sums up. "We were proud commie pinko queers."

When someone uttered the name Gay Liberation Front, Martha pounded her fist on the table and shouted, "That's it!" She volunteered to edit *Come Out!*, GLF's monthly paper.

The lesbians who joined the Gay Liberation Front in its formative months were practiced swimmers in the era's swift currents. Lois Hart, nicknamed Lovingheart for her gentle, passionate nature, was Martha's polar opposite, a former nun who had passed through Millbrook, Timothy Leary's spiritual center for attaining higher consciousness through LSD. Artemis March, a Vassar graduate who had contemplated a career in sociology, had dropped out of the system to make and sell leather sandals and belts. Karla Jay, an editorial assistant at Collier's Encyclopedia, thought it prudent to keep her newfound lesbian activism a secret from her Redstockings consciousness-raising group. Ellen Shumsky, a school librarian, had been deeply involved in the battle for community control of the schools in Ocean Hill–Brownsville.

"I'd been so active with the radical teachers," Shumsky reflects, "but it was a totally schizophrenic existence because my personal life was in the lesbian community and the lesbian bars. The times were so homophobic, so toxic, that there was no way I could come out to my radical friends, or to the black community in Ocean Hill–Brownsville, and especially not to the school system. I couldn't put myself at risk."

For her GLF activities, Ellen Shumsky became Ellen Bedoz, adopting the surname of a feisty old lady she'd met in France. Her friend Barbara Gladstone, a dancer, took Barbara XX as her nom de guerre in honor of the twin female chromosomes.

· · ·

Nineteen seventy was the year when the women's newspapers first blossomed. Offset printing, an inexpensive technological advance, had spawned a lusty counterculture press from Boston to Berkeley, but now it would be the women's hour. Marilyn Webb of D.C. Women's Liberation first broached the idea to Heidi Steffens, Marlene Wicks, Coletta Reid, and Norma Lesser when they convened one night at her dining room table. Seven months pregnant, Marilyn was the only one in the group who had actually done any newspaper reporting. She was the Washington correspondent for the *National Guardian*, the left-wing weekly, and she had four hundred dollars in a movement bank account that she figured might be enough to launch the new paper's first issue. The brainstorming session was joyous as the women scribbled down two lists of names—one for the paper and one for Marilyn's baby.

Jennifer, the baby, missed her deadline of International Women's Day, March 8, 1970, by twenty-four hours. *Off our backs*, a twelve-page tabloid, was right on schedule. Its premier issue, dated February 27, ran articles on abortion and the medical dangers of the Pill, plus an illustrated lesson in how to insert a diaphragm. During the first heady months, anyone who wandered into Heidi Steffens's basement to type or paste up a few lines of copy could become a member of the *oob* collective. "We paid no rent, we broke all zoning regulations because we had no idea there were any, and we got no salaries," Webb recalls. "We didn't want a formal hierarchy, so jobs were never assigned. An informal hierarchy developed instead, based on who did the most work."

The people who did the most work were Marlene Wicks (layout, production, subscriptions, fund-raising) and Marilyn Webb, who could knock out a story in two days while other *oob* collectivists often struggled for weeks to produce their copy. Resentments festered. Onka Dekkers, who came from a working-class background, was among the first to bring up Marilyn's class privilege.

"What class privilege?" Webb exclaims. "My father worked in the garment center! But it's true that I'd gone to a good college." The collective asked Marilyn to cut back on her writing and help the others improve their pieces. Reluctantly she redirected her talents toward speaking about *oob* to college and community groups.

Marriages within the *oob* community were breaking up, replaced by communal living arrangements. Some new women, burned-out activists for the defense in the Chicago Eight conspiracy trial, blew into town and into the collective, bringing heavy-duty emotions, and heavy-duty acid.

Marilyn's speechmaking became the subject of intense group scrutiny. "The specific issue," she recalls, "was my giving a keynote speech at a National Student Association convention where I shared the platform with Betty Friedan. They said the radical movement shouldn't have any stars." Before the year was out, Marilyn Webb, the founder of *off our backs*, had been expelled from the *oob* collective. "They said," she recalls, "that I was taking up too much space."

During the following years *off our backs*, which continues to publish, attracted a stream of new writers and editors for whom the departure of Marilyn Webb would be a distant, if uncomfortable, legend.

The women's takeover of the radical underground newspaper *Rat* in New York had its origins in a bombing conspiracy that featured Jane Alpert. Alpert had graduated from Swarthmore with honors despite a secret abortion, an arrest in a civil rights demonstration, and a year's suspension for what was in those days an illegal lover's tryst. The tryst had had an unusually painful end: trying to elude the campus police, she had slipped off the roof of a college guesthouse, winding up in a body cast with three cracked vertebrae. At twenty-two Jane had moved in with Sam Melville, a moody, guitar-strumming revolutionary on the far-out left. Jane and Sam dropped a lot of acid while they vented their anger at the Vietnam War. Sam talked often about explosives and the need for secret revolutionary collectives. Jane quit her job at a university press after helping two Quebecois separatists hijack a plane to Cuba, and signed on as office helper at the *Rat* loft on Fourteenth Street. She sold all her books because Sam said the last thing the revolution needed was bookshelves. One evening when Jane came home late, Sam told her he'd planted a timed explosive at Marine Midland, a bank she had never heard of. They heard on the news, that several people were wounded but no one was killed.

During the next few months Melville's small group was to carry out several more sorties against corporate America (Jane executed one solo mission), and *Rat* was always the first newspaper to get a copy of the press release that accompanied the actions. Alpert, Melville, and David Hughey were arrested in November 1969.

Out on bail and denying all charges, Alpert was treated as a heroine at *Rat*, promoted to writing front-page stories. Hurrying to a fundraiser for her defense case one evening, she grabbed the latest issue and saw that the men had produced a sex-and-porn special.

"I felt personally affronted," Alpert recalls. "I was the best-known name associated with the paper at that point—how could they do it? So I called Robin Morgan, whom I admired as the most compelling person on the subject of bridging the left and the women's movement. I said the *Rat* women wanted to put out an all-women's issue and we needed her help."

Robin set aside her unfinished anthology and a book of poems and started recruiting. She summoned a few former WITCH women and Martha Shelley from the Gay Liberation Front. To the women's surprise, the *Rat* men walked out and gave them the paper.

The easy takeover inspired Morgan to new heights of rhetorical eloquence. "Goodbye to All That," her rhapsodic farewell to the male-dominated New Left, appeared in February 1970 in the women's inaugural issue. With its tell-all litany of movement abuses ("Run it down, run it all the way down") and impassioned calls to "free" the New Left leaders' wives and girlfriends ("Left out, my sisters—don't you see?") it stands today as one of the most powerful documents of the emerging feminist era. The rest of the paper reflected the usual politico interests. Jane Alpert interviewed Afeni Shakur of the Panther Twenty-one at the Women's House of Detention, but a black fist superimposed on the page obscured some of the questions and answers. "A Weatherwoman" issued a call to smash male chauvinism and monogamy in the Weather Underground. Martha Shelley drew an allegorical comic strip about the storming of *Rat* with knives and rifles, which new volunteers would take as gospel, and Robin, under a pseudonym, saluted Jiang Qing, the wife of Chairman Mao, for her leadership in the Cultural Revolution. "My rhetoric in 'Goodbye' was ahead of my reality," Morgan ruefully concedes today.

Several other women's papers were born that year, some expiring almost as rapidly as the collective spirit fractured or the money ran out.

Seattle, already home to *Lilith*, a feminist literary magazine, gave birth to *And Ain't I a Woman?* The famous rhetorical question from Sojourner Truth's dramatic speech to a women's rights convention in 1851 inspired another *Ain't I a Woman?* in Iowa City. The Iowa paper announced, "We are a collective of ten women functioning either as a front for a worldwide conspiracy of Radical Lesbians or the house cornfield of the Women's Movement."

Everywoman in Los Angeles was started by Varda One, the movement name of Varda Murrell, a suburban housewife with grown children, and Ann Forfreedom (Ann Herschfang), a pioneer in women's studies at UCLA and a founder of the L.A. Women's Center. Produced at the Murrell home in Inglewood until neighbors filed a zoning complaint, *Everywoman* relocated to Venice, a move that led to the founding of Everywoman Bookstore. *Tooth and Nail*, the product of New York transplants, survived for four issues in Berkeley. It was supplanted by *It Ain't Me Babe*, a substantial twenty-page paper reflecting the lively voices of San Francisco Bay Area Women's Liberation (cartoons by Trina Robbins, poems by Alta, political essays by Lynn O'Connor and Susan Griffin) that managed to stay afloat for six months. The *Babe*'s guiding spirits were Bonnie Eisenberg and Laura Murra, better known as Laura X, a charismatic activist who subsequently ran through her small inheritance by founding the Women's Herstory Archives, the movement's first attempt to collect and microfilm its historical records.

Up from Under surfaced briefly in New York, where *Aphra*, a literary magazine founded by Elizabeth Fisher, lasted for several seasons. *KNOW, Inc.* was a fact-filled communique from Jo-Ann Evans Gardner in Pittsburgh. By 1972, Donna Allen in Washington was publishing her steady, reliable *Media Report to Women*. In time more papers and periodicals appeared: *her-self* in Ann Arbor, *Sojourner* in Boston, *Big Mama Rag* in Denver, *Plexus* in San Francisco, *The Feminist Voice* in Chicago, the *Women's Press* in Eugene. At the height of the movement in the mid-seventies, Donna Allen recalls, *Media Report* was trading subscriptions with 250 local, indigenous feminist publications.

•   •   •

In the fall of 1969, Shulie Firestone abruptly quit Redstockings, accusing Kathie Sarachild of an existential inability to act. She teamed up with Anne Koedt to found New York Radical Feminists, yet another new group committed to theory and, the two women hoped, to outreach and organizing. They invited seven others to join their "leadership brigade," named Stanton-Anthony to honor the heroines of the suffrage struggle. Casting themselves as the radical progeny of the suffrage movement was a defiant, clarifying tactic on the part of Firestone and Koedt, for leftists habitually denigrated the suffrage battle, belittling it as a racist, upper-class white women's campaign.

Of all the factions in Women's Liberation that were forming and dissolving like amoebae that season, Stanton-Anthony proved the most responsive to unaffiliated women who were desperately trying to find their way into, or reconnect with, the movement. Sorting through phone numbers on scraps of paper, the founders set out to organize consciousness-raising groups on a neighborhood basis. One of their ideas, that Stanton-Anthony would lead and the junior brigades would follow, proved less popular that season.

I wanted to reconnect with the organized movement after the demise of New York Radical Women, where my attendance had been sporadic because of the interminable "Is the enemy man or capitalism?" debates. Hearing that Redstockings was temporarily closed to new members, I joined the West Village–One brigade of New York Radical Feminists with my friend Sally Kempton, a gifted writer at *The Village Voice*. Sally brought in her friend Grace Paley, the dedicated antiwar activist and author of *The Little Disturbances of Man*. Grace was a vital presence among us for thirteen weeks before she went back to her antiwar work. Sally became my partner in feminist activism for eighteen months, until she embarked on the spiritual quest that became her lifelong commitment. I stuck with the program. West Village–One, with a changing cast of characters, became my home base in feminism for the next four years. Along with many others in NYRF, I went out and organized new consciousness-raising groups for those who wanted to join the movement. At its height three years later, New York Radical Feminists had four hundred members in neighborhood-based groups in Manhattan, Brooklyn, and Queens, and had staged pioneering speak-outs and conferences on rape, prostitution, marriage, motherhood, and the sexual abuse of children.

Small-group consciousness-raising took hold so suddenly and spontaneously among American women in the suburbs and the cities that it cannot credibly be called a New York invention, although Kathie Sarachild and Anne Forer did name it and the New Yorkers were the fiercest champions of its political importance. Not everyone was temperamentally suited to the c.r. process, which required a high degree of honesty about intimate matters in front of relative strangers. Many of the "naturals" had been in group therapy or just adored talking about themselves. Others (I include myself in this category) had to overcome an inbred reluctance to speak confessionally, thinking it somewhat narcissistic. But we all believed in the political importance of our task. We expected that the pooled information would clear our heads and lead to analysis and theory, and it did.

Mimeographed sheets of suggested c.r. topics put out by Redstockings and the Radical Feminists found their way around the country, where they were used as guidelines for new groups that were forming. The weekly gatherings in somebody's living room variably were called "my women's group," "my small group," "my support group," "my c.r. group," or "my rap group" in the day's parlance. By early 1972 a few NOW chapters had begun to offer "c.r. nights" in addition to their more structured programs; the first issue of *Ms.*, in July 1972, carried instructions on how to organize a consciousness-raising group, along with a list of sample topics. The free and simple technique of "going around the room and speaking from your own experience" on a given subject with no formal leader was the movement's most successful form of female bonding, and the source of most of its creative thinking. Some of the small groups stayed together for more than a decade.

As the new women's discourse reached into the mainstream during the next few tumultuous years, many original perceptions that the pioneer consciousness-raising groups had struggled to express would become received information, routine and unexceptional, to a new generation that would wonder what the fuss and excitement was all about. I can attest that in New York City during the late sixties and early seventies, nothing was more exciting, or more intellectually stimulating, than to sit in a room with a bunch of women who were working to uncover their collective truths.

CONFRONTATION

I HAD BARELY SETTLED into the rhythm of my Sunday evening consciousness-raising group when *The New York Times Magazine* asked me to explore the curious new rumble known as Women's Liberation. Then I found another group I wanted to organize for called Media Women. Writing about Women's Liberation while organizing for it gave me my first taste of the movement's ire.

The *Times* assignment came my way after the editors' first choice, a male journalist of some repute, informed them that some movement women would speak only to women reporters. Since I'd written for the magazine before, I got the nod, along with the suggestion that I might want to peg my piece to Jane Alpert's arrest. I replied that Women's Liberation was about women's issues, not about bombing, and confessed that I was *in* Women's Liberation. My editor was surprised. I seemed so well adjusted, he said. Not at all angry. And what gripes could I possibly have—wasn't I one of the few women writing for the *Times* Magazine?

Diving into the story, I sought out the leaders of the various New York factions. Kathie Amatniek Sarachild was the only leader to insist on a group interview, maintaining that the movement did not have leaders. My session with her and nine other women at a Redstockings apartment was stilted and awkward. Some of the Redstockings let me know that they were suspicious of the establishment press. Midway through the exchange I recognized my old sofa, which I'd last seen at New York Radical Women.

Rita Mae Brown introduced herself during the group interview and told me about her resignation from NOW after Friedan had called her a Lavender Menace. I confirmed the remark with Friedan and put it near the end of my story, to address the recurring charge that all feminists were lesbians. Since what I wrote had such immediate reverberations, I will quote from "Sisterhood Is Powerful," my *Times* article of March 15, 1970:

> The supersensitivity of the movement to the lesbian issue, and the existence of a few militant lesbians within the movement once prompted Friedan herself to grouse about "the lavender menace" that was threatening to warp the image of women's rights. A lavender *herring*, perhaps, but surely no clear and present danger.

I was proud of that invented phrase, "lavender herring." In political usage a red herring is a smokescreen or a diversion from the issue at hand, and the issue at hand, as I saw it, was the feminist movement. Conjecturing that "lavender menace" owed its inspiration to "the Red Menace," I played with Friedan's color scheme to poke fun at her fear. I did not anticipate that some lesbians in the movement would read "lavender herring" and "no clear and present danger" as a scathing putdown, or that what I considered a cute turn of phrase would come back to haunt me.

• • •

While researching my article I joined Media Women, a spin-off from an antiwar journalists' coalition that met in midtown at St. Peter's Lutheran Church. Media Women owed much of its energy to Lindsy Van Gelder and Bryna Taubman, two young reporters who had created a furor at the *New York Post* during the pennant season of the Amazing Mets. Assigned to write "Women in News" features on two baseball players' wives, they'd done the work grudgingly and refused bylines for the stories. When they were fired for insubordination, the entire *Post* newsroom rose up and went on a wildcat no-byline strike. "The guys may not have understood what we were doing, or why," Bryna Taubman recalls, "but they understood reporters' rights." The women were rehired after the Newspaper Guild stepped in.

So Bryna, in her pigtails, and Lindsy, pregnant with her first child, were leaders in Media Women, along with Pam Jones from the Sunday Morning News at CBS. The Associated Press contingent consisted of two peppy reporters, Jurate Kascikas and Lynn Sherr. *Women's Wear Daily* was represented by Trucia Kushner, a smart, able writer who happened to be the sister of Abbie Hoffman's wife. Eleanor Perry, the screenwriter, and Nika Hazelton, the cookbook writer, occasionally showed up with Nora Ephron, then at *New York* magazine. Claudia Dreifus, Lucy Komisar, and Sophy Burnham were among the free-lancers. A delegation of *Newsweek* women usually sat by themselves in a little huddle, immersed in a secret plot that would soon become public. A contingent of obstreperous radicals from Newsreel, a leftist filmmakers' collective, asserted itself as another faction. Quiet as churchmice in the male-dominated Newsreel, Esther and Lynn (I won't use their last names) underwent a remarkable personality change at our all-women's meetings.

Despite or perhaps because of its tensions, Media Women was a high-spirited group that got things done. At one meeting Lucy Komisar mused on how nice it would be to have stickers emblazoned "This Ad Insults Women" to slap on offensive public advertising in the subways.

"Do it, Lucy," I prodded.

She arrived at the next meeting hauling cartons of stickers. We divided the costs and became a slap-happy crew. Soon we were selling the stickers around the city.

At another meeting I proposed that we target one of the big women's magazines that had remained immune to the changing times. From *Seventeen* to *Good Housekeeping*, all the slick publications instructing their readers in the feminine arts were run by men, except for *McCall's*, where Shana Alexander was new on the job, and *Cosmo*, the brainchild of Helen Gurley Brown. Clubby male editors warred over circulation and ad pages while they pushed a happy homemaker line from the 1950s that was white-bread formulaic. In a make-believe world of perfect casseroles and Jell-O delights, marriages failed because wives didn't try hard enough, single-parent households did not exist, and women worked outside the home not because they wanted to, or to make ends meet, but to "earn extra income in your spare time." The deceitful ideology discouraged the full range of women's ambitions.

Okay then, which magazine and what action? From the lunch counters of Greensboro, 1960, to the occupation of Columbia, 1968, sit-ins had been an electrifying tactic in radical movements. I suggested we try one, knowing that we had a surefire story that would get major coverage if we pulled it off.

Sandie North clapped her hands. "The *Ladies' Home Journal*, I used to work there! Let's occupy the *Ladies' Home Journal!*"

Most of the journalists with staff jobs bowed out of the action, feeling it crossed a boundary that professionals shouldn't cross. They promised to do what they could to get us attention. The freelancers, used to living on the edge, held firm.

The Ladies' Home Journal Sit-In Steering Committee was chaired by Signe Hammer, a junior editor at Harper and Row, and the planning sessions, in various people's apartments, were volatile in the extreme. Esther from Newsreel wanted men in on the action. *No, Esther. No men.* Esther from Newsreel wanted a separate contingent "to stop the presses in Dayton," where the *Journal* was printed. *Esther, we don't have the woman power to stop the presses in Dayton.* Esther from Newsreel was opposed to chaired meetings and votes. Dealing with Esther, a self-proclaimed anarchist, led me to formulate a precept: "One movement crazy can do the work of ten paid *agents provocateurs.*" I would repeat that line like a mantra in the years ahead, whenever suspicions arose that our movement had been infiltrated by government agents. Obstreperous Esther did not show up on the day of the action, and I never saw her again.

Finally we picked an invasion date: Wednesday, March 18, 1970. Sally Kempton put together twenty pages of article suggestions, the kind of material that the *Ladies' Home Journal* never printed. The suggestions ranged from our idea of genuine service pieces—"How to get a divorce," "How to have an orgasm," "How to get an abortion"—to "What to tell your draft-age son" and "How detergents harm our rivers and streams."

We learned about the cast of characters we would be confronting from Sandie North and her friend Brook Mason, who still worked at the *Journal*. John Mack Carter, age forty-two, the urbane, southern-born editor and publisher, had built his entire career at women's magazines and was a member of Sigma Delta Chi, the fraternity of distinguished journalists that until 1969 had excluded women. Lenore Hershey, the *Journal*'s sole woman above middle management, belonged to a generation of tough lady editors who sat at their desks in flowered hats; it was unlikely that she would declare herself on our side. The *Journal*'s paid circulation was 6.9 million, with a readership four times that number, yet more than half its articles were written by men. Only one piece by or about blacks, a hometown memoir by Mrs. Medgar Evers, had appeared in the last twelve months, although the magazine estimated its black readership at 1.2 million.

The *Journal*'s slogan was "Never Underestimate the Power of a Woman." We kept that in mind as we worked on our "nonnegotiable demands." Everyone was making nonnegotiable demands in those days. Looking back, though, I'm impressed at how farsighted we were.

We demand that the *Ladies' Home Journal* hire a woman editor-in-chief who is in touch with women's real problems and needs.

We demand that all editorial employees of the magazine be women.

We demand that the magazine use women writers for all columns and freelance assignments because men speak to women through the bias of their male supremacist concepts.

We demand that the magazine hire nonwhite women at all levels in proportion to the population statistics.

We demand that all salaries immediately be raised to a minimum of $125 a week.

We demand that editorial conferences be open to all employees so the magazine can benefit from everyone's experience and views.

Since this magazine purports to serve the interests of mothers and housewives, we demand that the *Journal* provide free day-care facilities on the premises for its employees' children, and that the policies of this day-care center be determined by the employees.

✓   We demand an end to the basic orientation of the *Journal* toward the concept of *Kinder, Küche, & Kirche* and a reorientation around the concept that both sexes are equally responsible for their own humanity.

We demand that the magazine cease to further the exploitation of women by publishing advertisements that degrade women, and by publishing ads from companies that exploit women in terms of salary and job discrimination.

We demand that the magazine cease to publish "Can This Marriage Be Saved?" and all contributions by Drs. Bruno Bettelheim and Theodore Rubin.

We demand an end to all celebrity articles, all articles oriented toward the preservation of youth (implying that age has no graces of its own), and an end to all articles specifically tied in to advertising: e.g., food, makeup, fashion, appliances.

We demand that service articles perform useful services: e.g., real information along the lines of *Consumer Reports*, telling whether consumer goods really work.

We demand that the *Journal* publish fiction on the basis of its merits, not specially slanted, romantic stories glorifying women's traditional roles.

The Women's Liberation Movement represents the feelings of a large and growing mass of women throughout the country. Therefore we demand that as an act of faith toward women in this country, the *Ladies' Home Journal* turn over to the Women's Liberation Movement the editorial content of one issue of the magazine, to be named the *Women's Liberated Journal*. We further demand a monthly column.

The main problem, as I saw it, was getting out the troops. At that early stage in Women's Liberation there had been WITCH zaps and NOW pickets, but most of the movement's energy was being directed toward consciousness-raising, abortion rights, and theoretical papers. A large-scale assault, in the flesh, on a giant American institution had not been attempted since the Miss America Protest of 1968. The leftists' taunt that we were living-room feminists was not without truth.

A sit-in does not need a huge number of demonstrators, but it does require a high degree of commitment. We had to find people willing to take a day off from work or school for an action that exposed them to arrest for criminal trespass, but if we tried to spread the word openly, with flyers on lampposts, for instance, the *Journal* might get wind of our intentions. We needed to proceed in stealth for maximum security and a lightning strike.

I passed the word to Kathie Amatniek Sarachild, who took it back to her group and returned with a solid guarantee of two dozen Redstockings. Kathie glumly predicted that the *Journal* would call the cops, but I did not think John Mack Carter would risk a tabloid headline along the lines of "Male Boss of Women's Mag Sends Gals to Clink." Furthermore, our sit-in was going to be perfectly nonviolent with an emphasis on constructive editorial advice and moral suasion. My friends Jan Goodman and Marion Davidson, then in their second year at NYU law school, enlisted as our legal advisers. If the paddy wagons showed up, Jan and Marion would negotiate with the police to make sure that the less-committed militants could leave quietly if they wished.

West Village–One, my consciousness-raising group, was fully behind the sit-in—ten more fearless activists to count on—but the leaders of New York Radical Feminists were dragging their feet. That situation changed one Sunday when Shulie Firestone and Anne Koedt were chairing the monthly general meeting and a visiting leftist erupted with the predictable "What do you women *do*? What are your *actions*?"

Anne turned to me. "Susan, you have an announcement about the magazine sit-in?" The visiting leftist got her answer, and I got a sign-up sheet with twenty more names.

Madelon Bedell, a public relations consultant and a member of OWL, Older Women's Liberation, promised to bring a crowd and commandeer the *Journal*'s test kitchen. Representatives from Barnard and Columbia Women's Liberation pledged their support. Twenty-three women signed a recruitment sheet at New York NOW. Michela Griffo, an art student at Pratt, volunteered to do the cover for our mock magazine, the *Women's Liberated Journal*, and produced a witty graphic of a pregnant woman holding an "Unpaid Labor" picket sign. We reproduced it as a poster. Janet Gardner and Jo Tavener from NYU film school were ready to roll if I could get them a light meter. Marlene Sanders at ABC called me to confirm that she and a network film crew would be shooting.

The countdown was scary. I had set in motion an act of protest that was rude, antic, patently illegal, and guaranteed to make news. Two weeks before, the Weathermen had accidentally blown up their bomb factory on West Eleventh Street in Greenwich Village, killing three of their number. My plan to confront the system was hardly akin to theirs, but it, too, was hurtling forward on its own momentum. Several hundred people going about their normal routines had no idea that they were prisoners of a ticking clock. I wondered if terrorists were ever beset by twinges of misgiving.

On Wednesday morning, March 18, I put on my best dress, a sleeveless gray wool, and bade a solemn goodbye to Kevin Cooney, the man I lived with. Reuters, the international wire service he worked for, was sending a reporter. Alerted in advance, all the major media outlets were sending reporters, and as far as I knew they hadn't tipped off the *Journal*, not wanting to ruin the spontaneity of a very good story. The gnawing question, the eternal one for organizers, was how many demonstrators would actually show up. Fifty would be a disappointment; thirty would be a rout. Kevin made a joke about the Women's Massacre and wished me a slow news day so we'd get lots of press.

Outside my apartment building I linked up with Jan, Sally, her friend Helen Whitney, and Grace Lichtenstein of *The New York Times*, my neighbor and friend. We took the E train to St. Peter's Church, our convenient collection point at Lexington and Fifty-third, one block from the glass skyscraper that housed the *Journal*. By 9 A.M. fifty demonstrators were huddled in the church vestibule. Another twenty-five waited outside, hugging their arms in the chilly March air.

We had a liftoff! Signe Hammer and I distributed posters and fact sheets, and went over the logistics: Mingle with the flow of office workers boarding the elevators, get off at the fifth floor. Sandie North and Brook Mason had taken me on a tour of the *Journal*'s labyrinthine corridors a few days earlier so I'd be able to lead the troops directly to John Mack Carter's huge corner office.

Right on schedule at 9:15, the first wave of demonstrators streamed into the building and proceeded upstairs. An AP photographer was snapping away, dancing backward at the front of the line. We passed startled secretaries clutching Styrofoam coffee cups. They gazed at us numbly. Everything was going according to plan. Except for my miserable sense of direction. Nothing looked familiar. I was hopelessly lost.

"Perhaps it's the other way?" said the man from AP.

"The other way!" I shouted.

The surging line reversed course. Eventually we tumbled into Carter's office.

He looked up from his desk, expensively suited, thinner and smaller than I'd imagined. Lenore Hershey was at his side. True to the lady-editor dress code, she was wearing a hat, although it did not sprout any flowers.

"Good morning," I began. "We are the Women's Liberation Movement. We shall now read our demands."

We demand . . .

We demand . . .

Our numbers had swelled to more than one hundred, and Signe and I had read the demands a second time, wondering what to do next, when at precisely 9:30 Marlene Sanders and the ABC film crew strode in. It was like the cavalry coming over the hill.

"Carter!" Marlene thrust her microphone forward. "What is your response to what these women are saying?"

Swallowing hard, John Mack Carter worked his jaw. He swallowed again. In shock, the man who had built his career by speaking for women had lost his own voice.

One by one the demonstrators found theirs. Sookie Stambler, Diana Gould, Ada Pavletich, Alice Denham, Sara Pines, Susan Frankel, Barbara Joans, Sonia Robbins, Corinne Coleman, Vivien Leone, Jacqui Ceballos, Marli Weiss, Rosetta Reitz—these are the women I particularly remember. Everyone was eloquent. They talked about their lives; they talked about their mothers' lives and their mothers' thwarted aspirations. I stepped back and relaxed.

No vocal failure afflicted senior editor Lenore Hershey. She was a tiger at the gate, a bear guarding her cub, a magpie passing judgment on our clothes, our hair, our extremely rude manners. Sisterhood failed us badly with Lenore Hershey. I got the feeling that even Carter wished she'd just shut up and listen.

The occupation of the *Ladies' Home Journal* lasted for eleven hours, and I can't remember Carter ever leaving his desk. At its height, two hundred demonstrators milled freely on the premises, engaging secretaries and editorial assistants in earnest discussions, hanging a banner, THE WOMEN'S LIBERATED JOURNAL, outside a window, picnicking on the carpet, passing around Carter's box of cigars, explaining their philosophy and grievances to WINS All-News Radio, CBS, NBC, the *Daily News*, *The Washington Post*.

Shana Alexander from the rival *McCall's* sent her beleagured counterpart a condolence bouquet of flowers.

Grace Lichtenstein whispered to me that the *Times* loved her call-in report and wanted more.

Trucia Kushner commandeered a phone to give a running account to *Women's Wear Daily*.

Art Rust, Jr., of NBC made the mistake of shoving Claudia Dreifus of the *East Village Other*.

"Out! Out! Out!" the demonstrators chanted.

Idly I watched Tony Rollo of *Newsweek* lavish a roll of film on Holly Forsman, winsome in her granny glasses, as she rested her chin, just *so*, on a homemade poster. Holly, of New York Radical Feminists, was a former teen-fashion model for Eileen Ford.

In the media free-for-all, some of our more experienced firebrands who hadn't attended the planning sessions felt ignored. Only the night before, Ti-Grace Atkinson had purred into the phone, "I have decided to attend your demonstration. My presence will assure that you get media coverage." Now I watched her stalk the perimeter of Carter's office, unrecognized and unnoticed.

Shulie Firestone was in a snit, stamping her foot like Rumpelstiltskin.

"Am I your leader in New York Radical Feminists?"

"Yes, Shulie, you are."

"Then tell the reporters they must speak to *me*!"

"Shulie, they'll speak to whomever they want."

Minutes later I was standing near Karla Jay, a sturdy Redstocking with a sense of humor who was doubling that season as a rotating chair in the Gay Liberation Front. We were facing the sleek expanse of

Carter's wood desk when Shulie, egged on by Ti-Grace, made her move.

"I've had enough of this," Firestone screamed, leaping onto the desk and tearing at a copy of the *Ladies' Home Journal*. As the magazine's spine broke she received a smattering of nervous applause and suddenly I had the sinking feeling that something was about to go dreadfully wrong. Then she shouted, "We can do it—he's small," and took a flying dive at John Mack Carter.

I froze.

Carter froze.

Everyone froze except Karla Jay. With split-second timing she grabbed Shulie's right arm and expertly flipped her off the desk and out of danger. There was an audible "Oooooh" as Shulie sailed in an arc toward three waiting demonstrators who cushioned her fall. A phalanx of hands reached out to detain her while she blinked, looking sheepish. Her passion was spent.

Karla had been studying judo for all of three months. *I have to save this woman from going to jail and destroying her life*, Karla remembers thinking.

Without Karla Jay's intervention, the *Journal* sit-in might have turned into a disastrous melee. She was our heroine, the woman of the hour. As for Shulie, at the time I thought that the media opportunity had simply gone to her head, but in retrospect I believe that her lunge was the first public sign of her growing instability. Disgraced, she walked out the door with Ti-Grace Atkinson and Rosalyn Baxandall. The three veteran activists, accustomed to claiming their place at the eye of the storm, tramped down the back stairs agreeing that the Media Women was a finky bunch. Ros had seen us wave sheaves of paper at Carter and Hershey—our precious demands and article suggestions. With little effort she somehow convinced herself that we were brandishing resumés and angling for jobs.

Most people who were there believe that the unplanned drama of Shulie's dive and Karla's flip spurred John Mack Carter to begin negotiating with us in earnest. Whether that was the catalyst or not, his initial stance—"I will not negotiate under siege"—changed at midday to "I will not negotiate with a group larger than twelve."

Choosing representatives from the various factions—three Red-stockings, one OWL, four Media Women, Karla! Karla! etc.—was diplomacy worthy of the United Nations. We worked it out and repaired to a conference room while a weary Carter informed the lingering demonstrators, "Stay or leave as you wish." The man had great dignity. Afterward he said the experience had been the most interesting and transformative day of his career.

By 6 P.M. we were hammering out the basic terms of our settlement. The *Journal* editors agreed to hand over eight pages of their August issue, for which they'd pay us ten thousand dollars. They also promised to explore the feasibility of an on-site day-care center.

•   •   •

A month later Robin Morgan led a mini-assault on her former employer, Grove Press, a small publishing house that thrived on its backlist of fancy European erotica. A dozen militants, including Ti-Grace Atkinson and Martha Shelley, barricaded themselves in publisher Barney Rosset's office, demanding that "the millions of dollars earned from pornographic books that degrade women" be put into a prostitutes' bail fund, a child-care center on Grove's premises, and a salary raise for Grove's staff.

"We hung a banner out the window," Martha Shelley recalls. "And I broke into Rosset's liquor cabinet and took a drink, as a sort of symbolic gesture."

The absent Rosset, in Copenhagen on a business trip, gave the order by phone to call the cops. Nine of the invaders were arrested, trundled from one precinct station to another, strip-searched, and put in an overnight holding tank. Released the next day, they called a press conference. "The idea was that each of us was to speak for a couple of minutes," Martha Shelley recalls, "but Ti-Grace went on for an hour until the reporters drifted off. She wouldn't shut up."

•   •   •

Meanwhile, the articles for our *Ladies' Home Journal* supplement, produced by five independent collectives, were being read aloud in my living room and edited jointly, a horrendous process. Nora Ephron signed on as utility fielder, weeding out clunkers as best she could. The *Journal*'s ten-thousand-dollar payment was a hot potato. Susan Spivak at Paul, Weiss, Goldberg, Rifkind, etc., incorporated us pro bono as the Women's Liberation Writing Collective with tax-exempt status assuring the IRS we would not engage in any further shakedowns of the publishing community by means of picketing or sit-ins. Signe Hammer chaired an open meeting at the Women's Center on West Twenty-second Street to decide how to allocate the funds.

The vibes at the Women's Center—two rooms, a couple of desks, a bookshelf, a few broken armchairs—weren't exactly friendly. You'd ring the bell, identify yourself, and somebody would throw down a key from a window. On the night of the big vote, the place was jammed with women sitting cross-legged on the floor, three apiece in the armchairs. Most of them hadn't been near the *Journal* sit-in and weren't involved in writing the supplement either. One faction tried to swing the entire ten thousand to the Joan Bird bail fund. (Bird, a Bronx Community College student and black activist, was one of the Panther-Twenty-one accused of plotting to blow up several police stations, department stores, and the Bronx Botanical Garden. Ultimately the Twenty-one were acquitted.) Another faction wanted to put all the money into a revolving bail fund for city prostitutes. Signe Hammer recalls that I rammed through a parliamentary motion against bullet-voting. That sounds like me. The checkbook shows that the money was apportioned to a day-care center, an abortion project, a women's newspaper, a women's film collective, and yes, a bail fund. The largest chunk paid the rent on the Women's Center for a year. I thought I had done a great job in building the movement, but in fact I was attracting enemies and was too busy to notice.

The one-two punch of my Sunday *Times* article and the *Journal* action, an accident of timing, had given me a dose of media attention that was aggravated by an appearance on Dick Cavett. I'd been thrilled to be asked. Cavett's late-night talk show headlined every new cultural and political trend in the nation, and of course I wanted my chance to reach an audience of millions. I roped Sally Kempton into going with me, following the Women's Liberation model of appearing in pairs to avoid the leadership and stardom onus. Our mission was to confront

Hugh Hefner in fifteen minutes between the Jefferson Airplane and Rollo May. The band struck up the Cavett theme song, we sauntered in, and Cavett asked me to define Women's Liberation. I quipped, "When Hugh Hefner comes here with a cotton tail attached to his rear end, that's the day we'll have equality."

The audience roared, but my star turn was over too quickly. Cavett invited us back the following week for a serious conversation.

Sally, who had not enjoyed herself as much as I had, flatly refused to return for a second engagement. I pondered the wisdom of going on alone. Obviously one of my driving forces was an unquiet need for recognition. I believed I had it in me to do important work, but media celebrity as a talk show guest, "famous for being famous," was not what I had in mind. Besides, as Sally, now the Swami Durgananda, reminds me, the two of us knew we'd catch hell from the movement. So I joined Sally in declining to do a second program.

Holly Forsman and Diane Crothers, two standout women in New York Radical Feminists, were happy to take our place. They were promptly trashed by *Rat* for seeking stardom.

• • •

Michela Griffo, the art student at Pratt who had designed our poster, had not shown up on the day of the *Ladies' Home Journal* sit-in. She had gone ballistic over my phrase "lavender herring" in the *Times* the previous Sunday.

"I was incensed," she recalls. "I didn't see 'menace,' I just saw 'herring.' It was so dismissive, Susan, and you followed that line with 'no clear and present danger'! I'd always liked you before then, but now you were the enemy."

Twenty-one years old at the time, Michela was a convent-educated doctor's daughter from Rochester, New York. Engaged to a medical student, she had discovered her lesbian identity only a few months before, "when my friend Agneta, the most beautiful woman I had ever known, kissed me in my Horatio Street kitchen, and suddenly I knew what it was I'd been missing."

From the moment of that kiss, Michela also understood that "I had stepped into a world where I was going to be judged by who I slept

with, and I didn't have a choice whether or not to be political about it."
In January 1970 she resigned from NOW with Rita Mae Brown.
Teaming up like the Lone Ranger and Tonto, in Michela's description,
Brown and Griffo scoped out Redstockings, where they tried a c.r.
group, and lent a hand at the liberated *Rat*, where Rita Mae published
poetry and essays and Michela did pasteups and graphics. They sur-
veyed the scene at the Gay Liberation Front, where the GLF women,
outnumbered and outvocalized, were having their problems with the
GLF men.

"Rita and I came into GLF to start trouble," Griffo relates. "Our
sole purpose was to politicize the lesbians, to get them out of this male-
dominated organization and start our own lesbian political base. And
that was exactly what we did."

"We didn't really distinguish ourselves as lesbians during the first
few months of the GLF," says Ellen Shumsky, "but I guess some feminist stuff was filtering through. We were becoming aware at the meetings that the men were always the primary speakers. The weekend
dances, our big social forum, became the scene where the power struggles got enacted. We felt the dances were being conducted in a male
style, which at the time meant a dark, packed room, loud music, and
lots of raunchy, hot bumping and grinding. There was no place to talk,
no place where the lights were on and you could really see other people and be more contemplative, social, and playful. All this predated
the GLF Women's Caucus, and the split."

In a gut response to my words in the *Times*, Griffo made an "I Am
a Lavender Herring" T-shirt with iron-on letters and wore it to the
next Gay Liberation Front dance. "Everybody thought it was the funniest thing they had ever seen," she remembers.

"Michela had on a jacket over her shirt," says Artemis March. "She
was going around the floor sort of flashing 'Lavender Herring.'"

"Rita was so impressed that she wanted to plan an action around it,"
says Griffo. "Something that would embarrass the women's movement
for denying our existence."

"Well, some people might have seen it that way," says Artemis
March, who'd taken a seminar run by Cell 16 in Boston and had briefly
hooked up with THE FEMINISTS in New York. "We had this gay thing

over here, and there's that feminist thing over there, but there's no lesbian-feminist thing. Rita Mae proposed that we start such a process."

The GLF women coalesced around their new, unifying purpose. In April 1970 they sponsored the first of their own All-Women's Dances at Alternate U. The dances were joyful occasions. Beer sold for fifty cents and as many as three hundred women, drawn by leaflet actions in the Mafia-controlled bars, linked arms and kicked up their heels in large circles, stripping off their tops as the evening progressed. At the same time or even earlier, a small group of GLF women started meeting at Brown's fifth-floor walkup, where they made plans to disrupt the Second Congress to Unite Women, which NOW and the radical groups were convening in May with no mention of lesbians on the proposed agenda.

Early on, Griffo recalls, Brown decided that "Lavender Menace," not "Lavender Herring," would be the best slogan for their T-shirts "because that's who we were, or were going to be—a menace."

"We wanted to do something that would get their attention," says Artemis March. "Something funny and positive that would engage people and open up a space for us to make a statement. The notion was that we would collectively develop a position paper. Rita thought it was very important that we sign it with real names."

Around this time, the GLF women became the Radicalesbians, independent of the Gay Liberation Front. They made up a "Radicalesbian" button, chic with good lettering, in black and white.

"Radicalesbians? Why not Radical Radishes?" somebody quipped. And sure enough, somebody else made a "Radical Radish" button and wore it to the next meeting.

It fell to Artemis March to organize and synthesize the position paper that Rita Mae wanted, the paper that would define lesbian feminism for the first time in history. Artemis started composing her drafts, reading them aloud to the others, getting their input.

"Sidney Abbott came over to the little hole in the wall in Brooklyn Heights where I was living," she remembers. "I'm pacing around saying, 'Oh, this action at the Congress is going to happen in ten days and I'm stuck. It's not flowing.' 'March,' she says, 'you need a hook. How

are you going to get my attention?' Sidney used to work in public relations. Then she comes out with, 'A lesbian is the rage of all women
condensed to the point of explosion.' It was a beautiful statement. I
knew it was hyperbolic, but it was a beautiful opener and it broke the
logjam."

The Sunday before the Congress, a weary Artemis March read her
eleventh draft at a Radicalesbian brunch at Ellen Shumsky's. Linda
Rhodes came up with a title: "The Woman-Identified Woman."
Artemis typed the final version on an IBM Selectric after business
hours in Barbara Love's father's office. She appended six names to the
paper in order of the importance of their contributions: hers (as March
Hoffman, the name she then used), Ellen Shumsky (signed Ellen
Bedoz), Cynthia Funk, Rita Mae Brown, Lois Hart, and Barbara Gladstone (as Barbara XX). Then she added, because it was true, "with
other Radicalesbians," and put a price on it of twenty-five cents. She
ran off enough xeroxed copies to fill two cartons.

• • •

The ironically named Second Congress to Unite Women took place at
an intermediate school in Chelsea during the weekend of May 1–3,
1970. I will never forget the intensity of the emotions that were released at the Congress—some of them directed specifically toward me.

Two dozen "Lavender Menace" T-shirts had been dyed and silk-
screened at Ellen Broidy's apartment. Even counting the Vassar students who were coming down for the action (Rita Mae had read her
poetry at Vassar to great effect), the Radicalesbians did not expect to
exceed that number. Ellen Shumsky got a shirt with scrunched-up
letters. Artemis March, arriving with her cartons of "The Woman-
Identified Woman," got stuck with a shirt that came out bright fuch-
sia. On Friday morning Michela Griffo and Jessica Falstein talked their
way into the school, claiming they had been sent by NOW to check
out the auditorium's light board.

Four hundred women were in their seats for the Friday night opening session, listening to the welcoming address, when Michela, hiding
backstage, shouted, "Jessie, the lights!"

The auditorium was plunged into darkness. When the lights went back on, seventeen Lavender Menaces were on the stage and Martha Shelley had grabbed the microphone. Posters lined the sides of the hall: TAKE A LESBIAN TO LUNCH. LAVENDER JANE LOVES YOU. WE ARE ALL LESBIANS. LESBIANISM *IS* A WOMEN'S LIBERATION PLOT.

Jennifer Woodul, one of the Vassar students, watched in amazement as women unknown to the planners climbed onto the stage to join them. Others, some very well known to them, simply got up from their seats and formed an orderly line down below at the open mike. Sidney Abbott watched Ivy Bottini of NOW slowly made her way down the aisle. Then she spotted Kate Millett.

"I know what this oppression is all about—I've lived it," Millett said softly when it was her turn at the microphone.

The Lavender Menaces held forth for two hours that night, and conducted consciousness-raising workshops during the next two days of the conference. Artemis March sold out her supply of "The Woman-Identified Woman." A bunch of women, straight and gay, caroused happily on Saturday night at an all-women's dance at the Church of the Holy Apostles. Lesbians would be silent no longer in the women's movement.

•   •   •

I didn't get to the Congress until Sunday because I was working. When I walked in, looking for a warm bath of sisterhood, Susan Frankel from West Village–One, my consciousness-raising group, greeted me with a nervous warning, "They're organizing a petition against you."

"They" were a handful of women who'd run a Saturday workshop on class privilege and oppression. Marshaling their assorted frustrations, they'd come up with a resolution condemning Lucy Komisar and me for "seeking to rise to fame on the back of the women's movement by publishing articles in the establishment press."

Lucy and I were movement women. Our accusers knew us from scores of meetings. But now they couldn't see past our bylines. By no stretch of the imagination can a journalist's byline be construed as "fame," yet nothing threatened a particular kind of movement woman more than seeing another movement woman's name in print. The previous month a radical floater named Verna Tomasson had said of the

Ladies' Home Journal action in *Rat*, "Those of us who are writers and struggling just like Brownmiller et al. for recognition were especially resentful of being used by other writers to further their professional aspirations." She had followed her rebuke with a private letter to me complaining that an essay of hers had been rejected by *Look*. Apparently my ability to navigate in mainstream waters made me the enemy, while her motivations in seeking publication, of course, had been pure.

Lucy and I weren't the only reporters to have attracted resentment. Marlene Sanders of ABC had been sabotaged at the First Congress in November, but I hadn't heard Marlene's story and I couldn't find Lucy. My consciousness-raising group advised me to lie low when the damning resolution was read to the plenary session. I thought about the show trials in Eastern Europe when loyal Communists remained mute because they believed the people's revolution was more important than individual rights. I thought about the mass hysteria going on in China.

My accusers, some of whom I recognized, were trembling as they read their resolution aloud. When they got to the part about me, I leaped up and bellowed, "That's *my* name you're using, *sisterrrrs!*"

Necks craned. The Class Workshop women looked away and continued reading, arm in arm.

After they finished, discussion on the resolution was brief. Rita Mae Brown spoke for it. Eyes flashing, she skipped down the aisle, rapping about growing up in the South as poor white trash. For her finale she sassed, "We don't need spokespeople and we don't need leaders. All women can speak, and all women can write."

Her rhetoric brought down the house. Rita Mae, at twenty-five, was not yet a published author. *Rubyfruit Jungle* appeared in a feminist press edition in 1973 and became a mainstream paperback bestseller in 1977, proving that Rita Mae Brown, for one, could write up a storm. I believe she had her own potential in mind at the Congress when she made her demagogic pitch.

When the applause for Rita Mae died down, the NOW women rose in my defense. They were appalled by the Class Workshop's tactics, and their genuine outrage carried the day. The resolution was defeated by a comfortable margin.

Minutes later the Lavender Menace took over the stage again for a brief reprise of their Friday night action. The lesbian show of solidarity was so good-natured that the earlier ugliness was forgotten.

But not by me. I felt stamped on, repudiated, rejected by a movement I cared about more than anything else. When I got home that evening, Kevin handed me a Kurt Vonnegut short story, the one about an equalized society in which graceful people are burdened by leg weights and smart people wear electronic contraptions that scramble their brains every twenty seconds. Vonnegut's story was a tonic, though my misery lingered for months.

I was to watch the radical women's movement turn on its own people many times during the next decade. Eventually I grew fairly philosophic about it. A certain amount of cannibalizing seems to go with the territory whenever activists gather to promote social change. You need nerves of steel to survive in a radical movement, and you have to believe that the Sturm und Drang are worth it.

• • •

The entire country seemed to be in a state of upheaval. On May 4, four students at Kent State University in Ohio were killed by National Guardsmen trying to quell a campus protest against the extension of the Vietnam War into Cambodia. The same day, Jane Alpert jumped bail and went underground, hoping to connect with Weatherman. On the morning of her departure Robin Morgan supplied her with a thousand dollars in cash and a satchel filled with makeup and hair bleach to create a disguise. *Rat*'s next cover bore a sketch of a dripping faucet and a handwritten scrawl, "Jane, you left the water running."

Robin and Jane, torn between the new voice of feminism and the siren call of the radical left, would need another two years before they renounced armed struggle.

Robin's anthology, *Sisterhood Is Powerful*, was in galleys at Random House. She squeezed her last-minute "Letter to a Sister Underground" into her introduction, dropping "Goodbye to All That," her passionate critique of the male left, for Marge Piercy's more tempered essay on a similar theme. Morrow had acquired Shulamith Firestone's *The Dialectic of Sex*, which the twenty-five-year-old author was speeding to finish. Betty Prashker of Doubleday was oiling the gears for Kate Millett's *Sexual Politics*, believing she had an important book on her hands but not one that was likely to hit the charts. Everyone in book publishing seemed to be of the opinion that the women's rebellion, whatever it was, would last six months.

"ABORTION IS A
WOMAN'S RIGHT"

WOMEN'S LIBERATION FOUND its first unifying issue in abortion, and abortion became the first feminist cause to sweep the nation. From 1969 to 1972 an imaginative campaign—rash, impudent, decentralized, yet interconnected by ideas and passion—successfully altered public perception to such an extent that a "crime," as the law defined it, became a "woman's constitutional right." Its capstone was *Roe v. Wade*, the monumental Supreme Court decision of January 22, 1973.

Nineteen sixty-nine was a precisely defined moment, the year when women of childbearing age transformed a quiet back-burner issue promoted by a handful of stray radicals and moderate reformers into a popular struggle for reproductive freedom. The women had been dubbed the Pill Generation, and indeed, earlier in the decade many had heeded the persuasive call of the sexual revolution, only to be disenchanted. Exploring their sexual freedom with an uncertain knowledge of birth control and a haphazard employment of its techniques, they had discovered the hard way that unwanted pregancy was still a woman's problem.

Unlike the isolated women of their parents' generation who sought individual solutions in furtive silence, they would bring a direct personal voice to the abortion debate. They would reveal their own stories, first to one another and then to the public. They would borrow the confrontational tactics of the radical-left movements from which they had come. They would break the law, and they would raise a ruckus to change the law, devising original strategies to fight for abortion through the courts.

Before the new militance erupted, abortion was a criminal act in every state unless a committee of hospital physicians concurred that the pregnancy endangered the woman's life. Three states had extended the largesse to women whose health was threatened—broadly interpreted, health could mean mental health, if two psychiatrists so attested—but no more than ten thousand "therapeutic" abortions were performed in a year. To the general public, abortion was the stuff of lurid tabloid headlines that underscored its peril: A young woman's body found in a motel room; she'd bled to death from a botched operation. A practitioner and a hapless patient entrapped in a midnight raid on what the police dubbed "an abortion mill." There were shining exceptions like the legendary Dr. Robert Spencer of Ashland, Pennsylvania, who ran a spotless clinic and charged no more than one hundred dollars, but venality ran high in an unlawful business in which practitioners were raided and jailed and patients were pressured to be informers. Money was not the only commodity exchanged on the underground circuit; some abortionists extorted sexual payment for their secret work.

One million women braved the unknown every year, relying on a grapevine of whispers and misinformation to terminate their pregnancies by illegal means. Those lucky enough to secure the address of a good practitioner, and to scrounge up the requisite cash, packed a small bag and headed for San Juan, Havana, London, or Tokyo, or perhaps across town. The less fortunate risked septic infection and a punctured uterus from back-alley amateurs willing to poke their insides with a catheter, a knitting needle, or the unfurled end of a wire hanger. Still others damaged their health with lye or Lysol, the last-ditch home treatments. *Life* magazine estimated in 1967 that "five thousand of the desperate" died every year.

The writer Jane O'Reilly's story gives the lie to the too simple myth that "rich" women could always find a connection. In the summer of 1957, she was a Catholic debutante from St. Louis who was

looking forward to her senior year at Radcliffe when she discovered
she was pregnant. Dr. Spencer was in one of his periodic shutdowns,
Cuba sounded unreal and scary, and the trusted family doctor to
whom she appealed insisted that she tell her parents. A classmate finally came up with an address in New York and lent her the six hundred dollars. O'Reilly recalls that a man with a mustache placed her
on a kitchen table, prodded her with a knitting needle, and gave her
some pills.

A month later she fainted in her college dormitory shower. Whatever had been done to her in New York, Jane O'Reilly was still pregnant. Moving out of the dorm, she joked about putting on weight
and took her finals shrouded in a raincoat. The next day she gave
birth at a Salvation Army hospital and signed away her baby daughter. For the next thirty-four years on every May 10, her daughter's
birthday, O'Reilly plunged into a sobbing depression. In 1991 the
pain partially lifted when her daughter found her through an adoption search.

Women of my generation still need to bear witness; we still carry
the traumas. For my first abortion in 1960 I took the Cuba option that
had scared O'Reilly. Here's what I remember: Banging on a door during the midday siesta in a strange neighborhood in Havana. Wriggling
my toes a few hours later, astonished to be alive. Boarding a small plane
to Key West and hitchhiking back to New York bleeding all the way.
Bleeding? I must have been hemorrhaging. In which state did I leave
the motel bed drenched with my blood?

No movement is without heroic antecedents. In 1962 Sherri
Finkbine, the host of *Romper Room*, a franchised television show
for children in Phoenix, Arizona, went public with her insistence
that the medical establishment owed her a legal abortion. That was
the year thalidomide, a tranquilizer prescribed for morning sickness,
was found to deform the fetus. Finkbine, pregnant with her fifth
child, had taken the drug. A therapeutic procedure was approved for
her at a Phoenix hospital, but when she gave an interview to a newspaper reporter, the nervous doctors reneged. Finkbine stubbornly
pressed her case in an avalanche of media attention. With time running out, she flew to Sweden for a legal termination. Her public

odyssey ended her television career, but it opened the door to a national debate.

Four years later Patricia Maginnis, a survivor of three illegal terminations, two self-induced, founded the Society for Humane Abortion in California. Working with Lana Clarke Phelan and Rowena Gurner, she put out an abortion handbook of practical advice and took the brave step of offering referrals through the mail. Her mimeographed list of Mexican clinics bore a startling legend: "A woman has the right to control her own body." Few people knew the electrifying phrase had been voiced by Margaret Sanger, the birth control pioneer, at the turn of the century.

I was vacationing in London during the summer of 1967 while Parliament was moving toward passage of an extremely liberal Termination of Pregnancy bill. Nothing about this remarkable event had appeared in the American press, so I wrote a piece for *The Village Voice* and enjoyed watching *The New York Times* play catch-up. By then I'd been to Puerto Rico for my second and third illegal abortions. *Voice* writers seldom shrank from first-person journalism, but it never occured to me to tell my own story. The movement was to pioneer that strategy two years later. In 1967 I wrote simply that Britain's move toward legalization exemplified the civilizing influences one found in that country.

That year the Reverend Howard Moody of the Judson Square Memorial Church in Greenwich Village added abortion referrals to his long list of humanitarian missions. Two years later the liberal Baptist with a powerful commitment to social justice had inspired a loose federation of ministers and rabbis in six cities. Moody's Clergy Consultation Service sent women to local abortionists who passed its stringent tests, and also had working arrangements with doctors in London and Puerto Rico. Here and there at the major colleges, students increasingly found they could count on someone, another student or the wife of a professor, for a solid referral.

I wrote about the Clergy Consultation Service for *New York* magazine. The feminist movement was beginning to make itself heard, and my piece reflected a certain new surliness that was abroad in the land. One clergyman I interviewed had preened with self-importance, which did not sit well with my growing militance. I appreciated the fact that men of the cloth were risking arrest to help desperate women, but women were becoming infused with the urgent desire to help themselves.

Improved technology was reducing abortion's medical dangers. Dilation and curettage with a local pain blocker had become a quick, relatively painless procedure for abortion seekers under three months pregnant. The vacuum aspirator, developed in China, where condoms and diaphragms were unavailable, cleaned out the uterus by suction instead of scraping. Elsewhere in the world, saline abortions for more advanced pregnancies were proving effective, but few American doctors dared to explore the technique.

February 1969 was an important month in the abortion struggle. Larry Lader, a biographer of Margaret Sanger, summoned a handful of professionals in law and medicine to the Drake Hotel in Chicago for the organizing conference of NARAL, the National Association for Repeal of Abortion Laws. (NARAL became the National Abortion Rights Action League in 1974.) The conferees targeted specific states where they believed the repressive codes could be knocked down. New York, with its liberal constituency, was a top priority. Bills ranging from modest reform (in cases of rape and incest) to outright repeal of all criminal penalties were already in the legislative hopper.

Betty Friedan, one of the main speakers at the Chicago NARAL meeting, reflected the changing political climate. At NOW's founding convention in 1966, she had bowed to a clique that insisted abortion rights were too divisive, too sexual, and too controversial for the fledgling organization, but since then a groundswell of younger members had stiffened her spine. NOW was being inundated by "kids," one member observed. The "kids" from New York, Michigan, Ohio, Texas, and elsewhere pushed through an abortion plank at NOW's 1967 convention.

And the "kids" were forging ahead with their own tactics. On the same wintry day in mid-February when NARAL's founders were traveling to Chicago for their first conference six state legislators held a public hearing in Manhattan on some proposed liberalizing amendments to the New York law. Typical of the times, the six legislators were men, and the speakers invited to present expert testimony were fourteen men and a Catholic nun.

On the morning of the February 13 hearing, a dozen infiltrators camouflaged in dresses and stockings entered the hearing room and spaced themselves around the chamber. Some called themselves Redstockings, and some, like Joyce Ravitz, were free-floating radicals who were practiced hands at political disruptions. Ravitz, in fact, had been on her way to another demonstration when she'd run into the Redstockings women, who convinced her to join them.

As a retired judge opined that abortion might be countenanced as a remedy after a woman had "fulfilled her biological service to the community" by bearing four children, Kathie Amatniek leaped to her feet and shouted, "Let's hear from the real experts—women!" Taking her cue, Joyce Ravitz began to declaim an impassioned oration. Ellen Willis jumped in. More women rose to their feet.

"Men don't get pregnant, men don't bear children. Men just make laws," a demonstrator bellowed.

"Why are you refusing to admit we exist?" cried another.

"Girls, girls, you've made your point. Sit down. I'm on your side," a legislator urged, raising the temperature a notch higher.

"Don't call us girls," came the unified response. "We are women!"

The hearing dissolved in confusion. When the chairman attempted to reconvene it behind closed doors, the women sat down in the corridor, refusing to budge.

Stories appeared the next day in the *Times* ("Women Break Up Abortion Hearing"), the *New York Post* ("Abortion Law Protesters Disrupt Panel") and the *Daily News* ("Gals Squeal for Repeal, Abort State Hearing"). Ellen Willis slipped out of her activist guise to do a report for Talk of the Town in *The New Yorker*. Nanette Rainone filed for WBAI radio and the Pacifica network. Barely a month old, Redstockings, with an assist from the radical floaters, had successfully dramatized the need for "woman as expert" in the abortion debate.

Five weeks later, on March 21, 1969, Redstockings staged a public speak-out, "Abortion: Tell It Like It Is," at the Washington Square

Methodist Church, a hub of antiwar activism in Greenwich Village. For some Women's Liberation founders, the speak-out was the movement's finest hour. "Astounding," is the way Irene Peslikis puts it. "It showed the power of consciousness-raising, how theory comes from deep inside a person's life, and how it leads directly to action."

Peslikis had organized the panel and coached the women who were willing to speak. "The idea," she says, "was to get examples of different kinds of experiences—women who'd had the babies that were taken away, women who went to the hospital for a therapeutic abortion, women who'd gone the illegal route, the different kinds of illegal routes."

Three hundred women and a few men filled the church that evening as Helen Kritzler, Barbara Kaminsky, Rosalyn Baxandall, Anne Forer, and a few other brave souls passed a small microphone back and forth. Baxandall broke the ice with a touch of humor. "I thought I was sophisticated," she joked into the mike. "My boyfriend told me if he came a second time, the sperm would wash away, and I believed him."

Another woman recounted, "So there I was in West New York, New Jersey, and the doctor had these crucifixes and holy pictures on the wall, and all he wanted was nine hundred dollars. I took out a vacation loan and I'm still paying it off."

Judy Gabree hurtled forward. "I went to eleven hospitals searching for a therapeutic abortion. At the tenth, they offered me a deal. They'd do it if I agreed to get sterilized. I was twenty years old. I had to pretend I was crazy and suicidal, but having the abortion was the sanest thing I'd done."

More women added their personal testimony. I was one of those who kept quiet. Irene Peslikis had asked me to be one of the speakers, but I chose an easier path and played *Village Voice* reporter. My front-page story, "Everywoman's Abortions: The Oppressor Is Man," was the only substantive coverage the landmark speak-out received. Someone retyped it in Chicago for the *Voice of the Women's Liberation Movement* newsletter, which carried the news to activists around the country.

Another journalist, in aviator glasses and a miniskirt, was taking notes in the church that evening. She hovered near Jane Everhart, a NOW member, and whispered, "What's going on?"

Everhart whispered back, "Sit down and listen!"

Gloria Steinem was a friend of Women's Liberation in 1969, but she had not yet thrown in her lot with the movement. Her plate was already overflowing with causes. Gloria spoke out against the war in Vietnam on the late-night talk shows, raised money for liberal Democrats and for Cesar Chavez's farmworkers, and wrote earnest pieces on all of her issues for the popular magazines. Genetically endowed with the rangy limbs and sculpted features of a fashion model, Steinem glided through the rarefied world of radical chic expertly building her political connections. Beneath the exterior of the celebrity journalist was a woman who yearned to save the world.

Steinem received a shock of recognition when a Redstocking quipped, "I bet every woman here has had an abortion." Hers had been done by a Harley Street practitioner in London during the late fifties after she'd graduated from Smith. Later she would say that the speak-out was her feminist revelation, the moment that redirected her public path. That night, however, she was working on a tight deadline. She threw together a hasty paragraph for the political diary she wrote for *New York* magazine. "Nobody wants to reform the abortion laws," she explained in print. "They want to repeal them. Completely."

The Redstockings abortion speak-out was an emblematic event for Women's Liberation. Speak-outs based on the New York women's model were organized in other cities within the year, and subsequent campaigns to change public opinion in the following decade would utilize first-person testimony in a full range of issues from rape and battery to child abuse and sexual harassment. The importance of personal testimony in a public setting, which overthrew the received wisdom of "the experts," cannot be overestimated. It was an original technique and a powerful ideological tool. Ultimately, of course, first-person discourse on a dizzying variety of intimate subjects would become a gimmicky staple of the afternoon television talk shows, where the confessional style was utilized for its voyeuristic shock value. Back then, personal testimony was a political act of great courage.

As time speeded up during 1969, rallies and marches brought pro-abortion sentiment into the streets. Referral services directed by clergymen were augmented or replaced by referral services run by activist women. Bills to repeal restrictive abortion statutes were introduced in state legislatures by women, and lobbying efforts were directed by women. As it turned out, lawsuits brought by women attorneys provided the winning strategy in the intensified struggle.

•   •   •

Nancy Stearns was "ready for women's stuff" in the summer of 1969. The young attorney with horn-rimmed glasses lived in Greenwich Village on a modest budget that allowed few concessions to fashion. Noticing one season that skirts were climbing to mid-thigh, she shortened hers with a pair of scissors to keep in style. Stearns had chosen a low-paying job in advocacy law to advance the cause of civil rights. After receiving her M.A. in political science at Berkeley, she had spent a year in Atlanta with SNCC, stuffing envelopes, answering the phones, and going to jail for a sit-in at a segregated lunch counter. When SNCC began to purge whites from its staff, she did some fast thinking and concluded that "the only way a white person could do anything that wouldn't piss people off was to get a skill that they needed. At that point the skill seemed to be a law degree." Stearns enrolled at NYU law school and got one.

Her activism made her a natural for the newly formed Center for Constitutional Rights, where Arthur Kinoy became her mentor. Most civil rights attorneys specialized in defense cases, but Kinoy went on the offensive by initiating federal lawsuits with massive numbers of plaintiffs. "Arthur's babies," as Stearns called his protégés, were always on the lookout for a fresh constitutional angle that could involve huge numbers of people. A class action suit with a vocal constituency was the Center's favorite form of political action.

In 1969, Stearns knew, the legal front on abortion consisted of a handful of criminal defense cases. Among the most promising were *Belous* and *Vuitch*. Dr. Leon Belous, a prominent physician, had been arrested in California for making a referral. Dr. Milan Vuitch, respected on the grapevine for his compassionate low prices, had been arrested in Washington, D.C. People in NARAL and Planned Parenthood believed there was a chance, slim but entirely possible, that one of the doctors' cases could be decided favorably by the Supreme Court.

Stearns had begun to mull over another strategy. She had come across an article by Harriet Pilpel suggesting that abortion was a woman's constitutional right under a penumbra of privacy and liberty protections in the Ninth and Fourteenth amendments. A woman's right. Due process. Equal protection. Pilpel, a lawyer for Planned Parenthood, had left her revolutionary idea in the realm of theory. Stearns wanted to test it in court.

That August she found some likely confederates at a brainstorming session of Health/PAC. The inadequacies of medical care for poor people had activated a number of radicals around the country to make health and hospital issues their primary cause. Barbara Ehrenreich had founded Health/PAC from a socialist perspective, seeing the profit motive in medicine as the core problem, but her group was feeling the rumble of Women's Liberation from within. A women's collective in Health/PAC led by Rachel Fruchter and Dr. June Finer wanted to mount an assault on the sexism of doctors in obstetrics and gynecology. The question was, how?

Stearns proposed that they organize in a new way around abortion. Instead of waiting for rulings in *Belous* and *Vuitch*, they could go on the offensive in federal court. "Let's bring an affirmative case in New York on behalf of the people who are really harmed," she urged. "Not the doctors. The women."

She laid out her plan. Hundreds of women could sign on as plaintiffs—women who could not get a legal abortion, women who had resorted to illegal means, women who'd been forced to endure unwanted pregnancies for the full nine months only to give their babies up for adoption. Health/PAC could hold meetings all over the city, all over the state. Rachel could talk about the politics of health care; June could discuss the medical aspects of abortion: Nancy could talk about the law. Together, they'd encourage the women to speak about their own encounters with OB-GYN at city hospitals and clinics. It was the Arthur Kinoy strategy of activating the masses through the feminist process of consciousness-raising as applied to the Four-teenth Amendment theory of Harriet Pilpel. The women's collective in Health/PAC loved it.

Stearns enlisted four more women attorneys, including Diane Schulder, an early member of New York Radical Women, and Flo Kennedy, always on hand to "kick ass" (as she liked to say) and carry the banner for women of color. The Women's Health Collective trekked around the city holding meetings in people's living rooms and signing up names. *Abramowicz v. Lefkowitz* was filed in federal district court in October 1969 with 350 plaintiffs, nearly all women. Doubting her own strategy at the last minute, Stearns added a couple of doctors and clergymen to the list. She needn't have bothered. Three compan-ion suits were filed simultaneously, one on behalf of prominent physi-cians saying the abortion ban inhibited good medical practice, one on behalf of abortion counselors, who were breaking the law, and one rep-resenting indigent families. The four suits were consolidated by the court.

The lawyers for the women's suit won a huge concession in Janu-ary 1970 when they got the green light to take personal testimony at the federal courthouse. Diane Schulder, who had heard me blurt out my story at New York Radical Women, asked me to come down and be deposed. Flo Kennedy conducted the questioning. She neglected to tell me that a reporter for the *Times* was present in the hearing room; it was an odd sensation to read about my abortions in the next day's paper. Things were moving very rapidly, so rapidly, in fact, that in April the New York State Legislature passed a bill introduced by Constance Cook, a Republican assemblywoman from Ithaca and member of NOW, making abortion legal during the first two trimesters.

The lobbying in Albany had been heated and fractious, with accu-sations hurled and temperatures rising—on our side, that is. If our op-ponents also were split into hostile factions, we didn't know it. Cindy Cisler's New Yorkers for Abortion Law Repeal took an all-or-nothing position, urging legislators to vote No on the Cook bill because it fell short of total repeal. NOW and NARAL people converged on the state capitol by the busload to agitate for its passage. Connie Cook's office became a command post. Betty Friedan, arms churning, words tumbling in exhortation, was a tireless presence. The state's entire liberal establishment—bar and medical associations, church groups, Democratic reform clubs, Mayor John Lindsay of New York and Governor Nelson Rockefeller, both Republicans—fell into line and endorsed the new legislation.

Redstockings, whose first-person speak-out had revolutionized the abortion discourse the year before, had retired from the field. Excessively concerned that Women's Liberation was becoming a one-issue movement, the original consciousness-raisers had closed their doors to new members and were turning inward to reexamine their goals. Redstockings women were innovators and theorists, not conventional activists who wrote to and lobbied elected officials. As abortion rights in New York snowballed into a popular cause, they saw little need for further radical tactics. I believe that some of the movement's most creative founders were already beginning to feel co-opted. The phenomenon of pushing a new issue forward and watching the vision play out pragmatically was a dilemma for them, and would remain one for many of the early leaders.

Some of the radical fervor was picked up by People to Abolish Abortion Laws, an ad hoc coalition led by Ruthann Miller, a young Trotskyist organizer in the youth group of the Socialist Workers Party. People to Abolish was a precursor of WONAAC, the Women's National Abortion Action Coalition, which the SWP "helped originate," in its somewhat disingenuous phrase, at a tri-state conference at Hunter College the following year. Both groups attracted radical activists who disliked the intense personal revelations of consciousness-raising but felt at home carrying a placard and marching.

Unlike the tired old Communist Party and other sectarian groups of the left that were ignoring the new forces of Women's Liberation, the SWP and its youth group, the Young Socialist Alliance, leaped headlong into our midst, seeing "masses in motion" who needed their guidance. The Trotskyists were like sheepdogs whenever they sensed "masses in motion." Big public rallies where they could sell *The Militant*, the SWP paper, were their idea of revolution heaven. They were determined to get the "living-room feminists" into the streets.

The SWP's passion for marches and rallies added another dimension to the abortion struggle. Worried that legalized abortion might be employed as a form of population control by "the state," the activists carefully appended "No Forced Sterilization" to every WONAAC poster and flyer. At first WONAAC championed the provocative slogan "Free Abortion on Demand." Later it excised the "free" part as ultra-left and unrealistic. WONAAC's effectiveness was seriously undercut by its ties to the SWP. Whenever the hardworking, disciplined Trots moved into a group, they voted in blocs and tried to recruit for their party. They were accused of trying to take over the movement in a score of cities and college towns, and I don't doubt that they wanted to and would have if they could, but Women's Liberation was simply too amorphous, unstructured, and volatile for an SWP putsch.

A week before the Cook bill was brought to the floor in Albany, Ruthann Miller's coalition drew two thousand New Yorkers to Union Square, the famous old site of May Day rallies. The air was thick with FREE ABORTION ON DEMAND/NO FORCED STERILIZATION posters. Most of the women who filled the square had never heard of the Socialist Workers Party, but the new spirit was such that they wanted to stand up and be counted. *The Militant* was the only newspaper to give the rally significant coverage.

All eyes were on Albany the following week. The roll call in the assembly stood locked at a tie until George Michaels, an upstate legislator representing a heavily Catholic district, rose shakily to his feet: "Mr. Speaker, what's the use of getting elected if you don't stand for something? I realize that I am terminating my political career, but I cannot in good conscience sit here and allow my vote to be the one that defeats this bill. I ask that my vote be changed from No to Yes."

From the visitors' gallery there was an audible gasp followed by wild cheers.

Governor Rockefeller signed the bill into law on April 11, 1970, to take effect July 1. He credited Women's Liberation, including the wives of the assemblymen and state senators who voted Yes. George Michaels's gloomy prediction about the end of his political career proved accurate in the next election.

New York was actually the second state in the nation to legalize abortion. Hawaii had accomplished the feat one month earlier, although a ninety-day residency requirement limited its effect. Two weeks after New York, Alaska came through. New York, of course, garnered the national headlines, and an influx of abortion seekers from out of state. No residency requirement was attached to the New York law.

Pro-abortion sentiment triumphed in the Pacific Northwest during 1969 and 1970, when a radical women's movement lit a fire under the medical reformers to change Washington State's law by popular referendum. Their victory was extraordinary. While activists in a few states were to try a voter referendum, Washington was the only state where it actually succeeded.

Seattle Radical Women and Women's Liberation–Seattle had been spawned by antagonistic factions. Clara Fraser, an old-time Trotskyist, was the hurricane force behind Radical Women. Women's Liberation–Seattle came out of University of Washington SDS. "The important thing to remember is that we all came into the abortion struggle as politically sophisticated women," says Lee Mayfield, a mother of four, who had gone to Vancouver for two illegal abortions. The second time she had landed in the hospital, hemorrhaging badly.

"The splits make little sense in retrospect," admits Jill Severn. "Whichever faction you belonged to, it was very radical to say 'abortion' out loud." Severn, raped at sixteen by her brother's close friend, had given up her baby for adoption.

Women's Liberation–Seattle ultimately triumphed as the dominant feminist group in town, but both factions were instrumental in shifting the referendum's focus from health care reform, as the medical professionals had tried to frame it, to "Abortion Is a Woman's Right."

Clara Fraser organized busloads of demonstrators for lobbying trips to Olympia, the state capital, to jog the bill out of committee. Lee Mayfield wrote the campaign pamphlet, "One Out of Four of Us Has Had or Will Have an Abortion," for Women's Liberation–Seattle. The group sold a total of ten thousand copies. It was the first time in Mayfield's life as a radical that she had used a personal voice; the Redstock-

ings abortion speak-out in New York had given her the courage. Nina
Harding, an African-American student at the University of Washington, is credited by Seattle feminists as the first person to draw a wire
hanger on a LEGALIZE ABORTION poster to symbolize the danger from
back-alley butchers. The wire hanger was adopted as a pro-choice symbol from coast to coast.

Referendum 20, as it appeared on the ballot in the November 3,
1970 election, had a hero in Dr. Frans Koome, a Dutch-born physician who ran an illegal abortion clinic in Renton, near the Sea-Tac airport. Reformers and radicals alike used the YWCA building on the
University of Washington campus as their campaign headquarters.
Dan Evans, the state's Republican governor, endorsed the referendum. The women radicals did most of the leafleting, speaking, and
ringing of doorbells. "We were all over the state, in Bellingham, in El-
lensburg, at Rotary clubs, Democratic clubs," Mayfield recalls. Even
the Anna Louise Strong Brigade, a Maoist collective opposed to bourgeois electoral politics, found a way to pitch in with spray-painted slogans.

Opposition to the referendum was led by the Voice for the Unborn.
The advocates for the fetus had not yet developed the sophisticated
techniques they were to employ in the following decades. Their billboard slogan, "KILL Referendum 20, Not Him," backfired, and their
traveling "Life Van" with goat and pig embryos in jars was so tacky that
people dubbed it "the pickled-fetus-mobile." In their worst tactical error the Voice for the Unborn attempted a "Kill the Bill" march in
downtown Seattle on Halloween, three days before the statewide vote.
Five hundred Women's Liberationists, many dressed as witches, outnumbered and outyelled the rosy-cheeked parochial schoolboys who
were whooping it up with "Kill, Kill, Kill!"

Voters going to the polls the following Tuesday gave their overwhelming approval to Referendum 20.

Washington State's new law had a residency requirement and a
parental-consent clause for minors, and the abortions were not going
to be free, as the women had hoped. "But we'd seen public opinion
change by our efforts," says Lee Mayfield. "Oh, we came out of that
campaign feeling so darned good."

Back east, the legislative victory in Albany had mooted the New York women's lawsuit, but the concept of a federal challenge, which Nancy Stearns had pioneered, was taken up by feminists in four neighboring states. Activists signed up plaintiffs by the hundreds for class action suits in New Jersey, Rhode Island, Connecticut, and Massachusetts. A new wave of feminist law students recruited a slightly older generation of women lawyers and aided them in writing the briefs. New Jersey's challenge, with six hundred plaintiffs, took off when some Rutgers law students approached Nadine Taub, an American Civil Liberties Union lawyer in Newark. Working with Stearns, Taub copied whole sections from the New York suit before adding her own distinctive spin: an argument based on the Nineteenth Amendment (women's suffrage). After a roaring start, justice moved slowly for the New Jersey women. Two years were frittered away by a blanket of silence from the court before the case was decided favorably, too late to make it a contender for Supreme Court consideration.

Activists in Connecticut were opposed at every turn by the state's antiabortion governor, Tom Meskill, but they found the perfect attorney in Catherine Roraback, the New Haven lawyer who was handling the high-profile defense of Black Panther Ericka Huggins, charged with Bobby Seale in the murder of a Panther informer. A decade earlier the redoubtable Katie Roraback, a member of the National Lawyers Guild and an attorney for Planned Parenthood, had been instrumental in *Griswold v. Connecticut*, the landmark Supreme Court decision that legalized birth control for married women.

Women Versus Connecticut, the suit's organizing coalition, was based in New Haven, the home of community activist Betsy Gilbertson and Yale law students Gail Falk and Ann Freedman, the three main campaigners. Roraback invited Nancy Stearns to help write the brief, and added on female lawyers in Bridgeport and Hartford to strengthen the suit's geographic representation. A total of 850 plaintiffs signed on for the abortion-ban challenge that was filed in March 1971 as *Abele v. Markle*. Demonstrators waving banners and placards gathered on the steps of the New Haven post office to celebrate the occasion.

Abele was dismissed two months later, when a judge ruled that the 850 plaintiffs lacked legal standing because they were not pregnant and thus had "an insufficient personal stake in the outcome." The legal setback increased the group's militance. Roraback argued on appeal that all women of childbearing age in Connecticut had a direct personal stake in the outcome. While the lawyers "kept stuffing the court with paper," as Ann Freedman phrased it, a growing army of activists drummed up more litigants at public meetings throughout the state. Two thousand plaintiffs, including two verifiably pregnant women who later sneaked into New York for their terminations, signed the second version of *Abele*, making it the largest grassroots challenge to an abortion law in the country. The Connecticut suit was in district court when the Supreme Court agreed to hear arguments in *Roe v. Wade*, a single-plaintiff case that had gotten an earlier start in Texas.

• • •

Women's Liberation had come to the University of Texas at Austin by a familiar route—in reaction to the macho posturing at an SDS convention. Austin was a happening place in 1969. The pleasant state capital was the nerve center of Texas politics, while its university enjoyed a reputation as the Berkeley of the Southwest. Radicals and hippies read and wrote for *The Rag*, a brash counterculture gazette that was one of the best in the nation. When SDS converged on the Austin campus in March 1969, it was already in its death throes, beset by warring factions. Fistfights broke out on the convention floor as Progressive Labor battled Revolutionary Youth Movement II, soon to be Weatherman. After the SDS debacle, three graduate students in the school's zoology department started a consciousness-raising group to give voice to ideas they had not been able to express at the chaotic convention.

At five feet eleven with hair that fell below her shoulders, Judy Smith was the soul of the weekly meetings. Judy had majored in chemistry at Brandeis and had spent a year in the Peace Corps in West Africa before coming to Austin. Bea Durden, a mother of two, had a Ph.D. in biology from Yale. Victoria Foe was the third campus organizer. As the group coalesced it was joined by Sarah Weddington, a minister's daughter from Abilene and a recent graduate of the university's law school, where she was teaching. Sarah's bubbly presence in skirts and stockings in the usual pool of jeans and sandals was a sign to the others that Women's Liberation was attracting a mainstream constituency undreamed of by the left.

Austin Women's Liberation set up a table on the quad every morning to distribute a birth control handbook put out by McGill University students in Montreal. At their weekly meetings they discussed "Women and Their Bodies," an early mimeographed version of *Our Bodies, Ourselves* by the Boston Women's Health Book Collective. Their own feminist essays, most often Judy's, appeared in *The Rag*. Through Liberation News Service, a mail packet of leftist news *The Rag* subscribed to, they kept abreast of the movement in other cities.

By October the activists had opened a Women's Liberation Birth Control Center in space shared by *The Rag* at the YMCA across the street from the campus. For a slogan they chose "Every woman has the right to control her own body." As the need became clear, they took on abortion referrals, building a list of practitioners in Dallas, San Antonio, and the border towns in Mexico. Drawing on the testimony of five women, they held a Redstockings-style speak-out at the student center. Their next bold move was to challenge the state law through the courts.

Judy Smith came up with the idea of launching a legal assault. She knew *The Rag* had been successful in its lawsuit to keep the university regents from banning the paper on campus. In addition, she was vaguely aware that women had sued for abortion rights in New York. Smith and Bea Durden cornered Sarah Weddington in her backyard during a November garage sale for the Austin Birth Control Center. They told her they wanted the Center to serve as the plaintiff, and she was the only lawyer they knew who might take the case without a fee. Weddington protested that she lacked courtroom experience and the backing of a law firm before she allowed herself to be persuaded. She had a secret that she chose not to reveal for another twenty years. Before her marriage she had gone to one of those dismal border towns in Mexico for an illegal abortion.

By December, Weddington had found an eager co-counsel in Linda Coffee, one of two other women in her graduating class at the UT law school. "I've always said that Linda was smarter than me," Weddington laughs. "She was on *Law Review*, I wasn't."

Shy and retiring, Linda Coffee had taken a job in her hometown of Dallas with a firm that specialized in bankruptcy cases. More relevant to the women's incipient project, she had just finished a year clerking for Sarah Hughes, the federal judge who'd sworn in Lyndon Johnson aboard *Air Force One* after the Kennedy assassination. Hughes, in her mid-seventies, was known for her outspoken views on women's rights. The novice lawyers figured it would be a smart move to get their suit before her jurisdiction.

Linda Coffee did not think the Austin Birth Control Center would survive the hurdle of legal standing. Under her reading of the law, the best plaintiff would be a pregnant woman who could not obtain a legal remedy in the state of Texas. Any person or entity falling short of that procedural ideal could be mooted by the court. "When I'd worked for Judge Hughes, I'd seen some civil rights and First Amendment cases that had gotten into standing problems," Coffee explains. "Many times courts would use standing, a procedural point, to avoid deciding an issue they didn't want to meet head-on."

Weddington broke the bad news to the Austin activists, who agreed to hunt for an ideal plaintiff. They came up dry. The UT students who passed through the Center wanted a speedy termination, not a lawsuit, so they could get on with their lives.

In January 1970 a friend of Coffee's who handled adoptions steered the clientless litigants to Norma McCorvey, a hard-luck, itinerant bartender in Dallas who lacked the resources to cope with her third pregnancy in six years. McCorvey's first child lived with her parents; the second had been given up for adoption at birth. This time she wanted an abortion, and had cooked up a tale about gang rape on a dark rural road in Georgia, a story that could not have gotten her a legal abortion in Texas even if it had been true.

The twenty-two-year-old was already too late for a routine termination. Over four months pregnant and showing when she met the two lawyers at a Dallas pizza parlor, she still hoped they could lead her to one of those mysterious doctors she knew were out there. Delicately they confirmed that she was too far along for a Mexican D & C through the illegal route. Uncertain about the timetable of a court case but with nothing to lose, McCorvey agreed to be Weddington and Coffee's pseudonymous "Jane Roe." Coffee drew up the papers and paid the filing fee for *Roe v. Wade* in March 1970. (Wade was the district attorney for Dallas County.) To be on the safe side, she and Weddington later amended the documents to make *Roe* a class action on behalf of all pregnant women in Texas.

Roe was argued in May without the presence of McCorvey, by then eight months pregnant, before a federal panel of three judges that included Sarah Hughes, the jurist the litigators had hoped for. Less than a month later the panel reported its favorable decision, and the state of Texas appealed.

• • •

Another southern state was proceeding apace. In 1968 a group of physicians and social workers in Georgia had persuaded the state legislature to pass a law permitting therapeutic abortions in rape and incest cases and to preserve a woman's life and health. Two years later, in response to the new feminist militance sweeping the country, many of the same reformers were working to repeal the law, which now looked too restrictive.

Judith Bourne, a trained nurse in Atlanta and a central figure in the repeal campaign, picked up on the idea of a women's challenge through the courts. She found an enthusiastic attorney in Margie Hames, a volunteer counsel for the ACLU. Nine months pregnant with her second child, Hames turned to her colleagues, Tobiane Schwartz of the ACLU and Elizabeth Rindskopf of Legal Aid, for help.

The Atlanta lawyers did not have to wait long before they acquired an unhappily pregnant plaintiff. Twenty-two-year-old Sandra Bensing had put two kids in foster care and farmed out a third baby for adoption. Her husband had a criminal record for child molestation. Citing depression and a prior stay in a mental hospital, she had applied for a therapeutic abortion at Grady Memorial and had been rejected under the hospital's rigid quota system. An intake evaluator sympathetic to her plight put her in touch with the activists, who sent her on to the lawyers. In April 1970, Bensing agreed to be "Mary Doe." The activists then arranged for her to have a therapeutic abortion at another hospital in Atlanta, but the conflicted young woman failed to keep the appointment. She had skipped town with her husband, who was evading some fresh troubles with the law.

Margie Hames received a frantic call from her elusive client one week before *Doe v. Bolton* was scheduled to be heard in court. Stranded and broke in Oklahoma, Bensing was willing to come back to Atlanta and continue the suit if someone paid her airfare, but after feeling the baby kicking inside her she was no longer interested in having an abortion. Hames knew that her client's pregnancy made for a stronger case.

Doe v. Bolton drew an overflow crowd on Monday morning, June 15, when it was argued before a three-judge federal panel. Tobiane Schwartz had collected Bensing at the airport on Sunday and driven her to Margie's house for a fresh change of clothes and a briefing on what to expect in court. Leaving nothing to chance, Tobi made up a bed in her own house to seclude the jittery plaintiff for the night. By a prearranged plan, the following morning a dozen women in advanced stages of pregnancy deployed themselves around the hearing room to shield Bensing's identity from curious reporters. Seated at the counsel table, lawyer Elizabeth Rindskopf, too, was visibly pregnant.

"Mary Doe is present in court," Margie Hames announced in triumph. In the gravid context, the anonymous plaintiff was Everywoman. The court moved rapidly to hand down a favorable opinion at the end of July, just weeks after the *Roe* decision. As in Texas, the state of Georgia appealed.

•   •   •

Abortion militance in Chicago took a different direction. Perhaps its unique path had to do with the women's ties to the New Left, which remained stronger in Chicago than in most other places. Perhaps the political convulsions and warlike atmosphere in Mayor Daley's city were sufficient to induce an extreme form of action. Chicago had witnessed the crazily fractured 1968 Democratic Convention and the assault in Grant Park with clubs and tear gas ("The Whole World Is Watching"); Bobby Seale bound and gagged in Judge Hoffman's courtroom during the Chicago Eight conspiracy trial; the fatal shooting of Fred Hampton and Mark Clark in a Panther apartment; Weatherwomen in helmets rampaging through the streets.

Radical women in Chicago poured their energy into Jane, an abortion referral service initiated by Heather Booth, who had been a one-woman grapevine for her college classmates. In 1971, after's Booth's departure, some of the women took matters into their own hands and secretly began to perform the abortions themselves. Safe, compassionate terminations for a modest fee became their high calling—a model, as they saw it, for women's empowerment after the revolution.

Leaflets appeared in the Hyde Park neighborhood of the University of Chicago bearing a simple message: "Pregnant? Don't want to be? Call Jane at 643-3844." The number rang at the home of one of the activists who volunteered to be "Jane." As word spread and the volume of calls increased, the service acquired its own phone line and an answering machine, a cumbersome reel-to-reel device that was one of the first on the market. Volunteers, known inside the service as "call-back Janes," visited the abortion seekers to elicit crucial medical details (most important was "lmp," the number of weeks since the last menstrual period), then another level of volunteers scheduled an appointment with one of the abortionists on the group's list.

At first the service relied on "Mike in Cicero," who was fast, efficient, and willing to lower his price to five hundred dollars as the volume increased. Mike gradually let down his guard with Jody Parsons, his principal Jane contact, an artisan who sold her beaded jewelry and ceramics at street fairs and was a survivor of Hodgkin's disease. The clandestine abortionist and the hippie artisan struck up a bond. When Mike confessed that he was not in fact a real doctor but merely a trained technician, she cajoled him into teaching her his skills. Jody's rapid success in learning to maneuver the dilating clamps, curettes, and forceps demystified the forbidden procedures for another half dozen women in Jane. "If he can do it, then we can do it" became their motto.

Madeline Schwenk, a banker's daughter who had married at twenty, "six months pregnant with no clue whatsoever about how to get an abortion," moved from counseling to vacuum aspiration after Harvey Karman, the controversial director of a California clinic, came to Chicago to demonstrate his technique. Madeline was one of the few women in Jane who was active in NOW, and who stayed affiliated with the Chicago chapter during the year she wielded her cannula and curette for the service. "I'd get up in the morning, make breakfast for my three kids, go off to do the abortions, then go home to make dinner," she reminisces. "Pretty outrageous behavior when you think about it. But exciting."

Jane's abortion practitioners and their assistants were able to handle a total of thirty cases a day at affordable fees—under one hundred dollars. A doctor and a pharmacist among the women's contacts kept them supplied with antibiotics.

Fear of police surveillance in radical circles had its match among clandestine abortionists who relied on a complicated rigmarole of blindfolds and middlemen. Jane straddled both worlds. Abortion seekers gathered every Wednesday, Thursday, and Friday at a "front" apartment, usually the home of a Jane member or a friend, and were escorted by Jane drivers to "the Place," a rented apartment where the abortions were performed. The fronts and the Place changed on a regular basis. New volunteers, brought into the group as counselors and drivers, went through a probation period before they were told that women in Jane were doing the abortions. The news did not sit well with everyone. Turnover was high, from fear and from burnout, although the service usually maintained its regular complement of thirty members.

Jane lost most of its middle-class clientele after the New York law went into effect. Increasingly it began to service South Side women, poor and black, who did not have the money to travel out of state, and whose health problems, from high blood pressure to obesity, were daunting. Pressure on the providers intensified. Audaciously they added second-trimester abortions by induced miscarriage to their skills.

On May 3, 1972, near the conclusion of a busy work day in an eleventh-floor apartment on South Shore Drive overlooking Lake Michigan, Jane got busted. Seven women, including Madeline Schwenk, were arrested and bailed out the following day. The *Chicago Daily News* blared "Women Seized in Cut-Rate Clinic" in a front-page banner. The *Tribune* buried "Lib Groups Linked to Abortions" on an inside page. Six weeks later the service was back in business. Wisely, the women facing criminal charges selected a defense attorney who was clued in to and optimistic about the national picture. She advised them to hang tight—some interesting developments were taking place in Washington that could help their case. (After the January 1973 *Roe* decision, all outstanding charges against the seven were dropped.)

The activists of Jane believe they performed more than ten thousand abortions. It's a ballpark figure based on the number of procedures they remember doing in a given week. For security reasons they did not keep records.

· · ·

In contrast to the clandestine Chicago women, the rebellious self-help movement that originated in Los Angeles was flamboyant, messianic, and not without large doses of exhibitionism and high drama. In two words, it was "very California." Carol Downer and Lorraine Rothman were to add yet another creative dimension to the abortion struggle.

Carol Downer had no prior political experience when she joined the Los Angeles chapter of NOW, but her reproductive history encompassed six children, two miscarriages, and one illegal abortion. The divorced and remarried thirty-eight-year-old housewife gravitated naturally to Lana Phelan's abortion committee, where the older activist became her mentor. California's liberalized law, which had seemed so promising, had produced a mass of red tape and few abortions. One afternoon Downer paid a visit to Harvey Karman's underground clinic in Santa Monica to see how things worked. Karman showed her a speculum, a common tool in gynecological examinations for peering at the cervical opening to the uterus, and invited her to watch a vacuum aspiration, which Karman performed with a flexible, lightweight plastic tube, called a cannula, attached to a hand-held syringe. The cervical view and the cannula abortion struck Downer with the force of a mystical revelation, or rather a demystified revelation.

"I was bowled over," she recalls. "In shock. This wasn't exactly open-heart surgery. I realized that if women just had some basic information about our bodies, we could take care of ourselves."

Downer eventually became disaffected from Karman, but she took time to study his nontraumatic technique. Her first Self-Help Clinic was held at Everywoman Bookstore in Venice Beach in April 1971. About thirty women showed up. Climbing onto a desk, Downer nonchalantly pulled down her pants and inserted a speculum in her vagina, inviting the assembly to see what a cervix looked like. When the excitement died down, someone else showed the group Karman's cannula and syringe.

This was the revelatory moment for Lorraine Rothman, a former public school teacher and a mother of four. "Why go through the humiliation and frustration of trying to persuade the powers that be to legalize abortion?" she remembers thinking. "Why not take back the technology, the tools and the skills?"

Rothman tinkered with the borrowed cannula and syringe at her husband's science lab at Cal State. "Lorraine was very handy," Downer recalls with a chuckle, "but it took her a while to get it right." At the next Self-Help Clinic, Rothman appeared with an improved model. She had taken a mason jar and punched two holes in the rubber stopper. Fitted with two lengths of aquarium tubing and a bypass valve, the jar was tranformed into a miniature aspirator. An operator could pump the syringe with one hand while her other hand guided the cannula in its sweep of the uterine wall. Slower but less invasive than the pump-and-withdraw technique used in Karman's clinic, Rothman's contraption, when it was refined a bit further, emptied the unwanted contents of a uterus into the jar in thirty minutes. With sufficient training, a group of self-helpers could rid a woman of her monthly period in a single half hour. By the same means, they could do safe early abortions for each other, if they wished. Rothman took out a patent on her inventive device, naming it the Del-Em, a private acronym for "dirty little machine." She and Downer named their suction process "menstrual extraction." A trip up the coast to observe the brisk procedures of Seattle's famed abortionist, Dr. Frans Koome, who used metal curettes without anesthetic, convinced the two women that gentle suction performed in a sisterly circle with hand-holding and empathy was equally good or better.

Menstrual extraction and speculum exams became the unofficial highlight of NOW's 1971 national convention that September. Denied exhibit space among the regular vendors hawking books, T-shirts, and greeting cards, the usual fare at a NOW convention, Downer and Rothman held marathon demonstrations for interested delegates in their hotel room. That fall they took temporary leave of their husbands and children and went on the road with Colleen Wilson, another self-helper, calling themselves the West Coast Sisters. Traveling by Greyhound bus with a huge box of plastic speculums marked "Toys," the trio met with Women's Liberation groups in twenty-three cities during a hectic six-week tour. In Stamford, Connecticut, Lolly Hirsch and her daughter Jeanne became major converts. The Hirsches started a newsletter, *The Monthly Extract: An Irregular Periodical,* and went on the college lecture circuit. Mother Lolly did most of the talking on the lecture dates; daughter Jeanne did the cervical demonstrations.

While the show-and-tell meetings run by the Hirsches and the Los Angeles women usually generated near-mystical excitement, a brisk sale of plastic speculums, and much talk of empowerment, the self-helpers' promotion of menstrual extraction was controversial even inside the movement. A mini-summit between the West Coast Sisters and the Jane collective in Chicago turned into a frosty competition as each side turned up its nose at the other's techniques. The Janes dismissed the Del-Em as too amateurish and slow for their volume service; the West Coast Sisters retorted that Jane with its blindfolds and metal curettes had "bought in to the male model."

Downer's self-help clinic in Los Angeles held court every Wednesday evening at the Women's Center, a one-story building on Crenshaw Boulevard that offered space to various and assorted manifestations of Women's Liberation: a library and bookstore, weekly consciousness-raising groups, a car repair clinic, and women's dances. WONAAC

came to the Center to organize a national abortion rights demo in
Washington. "We had beanbag pillows and they had straight chairs,"
Downer remembers. "That says a lot, doesn't it? We all felt that change
was imminent, but our group didn't feel it was going to take place
through large numbers of women in the streets. We believed that can-
nulas were better than leaflets for threatening male power."

Carol Downer and Colleen Wilson were arrested at their clinic on
September 20, 1972, and charged, among other counts, with practicing
medicine without a license. Wilson pled guilty to one count (fitting a
diaphragm) and received a suspended sentence. Downer stood trial and
won an acquittal. The announcement of the *Roe* decision was four
months away.

• • •

In May 1971 the Supreme Court had sent notice that it would hear arguments on the merits of *Roe* in Texas and *Doe* in Georgia, the two
pregnant-plantiff cases that had sailed through their respective district
courts and gone up on appeal. Margie Hames and Sarah Weddington
conferred by telephone. They agreed that the Court might have chosen to hear any one of a number of abortion cases that were floating
through the judicial system. Some of the criminal defense cases had
been bumping along for a lot longer than the challenges brought on
behalf of pregnant women. By choosing *Roe* and *Doe*, the Court was
saying that it wished to focus on women's rights.

Roy Lucas in New York certainly thought so. At NYU law school,
Lucas had been a contemporary of Nancy Stearns's, the woman who
later initiated the strategy of suing the state on behalf of women,
although their paths had seldom crossed. The experience of accompanying a girlfriend to Puerto Rico for an illegal abortion lay behind an
article he wrote for the *North Carolina Law Review* in 1968 proposing a
federal challenge to the state codes; however, the strategy he put forward was a lawsuit filed by prominent doctors. Lucas subsequently became a maestro of litigation, initiating the doctors' suit in New York
that was consolidated with the women's class action, insinuating himself into *Vuitch*, popping up in a half dozen states after sensing physician interest, and departing more frequently than not with a retainer as

the attorney of record. His relations with Planned Parenthood and the ACLU grew chilly when lawyers in those organizations felt that the helpful young man had a nasty habit of hogging the credit, but nobody ever said that Roy Lucas was slow on his feet. Lucas had pinned his hopes and his place in history on the doctors' cases. Now it was apparent that he had been barking up the wrong tree.

Hastily he volunteered his services to Margie Hames in Atlanta, who curtly informed him that the ACLU was providing the help she needed. Next he placed a call to Sarah Weddington in Austin, who was delighted to be offered free lodgings in New York, a city she had never visited, while Lucas strengthened the technical points of her Supreme Court brief. It was an offer that Weddington soon regretted. Her lodgings were a lumpy sofa in the switchboard room of a rundown abortion clinic while the enterprising young man, behind on his numerous appeals in other cases, treated her like a secretary. "I was the best typist," she relates, "and I would have done anything to speed up the process. I just wanted to get the brief done and go home." By the summer's end, Lucas had badgered her into agreeing that he, with his vastly superior experience, should argue *Roe* before the Court for the good of the case and all that it stood for.

"He was really presumptuous," exclaims Linda Coffee, whose full-time job had kept her in Dallas. "He even sent the Court a letter saying that he was *Roe*'s lead counsel." Coffee and an entire chorus of outraged women, from Nancy Stearns in New York to Judy Smith and Bea Durden in Austin, set matters right again. *Roe* was a women's case, and a woman was going to deliver its message to the men of the high court.

On December 13, 1971, Weddington and Hames were in Washington for their oral arguments in *Roe* and *Doe*. Court watchers joked that it looked like Ladies' Day. Not only were the wives of five justices conspicuously present, the Georgia attorney general's office had selected a woman, Dorothy Beasely, to represent the state's interests. Only seven members were sitting on the bench. President Nixon's appointees for two vacated seats, Lewis Powell and William Rehnquist, were not to be sworn in until January.

Weddington began her thirty-minute presentation by stating the classic Women's Liberation position: "Pregnancy to a woman is one of the most determinative aspects of life. It disrupts her body, it disrupts her education, it disrupts her employment, and it often disrupts her entire family life. If any rights are fundamental to a woman, she should be allowed to make the choice whether to terminate or continue."

Under prodding from Potter Stewart, who wanted to hear the constitutional basis, Weddington said she rested her case on the Ninth and Fourteenth amendments, on due process, on equal protection, and on *Griswold*.

"And anything else that might obtain?" Stewart interjected, drawing a laugh.

Stewart drew laughter again when Texas district attorney Jay Floyd argued that a woman makes her choice "prior to the time she becomes pregnant."

"Or maybe when she decides to live in Texas," the justice retorted. "There's no restriction on moving, you know." The new freedom to secure an abortion in several states, and in the nation's capital under a stunning ruling in *Vuitch* by Judge Gerhard Gesell, lay behind the gibe.

Justice Harry Blackmun leaned forward during Margie Hames's presentation to question her intently about Grady Memorial's denial of an abortion to "Mary Doe." Dorothy Beasely devoted her time to an explication of the rights of the fetus.

The Court's deliberations remained a tight secret at the time. Now we know that when the justices took their informal poll, a majority of five—William O. Douglas, Thurgood Marshall, William Brennan, Stewart, and Blackmun—wanted to strike down the restrictive state laws, although their philosophic approaches were far from united. Chief Justice Warren Burger, in the minority with Byron White, assigned the majority opinion to Blackmun, his close ally. By doing so he finessed the last of the great liberals, William O. Douglas, who was itching to write the opinion on the broad constitutional basis of a privacy right, and who was entitled to the assignment, by Court tradition, as the majority's senior member.

Harry Blackmun was a slow and tentative writer who did not enjoy charting new paths for the law, but he was strong on medical issues from his years as counsel to the Mayo Clinic in his home state of Minnesota. Blackmun made little progress during the next few months and asked for an extension. Burger informed the justices that the abortion cases would be held over for reargument in the next calendar term. Reargument was rare in Supreme Court deliberations, but the chief justice was following his political instincts. The controversial decision would go down better with the American public if nine justices, not seven, were involved in the opinion.

While Burger stalled and Douglas fumed and Blackmun studied the *Roe* and *Doe* amicus briefs that spring, the *Women's Rights Law Reporter,* put out by feminist law students at Rutgers, heralded what it called an "onslaught" of litigation. Compiling a list of state and federal challenges to the constitutionality of abortion laws, the editors reported activity in twenty-nine states and the District of Columbia. Suits ran the gamut from *Tennessee Woman v. Peck,* brought by one pregnant plaintiff, to the huge class actions, such as *Beebe* in Michigan, with 830 women plaintiffs, and *Ryan* in Pennsylvania, on which more than one thousand women had placed their names.

In addition to the plaintiff suits, a pair of defense cases had become rallying points for feminists around the country. Dr. Jane Hodgson, the only female obstetrician in St. Paul, was appealing her Minnesota conviction for performing a therapeutic abortion on a patient exposed to rubella, the German measles virus known to deform a fetus; in Florida, Shirley Ann Wheeler, twenty-three, had been convicted of manslaughter and sentenced to two years' probation for having an abortion. Dr. Hodgson had deliberately put herself forward as a test case for the state of Minnesota, and a prominent physician at the Mayo Clinic was among her supporters. Shirley Ann Wheeler had staggered into the emergency room of a Daytona Beach hospital hemorrhaging from an incomplete abortion, and the law had moved in when she refused to divulge her practitioner's name. Aided and promoted by WONAAC, Wheeler became the subject of a *New York Times* profile. Dr. Hodgson went on a public-speaking tour.

Gloria Steinem's *Ms.* magazine made its debut with a test-run issue in the spring of 1972. Eager to make a mark in the reproductive rights debate, the editors borrowed a tactic from feminists in France and came up with a declaration, "We Have Had Abortions," addressed to the White House. Barbara Tuchman, Lillian Hellman, Anne Sexton, Judy Collins, and Billie Jean King were among the fifty-three signatories. Three years earlier both the declaration, and *Ms.* itself would have been inconceivable. (Gloria and I were on the list of signatories, but Jane O'Reilly, whose attempted abortion in 1957 had failed, felt she had to exclude herself. Still, her lead piece for the premier issue best defined the new mood. "The Housewife's Moment of Truth" captured the feminist awakening with an onomatopoeic "click." "Click" became a byword that season.)

Abortion rights entered the policy debate at the 1972 Democratic National Convention in Miami that August. New party rules, after the debacle of 1968, had opened the process of delegate selection. An unprecedented 40 percent of the delegates, counting alternates, were women. The six-month-old National Women's Political Caucus, started by Betty Friedan in a shaky alliance with Gloria Steinem, Bella Abzug, and Shirley Chisholm, set up a command post at the Betsy Ross Hotel. Jostling for media attention, the movement's stars were appallingly disunited. Outright warfare over tactics broke out between Friedan, cast in the outsider role, and the Steinem-Abzug constellation, overly optimistic about its back-door influence with presidential candidate George McGovern. Actress Shirley MacLaine, the candidate's Hollywood adviser on women, tried to suppress any mention of the A-word. Friedan managed to push the abortion plank to a floor vote, where it was defeated, more closely than the women anticipated, by McGovern loyalists unwilling to add another impediment to their candidate's uphill fight against Richard Nixon.

President Nixon had made his opposition to abortion perfectly clear on several occasions, most vividly in May when his letter to Cardinal Cooke in New York about protecting the unborn was released by the archdiocese. McGovern's rout was so overwhelming in the November general election that it is hard to see how a positive stand on abortion could have done him any damage, but the electoral process does not breed courage. The NARAL strategy of lobbying the state legislatures had foundered when it became painfully evident to legislators that a vote for abortion rights could effectively end a politician's career. That year a move to revoke New York's liberal law was beaten back by an uncomfortably narrow margin, while a voter referendum to repeal Michigan's restrictive law was defeated when a "Voice of the Unborn" campaign, considerably more sophisticated than the one two years earlier in Washington State, shifted public opinion at the last minute with a barrage of thirty-second televised spots.

But the court side of the picture was looking bright. Breaking its two-year silence, a three-judge panel voided New Jersey's abortion law in late February on grounds of vagueness and the right to privacy, and the Women Against Connecticut challenge, *Abele*, had a triumph in September (on the same day, coincidentally, that the Los Angeles self-helpers were arrested). Judge Jon Newman's opinion in the Connecticut case was particularly strong. His words about a woman's right to privacy and personal choice vis-à-vis the status of the fetus were read avidly at the Supreme Court by Blackmun and Stewart, and the forceful decision tipped Lewis Powell, one of the new Nixon appointees, into the affirmative column. Standing at 6 to 3, the Court was preparing to chart a national course, and to say what a presidential candidate dared not utter.

Weddington and Hames were back for reargument on October 13, 1972, hopeful but uncertain. The justices mused aloud about fetal viability and late-term abortions, ground they had raked over many times among themselves. They understood that what they were preparing to do came perilously close to legislative dictum. There was no way they were going to settle the debate among scientists and theologians about when life begins, but six men of the Court were prepared to act on their belief that the state had no compelling interest in preserving an embryo at conception when the life of that embryo was balanced against the lives and aspirations of women. To produce a meaningful set of guidelines, they needed to draw a line somewhere in the gestation process, and they would attempt the wisdom of Solomon according to their best understanding of safe medical practice. In one regard their task was simple. They were interpreters of the United States Constitution, and nowhere in the Fourteenth Amendment, which speaks of "persons born or naturalized," did a mention of the unborn appear.

"If it were established that an unborn fetus is a person," asked Potter Stewart, "you would have almost an impossible case here, would you not?" Weddington conceded that she would have a very difficult case.

Harry Blackmun had spent the summer in the library of the Mayo Clinic in Rochester, Minnesota. Among old friends, he firmed up his idea about a personal decision between a woman and her doctor, and devised a trimester formula for drawing the line. Stewart, Brennan, and Marshall sharpened and refined the drafts Blackmun circulated among the justices after the oral arguments that fall. Douglas was happy to have six votes. Chief Justice Burger was silent. At the eleventh hour he joined the majority, making it 7 to 2. With political delicacy he delayed the announcement of *Roe* until late January, after he'd sworn in Richard Nixon for what would be, in common metaphor, an aborted term.

Roe was astonishing news, even as it was eclipsed the same day by the death of the Lyndon Baines Johnson. Sarah Weddington told the first reporter who called that the Court ruling was "a great victory for women in Texas," too overwhelmed for a moment to grasp the national implications. Norma McCorvey read the story in Dallas and shouted to her current lover, a woman, "Hey, that's me!" Carol Downer in Los Angeles scoured Blackmun's decision and saw that the section on new technologies included a mention of menstrual extraction. "I didn't know about him, but he knew about me," she remembers thinking. Nancy Stearns in New York also found some familiar language in the Blackmun opinion. "The experiences of women got through," she says. "Our decision to influence the law by presenting the experiences of women was successful." Madeline Schwenk celebrated with crepes and champagne at a Magic Pan in Chicago. "I won't be going to jail," she cried. Then Madeline had a wild idea. "Hey," she said to a friend. "Since we put ourselves on the line and did all this work and now they're saying it's okay and legal, do you think they'll let us keep doing the abortions?"

Roe fostered the euphoric delusion that the women's revolution was an unstoppable success. A new day had dawned; anything was possible. Those at the heart of the fight understood that our enemies were marshaling their forces for a sustained counterattack. As I write these words, and you read them, abortion remains our most important and pivotal issue, the linchpin, then as now, of women's struggle for equality and reproductive freedom.

ENTER THE MEDIA

SHORTLY AFTER the Miss America protest of 1968, David Susskind had given Women's Liberation its first exposure on national TV. Taped in New York, where it aired on Sunday evenings, Susskind's syndicated talk show was a liberal institution, a sounding board for ideas from the serious to the kooky. The kook spot, as I called it, was an occasional feature at the end of the program.

Jane Everhart, NOW's liaison to the Susskind producers, remembers that they were "looking for the prettiest women who'd appeal to David." Anselma Dell'Olio and Jacqui Ceballos made the cut, as did Kate Millett, at work on *Sexual Politics*. Rosalyn Baxandall was picked to represent New York Radical Women. The panelists were asked to bring movement people to fill the audience. I was one of them.

Susskind announced, "We've got some angry women here," scratching his silvery head in genial bemusement, "and later in the show we're going to find out what their gripes are." Off-camera he said curtly, "You've got twenty minutes."

Twenty minutes? The kook spot! A slow rumble moved through the audience.

Susskind snapped, "Quiet in the studio!" He began again. "We've got some angry women here and they've brought their supporters with them."

"Hey, Susskind! Is twenty minutes what you think women are worth?"

"What are you afraid of, David?"

"David, tell us about your divorce!"

Susskind threw down his notes. The panelists walked off the set. The producers ran after them. Anselma Dell'Olio broke into tears. Out on the street a dozen militants surrounded Susskind's black limo and started to rock it.

A few days later the producers reassembled the panel for a full program's taping. This time when Susskind scratched his head and announced, "We've got some angry women here," he said it with conviction.

As the show began airing around the country, letters poured into the post office boxes for NOW and New York Radical Women. Heartfelt and handwritten on pink or blue notepaper, they basically asked the same question, "How do I find a Women's Liberation group near me?" Most of the letters went unanswered. The new movement was swamped.

One year after the *Susskind Show* the movement had grown sufficiently so that every important media outlet wanted large, interpretive stories. Through the fortunes of accident and serious campaigning, several of the assignments went to women who rallied to the cause. Their male editors had not expected such partisan allegiance.

Vivian Gornick, a wild-card intellectual at *The Village Voice* known for her cultural essays, was one of the first to declare herself in print. Ed Fancher, the *Voice* publisher, had approached her with the idea. He said, Gornick recalls, "All these chicks are gathering out there on Bleecker Street and every one of them has got a manifesto. They call themselves Women's Libbers. Why don't you do a piece?"

Gornick understood that she was supposed to produce a clever put-down of a lunatic fringe, a juicy plum for a freethinker from the Bronx whose Old Left childhood had made her allergic to ideologues of all stripes. As she pursued her quarry in tenement walk-ups and one-room studios from Greenwich Village to the Lower East Side, however, she experienced an epiphany.

"I truly felt that I was in the presence of revolutionary personages," she remembers. "I could see the movement taking shape in an allegorical form. A vision had suddenly burst on everyone, and these difficult, marginal, exaggerated creatures with their distinct, vivid, dramatic personalities all had a piece of it. *Only feminism would be the answer for women!* I was instantly persuaded by the truth, the beauty, the shining whiteness of it all. How did Arthur Koestler describe his conversion to Marxism? That comes the closest. Shafts of light were bursting across the top of my head and I knew that life would never be the same again."

An ecstatic convert returned to the office with her lyrical essay, "The Next Great Moment in History Is Theirs." Fancher cornered her with, "Jeez, are you sure you want to do this?" Dan Wolf, the *Voice's* silent, cryptic editor, looked up from his desk with a puzzled stare. "The Next Great Movement in History Is Theirs" ran on November 27, 1969, and its catalytic effect was stupendous. It was even reprinted in *Cosmopolitan* the following April.

"I got so much mail on that piece, it was unreal," Gornick remembers. "The mail just kept coming and coming and coming, on every conceivable type of stationery, from all over the country. Who knew that I would never get mail like that again as long as I lived?"

Several of us were happy soldiers marching on our own initiative that season. In December, Sara Davidson's "An 'Oppressed Majority' Demands Its Rights," with jubilant photos by Mary Ellen Mark, ran in *Life*. In February 1970 Lucy Komisar's "The New Feminism" made *The Saturday Review* cover. Over at *Newsweek*, my old place of employment, where women were researchers and men were writers, the male editors invited Helen Dudar of the *New York Post* to guest-write their March 23 cover, "Women in Revolt," because they had no woman with the requisite professional experience on staff.

Dudar, the wife of *Newsweek's* star writer, Peter Goldman, seemed like a safe choice, and indeed, she approached her assignment with a mind-set that hovered somewhere between ambivalence and annoyance. Stridency appalled her. She had forged a place for herself, so why couldn't others? As she dug into her interviews, she began to suffer anxiety-related headaches. She found it helpful to thrash things out with Lindsy Van Gelder, her young feminist colleague at the *Post*. By the time she sat down to write, Dudar had done a complete turn-around, concluding, "Women's lib questions everything; and while intellectually I approve of that, emotionally I am unstrung. Never mind. The ambivalence is gone; the distance is gone. What is left is a sense of pride and kinship with all those women who have been asking all the hard questions. I thank them, and so, I think, will a lot of other women."

The Sunday before Dudar's story appeared, *The New York Times Magazine* ran my own unambivalent exposition, "Sisterhood Is Powerful," with the subhead "A member of the Women's Liberation Movement explains what it's all about." *Esquire*, proudly billing itself as "the magazine for men," took the plunge in July with Sally Kempton's intensely personal "Cutting Loose." Sally's essay, like Vivian Gornick's, was an emotional knockout. Her memorable last line: "It is hard to fight an enemy who has outposts in your head."

Not every woman journalist that season cared to identify her interests with the ragtag battalions. Julie Baumgold, an up-and-coming writer at *New York*, wrote a mocking story on Boston's Cell 16 that the magazine illustrated with a composite cover photo of a woman flexing a grotesquely enlarged male bicep. Jane Kramer's heavily disguised profile of the Stanton-Anthony Brigade for *The New Yorker* kept its distance by focusing on the group's internal squabbles. A treacherous blow came from Diane Arbus, the celebrated photographer of freaks. Commissioned by the *London Sunday Times Magazine* to illustrate a feature that dismissed the American movement as "a crusade of neurotic, unhappy girls," the photographer employed a cheap bag of tricks. Arbus popped her flash at Roxanne Dunbar during a karate kick to capture a frightful grimace, switched to a wide-angle lens to portray Anne Koedt as a stark, solitary figure in an empty room, and crouched low for a shot of four Redstockings women to create the illusion of chubby legs. The Arbus pictures recirculated in *Time* and elsewhere. They weren't helpful.

A trusting freelancer named Susan Braudy learned the hard way that *Playboy* was not going to side with the feminists' camp. Her sympathetic story was killed by Hugh Hefner, whose bare-knuckled interoffice memo read "These chicks are our natural enemy. It is time to do battle with them. What I want is a devastating piece that takes the militant feminists apart." Hef got what he wanted in "Up Against the Wall, Male Chauvinist Pig" by another freelancer, Morton Hunt. An incensed secretary in the magazine's Chicago office leaked the Hefner memo to women's groups and the press, and was promptly fired.

Individual women asserted themselves in a positive fashion wherever they could. Mary Cantwell, the managing editor at *Mademoiselle*, commissioned a series of profeminist essays. Cantwell had an eager ally in Amy Gross, her young assistant. At ABC, Marlene Sanders constituted a one-woman corrective in television. Over at Metromedia, where no one like Sanders existed, an all-male unit produced "Women Are Revolting," a snide documentary fully in keeping with its double-entendre title.

It was one thing for a freelancer to write a piece that came down on the side of Women's Liberation. When women with staff jobs in the media began to rise up, feminism moved into another dimension. Their courageous actions were to change the face of journalism forever.

•   •   •

On Monday morning, March 16, 1970 (two days before the *Ladies' Home Journal* sit-in), forty-six women at *Newsweek* filed a sex discrimination complaint with the Equal Employment Opportunity Commission. Seizing upon a natural news peg, they'd timed their action to coincide with Helen Dudar's cover story, "Women in Revolt."

The *Newsweek* women were sedate, polite, composed, and grim. Eight months of whispered exchanges in the ladies' room and tentative feelers broached at lunch had preceded their decision to confront the magazine some of them had worked at for nearly a decade. No boisterous hijinks accompanied their press conference; they were happy to let their attorney, Eleanor Holmes Norton of the ACLU, do most of the talking.

Most of the women occupied a slot at the low end of the masthead called "editorial assistant," a code for researcher, although the men sometimes called them fact checkers, a term they abhorred. They'd also acquired an odious nickname, "the dollies." Before the "dolly" business gained currency, the women had reveled in *Newsweek*'s clubhouse vernacular. It seemed to define the collegial esprit of the place, along with the crazy hours, the intense, semipublic office affairs, and the Friday night dinners at a nearby restaurant before the team buckled down to close Nation and Foreign, the big front-of-the-book sections. *Newsweek* insiders called the top editors "the Wallendas," after the high-flying circus family that was prone to mishaps, but "Wallenda" was funny and "dolly" was not. "Dolly" was proof that the men did not think of the women as professional reporters, although reporting was the part of the job that the women loved. They prided themselves in producing files with colorful tidbits and sound assessments—good solid stuff—while young men barely out of college were brought in at a higher level, fussed over, and given a chance to write.

Judy Ginggold, a researcher in Nation, kicked off the women's revolt. Her impressive credentials (Phi Beta Kappa at Smith, scholarship to Oxford) were just what the magazine looked for in hiring women. That is, she'd gone to a good school and knew how to dress with understated taste. Maybe Judy took the lead in the women's rebellion because she wasn't afraid to bitch about the unjustness, the absolute unfairness, of her lot. Her weekly consciousness-raising group based on the Redstockings model had given her a fresh perspective.

"When I was hired," Ginggold relates, "they told me flat-out that women do not write at *Newsweek*. When they moved me from the library into research, they said I was the luckiest person in the world to get into Nation so fast. I didn't feel lucky. I felt I was wasting myself, but I didn't know what to do."

One evening she poured out her misery to Gladys Kessler, a Washington lawyer. "What *Newsweek* is doing to you is illegal," Kessler shot back. "Haven't you heard about Title VII of the Civil Rights Act? Call the EEOC."

Judy made the call. "First you organize," said the woman over the phone. "And," she added, lowering her voice, "you organize in secret so they don't pick you off one by one."

"I was terrified," Ginggold remembers. "I saw myself as a nice person, not as an angry feminist. But it turned out that I was an angry feminist after all."

Ginggold put forward some lunch-hour feelers to her best friends in Nation, Lucy Howard and Margaret Montagno. Lucy and Margaret had never done anything political in their lives, but they were heartsick from the years of being passed over. Next the nucleus of three approached Pat Lynden, a former researcher who'd returned to the magazine as a New York bureau reporter after a year of successful freelancing. "A man in the New York bureau with the same job I had was called a correspondent," Lynden remembers. "But I was just called a reporter."

Emboldened, the four conspirators extended their net to Lynn Povich, the daughter of a famous *Washington Post* sportswriter, who had just received a promotion to junior writer, the token woman, and treated as such, among fifty men. Lynn was following the Women's Liberation Movement on her own initiative and filing reports, but little of her work made it into the magazine. "I'd gotten my promotion," she laughs, "because none of the guys wanted to write about fashion. That was my big break. I seemed to be on my way, at least I hoped so, but I certainly understood that nobody else was." She offered her cubicle for the secret meetings.

When the women had a solid core of nine, they began soliciting lawyers. "Harriet Pilpel turned us down," Ginggold remembers. "She just didn't get it. Flo Kennedy got it, but she wasn't for us. She was wearing a big cowboy hat and we were such straight and square women. Then we met Eleanor Holmes Norton."

"Eleanor Holmes Norton was perfect for us," continues Pat Lynden. "She'd gone to Yale Law School, which was something *they'd* respect. She was black, with a decade of civil rights stuff behind her, and she was pregnant. That was delicious. And she understood exactly what we were after—an end to the unspoken caste system that was making us so unhappy. Eleanor spent a lot of time with us, whipping us into shape. She'd say, 'You gotta take off your white gloves, ladies. Take off your gloves.'"

The conspirators were wracked with doubt. *Newsweek* was like a benevolent, paternal family. The rule of the game was "Work for a couple of years, then leave and get married," but married or not, this crew had stayed on, lulled by the magazine's first-name civility, the delightful long lunches, the built-in overtime that allowed them to buy a good pair of earrings or a mink-paw coat while they performed their allotted tasks and waited to be noticed. In weak moments they told themselves that *they* were the problem—they were directionless wimps! Some of their former colleagues (Nora Ephron, Ellen Goodman, and I) hadn't hung around the research pool waiting to be discovered. Nora had cut out fast and never looked back. "Oh hell, Simone de Beauvoir could walk in here," somebody sighed, "and they'd put her in research."

The time to take off their white gloves arrived with Helen Dudar's invitation to guest-write the magazine's Women's Liberation cover. "It was remarkable," exclaims Lucy Howard. "The Wallendas did not see the irony in this at all."

Certain they would all get fired and have their names inscribed on an industry blacklist, the ringleaders attempted to involve every woman in the office in the EEOC complaint. Fay Willey, the crusty chief researcher in Foreign, came aboard; she had seen many a young male pup whiz by her in twenty years of faithful service. The letter writers in the backwater of Reader Mail wanted in. But despite Eleanor Norton's presence on their team, the organizers struck out with *Newsweek*'s five black researchers, whose entry into the magazine had been forged by the civil rights movement only a few years before.

"Our identification at the time was with a black movement, not a women's movement," Leandra Abbott recalls. "I remember going to a big meeting at somebody's house and sitting there feeling this wasn't my fight. I was thinking, *What about blacks who don't have opportunity?* It's interesting—the black women all came to the same conclusion that the petition wasn't about us."

"The black women didn't caucus," says Diane Camper, a *Times* editorial writer today. "We simply had this feeling that the petition wasn't going to help us. In retrospect I can say that I certainly benefited from it."

Oz Elliott, the editor in chief, got wind of the revolt two days before the women went public. He called Fay Willey at home on Saturday night, imploring her in the name of loyalty to stop the complaint from going forward. These were terrible times for journalists, he pleaded. Just recently Vice President Spiro Agnew had called them "a tiny and closed fraternity of privileged men," and the women's action was certain to play into Agnew's hand. Willey stood firm, and rushed to tell her cohorts the gist of the conversation.

"In those days an EEOC finding had no teeth, no enforcement procedures," Pat Lynden recalls, "so we had to go public as a militant tactic. We weren't the type for sit-ins or guerrilla theater, but we sure knew how to stage a press conference. We'd covered enough of them for the magazine."

As *Newsweek* with "Women in Revolt" emblazoned on its yellow cover hit the newsstands on Monday morning, March 16, Eleanor Holmes Norton, flanked by Pat Lynden, Lucy Howard, and Mary Pleschette Willis, read the EEOC complaint to a packed room of journalists at the ACLU. Thirty *Newsweek* women were present. They had chipped in to fly one of their number, Sunde Smith, to Washington to present a copy to Katharine M. Graham, the widowed socialite owner of *Newsweek* and the Washington Post Company, while the Wallendas' copies were delivered to the Wallendatorium on *Newsweek*'s twelfth floor. As it happened, Mrs. Graham was vacationing in the Bahamas at the historic moment when the rebels fired their guns. When the nervous editors reached her by phone, her half-joking response was "Which side am I supposed to be on?"

Oz Elliott issued a statement for the magazine. "*Newsweek* does not discriminate," he said. "We're talking about a newsmagazine tradition going back almost fifty years."

So it had, but this tradition was doomed to expire. To the researchers' great disappointment, Kay Graham did not throw her weight behind them. She took the position that the aggrieved women should have spoken to management first. Years would pass before Mrs. Graham could appreciate that the gathering feminist storm, already in evidence at *Newsweek*, did more than any other factor to recast her as a publisher of stature.

My former colleagues in Nation had invited me to witness their landmark press conference, knowing that it would warm my heart. And so it did. A few weeks later, however, I was startled to receive an urgent phone call from one of the Wallendas, inviting me to meet with them at the office.

I hadn't seen Lester Bernstein, Bob Christopher, and Kermit Lansner since 1964, and never before had I commanded their full attention. After we shook hands, they got right to the point. Conceding that there was merit to the researchers' case, they said that the women, bright and deserving, seemed paralyzed in informal tryouts when given a chance to produce the tightly compressed, formulaic newsmagazine prose. The editors wondered if the women had been held back too long. The men were familiar with the internal damage to people's psyches that resulted from years of conforming to low expectations—they had witnessed the same phenomenon in blacks. But I'd proven myself elsewhere. How would I like to come back to *Newsweek* as a writer in any department I wished?

I wouldn't. The moment for me as a *Newsweek* writer had passed. And talk about the damage from lowered expectations. I'd knocked out copy in two TV newsrooms and written for *Esquire* and the *Times*, but my idea of a cold-sweat nightmare was eighty-five lines for Nation on a Friday night. It still is.

With the recruitment business out of the way, Kermit Lansner, his shirttails rumpled as I'd remembered, confided that Kay—Mrs. Graham—was nagging them to put Gloria Steinem on the cover.

"Over my dead body," he or Christopher avowed, and everyone laughed. They were not in the habit of taking editorial cues from the diffident heiress. One year and five months later a steelier Mrs. Graham, buoyed by the feminist upsurge, got her Steinem cover, and no dead bodies were discovered on the floor.

Before we adjourned, Lester Bernstein, my old boss in Nation, asked if I'd mind answering a personal question. My relationship with Lester had been fine and flirty when I'd been a researcher in his department. I was one of his favorites; I'd thought he had understood my frustration and boredom. But now he inquired with puzzled sincerity, "When you worked here, Susan, did you have ambition?"

For two years not a week had gone by without my asking if I could "do more." He hadn't noticed.

Two months after the *Newsweek* rebellion, the women at Time, Inc., the empire of *Time*, *Life*, *Fortune*, and *Sports Illustrated*, filed sex discrimination charges with the New York State Division of Human Rights. The women of *The Washington Post*, the *Times*, and many other newspapers would organize soon after. Dissatisfied with the token progress at their magazine, the *Newsweek* women filed a second complaint with the EEOC in 1972. By then the federal agency and the women's movement had become forces to be reckoned with. Joseph Califano, for the magazine, and Harriet Rabb, for the women, hammered out a specific timetable for affirmative action. This time around the researchers were offered an in-house training program, and several would indeed become *Newsweek* correspondents and writers.

• • •

August 26, 1970, marked the fiftieth anniversary of women's suffrage, a piece of historical information most welcome to Betty Friedan, who was suffering that spring from a strong sense of repudiation. At NOW's fourth national conference, held in Des Plaines, Illinois, in March, 250 delegates had elected Aileen Hernandez and Wilma Scott Heide to the top two posts, denying Friedan a seat on the board in the process. Refusing to bow out politely, Friedan used the forum of her farewell address, a speech that was clocked at two hours, for an audacious proposal. She called for a "Women's Strike for Equality" to commemorate August 26 across the country. Acting unilaterally, the difficult visionary once again proved her prescience.

A national one-day work stoppage, Friedan's idea, proved too ambitious, although the planners were reluctant to part with their slogan, "Don't Iron While the Strike Is Hot." Coordinated events were, however, to take place around the country. Ivy Bottini, the president of the New York chapter, proposed a march and a rally, to begin after work on Wednesday, August 26.

Thrilled that the living-room feminists were taking to the streets at long last, Ruthann Miller, the young Trotskyist organizer from the So-

cialist Workers Party, opened a "march coalition" headquarters on
lower Broadway, at a physical remove from NOW's Lexington Avenue
office. The schism between "the bourgeois women" and "the downtown crazies," as the two factions called each other, was mended in late
summer. Bottini, who had raised two children while holding a full-time
job, felt a welling of motherly empathy for the young Trotskyist with
an infant strapped to her back. The warring headquarters were merged
when the women found they could agree on three basic principles: free
abortion on demand, community-controlled twenty-four-hour child-
care centers, and equal opportunity in jobs and education. Bowing to
the SWP's superior experience in staging marches, NOW accepted the
Trotskyists' parade route. They would assemble at the Grand Army
Plaza at Fifty-ninth Street, march down Fifth Avenue, and conclude
with a rally of speeches and songs at Bryant Park. The two factions
agreed on another piece of strategy. They would solicit Famous Names
to address the rally. Betty Friedan, of course. Bess Myerson? Bella
Abzug? Gloria Steinem? Kate Millett? They began making calls.
Everyone said yes.

As August 26 approached, Women's Strike for Equality Day
was billboarded in advance by newspapers and magazines with
a lavish generosity that surprised the young movement. It helped
that the press had a natural news peg. Prodded by visits from feminist delegations, mayors in several cities took note of the fiftieth anniversary of women's suffrage with official proclamations. The
House of Representatives roused itself to reconsider the dormant
Equal Rights Amendment, bottled up in committee for forty-seven
years.

For the first time since the passage of the Nineteenth Amendment,
newspapers and magazines seemed to expect women to stand up for
their rights. On the Sunday before the Wednesday march, *The New
York Times Magazine* ran a full-dress preview of the upcoming events;
the *Post* and the *News* followed suit. On the morning of the march, the
Times printed the parade route and the starting times of coordinated
events.

The parade down Fifth Avenue exceeded the organizers' wildest
estimates as fifty thousand marchers of all ages and occupations

swept past police barriers and claimed the thoroughfare as their own. Traveling into Manhattan by bus and subway with hand-painted placards, disgorging from office buildings and falling into the line on sudden impulse, the women seemed delighted by the newfound sisterhood, the unaccustomed militance, the coordinated release of anger and joy.

• • •

Few people were more exhilarated that week than Betty Prashker, the alert editor at Doubleday who had acquired *Sexual Politics* by Kate Millett. Summer was a slow time in publishing, ideally suited for a small printing of an intellectual treatise that bore the cover line "A Surprising Examination of Society's Most Arbitrary Folly." Millett's rigorous feminist dissection of D.H. Lawrence, Henry Miller, and Norman Mailer, three writers usually admired for their sexual daring, had inspired her editor to reexamine many of her own assumptions, including the way she viewed her career at Doubleday. Prashker had expected *Sexual Politics* to reach a receptive audience, stir debate, and change opinions, but she had not expected a media avalanche.

Christopher Lehmann-Haupt of the *Times* devoted two daily reviews to *Sexual Politics* because, he announced amid accolades, Millett's treatise on male-female relations was "one of the most troubling books" he had ever read. Lehmann-Haupt had never published a two-day review of any book before. Then *Time* magazine had put Kate on the cover, a stark, glowering portrait in oil by Alice Neel. The cover story reported that *Sexual Politics* was already in its fourth printing, and that Millett was the Chairman Mao of Women's Lib. The day after the August 26 march, the *Times* listed Kate's name immediately after Friedan's in its front-page coverage. Even better, a two-column profile pronounced Katharine Murray Millett the "principal theoretician and new high priestess of the feminist wave."

Kate, the avant-garde sculptor and reluctant academic, was on a merry-go-round that was spinning out of control. Her dark hair no longer confined in a braid or the prim bun she'd worn to her Doubleday meetings, the author of *Sexual Politics* was vomiting before public appearances and gulping bourbon to quiet her nerves. If the media needed one personality to stand for the movement, Kate Millett resolved to fulfill that obligation. If a group at a college somewhere needed a public figure to rally the troops, Kate Millett would get on a plane. By September she began to think she was going crazy. Why did she have to answer the same questions over and over? Didn't people listen? Had she really told the reporter from *Life* that she wasn't "into" the dyke trip, that it wasn't her bag? But the damning words were in print, along with a huge photo of her kissing Fumio, her husband. And who was behind the unsigned broadside that accused her of exploiting lesbians and ripping off the movement's ideas?

The neatly typed page, which scornfully called Millett "this woman," had blasted her for telling the *Times* that she was a bridge between the lesbians and the rest of the movement, and for publishing *Sexual Politics* at $7.95, "which few women can afford."

"Rita Mae Brown did this thing anonymously," says Martha Shelley, "and to my everlasting shame, I didn't stop her. We were having a meeting of Radicalesbians and we knew Kate was coming. I was there early, setting up the room, when Rita Mae put the unsigned paper on people's chairs. At that point I was as much a part of my time as other people. While I didn't do it, I didn't stop it either. Basically the statement attacked Kate for being a star and selling out to the male press, which of course as soon as Rita Mae could possibly do, she did."

"I never placed or wrote an unsigned statement regarding Kate Millett on people's chairs," Rita Mae Brown retorts in a blanket denial of Martha Shelley's assertion. "If I had a disagreement I was up-front about it—to your face or a signed paper. Also, I thought Kate's work critically important, and still do."

"Kate came into the meeting and everyone started discussing the paper," Ellen Shumsky remembers. "Some people were appalled, some people thought it raised interesting points—you know, opinions ranged as they always did. I felt very protective of Kate, I hope she knows this. I knew she was fragile."

"Kate looked liked a whipped puppy," Sidney Abbott recalls. "When it was my turn to speak, I defended her strongly. I was sitting near her, and I remember her staring at the floor."

Things came to an ugly head for Millett in November at Columbia, the school where she had written her doctoral thesis, taught in the English department, and organized the first campus meetings of Women's Liberation. The venue was a panel discussion on Gay Liberation and sexuality at the MacMillan Theater. "People were wearing little bracelets identifying where they placed themselves—heterosexual, asexual, bisexual, homosexual," Shumsky recalls.

Kate rushed in late from an out-of-town speaking engagement and took her seat on the stage. Minutes into the panel a voice from the back of the hall rang out, "Bisexuality is a cop-out!"

Sidney Abbott, another panel member, peered into the audience and recognized Ann Sanchez, one of the Radicalesbians.

The persistent voice catcalled, "Are you a lesbian, Kate? What are you afraid of? You say it downtown, but you don't say it uptown. Why don't you say it?"

"Yes," Millett wearily replied. "You think bisexuality is a cop-out, so yes, I'll say it. I am a lesbian."

A reporter from *Time* was at her door the next morning. The story ran in December. Millett's disclosure of her bisexuality, the magazine intoned, avoiding the word "lesbian," was "bound to discredit her as a spokeswoman for her cause."

Dolores Alexander and Ivy Bottini of NOW urgently called a "Kate Is Great" press conference. Artemis March and Ellen Shumsky of the Radicalesbians composed a statement of solidarity that was read to the reporters. Ann Sanchez showed up, horrified at what she had wrought and wanting to make amends. Sally Kempton and I were there. Gloria Steinem firmly held Kate's hand for a significant photo in the *Times*. Ti-Grace Atkinson broke ranks to thunder that the statement "did not go far enough." But the show of support did little to calm the fraying nerves of the woman who stood at the center of the media storm. "It was as if," she said later, "I was standing on a huge platform and suddenly this wind tore off all my clothes and the multitudes were looking up at me and laughing."

During the following decades Kate Millett would be honored and celebrated as *the* American feminist in London and Paris and points beyond. She would continue to make and show her avant-garde sculpture, she would experiment with photographs and film, she would employ a personal voice and a stream-of-consciousness style in a half dozen books, and she would rise up and recover from periodic bouts of manic-depression. To her relief, her private life would be private again, except when she chose to reveal it in her autobiographical works. *Sexual Politics* would never be dislodged from its place as feminism's first book-length bombshell, but the making and breaking of Kate Millett as the movement's high priestess had run its course in four months.

• • •

Unlike many of the founders of Women's Liberation, Shulamith Firestone was not ambivalent about wanting to be a national figure. Earlier that fall the young woman in a hurry who had helped initiate three signal groups in three years—Chicago's West Siders, New York Radical Women, and Redstockings—abruptly quit her fourth creation, New York Radical Feminists, after a split over leadership inside her Stanton-Anthony brigade. Anne Koedt left with her.

With her angry departure, Shulie gave up on meetings and organizations, telling everyone within earshot that the book she was about to publish, *The Dialectic of Sex*, would place her in the firmament next to Simone de Beauvoir. She watched the media circus engulfing Kate and champed at the bit, awaiting her turn.

Robin Morgan's anthology *Sisterhood Is Powerful* was also scheduled for publication that fall. Picking and choosing among the mimeographed outpourings, soliciting new pieces to fill the gaps, Morgan had remained faithful to her left-liberationist perspective. She ignored Dana Densmore's "On Celibacy" and Anne Koedt's "The Myth of the Vaginal Orgasm," two of the movement's most powerful essays, and selected nothing by Firestone, but she added an impressive range of multicultural voices, printing poems and essays by four black women, two lesbians, and one Chicana. The youngest contributors were identified as founders of High School Women's Liberation.

Dialectic and *Sisterhood* both reached reviewers and bookstores in October, too soon after Kate's triumph for another huge round of media attention, but just in time for a counterreaction. Critics who might have been charmed, if not dazzled, by a brash twenty-five-year-old's assault on Marx, Engels, and Freud recoiled at Firestone's excesses and overstatements. Shulie was pinned to the wall for asserting that women needed to be freed from childbirth, and for her flat-out challenge, "Men can't love." Even worse, she suffered the mortification of a group review in the *Times* along with her enemy Robin Morgan in a grumpy essay by the normally astute John Leonard, who declared that the feminist tracts lacked the grace and wisdom of *Don't Fall Off the Mountain,* an autobiography by Shirley MacLaine.

Sisterhood Is Powerful became the subject of some acrimonious inner-movement disputes. Kathie Amatniek Sarachild grumbled that Robin had appropriated *her* slogan for the title. Cindy Cisler charged that the book's bibliography owed a debt to *her* mimeographed list. Her feathers ruffled, Robin tried to tough it out. Cisler circulated an angry letter inside the movement and filed a lawsuit that was settled out of court. Taking her portion of brickbats and plaudits in stride, Robin Morgan soldiered on, returning to poetry and essays, hanging in at *Rat*, redoubling her efforts on the college lecture circuit.

I believe that Shulamith Firestone, given her expectations for her book, must have seen the mixed reception accorded to *The Dialectic of Sex* as a crushing defeat. The inner forces that propelled her forward as a radical visionary may have allowed for nothing less than universal acclaim. What I know is that she disintegrated rapidly, losing her emotional equilibrium and her sense of herself in the world.

Morgan's anthology and Firestone's *Dialectic* spoke the unpolished language of the vibrant young movement in ways that Millett's formal locutions had deliberately avoided. Read, debated, and studied in many editions and foreign translations, all three of these astonishing books from the watershed year of 1970 influenced thinking here and abroad and are acknowledged classics today.

·   ·   ·

Mary Catherine Kilday's women's rights committee at station WRC in Washington was making no headway as management kept spouting the same old defenses—"What do you mean, discrimination? No woman has ever applied to be an engineer." Steeped in politics since childhood—her father, Paul Joseph Kilday, represented his Texas district in Congress for twenty-three years—Mary Catherine had fallen in love with the business side of broadcasting. She had joined WRC, an NBC station, as a secretary, hoping to break into sales.

"They actually told me," Kilday remembers, "'How could you take a time-buyer to lunch? It would embarrass NBC to have a woman pick up the check.'" After ten years of persistence, Kilday had progressed to Community Affairs, a soft slot in management that was not on a career track.

Kilday had decided that the women of WRC should have an event of their own on August 26, 1970, to celebrate the passage of the Nineteenth Amendment. She approached Alison Owings in the cafeteria line one day. "Alison was the only woman in the documentary unit at the level of associate producer. I didn't know her very well, but somehow I knew she'd be simpatico to women's rights."

A whimsical, offbeat writer from Valley Forge, Pennsylvania, Owings was very sympathetic to women's rights. The new allies invited twelve of their coworkers to Mary Catherine's house for a lunchtime meeting.

Formed on the spot, the high-spirited women's committee did a survey and job count: WRC had no female announcers, no women in sales, no women on its film and videotape crews, no women engineers, no women directors, and only three tokens representing on-air talent. Armed with their statistics, Kilday and Owings circulated a modest "I am concerned" statement directed at management to every woman in the office. The three on-air tokens—Cassie Mackin, a gifted TV reporter, Betty Groebli, a daytime radio host, and Marilyn Robinson, a newly hired black reporter—were quick to sign.

"We got about one-third of the ninety women, including a lot of secretaries," Kilday recalls. "One person, an assistant in radio, became the group fink—isn't that typical? She used the leverage to deal with management on her own. I'm still angry when I think about it. Anyway, the rest of us confidently made our little pitch to management in a conference room on August 26. We expected they'd say 'Gee, yeah, something is wrong here, let's see what we can do about it.' We were really that innocent."

"We'll study the matter and get back to you," the general manager of the station said politely.

"We never should have given you the vote in the first place," another veep hee-hawed from the back of the room.

WRC's women were stunned. They had gotten a brush-off. The group fink was promoted to radio producer.

Two young feminists barely out of law school, Nancy Stanley and Susan Deller Ross, told Kilday bluntly that the WRC women would never get anywhere unless they filed federal charges. The best person to handle the case, they said, was Gladys Kessler.

Kessler, whose quick response to Judy Ginggold had triggered the *Newsweek* women's rebellion, had become a partner in a public interest law firm and was happy to take the broadcast case. Working with Ross and Stanley, she drew up three separate discrimination charges: for the EEOC, for the Federal Communications Commission, and for the Office of Federal Contract Compliance, the last a long shot worth pursuing because NBC's parent company, RCA, held government contracts.

"Filing charges was a big step," Kessler, now a federal judge, affirms. "The WRC women had hopes for advancement in a high-profile profession. They knew they might be jeopardizing their future."

March 2, 1971, was their D-Day. Barred by management from meeting in a station conference room, Mary Catherine Kilday rallied her troops via interdepartmental mail for an emergency lunch-hour session at the nearby Presbyterian Center. After listening to Kessler explain the ramifications, twenty-five women stepped forward to sign the complaints. Kilday and Alison Owings raced to the federal agencies with the documents while Bernice Sandler of the Women's Equity Action League and some NOW volunteers fanned out to deliver press releases, thoughtfully prepared in advance, to every media outlet in the city.

"I got back to the station," remembers Kilday, "and the phones started ringing—CBC, ABC, *The Washington Post*, the *Star, The Wall Street Journal*, our own news department. That night everybody came over to my house and we had TVs set up all around. It was a panic. Of course the newscasters all reported that NBC had no comment."

The complaint to the FCC was rejected; the Office of Federal Contract Compliance was silent. But after eight months of study the EEOC ruled that station WRC had indeed practiced discrimination. The ruling galvanized Marilyn Schultz, a production assistant with *NBC Nightly News* in New York, who set out to organize the network's women at 30 Rockefeller Plaza. Schultz, from Indiana, had started at NBC as a "guidette" after getting a degree in broadcast journalism.

Borrowing a tactic that had worked for Kilday, Schultz made use of NBC's interdepartmental mail. "A hundred women, mostly secretaries, came to our first meeting," she relates. "It was huge. We were shocked." The ringleaders initiated their protest on National Secretaries Day, when by company policy NBC's personnel department presented every female employee, regardless of her occupation, with a single red rose. That year several hundred NBC women placed their roses in office envelopes and routed them back to Personnel. Marilyn and some others scrawled "Bullshit" on theirs.

"We were angry about everything," Schultz recalls. "We wanted promotions, equal pay, access to technical jobs. We criticized the network's programming content, we monitored the language of the news broadcasts. We demanded a place to hold our meetings and were furious when they wouldn't let us put up signs in the bathrooms. We met with the personnel department for a long, long time. God, those were dreadful meetings. They'd say 'Oh, we'll get back to you next week,' and so we'd go back the next week and it would just drag on and on." Growing more sophisticated, the women created a slide show presentation, with facts and figures, for NBC's corporate executives. The executives countered with a slide show presentation of their own.

At an impasse, the women sought out my old friend Jan Goodman, just graduated from NYU law school and, with Nancy Stanley and Susan Deller Ross, a founder of the first women's law firm in the country. Goodman pushed her clients to file a class action suit in court. Fearful of the drastic adversarial step, only sixteen NBC employees were willing to sign on as plaintiffs. They received a big boost when the EEOC joined the case. It took seven years before NBC settled, distributing two million dollars in compensatory back pay to more than one thousand employees. News of the affirmative action settlement made the front page of *The New York Times*.

•   •   •

By 1971 the national media were no longer simply engaged in reporting a story. Newsrooms were being impacted directly by Women's Liberation, and the demands for a new order were reaching into the journalists' personal, as well as their professional, lives. If the movement's disputes with the left were too abstruse for public consumption, if its desire to function without leaders was unfathomable and erratic, its radical analysis that men were the core of the problem rang loud and clear.

The stage was set for an uninhibited six-foot Australian who strode into view with a thrusting jaw, high cheekbones, and trendy designer costumes. Her name was Germaine Greer and she arrived from London bearing *The Female Eunuch*, a romping success in her adopted country due in no small part to the author's virtuoso talent for self-promotion. Greer had an uncanny knack in her public appearances for switching from erudition to raunchy wit while she crossed a bare leg and adjusted her stole.

Germaine was an improbable, self-made creation, a woman with a steel-trap mind and a self-professed lust who spun curious appellations for herself such as "Supergroupie" and "Intellectual Superwhore." A decade earlier she had migrated from Melbourne to Sydney in search of kindred spirits among the Push, a small counterculture movement devoted to libertarian sex, anarchist politics, and hoisting a glass at dockside pubs. Almost immediately she became one of the Push's leading female figures, admired for her quick mind and eccentric exhibitionism. "The thing about Germaine," a young Push woman once remarked, "is that she never menstruates. She hemorrhages once a month and gives you a drip-by-drip description."

It was a cardinal tenet among the Push to eschew careers and ambition, but Germaine left Australia for England in 1964 to pursue a doctorate in Shakespeare's early comedies at Cambridge. The university drama society voted her Actress of the Year. With the doctorate under her belt, she took a teaching job at Warwick, a provincial university within striking distance of London, and became a star contributor to *Oz*, a raucous journal of rock music, satire, and freewheeling sexuality started by one of her countrymen. Her piece "In Bed with the English" created a big stir. Television appearances followed. She had a go at helping to start *Suck*, a journal as short-lived and sexually explicit as its name. Tom Wolfe, the novelist and caustic social observer, had a memorable dinner with Greer during her *Suck* phase. As he recollected, she had "a tremendous curly electric hairdo and the most outrageous Naugahyde mouth I had ever heard on a woman." When the conversation palled in the King's Road restaurant, Germaine lit a match and set fire to her hair. Wolfe recalls that solicitous waiters rushed over with napkins to beat out the flames while she grinned.

Greer's wacky exuberance made a fan of Sonny Mehta, the head of a new paperback imprint in London, who shrewdly assessed that her firecracker mind and offbeat exhibitionism could be profitably harnessed. He offered her a contract to write a book that would illuminate the growing mood of Women's Liberation. Keeping aloof from the small British women's movement—too square, Marxist, and dowdy from her anarchist-libertarian perspective—she vacuumed up facts and quotations and let it rip.

McGraw-Hill picked up the American rights to *The Female Eunuch* and planned for an April 1971 publication. In a clever stroke, editor Robert Stewart sent a copy of the British edition to Norman Mailer, who happened to be at work on *The Prisoner of Sex*, a windy broadside intended to demolish Kate Millett and the entire feminist movement. (Among the many choice Mailerisms in *Prisoner*, my favorite remains "the women were writing like very tough faggots.") Slipping a few choice lines from Greer into his humongous diatribe, which first appeared in *Harper's* magazine, Mailer delivered the news that here was a liberated lady a fellow could admire.

Next Mailer proposed a fund-raising benefit for the Theatre for Ideas, an intellectuals' public forum. He volunteered to chair a debate between Millett and Greer, two radically different voices of Women's Liberation.

Kate prudently turned down the invitation, but Germaine grabbed at the chance and took aim at Kate by declaring that Mailer was *not* the enemy. She put out the word that she rather looked forward to a tumble with Norman. The Town Hall evening, a circus beyond anyone's expectations, became the linchpin of Greer's triumphal American tour, which reaped a week as guest host on Dick Cavett among other publicity bonanzas.

The Town Hall evening starring Greer and Mailer was filmed by D.A. Pennebaker. I didn't go, but I saw the movie. It was memorable mainly for a piece of excess in the presence of reporters and cameras that was typical of that volatile time. Jill Johnston, a dance critic for *The Village Voice* and a pioneer in performance art, had attracted a devoted following through her stream-of-consciousness musings without punctuation. More recently she had come out in print, turning her weekly column into a lesbian forum. Johnston had been invited to represent the lesbian point of view at Town Hall. Knowing she was up against some practiced spotlight hogs, she choreographed a surprise. Two women friends leaped on stage to join her in a simulated group grope, prompting Mailer to bark, "Cut it out, Jill. Be a team player. Be a lady."

I have to confess that I was the person who recommended Jill Johnston to the Theatre for Ideas. I figured that she was the only woman in the city who could steal a scene from the top-billed performers.

Life heralded Greer's arrival with a cover story, "The Saucy Feminist That Even Men Like." Christopher Lehmann-Haupt trumpeted *The Female Eunuch* in the *Times* by saying he wished "the timing of the publication of this book had been such that it could have caught the lightning that struck *Sexual Politics*, for it is everything that Kate Millett's book is not." His review was titled "The Best Feminist Book So Far." Betty Friedan was persuaded to host a publication party that is remembered by guests for Germaine's opening salvo. "Betty!" she boomed, "A talk show host told me it was so nice to have a spokesperson for Women's Liberation who was good-looking for a change. But I stood up for you, Betty, I did."

I must say my heart leaped at the book's opening chapters: fresh, sharp disquisitions on bones, curves, hair, womb. *Eunuch* was strong on economic injustice, scathing in its analysis of male hatred. Further into the text I experienced doubt. It was apparent to me that as much as Greer thrilled to the vision of bedding down men in multiples while retaining her personal autonomy, she did not particularly like or respect women. Neither did she believe in organized movements. Hers was a personal, idiosyncratic declaration of independence, true to her anarchist-libertarian ideals. The woman went out of her way to scatter shots across the wide bow of the American movement, slamming Anne Koedt's "The Myth of the Vaginal Orgasm," a sure way to curry favor with men, while producing such odd irrelevancies as "If you think you are emancipated, you might consider the idea of tasting your menstrual blood—if if makes you sick, you've got a long way to go, baby." Oh?

Eunuch zoomed to number one on all national best-seller lists. Never mind the absence of sisterhood, the disregard for a radical movement as the prime vehicle for social change—the book, and Germaine, struck a loud chord among huge numbers of women who were fearful of feminism unless it came wrapped in a glamorous package. I witnessed this phenomenon one afternoon in the book alcove of a chic department store. Two young women were daring each other to buy a copy. "Oooh," said one, entranced by Germaine's picture, "she looks like a *Vogue* model." That night a friend at CBS called to report, "She came into the office wearing Jean Muir! I recognized the jacket!"

Only one American feminist, Claudia Dreifus writing in *The Nation*, dared to take on *The Female Eunuch* in print. Everyone else, so willing to bash and trash inside the movement, was unwilling to appear unsisterly in public. Germaine had a free license that season. She flummoxed the men and hamstrung the women. It was an amazing tour de force. Yet for all its flaws, *Eunuch* made it easier for hundred of thousands of the uninitiated to overcome their nervousness and declare themselves in the feminists' camp.

I met Germaine twice, both times on television programs where I was asked to be part of the window dressing. Our interesting exchanges took place off-camera during the breaks. At Channel 13, the public broadcast station, she looked me in the eye and leveled: "I've worked too hard all my life for this chance and I'm not going to blow it." Our second encounter occurred on a *David Susskind Show*. Germaine had stripped to a sexy tank top, the male and female guests were trading insults as expected, and the invited audience of movement women was keeping up the heat by screaming at Susskind to take his hands off Germaine's bare shoulder. At me they yelled, "You shouldn't be up there, Susan."

My movement sisters were saying: Germaine comes to us as a star so we accept her status and protect her, but you have no right to the spotlight unless we all do. It was a rather obscure movement point, but Germaine understood it perfectly and was enjoying my discomfort. At the close of each segment, she leaned over to whisper, "Hmmm, you held your own with me that time."

Germaine Greer soon tired of explaining feminism to Americans. She grew increasingly testy on the lecture circuit, drank more than she should have, snapped at the repetitive questions, ducked the well-meaning professors and earnest students who had arranged her visits. Eventually she went back to London. Most of us weren't sorry to see her go.

• • •

Gloria Steinem never shared a lecture platform or TV panel with Germaine Greer during the promotion of *The Female Eunuch*, although they were an obvious matchup. I believe Gloria was too media-wise to place herself in that windstorm, but her ascension was coming. In fact it arrived in August 1971, five months after Germaine's triumph and one year after Kate's. The deus ex machina was the *Newsweek* cover that Kay Graham had been hankering for. Pegged to the emergent "New

Woman," the story declared Steinem the "unlikely guru" of Women's Lib. No one was more surprised, I think, than Betty Friedan. It was the beginning of the bad blood between them.

A generational difference of fourteen years and the politics of the Cold War separated these two ambitious, talented women whose public careers would be so entwined, and whose animosities would run so deep. Each had escaped from a medium-sized industrial city in the heartland to graduate Phi Beta Kappa from Smith (Betty in 1942, Gloria in 1956). Betty was Jewish, the precocious daughter of a shop-keeper in Peoria, Illinois, who sold jewelry and fine china. Radical-ized at Smith during the Second World War, she had hurled herself into left-wing activism as a labor writer for the *UE News*, the boldly political paper of the United Electrical, Radio and Machine Workers of America. UE was red-baited, expelled from the CIO, and nearly hounded out of existence during the fifties, but Betty stayed on until 1952, when she became pregnant with the second of her three chil-dren. From there she segued into issue-oriented freelancing for the women's magazines.

Gloria grew up in Toledo, Ohio, the child of a mixed marriage be-tween an erratic, entrepreneurial Jewish father and an aspiring jour-nalist mother, of French Huguenot ancestry, whose mental illness had required hospitalization. Her precarious adolescence after her parents' divorce had been offset by the advantage of breathtaking beauty. Glo-ria's path after Smith was no less political than Betty's, but her activism as an atypical rebel of the Silent Generation tilted to the establishment side of the Cold War divisions. Returning from a government fellow-ship in India, she took a recruiter's job with the Independent Research Service of Cambridge, Massachusetts, a CIA front. Her mission was to lead student delegations into the jaws of Communist-sponsored inter-national youth festivals in Vienna and Helsinki to argue the case for American democracy. During the seventies this job would come back to haunt her.

By sheer coincidence the two women both entered the public con-sciousness in 1963, the year of bloody southern civil-rights battles and JFK's assassination. Betty, of course, had come out with The Book, tailoring her message somewhat to reach an audience of suburban

housewives. Gloria made a splash in *Show*, a glossy, short-lived journal of the arts, with a two-part exposé of her undercover life as a Playboy Bunny.

I'd admired and envied the Bunny story. It was gutsy, and it
observed something fresh about the chameleon qualities of feminine
identity. Donning her Bunny ears and stuffing her bosom for her first
night on the job, Gloria had looked in the mirror and seen, not
herself, but a Playboy Bunny. The anecdote reminded me of an experience in my past when I'd tried on a Las Vegas showgirl's plumes
and feathers and seen an eponymous Showgirl in the mirror's reflection. *Steinem is wise*, I concluded. That August, however, Gloria
suffered one of her few accidents of bad timing. During a month
when 350,000 Americans (including me and everyone I was close
to—and Gloria, too) trekked to Washington for civil rights and were
privileged to hear Martin Luther King's "I Have a Dream," she published *The Beach Book*, with unfolding reflector covers for sunning.
I chalked her off as a frivolous jet-setter. When she began tackling
political causes for *New York* magazine, I revised my judgment
again. But there were aspects of Gloria Steinem—the fashion
model glamour, the pop celebrity, the famous men she was linked
with in the gossip columns—that didn't jibe with my idea of a serious
person.

My first encounter with Friedan and Steinem, in the flesh, took
place during the fall of 1967 at Friedan's apartment in the neo-Gothic
Dakota on Central Park West. Betty was hosting a fundraiser for a
writers' group against the war, and Gloria was a cohost, although they
had not met before. The big news in the room was Senator Eugene
McCarthy's decision to run in the Democratic primaries as an antiwar
candidate against Lyndon Johnson. This was four years after the publication of *The Feminine Mystique*, two years after the formation of
NOW, and a year before the Miss America Protest officially kicked off
Women's Liberation. In other words, as Friedan and Steinem and I
formed our conversation node amid the buzz and flutter of peace activists and writers, only one of us, the oracle Friedan, possessed a vision
of a mass feminist movement.

Betty was bedecked in a flowing caftan. Gloria was sinuous and smashing in a mini. I walked over to say hello. Betty, my icon at a distance, who'd rebuffed my early attempt to join NOW, was full of herself and distracted, as she would continue to appear full of herself and distracted whenever I introduced myself, or reintroduced myself, over the next thirty years. That was Betty. Her lack of diplomacy went as a package with her Cassandra-like prescience, the way her rapid-fire delivery, with sentences left unfinished as thoughts sped ahead of thoughts, made her sound at times as if she were speaking in tongues. Gloria's emblematic response to my interruption was generous and friendly. Putting my name through her mental calculator, she clicked her long fingers and paid me a compliment on something I'd written. I returned the compliment by saying that her statements against the war had been terrific on Carson or Cavett a few nights before.

She then treated me to a self-assessment that I would mull over many times during the next few years as she soared into prominence as the movement's anointed leader. That evening I learned that Gloria was a keen student of her own natural powers, which she worked tirelessly and attentively to improve. She was aware that she had a rare gift to make things go down palatably in the "cool" medium of television, as Marshall McLuhan had defined it, but she did not yet comprehend how far it might take her.

"I call myself the Great Stone Face," she confided. "But am I getting through or doing it wrong? I joke that I could call for a victory for the Viet Cong and Johnny would say 'That's nice, Gloria. We'll be right back, folks, after this message.'"

"I was telling Gloria," Friedan broke in, "that McCarthy has to put a plank on women's rights in his platform."

"Oh, *Betty!*" Gloria and I chorused, giving each other a sisterly wink. "Leave him alone. It's enough that he's running against the war."

"You're wrong, you're both wrong. I'm in touch with women across the country. I know what's happening."

Betty did know, and we didn't.

McCarthy did not put a women's plank in his platform, and Friedan, riding a crest in NOW, had little time for his campaign.

Steinem's peregrinations during the next few months were all over the lot. She endorsed McCarthy, switched to Bobby Kennedy when he announced, and jumped to McGovern after Bobby's assassination. Gloria wasn't alone in playing musical chairs during the swift, unexpected events leading up to the Chicago Democratic Convention, yet when McCarthy came to New York to read his poetry after his defeat, I was taken aback by his mockery of Steinem, and Steinem only, from the lectern. The man was known for his waspish spite, but I felt this was pure sexism, although the word had not yet been invented.

By then Gloria was soaring into the stratosphere as a friend of the California grape pickers, a booster of the antiwar movement, a fundraiser for a clutch of candidates and causes, and a journalist with impressive ties to the liberal wing of the Democratic Party. She was a contributing editor at Clay Felker's *New York* magazine, where her photograph graced an early cover, she had a contract at *Glamour*, and she represented *Seventeen* in speeches to campus groups. Welcomed into the fold by the celebrity male journalists, she was drafted in 1969 by Norman Mailer and Jimmy Breslin to run for comptroller in their waggish "Make New York the Fifty-first State" mayoral campaign. After the initial round of publicity, she eased out of her candidacy for a lesser role in the rampantly egotistical campaign. That April she took note of the new stirrings among the radical women in her City Politic column for *New York*, reporting on some WITCH zaps and the Redstockings abortion speak-out. Her piece was titled "After Black Power, Women's Liberation."

Steinem's cheering section among the male journalists turned into a veritable drumroll in 1970. I believe the men knew that something cataclysmic was happening and desired to shape the new movement to her image before the hot lava ran over. Writing in the *New York Post* on the occasion of the August 26 Women's March for Equality, when Gloria introduced the speakers at Bryant Park, Pete Hamill, who seldom missed a chance in those days to disparage the female anatomy from fat ankles to big nose, allowed that "most of the men I know are in love with Gloria Steinem, and it isn't difficult to understand why." In *The Prisoner of Sex*, Mailer juxtaposed the legions of his heated imagination—"thin college ladies with eyeglasses, no-nonsense features, mouths thin as bologna slicers"—with a chummy lunch at the Algonquin he had shared with "Miss Steinem," who broached the idea of his running for mayor and teased about needing "to explain you to my friends at Women's Lib." Noting that Steinem was missing from *Sisterhood Is Powerful* and another feminist anthology published that season, John Leonard complained in the *Times*, "That's sad."

A year later, in August 1971, when *Newsweek* ran its cover story on Gloria, the magazine did more than present her as the personification of the women's movement; it declared in so many emphatic words that she was its leader, or in Newsweek-ese its "unlikely guru," and painted an apocryphal picture of humble acolytes sitting at her feet. At the time I was furious. From my vantage point among the radicals, the characterization was typical newsmagazine hype, short on facts and long on burble, and an insult to the thousands of women across the country who were making the revolution. Gloria herself was uneasy with *Newsweek*'s claims, and thought it best not to sit for a cover photo.

Yet in an incredibly short space of time, *Newsweek*'s proclamation of Gloria's ascendancy became fact. The transformation of Gloria Steinem from media darling and invented leader to the tireless, preeminent, unifying spokesperson for feminism was a remarkable personal journey that helped to shape the extraordinary times. Looking back, I can see that while the radicals were insisting, "We don't need leaders," mainstream women needed to have Gloria up there—a golden achiever who wore the armament of perfect beauty, was wildly attractive to men, and spoke uncompromising truths in calm, measured tones that seldom betrayed her inner anger. And Gloria, for all the complex reasons a person seeks heroism and stardom, needed to become what people wished her to be. During the seventies I often grew cross as I saw hard-won, original insights developed by others in near total anonymity be turned by the media into Gloria Steinem pronouncements, Gloria Steinem ideas, and Gloria Steinem visions, but recognition and credit have a way of evaporating in the heat of political movements, and Gloria, with her inner toughness, external composure, and shrewd diplomatic skills, filled a public space no one else in our fractious movement could possibly hold. Her yearning to approach the sainthood of Joan of Arc, short of consummation by fire, was to mesh brilliantly with her chosen role.

FULL MOON RISING

Women's Liberation became a cultural phenomenon as well as a political movement as the explosive vitality of women interacting with women blossomed into new forms of community and creative expression. From the radical left to the Democratic Party, men had begun to concede with grudging respect that women, of all people, had become so articulate and interesting. Even the "Women's Lib look"—the brazen disregard for makeup and bras and a preference for jeans and long, unkempt hair that affronted Middle America—was taken up by fashion trendies as a sexy statement.

The restless energy spilled into women's bookstores, to accommodate a volcanic eruption of publications, women's newspapers, theater groups, art collectives, and coffeehouses. In May 1972, Dolores Alexander, NOW's first executive director, and Jill Ward, an organizer of the 1970 March for Equality, opened Mother Courage, a restaurant for movement women and their friends, in Greenwich Village. Neither of the novice restaurateurs had thought much about the menu beyond spaghetti and meatballs.

By then I was spending my days and a good part of the evening writing my book on rape, so I often dropped in for a late meal at Mother Courage, usually with Florence Rush, who at my urging was writing a history of the sexual abuse of children. Dolores, bubbling with good cheer, was the official meeter and greeter. Joyce Vinson would stop

washing dishes to give us a soaking wet hug. On a typical night Kate
Millett might be deep in conversation with Diane Cleaver, who was
waving to Susan Rennie and Kirsten Grimstad, while Phyllis Chesler,
nibbling bread sticks, urgently addressed Jill Johnston. At another table
Kate Stimpson, dean of women at Barnard, shared a bottle of wine with
Marcia Storch, the feminist gynecologist. Across the room Gloria
Steinem picked at a green salad with the lawyer Brenda Feigen Fasteau.
The mise-en-scène at the little restaurant on West Eleventh Street was
unselfconsciously authentic. The whole place erupted in a spontaneous
party on the night in January 1973 when the *Roe v. Wade* decision came
down.

• • •

I don't remember Betty Friedan ever dining at Mother Courage, but
around that time she exercised her visionary powers yet again, initiating the Manhattan Women's Political Caucus with an eye toward se-
curing a feminist presence within the Democratic Party. In the first
phone call I ever received from the author of *The Feminine Mystique*,
she asked if the Radical Feminists could help her put out the Caucus's
first mailing, which we did in exchange for folding in a flyer about our
prostitution conference. (We had the woman power that season; Betty
had the lists.)

The Manhattan Women's Political Caucus eased the way for the
National Women's Political Caucus, with Friedan, Gloria Steinem, and
Congresswomen Shirley Chisholm and Bella Abzug as its founders. Its
presence at the 1972 Democratic Convention in Miami was a mile-
stone in electoral politics, but the tactical alliance among the four
founders failed to hold. Friedan by then was feeling usurped by
Steinem, and in her usual manner Betty had struck back intemperately,
complaining to a college audience that Gloria's enlistment in the feminist cause had been tardy. "The media tries to make her a celebrity,"
Friedan said in the presence of a UPI reporter "but no one should mistake her for a leader." The nasty assessment was one of several wild
misfires aimed at Steinem that Friedan would make in the years to
come. Gloria, a very deft infighter, always took the high road in her
public responses. Friedan would get her excruciating comeuppance in

Ms. magazine, where she would be treated as something akin to a non-person. (NOW, in a case of guilt by association, would also be slighted in *Ms.* as a distant, cooperating entity somewhere off to the side.)

Ms. started publishing in July 1972, about a month before the Democratic Convention. Its fait accompli was my moment to feel bested by the larger, more powerful, and more effective personality of Gloria Steinem.

After the 1970 *Ladies' Home Journal* sit-in, Sally Kempton and I had tried unsuccessfully to start a mass-circulation feminist magazine. The idea part was easy. We planned to run book excerpts, movie reviews, theoretical pieces, profiles, investigative reports, and resurrect the old Wonder Woman comics. I roped in Nora Ephron and my friend Doris O'Donnell, who believed she could raise some money. Doris and I visited some professional consultants and drew up a prospectus. We called our putative magazine *Jane*, imagining monthly columns titled Plain Jane and Crazy Jane and Jane Goes to the Movies. There was only one problem: we couldn't raise any money. A year later I heard that a California woman named Elizabeth Forsling Harris had come east to launch a mass-circulation feminist magazine with Gloria Steinem as her editor. I met with Harris with the idea of joining forces and got a curt rebuff. "Gloria is my horse and I'm riding her," said the lady, "and I have access to money."

As it turned out, Harris was a flop in the money department. Gloria, with extraordinary skill and determination, pieced together the financial package with an assist from Letty Cottin Pogrebin, who knew somebody at Warner Communications. Pat Carbine came over from *McCall's*, where she had been editor in chief, to handle the business side. Clay Felker, who had created *New York* and made it a huge success, ran the first trial-run issue of *Ms.* as a special supplement folded into his magazine. Scores of young journalist hopefuls were eager to work with Steinem, a captivating role model, at whatever pittance she could offer. My team never got off the starting blocks. Elizabeth Forsling Harris, cranky and out of touch, was removed from her post as publisher and given a money settlement six months down the line. She had played her historic role and would grumble about its denouement ever after.

Depending on your perspective, *Ms.* was dangerously subversive, a crucial lifeline, or predictable and boring. I fell into the last category, although I never doubted the magazine's importance, at least in the seventies, when every articulation of feminism was fresh to somebody out there. Its increasing lack of relevance in the eighties was inevitable as the movement ran out of steam and lost the public's attention.

Gloria's charisma kept *Ms.* afloat. In return, *Ms.* gave her a solid base as a feminist leader. Knowing her strengths, she chose from the outset not to get bogged down in the daily chores and executive decisions of an editor in chief. She was more effective writing her monthly pieces, intervening to settle internal squabbles, and speaking for the magazine in public. Everyone in the office seemed a little in love with her and eagerly awaited her return from her hop-skips on the road. In that respect *Ms.* was like the chaotic headquarters of an election campaign where loyal, devoted workers and "issue people" vie with one another and jockey for access while the popular candidate tries to appease all factions and remain above the fray. The clubhouse atmosphere grew more pronounced as Gloria's fame and effectiveness spread. Her natural generosity and shrewd understanding of political loyalty encouraged a sort of patronage system, the only one of its kind in the movement. Small, unsolicited perks that flowed steadily into the office—paid speaking engagements, television appearances, free trips abroad to represent American feminism—that could not be fit into Gloria's schedule were apportioned to staffers, who were grateful for opportunities that otherwise would not have come their way. Not everyone who passed through *Ms.*, of course, was constitutionally cut out to be a lesser moon in Gloria's orbit. Some of the most talented writers, typically possessed of the most stubborn egos and prickly personalities, made angry departures. Ellen Willis and Alice Walker both quit their posts, irritated by the magazine's mainstream posture, although Walker and Steinem continued to be friends. To my surprise, Robin Morgan, shedding her *Rat* persona, found a comfortable home there for many years.

I liked Harriet Lyons, Joanne Edgar, and Mary Thom, three behind-the-scenes people who were selfless in their devotion to Gloria and the magazine, and I enjoyed the writing of Jane O'Reilly, Susan

Braudy, Letty Pogrebin, Mary Kay Blakely, and a few others, but I have to say that only one piece in *Ms.* ever knocked me back in my chair, an edgy personal essay on bisexuality written under the pseudonym "Orlando" by Lindsy Van Gelder. As a rule, the individual writer's voice was not treasured by the inexperienced editors, while some major cover stories that sent potential advertisers scurrying for the hills seemed unnecessarily bland to me. *Ms.* picked up trends originated elsewhere and tried to cover all bases. Too often the end result was porridge.

Today I think some of the former editors would concur that too much energy was spent in trying to make feminism palatable to the broadest number of women while straining all the while to be politically correct. Gloria was brilliant at embodying these two goals in her person—it was her genius—but her seductive complexity and wry humor were never apparent in the magazine's pages, where the pedagogical side of her personality was what came through. The cumbersome group-editing process, in keeping with movement values, alienated many writers, professionals and beginners alike. Five or six people scrutinized every manuscript, each convinced that her cuts, adds, and queries vastly improved the beleaguered author's perspective. Often the suggestions were contradictory. One magazine simply couldn't be all things to all people, let alone to a bunch of disagreeing editors, some pulling toward the mainstream and some tugging hard in the opposite direction. So glowing accounts of five successful career women would wind up next to a report on clitoridectomy in Africa, and black, lesbian, and working-class concerns, anathema to the corporate advertisers, vied for attention with Alan Alda. Still, I'm glad *Ms.* was there; its longevity was a miracle. The magazine promoted the early work of Alice Walker and Mary Gordon, offered a chance to hundreds of previously unpublished writers, and gave its loyal subscribers a critical link to the larger movement. For many, the sheer act of reading the magazine at work or at home was an open display of courage.

• • •

While *Ms.* was undertaking its mission to reach the broad multitudes, some evangelistic lesbian feminists were steering a course in the opposite direction, toward separatism and exclusion. The Lavender Menace action at the Second Congress and their "Woman-Identified Woman" position paper had inspired a coming-out fervor akin to a tidal wave. At the time, I was bewildered by the overnight conversions and sudden switches in overt orientation by many of the activists I knew. Now I think I understand the phenomenon better.

There is a saying that armies run on their stomachs and political movements run on sex. Romance and sexual attachments flourish in the heated cauldron of common cause; flirtation, intrigue, and attraction are compelling reasons to get out of the house and go to a meeting. As a movement seeps into one's veins and takes over one's life, who else exercises any hold on one's imagination but other movement people?

Women's Liberation was a one-sex movement. The dissatisfactions with men that propelled women into the cause found expression and support in the vital community of activists, but activism cannot quell emotional loneliness or bury the need for sexual connection. Many women who came out as lesbians in the seventies were driven by a deep yearning for emotional and sexual connection. Caught in the powerful wave, some others merely wished to experiment, try a lesbian experience, have an adventure, explore their bisexual dimensions. Several were persuaded, at least temporarily, by the lesbian-feminist argument, emphatically presented, that radical feminism led logically to lesbianism and a woman was wimpy if she wanted to sleep with the enemy. ("Political lesbians" were viewed with suspicion by hard-core dykes who insisted that *they* did not have a choice.) But the overarching truth is that a large number of women had simply found their true sexual identity at last, not knowing or believing before the seventies that the option existed.

One popular manifestation of the lesbian input into radical feminism was the All-Women's Dance. Illegal back-room dancing was the ostensible reason behind the notorious police raids of the old-style gay bars, so defiant open dances in nonbar spaces became a prime organizing tool of Gay Liberation. In a cross-fertilization, open dances were adopted by the women's movement much as the technique of small-group consciousness-raising was adopted by the Gay Liberation Front.

Flyers announcing the dances became nearly as prevalent as flyers announcing political actions, and it soon became the custom to hold a women's dance nearly every weekend and at the conclusion of every important conference. A tremendous release of sexual energy was apparent in the spirited circle dances and conga lines, and there was a sweet, innocent bacchanalian aspect to tearing off one's shirt and dancing bare-breasted in a room full of women, but I was one of those who demurred. Despite that apocryphal saying attributed to Emma Goldman—"It's not my revolution if I can't dance to it"—I felt the dances were irrelevant to the pursuit of feminism's serious political goals. For those who were interested in exploring the possibilities of a women's community independent of men, the dances were extremely relevant. They became a bone of contention in what came to be called the gay-straight split.

The gay-straight split went down differently in every group in every city. In New York Radical Feminists it went something like this: There came a time at the general meetings when anyone who stood up to address a heterosexual issue was met by a fusillade of stamping feet and a chorus of "Come out, come out!" Lesbian life was put forward as the new political utopia, free of hampering sex roles and unequal status. The idea was very exciting to women in the process of discovering their lesbian identity, but those of us who loved women as friends, not as sexual partners, were upset by the logic and the clamor. We desired to change men, not our sexual orientation. I watched in frustration as heterosexual women left the movement in droves, not primarily out of homophobia, as some of the lesbian theorists insisted, but more from a sense that the movement had exhausted its usefulness for them. They were replaced by newly uncloseted lesbians from all walks of life, from the gay bars to elite, quiet cliques in academia, who previously had not felt welcome in the movement's ranks.

I stayed, and developed a lasting reputation in certain lesbian circles as an unregenerate homophobe, an assessment that genuinely distressed me. My refusal to accept the lesbian nirvana was a political as well as personal position, deeply felt. I thought it was ridiculous to gauge feminist commitment by sexual preference. So did many lesbian feminists, but their voices got lost in the furor of the times.

Lesbian separatism was a further step. It took hold most dramatically in Washington D.C., where *The Furies*, a newspaper put out by a collective of the same name, took aim against heterosexual feminism for a year and a half. Once again the catalyst was Rita Mae Brown, this time in conjunction with Charlotte Bunch, the dedicated antiwar activist and popular leader of the dominant left wing in D.C. Women's Liberation. The extreme lifestyle changes that Bunch came to embrace were emblematic of the times.

Open-faced and bespectacled, the daughter of Methodist missionaries who ran medical clinics in the mountains of North Carolina and New Mexico, Charlotte Bunch had been a liberal Christian student leader at Duke University during the mid-sixties. "My moral fervor went directly into the civil rights movement," she remembers. "My first protest was to hold a pray-in at the segregated Methodist church in Durham." In 1966, Charlotte moved into a black neighborhood in Washington to organize a project against poverty and racism. She married her coworker Jim Weeks, a Presybyterian student organizer from Berkeley, the following year.

"Like many of those early marriages in the sixties, we were political comrades who also had a sexual life," Bunch reflects. "I was heterosexual just like anybody who never thought about being anything else."

In quick succession Charlotte received a fellowship at the leftist Institute for Policy Studies, joined a Women's Liberation study group started by Marilyn Webb, and took part in the 1968 Miss America Protest. Moving to Cleveland with Jim, she started a women's group there and helped Marilyn organize the Thanksgiving conference at Lake Villa, Illinois, where she was sickened by the angry clashes between the radical feminists and her ideological allies, the anti-imperialist women. The Cleveland sojourn was an unhappy time for her, and she and Jim returned to Washington. In May 1970 she flew to Hanoi with an antiwar delegation. Webb had started *off our backs* earlier that year, but Charlotte kept her distance from the newspaper collective, viewing it as "Marilyn's thing." It was so typical of Marilyn, she thought, to dash headlong into a new project without consensus-building. Charlotte's new group was Women and Imperialism. With others she made plans for a "solidarity conference" with North Vietnamese women, to be held in Toronto in the spring of 1971.

Few of the radical feminists were interested in the prospect of meeting with the Vietnamese women even though as individuals we were strongly opposed to the war. The struggle to wrench free of the male left's priorities had succeeded in focusing us on a strictly feminist agenda: abortion was our issue and rape was on the horizon. From our point of view the Toronto conference was just another of the left's unceasing efforts to assert antiwar work as the chief priority in Women's Liberation. Feelings ran especially high in Detroit, where six movement feminists signed the "Fourth World Manifesto," a sophisticated analysis of the anti-imperialist women's tactics. It offered instead: "The demand for an end to sex roles and male imperialist domination is a real attack on the masculine citadel of war."

Charlotte Bunch was not perturbed by the Fourth World Manifesto, but her careful construct of political certainties began to implode when Sharon Deevey, her best friend and sturdy partner in antiwar work, made a stunning revelation. Deevey, in a movement marriage similar to Charlotte's, confided that she had become a lesbian after falling in love with Joan Biren, another antiwar activist they knew, who had taken up photography in Washington and started calling herself by her initials, JEB.

The intense romance between the two women kicked off what Bunch calls in retrospect "the summer of madness." Charlotte and her husband joined a commune built around JEB, Sharon, and Sharon's husband, but JEB and Sharon abandoned it for an all-lesbian house, leaving Charlotte behind with the men. Coletta Reid, a founder of *off our backs*, left her husband to start a new lesbian life. Three more women at *oob* began to wonder if they might be lesbians, too. What impressed Charlotte was the energy, "a political, sexual, emotional energy that was just popping all around, everywhere, an intense personal experience of women figuring out their sexuality overlaid with this political, intellectual discussion about the meaning of lesbianism and heterosexuality." She wanted to be part of it. Intellectually she felt she was part of it already.

That fall Rita Mae Brown and her current lover, tiring of New York, piled their belongings into a van and moved to D.C. to join one of the communal lesbian houses. After six weeks of sustained courtship, she seduced Charlotte Bunch. In an agonizing decision, Charlotte left her husband four months later. "Rita Mae was a good introduction to the potential of lesbianism for me," she reflects, "although I knew enough about her to realize that she was being opportunistic. She made an assessment of the D.C. Women's Liberation scene and figured out how to get her alliances."

Swallowing her mortification when Rita Mae jilted her for another lover, Charlotte took her newfound lesbian-feminist evangelism back to her Women and Imperialism group. "I pushed my view that lesbianism had to be on the agenda for the Toronto meeting with the Vietnamese," she remembers. "I felt the Vietnamese women needed to know about it." The anti-imperialists went berserk. The issue, they reminded her in a set of screaming matches, was how to get more American women to work against the war.

Charlotte did not go to Toronto. Instead she broke with the anti-imperialists and formed a lesbian-separatist collective with Rita Mae Brown, Ginny Berson, Coletta Reid, Sharon Deevey, and JEB that became The Furies. She relates, "There were people in it like Nancy Myron and Dolores Bargowski, lesbians forever who were feeling this incredible release—instead of the old shame they were suddenly the vanguard. Others weren't sure they were lesbians at all and eventually decided they weren't. And I, with my whole history of political work, had to believe that lesbianism was a political cause. I had to make it a political cause."

The first issue of *The Furies*, dated January 1972, carried bold separatist statements by Ginny Berson and Charlotte Bunch. "Lesbianism is not a matter of sexual preference," Berson wrote, "but rather one of political choice which every woman must make if she is to become woman-identified and thereby end male supremacy." Bunch proposed that "organized lesbianism is central to destroying our sexist, racist, capitalist, imperialist system." Then she threw down her challenge to the movement's confused and bewildered straight ranks: "As long as women still benefit from heterosexuality, receive its privileges and security, they will at some point have to betray their sisters." In one bitter sense Charlotte was speaking personally. Both she and Sharon Deevey had been ostracized by many of their straight friends on the left when they'd abandoned their husbands for women.

Lesbian separatism becomes more understandable in the context of other holier-than-thou separatist organizations of the era, from the Black Panthers to Weatherman, in which there was a narrowing of the core goup and an intensification of the rhetoric. *The Furies* was not the sole advocate of separatism to emerge in the women's movement. *Ain't I a Woman*, begun by "a conspiracy of Radical Lesbians" in Iowa City, was committed at first to printing a range of Women's Liberation voices in the Midwest; as the paper changed gears it announced it would print only those articles its shrinking collective of eight, then six, agreed with. *Spectre*, a voice of "white revolutionary lesbians" in Ann Arbor, doused its pages with expletives, dropped final consonants to affect a tough working-class style, and declared war on everyone, including *The Furies*. During the same period in New York, *Rat* was taken over by a lesbian collective, then by a third-world lesbian collective, and finally ceased to publish.

When she raised her head from her *Furies* evangelism, the sober fact slowly dawned on Charlotte Bunch, the former consensus-builder, that separatism was not only frightening vast numbers of heterosexuals in the feminist movement, it wasn't making any friends in Washington's lesbian population either. Rita Mae Brown's favorite outreach program was to invite bar lesbians to screen one of the old Hollywood films she loved, and then hit them with a political analysis, but the tactic usually resulted in a mass exodus once the movie was over. As the spring of 1972 rolled around, Bunch and the others felt a need to confront their catalytic rogue on her individualistic tendencies vis-à-vis the collective. This wasn't the first time *The Furies* women had turned on each other; Sharon Deevey and JEB had already been expelled on an assortment of charges.

"Rita Mae really did have style," Bunch laughs. "She came to the confrontation in a military jacket and sunglasses to show us that she was not the sort of leader who would take a trashing and cry. Later she said that she had been purged, but it wasn't a purge, it was a classic confrontation with the leader-person of the moment. We were all so incestuous that we were cutting each other up alive." That fall and the following winter Bunch wrote a pair of essays for *The Furies* on the limits of separatism, in which she broke with her previous thinking. After nine issues in fifteen months, the newspaper ceased publication in the spring of 1973, but the creative energies it had unleashed found their way into new outlets. Some of the former collectivists went on to found *Quest*, a nonseparatist arts journal; Rita Mae Brown, on a grant arranged by Charlotte, began work in earnest on *Rubyfruit Jungle*; Ginny Berson became a founder of Olivia Records.

Jill Johnston also positioned herself in the separatist camp for a couple of tumultuous years. Unlike most of the other evangelists, Jill had come into the lesbian-feminist movement as a fully formed personage, a celebrity in the art world's avant-garde. Divorced from her husband, who took the two children when he remarried, she had joined the *Voice* as its unpaid dance and art critic in 1959, when the struggling paper had very few readers. A decade later the *Voice* was triumphantly riding the counterculture wave and Jill was earning eighty dollars a week for a column that had evolved into a stream-of-consciousness pastiche with lower-case spellings, eccentric punctuations, and dazzling, inventive wordplay. She was the *Voice's* most original writer, and its funniest too. "A close reader could detect some occasional sapphic meanderings," she laughs. "The *Voice* printed whatever I wrote, including the stuff from my time in the mental hospital."

Invited by Lois Hart and Suzanne Bevier, two of her avid fans, to join the weekly dances at the Gay Liberation Front, Johnston initially had not been impressed: "I had been hanging out with the trendy, beautiful people at Max's Kansas City, and the women at the GLF were definitely not *Vogue* cover models. They looked funny to me." She was even slower to grasp the feminist part of the "lesbian-feminist" hyphenation when the Radicalesbians broke away from the GLF. "I had made my own way," she reflects, "so my attitude in the beginning was just like a man's—*What do these women want?*" When she figured it out, Johnston boldly announced "Lois Lane Is a Lesbian" in a March 1971 *Voice* column.

Jill had a knack for raising the lesbian banner in unusual venues whenever members of the press were present. Her gambits, fortified in those days by seriously excessive drinking, were essentially a form of performance art. She splashed topless in the swimming pool at a 1970 fund-raising party for NOW at art collector Ethel Scull's house in the Hamptons, upstaging Betty Friedan and Gloria Steinem on that occasion, and attempted a similar coup, with disastrous results and great personal embarrassment, at the 1971 Town Hall extravaganza starring Norman Mailer and Germaine Greer.

"The Radicalesbians hadn't wanted me to be on the stage because the Town Hall event was elitist," Johnston relates, "but I thought I had a great way to disrupt and destroy it. I'll confess that *Marmalade Me*, my first collection, had just been published, and hell—we were living in a time of freaky, neo-Dada actions when any attention you got gave you a certain cachet. I wanted a whole bunch of people to join me onstage for my group grope, or happening, but the only ones who would do it were two friends from the dance world. One wasn't even a lesbian. Maybe it would have been better if we'd just released some balloons."

In the wake of Town Hall, Johnston came out on *The Dick Cavett Show* as America's first nationally televised lesbian. She looked petrified during her segment, I distinctly recall. Her *Voice* column had already evolved into an open lesbian forum, or rather into a forum between Jill the stream-of-consciousness writer and Jill the improbable activist putting her column at the movement's service. The pieces, augmented by jottings from her diary, were collected and published by Simon and Schuster in 1973 under the title of *Lesbian Nation: The Feminist Solution*. "Lesbians were natural outsiders to begin with," she says in reflection, "so separatism seemed normal to me, or a least a normal development at the time. I guess it ran its course and served its purpose."

Two years after her book appeared, Johnston began slowly and painfully trying to reintegrate herself into the avant-garde scene she had summarily abandoned. Her individualism and erratic behavior had antagonized many of the movement people she was championing in her writing, and her ventures on the media barricades had driven her over the edge of her precarious emotional balance. "I was outing myself continuously," she sighs, "for six fucking years. Well, it wasn't all terrible."

"Collective" was always a word with variable meanings in Women's Liberation. The utopian desire to submerge individual ego for the greater political good led to a range of experiments such as fitful stabs at group writing and the founding of communal houses where personal lives intermingled at every conceivable level and food, clothes, and money were shared. Of all the experiments that marked the era, foolish and grand, to me the Boston Women's Health Book Collective stands as the one unqualified success. It became the heroic achievement of a lifetime for the twelve little-known women who wrote and edited the feminist classic *Our Bodies, Ourselves*.

Nancy Hawley had grown up in radical politics. Her mother had been in the Communist Party, and Nancy herself was a charter member of SDS at the University of Michigan. After an inspiring conversation in 1968 with her old chum Kathie Amatniek, she started one of the first consciousness-raising groups in Cambridge, enlisting the young mothers in her child's cooperative play group. Happily pregnant again, she attended the stormy Thanksgiving conference in Lake Villa, Illinois, but unlike Charlotte Bunch and many others, Hawley came away from it euphoric. After hearing Shulamith Firestone call pregnancy "barbaric" and assert that women would be equal only when science offered alternatives to biological reproduction, Hawley knew that the movement needed her pro-motherhood voice.

In May 1969, a month after giving birth, Hawley chaired an overflowing workshop called "Women and Their Bodies" for the New England regional conference on Women's Liberation, which took place at Emmanuel College. Summoning an incident fresh in her mind, she repeated a glib sexist remark by her obstetrician. "He said," she recalls, "that he was going to sew me up real tight so there would be more sexual pleasure for my husband." Hawley's outrage unleashed a freewheeling exchange on patronizing male doctors, childbirth, orgasm, contraception, and abortion that was so voluble and intense nobody wanted to go home.

"Everybody had a doctor story," exclaims Paula Doress, who was scheduled to give birth two weeks later. "We put aside our prepared papers and did consciousness-raising."

Vilunya Diskin, who had been in another workshop, received an excited report from Hawley that night. Diskin, a Holocaust survivor, had undergone two traumatic childbirths with severe complications as a young married woman in Boston. Her first baby lived, but she had lost her second to a lung disease that the hospital had failed to monitor in time. "I was solidly middle class and well educated, and my health care had been appalling," she says. "So I could imagine what it was like for others without my resources."

A fluid core of activists from the Emmanuel conference agreed to continue meeting and compile a list of doctors they felt they could trust. They resolved as well to take the "Women and Their Bodies" workshop into the community, wherever they could find free space in church basements and nursery schools. "Our idea," says Diskin, "was to go out in pairs. We hoped that the women who attended the workshop would then go on and give it themselves."

To the core group's bewilderment, the Doctors List kept dwindling. Every time it got up to four seemingly solid, unimpeachable names, somebody new showed up to exclaim, "Oh, do I have a story about *him!*" But the workshop project soared. As the summer turned into fall, the women amassed enough hard medical information, and confidence, to install themselves in a lounge at MIT where they offered a twelve-session course in women's medical and sexual issues. Venereal disease and "Women, Medicine and Capitalism" were added to the program.

Ruth Bell, a stranger to Boston, went to the course at MIT in an oversized pair of denim overalls, her maternity outfit. "Fifty women were talking about their lives, their sexuality, their feelings," she remembers. "I raised my hand and said, 'I'm pregnant for the first time and I don't know much about this and I'm having nightmares.' Three or four other women got up and said, 'That happened to me too. Let's meet after and talk about it and maybe we can figure something out.' That's how it was. Somebody had a concern, she raised her hand, and three or four others said, 'Boy, that happened to me too.'"

Joan Ditzion, married to a Harvard medical student and debating whether to have kids, was transfixed by a large, detailed drawing of a vagina with labia and clitoris that the women had placed on an easel. "I'd only seen pictures like that in my husband's textbooks. These women were speaking so easily, without shame. I got my first sense that women could own our own anatomy."

Wendy Sanford, born into an upper-class Republican family, was battling depression after the birth of her son. Her friend Esther Rome, a follower of Jewish Orthodox traditions, dragged her to the second MIT session. Wendy had kept her distance from political groups. "I walked into the lounge," she recalls, "and they were talking about masturbation. I didn't say a word. I was shocked, I was fascinated. At a later session someone gave a breast-feeding demonstration. That didn't shock me, but then we broke down into small groups. I had never 'broken down into a small group' in my life. In my group people started talking about postpartum depression. In that one forty-five-minute period I realized that what I'd been blaming myself for, and what my husband had blamed me for, wasn't my personal deficiency. It was a combination of physiological things and a real societal thing, isolation. That realization was one of those moments that makes you a feminist forever."

Ruth Bell gave birth to her daughter in the middle of the course and returned to become "a second-stage original member" of the amorphous collective, along with Joan Ditzion and a renewed, reenergized Wendy Sanford. "There was an open invitation to anyone who wanted to help revise the course notes into a more formal packet," Bell remembers. "If you wanted to work on writing, you'd pair or triple up with people who could do research."

"We had to get hold of good medical texts," remembers Paula Doress, "so we borrowed student cards to get into Countway, the Harvard Medical School library. It was very eye-opening to realize that we could understand the latinized words."

"Then we'd stand up at a meeting and read what we had written," Ruth Bell continues. "People would make notes. Somebody would raise a hand and say, 'I think you should add this sentence,' or 'You need a comma here.' This was how the first editing got done."

Xeroxed packets of the course material made their way around the country. Judy Smith of Austin Women's Liberation remembers getting the packet and building a "Women and Their Bodies" course around it. "The ideas were out there but the Boston women crystalized our thinking," she says.

Closer to home, some of the women connected with the New England Free Press, a leftist mail-order collective in downtown Boston. "Basically they were a bunch of men, conventionally Marxist, who printed and sold pamphlets at ten to twenty-five cents," Jane Pincus sums up. "They didn't see us as political." The mail-order collective grudgingly agreed to publish and distribute the health course papers if the women paid their own printing costs. "So we raised fifteen hundred dollars from our parents and friends," Pincus relates. "And then we had to hire somebody to send out the orders because the demand was so great."

Five thousand stapled copies of "Women and Their Bodies" on newsprint paper with amateur photos and homey line drawings rolled off the press in December 1970 bearing a cover price of seventy-five cents. The blunt 136 page assault on the paternalism of the medical establishment, a juxtaposition of personal narratives with plainspoken prescriptives, immediately sold out. A second edition of fifteen thousand copies, with the price lowered to thirty-five cents, bore an important change. In one of those eureka moments, somebody had exclaimed, "Hey, it isn't women and *their* bodies—it's us and our bodies. *Our Bodies, Ourselves.*"

Women's centers in big cities and college towns were thirsting for practical information and new ways to organize. The Boston women's handbook with its simple directive, "You can substitute the experience in your city or state here," fit the bill. Subsequent press runs for *Our Bodies, Ourselves* were upped to twenty-five thousand copies each in an attempt to satisfy the demand. Three printings in 1971 were followed by six printings in 1972.

"We are working on revisions," the Collective declared. "We want to add chapters on menopause and getting older and attitudes toward children, etc., etc., but we haven't had time."

There was no shortage of feedback. "The first edition was weak on the dangers of high-dose-estrogen oral contraceptives," Barbara Seaman remembers. She mailed the women a copy of her book, *The Doc-*

tors' Case Against the Pill, and was gratified to see that the next edition reflected her concern.

"A woman in Iowa wrote in and said, 'You didn't mention ectopic pregnancy.'" remembers Jane Pincus. "And we said 'Great, write about it and we'll put it in.' This is really how the book evolved."

It was only a matter of time before New York publishers learned of the phenomenal underground success. In the fall of 1972 both Random House and Simon and Schuster came courting with modest offers. For the first time in their experience as a working collective, the Boston women were unable to reach a consensus. Random House was owned at the time by RCA, a conglomerate with huge government defense contracts, rendering it complicitous in the war machine. An independent company and seemingly purer, Simon and Schuster won the agonizing vote by a narrow margin.

Freezing their ranks, the women incorporated as a nonprofit foundation. Judy Norsigian, their "baby" at twenty-three, and Norma Swenson, their "old lady" at forty, were the last to come aboard. They were to become the public face of the Collective in the years to come.

When the news of the commercial sale appeared in the penultimate New England Free Press printing, the mail-order leftists commandeered a page of their own to cry foul, warning that a capitalist publisher would impede the building of socialism. The women dodged the ideological brickbats as best they could while they readied their beloved creation for its aboveground debut. "Everything had to be decided by consensus," Simon and Schuster editor Alice Mayhew remembers. "It took a long time. But we knew they were in touch with a generation of young women who wanted to be talked to straightforwardly. We would have been dopey to interfere."

Rape, an emerging issue for feminists, became a chapter in the handsome, large-format 1973 Simon and Schuster *Our Bodies, Ourselves.* Judy Norsigian, who'd been in the commune movement, wrote a chapter on nutrition. Mindful of the rising tide of lesbian consciousness, the OBOS women—who were then all heterosexual—sent out a call for the appropriate expertise. A Boston gay women's collective responded with "In Amerika They Call Us Dykes," insisting on anonymity and complete editorial control of their chapter.

Illustrations for the aboveground *Our Bodies, Ourselves* included many drawings and photographs of African-American women, in keeping with the politics of the newsprint editions. A sharp dig at the U.S. military presence in Vietnam survived, but the proviso "Don't forget that Ortho and Tampax are capitalist organizations pushing their own products for profits" got axed. "Women, Medicine and Capitalism," a lengthy polemic in the earlier versions, shrank to a paragraph that was buried amid the nitty-gritty on yeast infections, cystitis, and crabs. Softer rhetoric was a Collective decision, in line with the women's desires to reach the mainstream and include more facts. However, they resisted the ladylike language a copy editor they nicknamed Blue Pencil wished to impose. "Where we wrote 'pee,'" says Jane Pincus, "Blue Pencil changed it to 'urinate.' We changed it right back."

Our Bodies, Ourselves sold more than a million copies and earned more than a half million dollars in royalties during its first five years of commercial distribution, and became the premier sourcebook for a generation of sexually active young women, crossing all lines of race and class. Copies were deeply discounted or given out free at birth control clinics; the book found an audience among hard-to-reach teenagers when it was adopted as a teaching tool in hundreds of high school sex-education programs. With aching honesty the women dispersed their royalty money to movement projects, except for the pittance they paid to their staff people, chiefly Norsigian, Swenson, and Rome. By the end of the seventies the Boston Women's Health Book Collective, convening periodically to work on updated editions, had witnessed four divorces and three second marriages. Jane Pincus and Ruth Bell were living with their husbands in other parts of the country; Wendy Sanford had discovered her lesbian identity; Nancy Hawley had developed a deep interest in Buddhism. All told, the women reared nearly two dozen children. "People used to come from overseas and ask to see the house where the Collective lived," says Norma Swenson. "I think they were disappointed to find that we led individual lives."

•   •   •

In the summer of 1973 a singer-songwriter named Helen Reddy released "I Am Woman (Hear Me Roar)," a hit record that reflected the chang-

ing times. On another front, Billie Jean King trounced an aging
male chauvinist braggart, Bobby Riggs, in a nationally televised tennis match billed as "The Battle of the Sexes." The women's movement had rapidly moved beyond the initial phase of mimeographed position papers. Abortion rights, electoral politics, and
legislative campaigns were commanding many women a full-time attention.

Yet the search for community, the warmth and support of kindred
souls, was still uppermost in many radicals' hearts, and so was the opportunity to grapple with new ideas through writing, feminism's chief
means of expression from the beginning. These two abiding interests
merged in the founding and running, on a shoestring basis, of another
wave of women's newspapers. Defiantly countercultural, the papers'
writers and editors cared little for establishment values and mainstream success. They represented "the movement" on its most basic
level. For at least a decade, until the advent of the Reagan era, there
was a political and economic climate that permitted their voices to be
heard.

Berkeley native Becky Taber, five feet tall with waist-length hair,
who founded *Plexus* in San Francisco, called herself a cosmic tramp. A
college professor's daughter, she was go-go dancing in Portland,
sewing her own costumes, when she happened upon New York Radical Feminists' *Notes from the Second Year*. It changed her life. Quitting
the go-go life, she took a job selling water beds in San Mateo, managing a store. In February 1974 she had a deep talk with Sandra Dasmann, her childhood chum, in East Oakland.

"The Full Moon women's coffeehouse was opening, women's music
was happening, A Woman's Place bookstore was going strong, and
Patty Hearst had just been captured by the SLA," Taber relates. "Sandra was scared, she was freaking. The papers were full of the lifestyle
of the SLA women—their former boyfriends, their female lovers, their
black lovers. It was too close to home for us, right down to their cats
and their plants. Sandra said the Bay Area needed a women's newspaper—we needed to sort things out."

The first issue of *Plexus* appeared the following month. It carried
Dasmann's review of *Women and Madness* by Phyllis Chesler, and

Taber's Open Letter to "Fahizah," Nancy Ling Perry of the SLA, with whom she felt a bond. Perry, who was tiny in stature like Taber, had also worked as a topless dancer. "I think honesty and bravery, not weapons, differentiate the free person from the oppressed and the oppressor," Becky wrote to her counterpart in the SLA.

Copy for *Plexus* was typed with ragged right margins on an IBM Selectric and pasted up with rubber cement. Transfer letters were used for headlines. Robin Cox, into spiritual art, did the layout and illustrations. Ann McConnell, a single mother volunteering at Friends of the Earth, donated three hundred dollars from her welfare check to pay the printer for five thousand copies of the premier issue.

"We built *Plexus* around news, poetry, and a calendar of upcoming women's events," Taber reminisces. "Sixty women came through as volunteers the first year. I ran all over San Francisco, collecting ideas for articles and gathering lists of resource groups and events on scraps of paper. I fetched and carried for *Plexus* as though I was carrying the sacred fire. 'Write it up, the deadline's the fifteenth' 'Would you like to learn layout?' The advertising people got a commission that turned into a minimum wage for them. They were the only ones who got paid."

"Joining the *Plexus* collective was definitely not a career move," says Toni Mester, a college English instructor who wrote book reviews and cultural reports as Toni Chestnut. "It was a community-building exercise and a new way to express ourselves. We published everything interesting that came in that was feminist, lesbian, spiritual, environmental. Because we weren't ideological, the Marxists held us in contempt."

"I have so many vivid memories of *Plexus*," says Nancy Stockwell, writer, editor, and ad seller. "I met Becky Taber in A Woman's Place bookstore just after I'd moved to the Bay Area from Boston. Right on the spot I volunteered my unemployment check to cover the third issue. It turned out we didn't have to use that money because we sold enough ads.

"I was in the office when the FBI came looking for a tape we'd been sent by Bill and Emily Harris, who were part of the SLA group that kidnapped Patty Hearst. We told them we threw the tape out because it had a man's voice on it. That seemed to satisfy them, but they followed us for weeks and then they arrested Jackie McBee, my neighbor, thinking she was Patty. I guess they thought we were all one big conspiracy.

"And I remember getting up in the middle of the night to help photograph the huge, lit-up Smirnoff billboard on top of the department store in downtown Berkeley. We knew women were going to change the sign from 'What's an Ice Pick? Smirnoff Vodka' to 'What's an Ice Pick? One Answer to Rape!'"

A photo of the altered billboard appeared on the *Plexus* cover for September 1975.

Hoping to get a friend's poetry published, April McMahon went to an open meeting for *Plexus* at the Bacchanal, a women's cafe in North Berkeley. The scholar of French literature ended up working at the paper for ten years. "First as the classical music critic," she relates, "and then as the bookkeeper. We're talking tiddlywinks money, but after we incorporated, suddenly there were quarterly payroll taxes, corporate taxes, county property taxes. I took a bookkeeping course at Contra Costa College and slowly got an accounting degree."

At its peak the print runs for *Plexus* reached eight thousand copies. The women had a monthly budget of eight hundred to a thousand dollars, depending on the number of paid ads, and were able to rent three small rooms from a Baptist seminary on Dwight Way overlooking People's Park.

"We had collectives for everything," April McMahon laughs. "News, Reviews, Features, Letters, and Calendar. Also an Office Collective, and a coordinating council. Every collective was supposed to send one person to the council meetings, which would go very late sometimes. Poor Jane Bicek, who had to get up very early in the morning, would fall asleep."

"We discussed stuff like how do we bring women of color into a largely volunteer organization, and oh, lots of serious things," says production manager Chris Orr. "Often someone would create a crisis and call a special emergency meeting. Once the whole News Collective walked out. I ran to the Bacchanal to find Nancy Stockwell—'Nancy, Nancy, we're not going to publish the next issue!' Stockwell slammed her beer on the bar and growled, '*Nothing* stops *Plexus!*' Sometimes the meetings were so disruptive we wondered who the disrupters were working for. We evolved an m.o. that I called Roberta's Rules of Order, with a chair and motions and calling the question. That helped."

Sandra Dasmann drifted away after the first year: "People were becoming lesbian; I wasn't. If I had a choice, believe me, I would have jumped over the line, just for the community. But I was pregnant and I wanted to do what was best for me and my baby, so I joined the back-to-the-land movement, which I regret to say was very male dominated."

Nancy Stockwell stayed with *Plexus* for three years, until she moved back east: "Becky Taber always said that the most political thing we could do was to run the calendar so women could find each other and have places to meet. She was right. It led to the whole Lesbian Nation and women's music scene. I think at the time we didn't quite realize how much the women's presses did change things for women in this country."

Becky Taber burned out after three years: "Okay, the first major split was 'Who are we and what do we believe?' Some people wanted us to stop publishing and go on a retreat to figure it out. In the middle of the meeting I walked into the bathroom and saw running sores all along my jawline. That fight I won. We continued to publish. The next big split was over the voting rights of new people. I thought the interns should be included. That fight I lost. It took me another three years to recover, but my three years at *Plexus* were the most exciting in my life."

Toni Chestnut stayed for four years: "Sexuality took over and frankly I got real sick of it. I went into environmental and labor work."

Chris Orr stayed for seven years: "I was getting tired of holding the paper together, pasting on the damn mailing labels. The center wasn't holding anymore, we weren't getting the next generation of volunteers. This was the early eighties and Reaganism was taking its toll. I was working as a waitress and I needed to earn a better living."

"I stayed till the bitter end in 1986," says general manager KDF Reynolds. "Drove a cab to support myself. Still do."

• • •

Denver's pioneer spirit attracted a crew of adventurous women who were to devote themselves, heart and soul, to *Big Mama Rag*. Choco-

late Waters, a Navy brat from Pennsylvania (she legalized her childhood nickname), got dumped in the city by her old college boyfriend.
"Yeah, we were traveling across the country and he took off and left me
with no money in one of those old-timey women's bars. I was bisexual
then, so I started hooking up with the dykes. At a women's festival
somebody had an idea about doing a newspaper. We passed around a
sign-up sheet."

Jackie St. Joan—then Jackie Bryson—arrived in Denver with
her husband and two children. Her interracial marriage, the first
in Virginia after the Supreme Court struck down the state's notorious
antimiscegenation statute in 1967, began to founder when the couple
moved west. Jackie swallowed her pride and went on welfare for
five months before she found work as a secretary. At a potluck
dinner sponsored by the Denver Peace Coalition, she heard about
plans for a women's paper. "It was an ongoing conversation for
nearly a year," she recalls. "Eventually we got three hundred dollars
from a private foundation, enough for an X-Acto knife and a light
table."

Big Mama Rag came to fruition late in 1971. Maureen Mrizek, radicalized at college in Carbondale, Illinois, set the tone of the first issue
by asking, "How can you conquer an oppressor when you sleep with
him every night?"

"My Anabaptist cousin saw that and wrote she was praying for me,"
Chocolate Waters laughs.

After leaving her husband, Linda Fowler from North Carolina had
taken her child to a commune in the Colorado Rockies, burrowing into
Russell Gulch, a miners' ghost town with no electricity or running water. "Those were my days of pot and acid," she says. "I was smoking
dope, chopping firewood, learning carpentry, and trying to figure out
who I was, and how lesbianism fit into feminism." On a trip into Denver she stopped into a radical bookstore and saw *Big Mama Rag*. "The
fog lifted," she exclaims. "Within a month I left the mountains and got
involved with the paper."

Denverite Carol Lease had been the editor of her Catholic high
school paper and had worked on the *Daily* at the University of Colorado. "One day back in Denver, I saw something on a lightpost: 'We

are a women's newspaper and we need help.' So I went to a meeting and there was Chocolate Waters, dressed in black. She scared the hell out of me. At that point I was living with a man. I mean, I knew what a lesbian was, but she was kind of fierce and arrogant. I figured I was a better writer, though!"

Working in the basement of a house on Seventeenth and Gaylord in Denver's old mansion district, a dozen to twenty-five volunteers produced one thousand copies of *Big Mama Rag* on a monthly or bimonthly schedule, reporting on the feminist issues of the day: lesbian separatism, rape, spirituality, women in prison, the movement's internecine struggles. The sixteen-page paper was priced at twenty-five cents, or five dollars for a year's subscription mailed in a plain envelope. Unsold copies were handed out at supermarkets in an effort to reach Denver's housewife population.

"We paid maybe twenty-five dollars in rent," Lease remembers. "We had little ads and a good distribution network, and we ran frequent fundraisers. If our budget was more than one hundred dollars per issue, I'd be surprised. Bourge Miller—now she's Jean Hathaway—did the logo and was our art director. She was always saying 'More white space.'"

Some of the women paired off: Carol with Linda, and Chocolate with Jackie, who solemnly chose St. Joan as her new last name. "Janet Sergi said, 'Do you have a costume to go with it?'" she laughs. "But I've been Jackie St. Joan ever since."

"We were always having battles," remembers Chocolate Waters. "Either about sexuality or race or class. A lot of us were going through our processes or whatever, becoming lesbians, you know, if we weren't already. The permutations on these themes drained a lot of our energy, but I guess it was part of trying to define ourselves. We were so busy having collective meetings about what was right and what was wrong that the paper almost fell apart. For a year and a half the main core people—me, Jackie, Linda, Maureen Mrizek—rented a house on South Pearl Street that turned into a workable commune. We shared secretarial and house-painting jobs, gave ourselves twenty dollars a week for spending money, and put the rest into keeping *Big Mama* alive."

The paper's one moment of solvency came in 1975, when the United Methodist Ministries of Denver gave it a grant. Chocolate Waters, developing her identity as a lesbian erotic poet and performance artist, received $125 a week as *Big Mama* staff editor. Jackie St. Joan used a small portion of the grant to report on Sagaris, a feminist think tank that convened in Vermont that summer. Carol Lease and Linda Fowler drove down to the International Women's Year Conference in Mexico City. On the way home they swung though North Carolina to cover Joan Little's murder trial.

"The trial was not something the *Denver Post* was covering," says Lease. "We'd learned about it through Liberation News Service. Basically I wrote that the issue of sexism was not addressed in terms of the rape. The defense only dealt with the issue of racism. So it kind of brought to the surface issues that are still with us today."

That same year the women learned via the establishment media that "Carla Weinstein," who'd been in on their start-up, was the fugitive Jane Alpert, wanted in New York on bombing charges. "She was obviously very smart and intellectual, but I'd thought there was something closed and standoffish about her," Jackie St. Joan recollects. "When *Ms.* printed her essay 'Mother Right,' I was so excited, I thought it was brilliant. I insisted she read it, but of course she never let on that she wrote it."

"And that explained the odd behavior of Robin Morgan when she came to town," Chocolate Waters laughs. "Maureen and I were driving her all over the place and all she wanted to do was get away and meet up with Jane."

The following summer *Big Mama Rag* went to Omaha, Nebraska, for a national Women in Print convention organized by June Arnold of Daughters, Inc., publishing house and Charlotte Bunch of *The Furies* and *Quest*. For a week the Denverites traded shop talk with two hundred of their counterparts from *Plexus, off our backs, Majority Report*, Diana Press, Womanbooks, and other alternative publishing houses, bookstores, journals, and papers.

Big Mama expired in the early eighties, long after the original crew had departed. Chocolate Waters moved to New York to pursue her writing. Jackie St. Joan put herself through law school and eventually became a Denver county court judge. "A lot of us had to reconnect with the need to make a living," sighs Linda Fowler, who started a successful construction company. "The paper was too utopian to succeed—it was one of those things that burns brightly and can't go on forever. But nothing has ever been like that time."

"RAPE IS A POLITICAL CRIME
AGAINST WOMEN"

RAPE THEORY WAS CONCEIVED of and developed by the American movement. The international campaign against battery, or domestic violence, originated in England. In my opinion these issues were radical feminism's most successful contribution to world thought.

Odd as it seems, although women had been living with the terror, their lives shaped and aspirations curtailed by the terror throughout recorded history, the pervasiveness of male violence had never been confronted by political action until the bold, creative organizing efforts of the 1970s. For obvious reasons. Militants of previous generations had been denied the social sanction to speak openly of sexual matters. The rules of polite feminine propriety, the universal bans on the use of forthright, realistic language in public forums, had kept the violence issues dormant, consigned to allusions spoken in hushed voices, relegated to the private, the personal, the shamefully unmentionable, until a freer climate permitted such things to be articulated aloud. Women in the seventies, after giving voice to such formerly unmentionable issues of physical autonomy as sexual satisfaction, birth control, abortion, and sexual preference, were finally ready to speak about rape and battery too. The brilliant, visionary strategy of radical feminism was to conceptualize sexual violence as a key link in the pattern of male domination and to attempt to put an end to it for all time.

Rape theory started for me in the fall of 1970 inside my conscious-ness-raising group, as part of a germination process that was taking place all over the country. Looking back, I can see that Cell 16 in Boston was ahead of the curve as usual with its classes in self-defense and the essay on rape-murder, "More Slain Girls," in *No More Fun and Games*. Working independently in New York, Kate Millett, a pioneeer in so many respects, had identified rape as a "weapon of the patriarchy" in *Sexual Politics*.

What was to become a major, sustained feminist campaign against sexual violence began percolating at the edges, where I think new ideas and great discoveries always begin. Street harassment, a relatively mi-nor but pervasive piece of the sexual abuse continuum, drew the move-ment's first open confrontations.

Every woman in a big city lived with routine street harassment. You couldn't make your apppointed rounds during a typical day without an incident of some kind or another, a catcall, "Oh, sweetheart, what I'd like to do to *you!*" from a truck driver, a murmured "Suck my dick" from an innocuous-looking fellow walking by in a business suit. And God forbid you had to pass a construction site when the guys were tak-ing their break at lunchtime. Pam Kearon of THE FEMINISTS said it was like being under twenty-four-hour-a-day surveillance.

Many of us, made bold by our heightened consciousness, had de-veloped individual strategies for coping with the harassment instead of scurrying by quickly with a lowered head as we had done in the past. Some women halted in their tracks and patiently tried to explain to the bewildered offender why an explicit sexual comment made by a stranger was so unpleasantly intrusive. My response had become a snarled "Fuck *you* up *your* ass," a hollow threat to be sure, and one that dangerously escalated the confrontation on a couple of occa-sions.

In 1970 the movement began to politicize street harassment with collective action. The Ogle-In was a popular tactic. A bunch of us would gather on a street corner and turn the tables on leering, lip-smacking men by giving them a taste of their own medicine. After the newspapers reported that a bunch of stock exchange employees had de-veloped a "fun" morning ritual before work, gathering on the street to watch a particular secretary with large breasts emerge from the subway station, Karla Jay organized a retaliatory Ogle-In on Wall Street. She chose a March afternoon at lunchtime. It was incredibly liberating to reverse the wolf whistles, animal noises, and body-parts appraisals that customarily flowed in our direction. Wendy Roberts, a free-spirited hippie who called herself Wendy Wonderful, was my heroine that day. She sauntered up behind an unwitting passerby and grabbed his crotch. Oh, retribution! Los Angeles feminists struck in September with their Ogle-In during Girl-Watching Week, an official Chamber of Commerce promotion. Trailed by the local media, the women boy-watched at several locations in Century City. One activist wielded a tape measure: "Too small!" "Too skinny!" "Hey, fella, can you type, file, and make coffee?" The Los Angeles boy-watchers dubbed themselves Sisters Against Sexual Slavery, or SASS.

After the Second Congress to Unite Women, where I'd been trashed for "seeking fame," I had chosen to be less visible in the movement. I stopped going to meetings of Media Women and turned down offers to explain Women's Liberation in print. There wasn't much else I wanted to write about, however, aside from a children's book on Shirley Chisholm. I fooled around with a screenplay. My income plummeted. I still believed in the potential of radical feminism with all my heart, and I never missed a meeting of West Village–One.

Tuesday had become our appointed night for consciousness-raising. One of our new members was Diane Crothers, an impatient, visionary activist from the defunct Stanton-Anthony brigade. Diane more than anyone else kept us clued in to the nuances and tremors of the national movement. One evening she arrived with a copy of It Ain't Me Babe from San Francisco.

Earlier in the summer, the July 23, 1970 Babe had run an unsigned, tape-recorded account, "Anatomy of a Rape," by a young artist in Marin. Buoyed by the experience of going to her first women's meeting in Berkeley, the artist had waved off suggestions that she stay overnight, preferring to hitchhike home. Her first ride left her on Van Ness. Almost immediately two Vietnam vets in a truck pulled up. "Okay, now, we're not gonna hurt ya, we're just gonna take ya out and ball ya," one said as they approached the bridge. A couple of hours later they dumped her at a bus station.

"Two of them! You must've been nice and slippery," her boyfriend teased in a lame attempt to cope with her trauma when she got home.

"That was the line that really got to us," recalls Laura X, who taped the story for the *Babe* collective.

It Ain't Me Babe surrounded the account of the evening with two exhortive essays, "Disarm Rapists" and "Fight!"

The September 4 *Babe* that Diane brought to our meeting carried a second rape story, news of a stunning retaliatory action. "Jack the Raper" was a report by a women's group calling itself, with all due bravado, the Contra Costa Anti-Rape Squad #14. A go-go dancer hired to perform at a bachelor party in Pinole had been roughed up by the groom's drunken friends, dragged into a bedroom, and raped by the sodden guest of honor. In a free-for-all, her gown was ripped, she was doused with wine, and her seventy-five-dollar dancing fee was stolen from her purse before her friends came to the rescue. The dancer, who considered herself a tough professional, filed a complaint that night with the Pinole police, but the district attorney in Richmond declined to prosecute under the boys-will-be-boys logic. He said it was the men's word against hers, even though a hospital test showed evidence of semen.

On the day of the wedding reception at the Stockton Inn, the Contra Costa Anti-Rape Squad plastered the guests' cars in the parking lot with a leaflet headlined "How Jack and His Friends Play When 'Their' Women Aren't Around." The flyer named names, including the groom's friends and the dismissive D.A., and ended with the words "Sounds ugly? Well, it is. It goes on all the time, one way or another. These pigs know the law won't touch them, they can always insist the woman is a liar or slut or crazy. We women are learning to see through that nonsense. We hope you learn to, too."

After we read this story in *It Ain't Me Babe*, Diane announced that rape was an important new feminist issue and proposed that we should begin to explore it through consciousness-raising. I wasn't convinced. The prevailing opinion, which I'd absorbed without question, held that rape was a murky, deviant crime any alert woman could avoid. Rape was political, I argued, only when it was "rape" in quotation marks, as the Old Left wrote it—the false accusation of white women against black men that lay behind some accounts of southern lynching. In fact, three years earlier I'd done a story about capital punishment and a Maryland interracial rape case for *Esquire* with no demonstrable sympathy for the victim. Our group had been analyzing femininity for months, and I was finding the revelations very helpful. I did not want to switch gears and talk about rape.

The others definitely wanted to talk about rape. Sara Pines quietly offered to begin the process. Sara was married, a professional psychologist, and the calmest woman in our group. Fifteen years earlier, she told us, she had been hitchhiking back to her school after a weekend at Harvard. The young man who picked her up asked where she was headed, and then said he wanted to make a detour to pick up a friend.

"*Pick up a friend?*" I interrupted. "And warning bells didn't go off your head?"

"No, he seemed okay."

"In my hitchhiking days I'd never ride in a car with more than one man! I'd have gotten out right then."

"I trusted him," she said simply.

Sara was raped in a deserted park by the man and three of his buddies. "I was told to be quiet or I'd be buried there and no one would know," she recounted. The worst part of her ordeal had been at the police station. "Aww, who'd want to rape you?" an officer teased. Another said she was too calm to be credible—in his view she should have been crying hysterically. After several postponements there was a trial that Sara did not attend, and the men were given suspended sentences.

Listening to Sara Pines was the moment when I started to change my mind about rape. She was a trusting person; I wasn't. I had to accept that not every woman viewed the world with my suspicions and caution. After Susan Frankel and Lucille Iverson finished their accounts of lucky escapes from threatening situations, I proposed that New York Radical Feminists hold a conference on rape with research papers and panel discussions. The others argued that personal testimony in a public speak-out was the proper way to begin, the way abortion had been politicized by Redstockings the previous year. I doubted that we could find enough women willing to go public. Once again I was wrong.

West Village–One presented the two plans at the next general meeting of New York Radical Feminists. The bold idea of summoning women to gather in public to talk about rape, as authorities, to put an unashamed human face on a crime that was shrouded in rumors and whispers, or smarmy jokes, had never been attempted before, anywhere. In their wisdom the affiliated consciousness-raising groups of New York Radical Feminists voted to hold a speak-out on rape at the earliest possible opportunity, to be followed by a conference on rape three months later. We chose as our slogan "Rape Is a Political Crime Against Women."

The speak-out took place on Sunday afternoon, January 24, 1971, at St. Clement's, a tiny Episcopal church on West Forty-sixth Street that doubled as a home for off-off-Broadway productions. A one-page flyer, in Spanish on the reverse side, had been circulated to women's groups, inviting everyone who'd had an experience with rape to testify. Admission was free, cameras and tape recorders were banned, and men could attend only if they paid two dollars and were accompanied by a woman. My job was to take tickets at the door. I collected thirty dollars, which meant that fifteen men actually showed up. Or maybe it was sixty dollars and thirty men. I do know that more than three hundred women crammed into the small circular arena, arriving early to fill the seats above a multilevel stage set designed for a less memorable drama. Latecomers hugged the walls, hunkered down in the aisles. Somebody commandeered a wheelchair, a production prop, for the last seat in the house. The ten women who were prepared to testify arranged themselves as best they could on the dimly lit stage.

In the hush, they began speaking. I took notes, which I've saved to this day, but the drama was too intense for pen and paper. Sara Pines recounted her hitchhiking story. Alix Kates Shulman described the childhood ritual of "pantsing," getting caught by a gang of boys as she tried to run past a vacant lot near her home in Cleveland. (The incident appears in *Memoirs of an Ex-Prom Queen*, published the following year.)

A dark-haired woman told of her date with a medical resident, arranged with great expectations by his aunt and her mother. The future gynecologist assaulted her in his room at the hospital. "I was so hung up on propriety," she confessed, "that I went to dinner with him afterward as if nothing had happened. I didn't tell my mother, much less the police."

Another woman spoke of rape by her therapist—"Not a real doctor, a lay analyst," she said amid groans—who continued to charge her for the weekly sessions. "When I took sleeping pills to kill myself, he dropped me," she finished.

A gray-haired woman in her sixties told of being assaulted in her apartment after opening her door to a man who said he was delivering a package.

A modern dancer graphically described a street encounter that happened one evening as she returned home after a class. "He slammed me against the wall and clawed at my leotard. The leotard kept snapping back. This seemed to enrage him. Then I kicked him in his precious groin. The people on the street didn't help, and the police talked me out of pressing charges. They said, 'You did enough to the poor guy.'"

The kaleidoscope of revelations continued:

"I got into the elevator with him because he was wearing white shoes. In my prejudice I thought it's all right, he's a doctor."

"It's funny what goes through your head. I was thinking, *Please God, don't let him rip my new dress which I just charged and haven't paid for.*"

"Those teenagers weren't sexually attracted to me. They wanted to degrade me in an asexual way. This was all about power."

"I was afraid he'd kill me. The fear of murder was worse than the rape."

In all, thirty women were inspired to speak out that afternoon, and their words were to reverberate far beyond the confines of the tiny church. So many varieties and aspects of rape had been revealed at St. Clement's. Sexual assault was a crime of power that crossed all lines of age, race, and class; women feared they would be killed; resistance was possible; the police were dismissive. All of us were reeling from the new knowledge.

Carolyn Flaherty of our Brooklyn Brigade #5 had done a great job with publicity, corralling Gail Sheehy of *New York* magazine and a husband-and-wife reporting team from *Vogue*. Sheehy's piece, which augmented the speak-out accounts with statistics and interviews with law enforcement people, was superb.

I'd been too much of an insider even to think of writing something.

Plans for our next event, the Conference on Rape, took over the general meetings of New York Radical Feminists. Lilia Melani, a professor of English at Brooklyn College, led the steering committee with Mary Ann Manhart, an opera student. (Melani went on to organize the CUNY Women's Coalition in its successful discrimination suit against the city university system a few years later.)

I freely offered my advice on how the rape conference should be organized. We needed workshops on the psychology of the rapist, the psychology of the victim, rape and the law, rape in marriage, rape and sexuality, rape and the cultural climate, rape during wartime (we could discuss Vietnam). The more I talked, the more I saw that workshops by themselves could not produce the comprehensive research that an analysis of rape deserved and required. I realized that I'd begun outlining chapters for a book in my head, a book I very much wanted to write.

Joan Mathews from West Village–Four proposed that we invite Florence Rush from Older Women's Liberation to be a speaker. Florence, a social worker in Westchester, could give a paper on the sexual abuse of children. Child molestation and incest? Once again I was slow on the uptake.

•   •   •

Minda Bikman and I were on Eighth Street, distributing flyers for the conference, when a guy goosed me. Maybe I was thinking of that dancer at the speak-out who had kicked her assailant in his "precious groin," maybe I was thinking of Emma Peel in *The Avengers*, maybe I was just in a bloody rage from a lifetime's accumulation of these petty assaults, the furtive hands reaching out to destroy my dignity on the subway or on the street when moments earlier I'd been happily engaged in my own reflections. Maybe being the target of a lightninglike molestation while I was handing out flyers for a rape conference was just too ironic. Whatever, I galloped after my assailant's retreating figure, swung my leg in a fancy arc, and sprained my ankle after connecting full force with his gluteus maximus.

"On Goosing," my story in *The Village Voice*, began, "I am sitting here with my ankle in the air, elevated, as they instructed at St. Vincent's." The rape conference was announced in an accompanying box. "On Goosing" was an intentionally funny parody of ideological tracts even as it laid out the sexual abuse continuum, but *Time* promptly cited it as an example of the humorlessness of the women's movement. Oh, those feminists making issues out of everything! By then I knew I had found my mission. I laughed when I read a letter to the *Voice* signed by a Maryland college student named James Wolcott, who wrote in the sepulchral tones of the future critic, "God help us if she is ever raped—we will be buried under an avalanche of rhetoric."

I hobbled on crutches into Washington Irving High School on Saturday morning, April 17, for our New York Radical Feminist Conference on Rape. My memories of the day are vivid and fragmentary. Rosemary Gaffney and Sheila Michaels had netted a swarm of reporters. Thomasina Robinson, a self-assured black karate teacher, demonstrated some basic flips and holds on her white partner. Phyllis Chesler, stomping the stage in blue jeans, full of pizzazz, gave a paper on rape in therapy, which she later expanded in *Women and Madness*. Germaine Greer, in town to promote *The Female Eunuch*, slipped into a workshop to speak of her rape in Australia when she was eighteen, pregnant, and searching for an abortion. A former Black Nationalist addressed the problem of not reporting her rape, because the assailant was Puerto Rican "and I felt it would be wrong somehow to retaliate against another third-world person."

Most vivid of all was the appearance of Florence Rush, the social worker from Westchester, diminutive, clad in a tailored dress and ankle-strap shoes, who peered over the lectern and read her analysis of the sexual abuse of children.

A civil rights activist in New Rochelle and the mother of three grown children, Florence was one of the few women of her age—fifty-five—and background to make a successful transition from the Old Left to radical feminism. "Once I started reading the literature, the stuff from Cell 16, Kate Millett's book, that did it," she recalls. "Everything seemed to fit my own experience—my dissatisfactions with my marriage, the arrogance of the New Left and its contempt for older women, that "Don't trust anybody over thirty' line. So I came to New York, attended a few consciousness-raising groups there, and went back and organized more consciousness-raising groups in Westchester County."

Florence had been in the audience at the rape speak-out in St. Clement's. "I sat there and began remembering that I had been molested as a child," she relates. "My uncle Willie, our family dentist, the men who exposed themselves in the movie theater, on the subway, in the street. The pinching and feeling were so prevalent, yet nobody ever mentioned it. As my personal experience came flooding back, I began to feel that I could talk about child sexual abuse with some authority."

At the lectern she calmly dissected four current academic studies and their "psychiatric mumbo jumbo": Under the prevailing Freudian logic, exhibitionists and molesters were to be pitied rather than feared, sexual assault was not particularly detrimental to the child's subsequent development, and the "unusually attractive child," as one study phrased it, was often the actual seducer. Children's silence after an assault probably stemmed from their guilt in succumbing to a forbidden attraction.

Jettisoning this Freudian interpretation with utmost dispatch Florence laid out her feminist conclusion: "The sexual abuse of children, who are overwhelmingly female, by sexual offenders, who are overwhelmingly male adults, is part and parcel of the male-dominated society which overtly and covertly subjugates women."

No one had ever said this before. Nineteenth-century feminists and social workers had battled to protect and shelter abused and abandoned children, but no one before Florence Rush had connected sexual abuse and its societal rationalizations with male dominance and the educative process of becoming a female. The applause for Florence broke like thunder as everyone stood up and cheered. That in itself was a first for a radical feminist conference.

I was hopping around in high gear for the rest of the day. "Think of the lynching analogy," I instructed a reporter for *Good Housekeeping*. "Rape is to women as lynching was to blacks. It's a conscious process of intimidation that keeps all women in a state of fear."

On Monday morning I was in the office of literary agent Wendy Weil with a four-page proposal for a book on rape. Simon and Schuster, the first publisher Wendy approached, offered a contract for ten thousand dollars. In my naïveté I agreed to deliver the manuscript in one year. That seemed right to Jonathan Dolger, my laid-back editor.

I spent the next four years writing *Against Our Will* in the New York Public Library, where the card catalogue had more entries for rapeseed than for rape but the stacks held treasures that could be retrieved if I followed a dim trail of footnotes and trusted my instincts. The book surprised me as it grew. All reporters are sleuths, but few are privileged to start their work at the beginning of a great discovery. I was finding answers to questions that no one had ever asked before. Hot on the trail of an elusive case or a legal point, sometimes I'd leave the Forty-second Street library at closing time and dash to the law library at NYU to browse undisturbed for another few hours. Occasionally I suffered paroxysms of doubt. Was it legitimate to isolate rape in war? Could I find the precise moment in English law when rape evolved from a crime of property to a crime against a woman's body? Should I make fewer enemies and perhaps gain some friends by skirting the minefield of race and sex? Indeed, could I argue the premise that rape had a history without becoming the laughingstock of historians everywhere?

The movement, of course, was my buttress. In April 1971, coincidentally the month of our New York rape conference, the *San Francisco Chronicle* gave extensive coverage to the rape-and-kidnap trial of one Jerry Plotkin, a local jeweler. Plotkin was portrayed by his defense lawyer as a persuasive libertine. His victim testified that he had accomplished his feat of "persuasion" with the aid of a gun and several buddies. On cross-examination she was raked over the coals for her prior sexual activity. After a full day of intrusive questioning, she blurted out on the stand, "Who is supposed to be on trial here? I did not commit a crime."

"Grueling Day for a Rape Case Victim" was the *Chronicle* headline. The next day an ad hoc group of San Francisco feminists held a protest demonstration at the courthouse. As it happened, Plotkin was acquitted, in a verdict that was typical of the times, but the verdict had a galvanizing effect on Bay Area women.

In September 1971, Susan Griffin, a poet and past activist with the Berkeley Free Speech Movement, and a founder of Bay Area Women Against Rape, published "Rape: The All-American Crime" in *Ramparts*. Griffin's trailblazing article, the first in a national publication to put rape in an historical context, was passed from hand to hand inside the movement.

Diana Russell, a Harvard-trained sociologist, had been among the protesters at the San Francisco courthouse for the Plotkin trial. A statuesque white South African from a proper Anglican family, she had joined a small, underground antiapartheid cell while she was a student in Cape Town. "My first impulse after the Plotkin verdict was to throw a brick with a message on it through the window of his jewelry store," she recalls with a faint laugh, "but I started doing research instead. I read the existing literature and found it was all victim-blaming." Newly appointed to a professorship at Mills College in Oakland, Russell began to interview victims of rape for a feminist sociological study. For Diana this would be the start of a lifelong commitment to a scholarly examination of sexual abuse.

Women Against Rape groups, taking WAR as their acronym, sprang up in several cities during 1971. In Detroit, Kathy Barry, Joanne Parrent, Cate Stadelman, and eight other feminists compiled *Stop Rape*, a fifty-page handbook of theory and practical advice. The two-word title emblazoned on a red traffic sign packed its own consciousness-raising wallop. *Stop Rape* was sold by mail through Women's Liberation of Michigan for twenty-five cents a copy, upped to sixty cents for a fourth printing one year later. In Boston, Betsy Warrior of Cell 16 produced the antirape movement's most riveting poster, a powerful drawing of a barefoot woman vanquishing her assailant with a well-aimed kick to the balls, and the legend DISARM RAPISTS/SMASH SEXISM. The widely distributed poster was reprinted in issue 5 of *No More Fun and Games*.

A fresh concept was born in the nation's capital early in 1972 when eight women in consciousness-raising groups loosely attached to D.C. Women's Liberation formed a special support group for rape victims. The prime movers were Liz O'Sullivan and Karen Kollias. O'Sullivan, quietly efficient, had been in the antiwar movement and was teaching political science at Dumbarton College while she worked on her doctoral degree. Karen Kollias, at American University on a financial-needs scholarship, grew up in a poor Greek neighborhood in Chicago. Karen partied hard, took a dim view of classroom assignments, and had sat in at the college president's office to protest the lack of birth control services on her campus.

"We came together from these different streams," O'Sullivan sums up. "Rape was our issue and counseling was an accepted form of political action. This was pre–*Roe v. Wade*, so we had some good precedents. We knew of counseling hot lines out there that told women where they could get an abortion."

Assembling as a collective, the eight women began meeting intensively after taking part in a Women's Liberation Conference on Rape held at George Washington University in April. (The George Washington University conference followed the model we had pioneered the year before in New York.) O'Sullivan and Kollias came up with a plan to offer emergency medical information and advice on police procedures by means of a rape hot line. They decided to staff their telephone service twenty-four hours a day, so volunteers would always be available to accompany a caller to the hospital or to the police, if that was what the caller wanted and needed. An all-day, all-night hot line would also ensure that raped women who had lived silently with the trauma for years could dial in at any hour and find somebody to talk to. With genius, they named their service a Rape Crisis Center.

The D.C. Rape Crisis Center was ready to go public in June, when a dedicated phone line—333-RAPE—was installed in the rented townhouse on Wisconsin Avenue that Kollias shared with a bunch of friends. "A typical student flophouse," O'Sullivan explains.

"My house was the Center," affirms Kollias. "First on Wisconsin, then when we moved to Fifteenth and Q, that house became the Center. Whoever lived there was part of it, but we never handed out the address. We put an extra bed in the hall in case a raped woman didn't want to go back to her house and needed a place to stay." Somebody gave them an old car to transport victims to the hospital or police station if need be, but the vehicle lacked registration and insurance. Volunteer counselors, augmented by Karen's roommates, were assigned to phone shifts. They earnestly practiced their script:

US: Crisis Center.
CALLER: I was raped.
US: When?
    a. if just raped: offer to call a cab to bring her to the Center; possible that Jan or Sue will be able to go to the hospital or police
    b. if a past rape: try to get her to talk somewhat about her feelings

The crisis collective printed up cards with the hot line number. Hoping to garner some helpful publicity, the women wrote a press release for the local newspapers and television stations.

"Nineteen seventy-two was President Nixon's runaway reelection year," O'Sullivan relates, "and we are in Washington D.C., with a lot of reporters who have nothing to do. So we open on June 1 and we get a five-part series on local TV and a lead editorial in *The Washington Post*. The editorial writer called us at one minute after midnight just to make sure we were really operating." Within days, reporters from National Public Radio, *Time*, and a gaggle of local newsrooms were lining up to do stories on the D.C. Rape Crisis Center.

According to O'Sullivan's analysis of the phone logs, 333-RAPE received between two and three hundred calls a month, discounting pranksters and hang-ups, after its media debut. A third of the calls were from actual rape victims, past or present, needing to hear a supportive voice, and from friends of rape victims seeking advice on how to be helpful. The rest were from eager reporters, women inquiring about self-defense classes, and groups around the country requesting a speaker.

"From the beginning we saw our mission as political education *plus* practical service," says Karen Kollias. "Nobody got paid; we weren't a line item in some other organization's budget. The speaking fees financed the operation. Liz was the quiet one, so I ended up doing the traveling. I went to places I'd never dreamed of, like Saskatchewan, Canada, saying "Rape isn't about sex, it's about power,' and telling people how they could start their own center."

Liz O'Sullivan's unsigned forty-page booklet "How to Start a Rape Crisis Center," including a sample press release, was ready in August. She mimeographed five hundred copies to fill the national demand. Jan BenDor at the University of Michigan opened a rape crisis center in Ann Arbor. A third center started in Philadelphia. After that the proliferation was extraordinary. Four years later O'Sullivan compiled a list of more than one hundred functioning rape crisis centers around the country, and the record was far from complete. By then she and Kollias, succumbing to the inevitable burnout, had passed the baton to others at the D.C. Center, and the burgeoning rape crisis movement had moved beyond its volunteer origins to attract mental health professionals and federal funding.

"What blows me away," says Kollias, "is if you watch a movie or TV show now and there's a woman that's raped, automatically they're contacting the rape crisis center. It's become normal, routine behavior."

• • •

With rape successfully launched as an issue, New York Radical Feminists turned to other projects. One afternoon a bunch of us staged a roving sit-in at four popular drinking establishments that refused to serve "unescorted" women. Based on the quaint assumption that women unaccompanied by men were likely to be prostitutes, the humiliating policy was enforced by bartenders with uncommon zeal.

For our first assault we leaped over the sidewalk railing of the Cafe de la Paix, the elegant outdoor terrace at the Hotel St. Moritz. Once my mother had tried to take me to this famous landmark on Central Park South as a birthday treat, but we had not gotten past the maître d'. I wish she had been alive to see the outcome this time. Faced by twenty implacable feminists occupying his tables, the haughty manager caved in. Next we lined up shoulder to shoulder along the polished bar at the glitzy Russian Tea Room. After a protracted spell of "I'm sorry, mesdames, we do not serve unescorted women," we got our drinks. P.J. Clarke's, a venerable hamburger joint on Third Avenue, took longer to crack. An angry bartender threw a glass of water at Claudia Dreifus and Claudia threw a cocktail napkin at the bartender, or perhaps it was the other way around. Whichever, the situation grew incredibly tense before the management capitulated and the walls of segregation came tumbling down at P.J.'s. By then our unbroken string of victories had left us a little tipsy. Weaving unsteadily to our last destination, the "no unescorted women" bar at Gallagher's steak house, we entered to hear the owner peal, "Welcome, ladies, welcome! Order what you want! I'll call Leonard Lyons."

The *New York Post*'s grand old man of the Broadway buzz materialized in minutes and gave us a full column. Robin Reisig did a fine story for *The Village Voice*. Never had a feminist action accomplished its objectives so swiftly. We went home to sleep it off. Blatant discrimination against women in public accommodations was doomed to tumble once enough women kicked up a fuss. A few months later the city council passed a law forbidding a public bar to refuse service to women.

We were totally unsuccessful in our next major campaign, a quixotic attempt to make the elimination of prostitution a feminist goal. The immediate impetus was a series of nightly street sweeps conducted by the New York City police during the summer of 1971. Vast numbers of street hookers on Times Square and Broadway were being chased by cops, hauled into vans, and shuffled through the judicial system, while their pimps and johns went scot-free. The city fathers were concerned about the rising rate of prostitute-related crimes, muggings and wallet heists, which were bad for tourism. While the cleanup campaign was creating headlines, some liberals suggested that legalized prostitution might be a more enlightened approach than nightly roundups. The mayor appointed a committee of six men to study the problem, and an all-male state legislative committee held a hearing on "Prostitution as

a Victimless Crime." We feminists were in favor of the decriminaliza-
tion of prostitution, but we were adamantly opposed to its legalization.
The state, in our opinion, should not sanction the buying of women's
bodies.

I wangled an invitation to address the legislative committee with
a speech that began "Prostitution is a crime, gentlemen, but it is
not victimless. There is a victim, and that is the woman." Then we
began our filibuster. Alix Kates Shulman read from the writings of
Emma Goldman; somebody else jumped on a table and recited a
poem. The filibuster went on all day; we were sixteen demonstrators
with plenty of material. Our main point was that no one should have
the right to buy another person's body. It was a good point, and I still
believe it.

New York Radical Feminists, in coalition with THE FEMINISTS and a
women's caucus of reform Democrats, held a weekend conference on
prostitution at Charles Evans Hughes High School in December. Mary
Daly, the feminist Catholic theologian and author of *The Church and
the Second Sex*, came down from Boston to give a keynote address;
speakers from the Fortune Society and the National Welfare Rights
Organization added their weight.

Things seemed to be going well until a half dozen high-priced call
girls—white, expensively dressed, one a "baby pro" who had been in
the life since her fifteenth birthday—walked in and let us have it between the eyes. It is funny in retrospect, but it wasn't funny at the time.
Our crisp, clean analysis of why men buy women's bodies, and why
they shouldn't, had neglected to anticipate that the prostitutes would
resist their depiction as downtrodden victims of male exploitation.
Understandably they saw us as a threat to their livelihood. Well versed
in left-counterculture rhetoric, they handed us the line that all work
was exploitative, so what was the difference if one woman sold her
body and another sold her mind to a big corporation? When that argument failed, they screamed, "Don't you know that Weatherwomen
are working in brothels to finance the revolution?"

Even if true, the information didn't cut any ice with us. Barbara
Mehrhof of THE FEMINISTS was eloquent about the honorable choices
she'd made in her life, insisting that working a nine-to-five job for low

wages was preferable to selling her body. The call girls jeered. Holly Forsman, the former fashion model, gave an impassioned speech about how society rewards men for using their bodies with athletic scholarships and well-paying construction jobs while denying women those options. The call girls snickered. I volunteered some painful memories from my struggling years as an unemployed actress. "Your men come to us because you're a bunch of tightasses," the prostitutes shouted. Looking for a brawl, their ringleader took a sock at Minda Bikman, who started to cry. The conference broke up with Kate Millett standing on a chair, an unheeded figure, pleading for reconciliation.

That ended our campaign to eliminate prostitution. The prostitutes had "spoken from their own experience." Our rhetoric, in contrast, sounded like a prudish condemnation of their behavior rather than a sharp analysis of economic injustice and male privilege. Eight years later we would run into similarly wrenching conflicts when we launched the feminist antipornography movement.

●   ●   ●

After the disastrous prostitution conference, I returned to the library and *Against Our Will.* I continued to gain sisterly support from the Tuesday night meetings of West Village–One until one evening in 1973, when I felt the heat of another blast of anti-elitist wrath. Jan Peterson, from a small town in Wisconsin, was one of the group's original members; previously she had worked in CORE (Congress of Racial Equality), as had I. I respected Jan as a good, sturdy feminist, but we weren't close. On the night in question I offered the good news that my book was coming together and the end was in sight.

"Do you have to put your name on your book?" Jan exploded. "Rape doesn't belong to you, it belongs to the movement. You should take a stand and be the first feminist author to do away with personal ego."

A gifted organizer, Jan went on to make a name for herself in Brooklyn as the founder of the National Congress of Neighborhood Women. That night as the movement's familiar demons of fame and public recognition rose to the surface in her righteous anger, I knew I had reached the point of diminishing returns in West Village–One.

I never went back. New York Radical Feminists continued to publish a newsletter and hold speak-outs and conferences from time to time on subjects like marriage and motherhood, but its vanguard role in forging new issues had peaked with its work on rape. Its last stunning event, in my view, was a speak-out on sexual abuse conducted jointly with the National Black Feminist Organization.

● ● ●

During the late sixties a small number of black female activists on the left had tried to establish a Women's Liberation presence inside their male-led organizations. Frances Beal of New York SNCC was a notable example. Her powerful paper, "Double Jeopardy: To Be Black and Female," directed some of its strongest arguments at white women. "If white groups do not realize that they are in fact fighting racism and capitalism," she wrote, "then we do not have common bonds." Beal was instrumental in forming the short-lived Third World Women's Alliance, which included revolutionary anti-imperialism among its principles and goals.

In the summer of 1973 a dozen black women in New York of varying ideological persuasions started a promising new entity called the National Black Feminist Organization. Doris Wright, Margaret Sloan, Jane Galvin-Lewis, and Deborah Singletary were the founders. Wright, the studious author of an early mimeographed paper addressed to black men, was serving on the board of NOW while she attended Hunter College at night and worked a day job at Rockefeller University. Sloan had been plucked from the South Side of Chicago to be the first black writer-editor at *Ms*. She was one of a number of women, black and white, whose lives were transformed on a direct, personal level by Gloria Steinem.

Sloan's activism had started early. At the age of fourteen she was picketing for CORE at a local Woolworth's to support the southern sit-ins. A few years later, as an unwed mother and a lesbian, she was working with her lover on the start-up of *Lavender Woman*, Chicago's lesbian-feminist paper. When the Panthers Fred Hampton and Mark Clark were ambushed and killed by the Chicago police, she was invited to be a jurist on a People's Tribunal.

"Flo Kennedy was also on the panel," Sloan relates. "She was talking feminism, and I was amazed. At that point the media was polarizing black and white women, as it usually does, and very few black women on a national level were articulating feminism as it related to black women. So we sort of became friends. She wanted me to meet Gloria Steinem."

In constant demand on the lecture circuit, Gloria customarily went on the road with a black speaking partner, alternating between Flo Kennedy and Dorothy Pitman Hughes, to link the oppressions of race and sex. One day when Flo was unavailable for a scheduled date in Rippon, Wisconsin, she recommended the young firebrand she'd met in Chicago. "Then Gloria got snowed in at some airport," Sloan laughs. "These people were expecting Gloria Steinem and Flo Kennedy and they got no-name me! But I pulled it off okay."

A few months later Margaret Sloan and her daughter were ensconced in a New York apartment, and Margaret had a contract with a lecture agent as Gloria's new speaking partner in addition to a job at *Ms.* "The speaking thing worked, it really worked, it was a very interesting combination," she relates. "I was twenty-one or twenty-two, a woman who came from nothing, and suddenly I was making big money. Somebody needs their rent paid? Sure, I'll pay your rent for a couple of months. The household workers union needs a thousand dollars? Sure! It was like a dream come true. And oh God, I was also in this famous-women's c.r. group that we had, with Gloria, Marlo Thomas, and Judy Collins. Insane, absolutely insane. But nobody ever told me I should save my money."

Brash, effervescent, and wildly undisciplined in the face of her changed fortune, Sloan hit New York with a full head of steam and became the propulsive force behind the National Black Feminist Organization. "You'd go to these various things and you'd see a couple of sisters and you'd wave hello," she remembers. "One day Doris Wright says to me, 'Let's have an all-day gathering so we can get to know each other.' Doris was able to get NOW space because she was a NOW member. She invited about sixteen of us and it was so beautiful. We talked about the differences between our skin color, our differences in growing up. We talked about our self-hate. We talked about white women, black men, everybody and everything. By the end of the day we were saying, 'Why don't we work on a black feminist conference?' I was the one who said let's do a press statement first. Around this time, Jesse Jackson was saying, 'Thank God my mama didn't have an abortion because I wouldn't have been born' and the press was always asking some nonfeminist black woman to give them a quote about feminism. I figured if we just came out with a strong statement, we'd shut them all up."

Jane Galvin-Lewis, another of Gloria's black speaking partners, arranged for the women to meet the press at the Women's Action Alliance, where she had a staff job. Started by Steinem and Brenda Feigen Fasteau as a sort of clearinghouse project, the Alliance predated *Ms.* and was located in the same building. The small office kept an up-to-date list of media contacts.

"Jane, myself, Eleanor Holmes Norton, lots of us came to the press conference," Sloan remembers. "And oh boy, did the press show up for this important statement by black feminists. Who knows, maybe they thought we were going to announce midnight castration parties—even fucking *Der Spiegel* was there. So the next day I thought it was my duty to go downstairs to the Women's Action Alliance and thank them for letting us use their space, and somebody said, 'Margaret, who is going to handle these phone calls?' The phone was ringing off the hook! I picked up the next call and a woman says, 'Hi, I'm from Montana and where is your chapter in Helena?' She wants to know the date of the next meeting, and I'm thinking, *I didn't know there were any blacks in Montana.*"

That week Galvin-Lewis and Sloan collected the names and addresses of two hundred callers wanting to join the National Black Feminist Organization. By the end of the month they had five hundred names. Concentrating on the New York, New Jersey, and Connecticut people, the excited women got free space for meetings at Harlem Hospital and sponsored a huge conference at St. John the Divine with a grant from the Eastman Fund. Thanks to Gloria Steinem's efforts, they acquired a free midtown office for a time. The core group set up a national board, to which Flo Kennedy, Eleanor Holmes Norton, and Shirley Chisholm lent their names and prestige, and accepted the affiliation of self-starting chapters in Los Angeles, Philadelphia, Chicago, Detroit, Boston, and Newark.

Some of the National Black Feminist Organization's best work was in rape awareness. The women campaigned with Julia Tucker's mobile van when it toured through Harlem. (A police detective with the rank of lieutenant, Tucker had set up a Sex Crimes Analysis Squad for the New York Police Department in response to feminist agitation.)

On August 25, 1974, I sat in the auditorium at Junior High School 104 and listened to the New York Radical Feminist–National Black Feminist Organization Joint Speak-out on Rape and Sexual Abuse. One after another, black women and white women took the microphone to offer their personal testimony. The official tape recording of the speak-out has been lost, but some of the stories appear in *Against Our Will.* I still recall the gutsy black speaker who told of being raped in her housing project when she was twelve: "Four detectives got me in a room and asked how long was his penis—like I was supposed to measure it. Actually they said, 'How long was the *instrument?*' I thought they were referring to the knife. *That* I could have told them 'cause I was sure enough looking at the knife." A second woman of color, tall, slim, and elegant, began, "My girlfriend and I took a vacation to the Virgin Islands," and then winced. I think the smarmy jokes associated with "virgin" must have flooded her mind. Tossing her head, she started over. "My girlfriend and I went to St. Thomas . . ."

The testimony that afternoon was powerful stuff, and the movement was never more perfectly integrated than it was that day.

But the National Black Feminist Organization would prove short-lived. Organizationally the NBFO was always chaotic, though no more so than the rest of Women's Liberation, where new faces showed up at every meeting and old faces vanished. Doris Wright quit the group even before she moved to Wisconsin for her graduate studies. Michele Wallace, soon to embark on *Black Macho and the Myth of the Superwoman,* black feminism's strongest book-length statement, had kept her distance from the outset, and chose to write critically about the organization. Margaret Sloan split town after a blowup at *Ms.,* when she was taken off staff for slighting her magazine duties. "I was hurt by the way it was done," Sloan reflects, "but I understood their position. Maybe it was just a big fantasy that you can take somebody in and teach them editorial skills when they're away four days a week speaking and organizing. I knew I was running amuck and wasn't being a writer-editor, which was what I was paid to be."

After the initial flush of excitement, trouble started brewing in the NBFO's affiliated chapters. The critic Margo Jefferson, a faithful attendee at NBFO meetings, ticks off the usual movement problems— anger at the top-down directives of the New York board, mainstream-left schisms, gay-straight splits. "Some of it," Jane Galvin-Lewis sighs, "was just oppressed people's bickering." The end came in 1975 when the New York board was ousted in what passed into history as the NBFO's final convention. (Some of the New Yorkers went into Salsa Soul, a group for lesbian women of color. The Boston chapter formed the Combahee River Collective, named for Harriet Tubman's military action in South Carolina during the Civil War. Writer-editor Barbara Smith of Combahee later joined poet Audre Lorde to found the Kitchen Table: Women of Color Press.)

•   •   •

The large place in my life that had been occupied by activism came to be filled by the company of a disparate group of writers who worked every day in the Allen Room of the New York Public Library. In that calm oasis on Fifth Avenue and Forty-second Steet where I kept my typewriter, I found a new community of peers, male and female, who were devoted to the slow, steady grind of pounding out pages. Two small foundation grants kept me afloat. When that largesse ran out, I borrowed two thousand dollars from my friend Jan Goodman, by then a founder of the nation's first women's law firm. Dolores Alexander offered to put me on the tab at Mother Courage, but the wolf wasn't that close to the door; Kevin was still sharing the rent, although we were growing apart. Convinced that I needed to study the efficacy of self-defense, I enrolled in a judo class and broke my collarbone while practicing the "forward fall from the running position." Ouch. The collarbone mended badly but my convalescence coincided with the Watergate hearings, so I managed to catch every word.

While I worked in relative isolation, the rape crisis center movement continued to grow, with every new counseling-service hot line attracting its own local publicity. Operating from her NOW chapter in northern Virginia, Mary Ann Largen almost singlehandedly placed rape on NOW's national agenda. Jan BenDor in Ann Arbor, a founder of one of the earliest crisis centers, began advancing ideas for new state legislation. Her Michigan Women's Task Force on Rape descended on the capitol in Lansing to pioneer an overhaul of sexual assault statutes that had gone unchanged for 117 years.

BenDor's ideas helped me enormously. Antirape people in several states had begun to lobby for more realistic legislation, but the Michigan Women's Task Force was amazing. Earlier than most, they saw the need to eliminate the archaic and sexist evidentiary requirements in the criminal codes that virtually guaranteed few prosecutions and even fewer convictions. Two practical goals that activists in many states fought for were the abolition of a corroborating witness rule and a restriction on testimony regarding the victim's prior sexual history (now called the rape shield law). BenDor's group was among the first to propose extending the assault statues to cover rape in marriage.

Today people forget what a sharp attitudinal reversal these legislative reforms signified. When I began researching law review articles back in 1971, cutting-edge theory on criminal justice was devoted to making arrests and convictions more difficult in order to safeguard defendants' rights. That was the accepted liberal thrust, in harmony with a string of important Warren Court decisions such as *Mapp, Gideon, Escobedo*, and *Miranda*. Prospering in that climate, criminal defense lawyers out to win acquittals in rape cases had a field day in court mocking "the prosecutrix," dragging her through the mud, and plumping the twin dangers of false accusations and mistaken identifications of assailants. The antirape movement, on the other hand, was determined to make the law and the courts work for victims. This stunning break with conventional liberal thinking was not easy for everyone to manage, even inside Women's Liberation.

I remember when I joined Barbara Mehrhof and Pam Kearon of THE FEMINISTS in 1971 to monitor a rape trial in a New York courtroom. Within a few years monitoring rape trials would be a standard procedure for the antirape movement, but back then it was a novel sensation to be on the side of the prosecution. I also recall that some of the early rape crisis centers were leery about developing cordial relations with the police. Sensitive to issues of police brutality, the support counselors could not shake their distrust of the law enforcers.

Thousands of radical women found another way to articulate their outrage about rape, one that was more in keeping with their anti-establishment values. They rallied around a trio of murder cases that utilized a "rape defense." The best known of the three cases was the trial, during the summer of 1975, of Joan Little, a twenty-year-old black woman in North Carolina charged with the murder of her white jailer.

Unable to make bail on a minor burglary charge, Joan Little had been the sole female inmate in the Beaufort County jail when her troubles began their drastic escalation. Clarence Alligood, the night-duty jailer, was found dead in her empty cell one evening with his pants around his ankles and his hand clutching the murder weapon, an ice pick he was known to keep in his desk drawer. Little hid out for a week before she turned herself in, and was represented at her nationally publicized trial by the Southern Poverty Law Center. By her account, she had been subjected to repeated sexual assaults by the sixty-two-year-old jailer, who granted her small favors, such as telephone privileges, in return for her forced compliance. The scenario of murder in self-defense against a background of historic white southern injustice was sufficiently vivid to win Joan Little an acquittal. She was promptly claimed as a heroine by Black Panthers and feminists alike.

Inez Garcia in California was hailed as a movement cause and a heroine from 1974, when her case first surfaced, to 1977, when she was acquitted at her second trial. Garcia had tracked down and then fired six rounds into Miguel Jimenez, the three-hundred-pound accomplice of Luis Castillo, a seventeen-year-old youth she asserted had raped her half an hour earlier, when the two men had been visiting her housemate.

The volatile thirty-year-old beauty of Cuban and Puerto Rican descent possessed a short attention span and had never learned to read, write, or tell time. After marrying Juan Cardenas Garcia, an anti-Castro Cuban, when she was fourteen, she moved to Miami, where Juan stepped up his anti-Castro activities, and Inez gave birth to a son. When she shot Jimenez, she was renting part of a house in Soledad, California, to be near Juan, then in prison for bombing a branch office of Air France. His right-wing passions notwithstanding, Juan persuaded his family to hire Charles Garry, the famed San Francisco lawyer who represented the Black Panthers, to defend his wife. The prosecution contended there was no evidence of rape, and that Inez had fired her .22-caliber semiautomatic rifle in the aftermath of a violent quarrel over drug territories between her housemate and Jimenez and Castillo.

"To know Inez was to know she was telling the truth," says Susan Rothaizer, her eyes widening as she recounts the story. One of the mainstays of Berkeley's Inez Garcia Defense Committee, Rothaizer had been raped while hitchhiking during her sophomore year at Brandeis. "Two steeplejacks from Worcester, Massachusetts," she winces. "I knew I was in trouble the minute I jumped into the truck. I was a practicing heterosexual then, so when they took me into the woods, I pulled my diaphragm out of my backpack and loaded it up with cream. 'What's *that?*' said one of the guys. 'There's no way you're going to make me pregnant,' I told him. He said, 'So lick my balls.'" She still shudders at the memory of the humiliation.

Rothaizer did not report her rape, "but I used to fantasize about going to Worcester and finding those guys." Three years later in Berkeley, when she heard about Inez Garcia, "It crystallized something for me," she says. "I could channel my rage in a positive way." She began writing about Garcia for *Plexus*, the Bay Area feminist newspaper.

Several of the core group of eight women on the Garcia defense committee had been raped. "And most everybody was left-leaning," Rothaizer elaborates. "I was a Red Diaper Baby and I'd marched in every major antiwar demo. About half of us were Jewish and half were lesbians—not necessarily the same ones." Hedy Sarney, another of Garry's clients, was out on bail and awaiting her own trial; she had been dragooned into an ultra-left sect and forced to rob a bank, à la Patty Hearst. Sheila Farrell's boyfriend helped steal the Pentagon Papers. Stacey Fulton, from Oklahoma, had organized for the Berkeley Free Speech Movement and the San Quentin Six. Pat Richartz was Garry's paralegal, Mary Sundance was in law school, and Nan Blitman already had her degree.

A few weeks before the trial, Garcia moved into a communal house in Berkeley that was shared by some of her supporters. She baked flan for them, appeared with them on radio and television programs, starred at "Viva Inez" benefits, and was iconized on "Viva Inez" buttons and T-shirts. At late-night bull sessions the women traded their life stories. "Inez had grown up with all the usual prejudices," Rothaizer relates. "She thought Jews had horns and she had never met any lesbians." For their part, the blue-jeaned militants refrained from criticizing Garcia's false eyelashes and painted toenails.

In August 1974, Garcia went on trial in Monterey, one hundred miles down the coast from Berkeley. Stacey Fulton and Hedy Sarney spread the word via sign-up tables and bulletins on KPFA radio. Susan Rothaizer organized a bus and car shuttle from Provo Park that hauled one hundred supporters to and from the courthouse each day. (Rothaizer's boss let her do her paying job, a health survey, on the weekends.)

Sheila Farrell found an unfurnished three-bedroom house near Monterey that the defense committee was able to rent on a short-term basis. The women brought in sleeping bags and stocked the kitchen with bean sprouts and peanut butter, augmenting their veggie fare with inexpensive locally grown artichokes. Hedy Sarney posted the house rules on the refrigerator: no dope, clean up after you eat, kick in a dollar a day (food stamps acceptable), and no long-distance calls without the committee's approval.

The first rule at the defense house was "Don't bug Inez." Garcia had her own room, where she tended to the mysterious cups of red wine and water she kept in the closet. A devout Catholic in public, the private Inez put her faith in Santeria, the old Caribbean religion, to cast a spell over Judge Stanley Lawson, who was determined to keep the trial focused on murder, not rape. Jim Wood, a sympathetic reporter on the *San Francisco Examiner*, was a popular guest at the house (no one suspected he was writing a book). As the trial progressed it attracted national interest, including a team from *People* magazine.

Santeria or not, things went badly for Garcia. "I killed the mother-fucker because I was raped, and I'd kill him again," she shouted from the defense table in one notable courtroom outburst. "Judge," she continued, approaching the bench, "why don't you just find me guilty and put me in jail?"

Lawson ordered her removed. *"Pigs! Take your hands off me!"* she screamed at the bailiffs as the judge rapped his gavel to adjourn for the day. Everything happend so fast that Susan Rothaizer was in a state of shock, she reported in *Plexus*, but she and most others on the defense committee thought it was good for the jury to see the depth of Inez's feelings.

Goaded on cross-examination a few days later, the defendant erupted again, defiantly sputtering, "The only thing I am sorry about is that I missed Luis Castillo."

The jury found Inez Garcia guilty of second-degree murder. In the recriminations that followed, some militants blamed Charles Garry, some blamed the defense committee, and still others, including Garry, blamed Inez for playing to the militants in her courtroom outbursts. "Even I got trashed," Rothaizer remembers. "The Oakland Women's Health Collective blamed *me* for Garry's defense."

While the prisoner did time in Frontera, where she went to begin her five-year-to-life sentence, the defense committee redoubled its efforts. Garcia appeared on the cover of *Ms.* with a story by Nan Blitman and a sidebar by Gloria Steinem asking "What do we do with our rage?" Susan Jordan, a young lawyer who represented Emily Harris in the Patty Hearst case, took over the appeal.

"I felt," says Jordan, "that Garry had done it wrong. Inez hated that he argued diminished capacity and presented her as a crazy woman. There wasn't much communication between them. He couldn't see that this was a classic self-defense case, imminent threat, even with the half-hour time lapse after the rape."

To fast-forward, Garcia was acquitted at her second trial in March 1977, thanks to the defense strategy of Susan Jordan, who at one point had been fired by the volatile defendant and then rehired after the trial was underway. The feminist lawyer convinced the jury that her client shot Jimenez because she feared that he would return after the rape and kill her. Inez was a model of decorum this time around. She forsook her false eyelashes and wore a demure jacket; there was no grandstanding in the courtroom to her militant supporters. Jordan also wore a demure jacket, set off by a pretty, feminine scarf. Of course, by 1977 rape consciousness was riding high; in addition, several prosecution witnesses from the first trial failed to show up.

Lawyer and client posed for a victory picture on the courthouse steps. "And then Inez went off into the sunset," Jordan laughs. "I never saw her again." Neither did the defense committee, although one of the women once got a Christmas card from Miami.

The third of the trio of rape defense cases concerned Yvonne Wanrow, a Colville Indian in Spokane, Washington. Hobbling on crutches with a cast on her leg, Wanrow had shot and killed a neighborhood drunk, known as Chicken Bill, after hearing he had molested her son and raped a friend's daughter. After her trial and conviction the Native American movement publicized her plight and brought it to the feminist movement's attention. In 1977 the Washington State appeals court overturned Wanrow's conviction in response to briefs filed by Susan Jordan and New York lawyers Liz Schneider and Nancy Stearns, who raised fresh issues about a woman's perception of physical danger and self-defense. "We worked out a deal for her," Jordan recalls. "Something like three hundred hours of community service. She didn't serve any time."

Some people felt that the rape defense cases, and the battered women's defense cases that followed in their wake, were tantamount to giving women a license to kill. I did not share this alarmist perspective, but neither did I feel that fund-raising concerts for murder defendants were the best way to promote rape consciousness. However, I certainly understood the cases' popularity. Each defendant had a double constituency: each represented both an oppressed minority *and* the growing awareness about sexual assault.

• • •

Richard Nixon resigned in the summer of 1974 and Gerald Ford became president. In another development, admittedly of less earth-shaking significance but of avid interest to me, a few fast-moving men alert to the new interest in rape dashed into print but most of them were unable to write about sexual assault without eroticizing its violence. Their books sank without a trace.

Well, that's not exactly true. One fellow had to be torpedoed several times. Frederic Storaska wrote *How to Say No to a Rapist and Survive*, in which he exhorted victims to urinate, defecate, or vomit in a rapist's face. He claimed he ran a national organization for the prevention of rape and had studied four thousand cases. Anatole Broyard, one of the critics taken in by Storaska, gave *How to Say No* a respectful review in *The New York Times*. Armed with this testament and a few other glowing commendations, Storaska started lecturing at colleges across the country until the real antirape movement hounded him off the circuit.

Rape: The First Sourcebook for Women, edited by Noreen Connell and Cassandra Wilson, was the first feminist book wholly devoted to sexual assault to appear via a mainstream publisher. The *Sourcebook*, published in 1974, drew on the testimony and speeches three years earlier of the pioneering New York Radical Feminist speak-out and conference. A major breakthrough occurred in network television that February when *A Case of Rape*, starring Elizabeth Montgomery, was broadcast on NBC. The heavily promoted TV movie with its sympathetic treatment of a rape victim received the week's highest Nielsen ratings. *Against Rape* by Andra Medea, a self-defense instructor, and Kathleen Thompson, a member of Women Against Rape in Chicago, was the next feminist book to arrive, followed by Diana Russell's *The Politics of Rape: The Victim's Perspective*. Russell went on to organize the International Tribunal on Crimes Against Women in Brussels, which drew two thousand women from forty countries.

Against Our Will was published in October 1975. Seven years after attending my first Women's Liberation meeting, five years after

I'd begun to think about rape and to organize against it, I was about
to be thrust into national prominence as a movement theorist and
leader. Rape awareness was entering mainstream thinking, thanks to
the movement's efforts, but the movement itself was struggling to recover its balance after a painful internal crisis that had begun that
spring and had lasted all summer.

INTERNAL COMBUSTION

IN 1975 THE WOMEN'S MOVEMENT was at its height, with antirape strategies at the forefront of the revolution's new thinking. Abortion rights seemed inviolable two years after *Roe v. Wade*. Ratification of the Equal Rights Amendment appeared imminent. NOW, with Eleanor Smeal and Karen DeCrow at the helm, had pledged its forces to a state-by-state campaign, and President Gerald Ford and his wife Betty had given the ERA their endorsement. With such broad-based support, what could possibly stop it? Feminism had gone global. Acknowledging the movement's indigenous strength, the United Nations declared 1975 International Women's Year and sponsored a conference in Mexico City. In the literary world, Erica Jong's *Fear of Flying* had put "zipless fuck" into the lexicon; while *Newsweek* declared that a new wave in fiction was wrenching the image of women from male hands.

Change was afoot on many fronts. Ella Grasso in Connecticut became the first woman to govern a state without following a husband into the job. Bella Abzug, the first voice in congress to call for Richard Nixon's impeachment, was preparing a run for the Senate. Billie Jean King, with Martina Navratilova and Chris Evert, had led women's tennis into the main court in sports. The circulation of *Ms.* topped 400,000. Women-owned businesses were springing up all over the place. In New York some people I knew even opened the First Women's Bank.

The New Left, however, was in disarray and confusion. The war in Vietnam was over, but a decade of militant upheaval had taken its toll. Of the name-brand radicals from the Chicago Eight conspiracy trial, Abbie Hoffman was in hiding after a drug bust, Jerry Rubin was exploring yoga, meditation, and est, Rennie Davis had found spiritual peace with the Maharaj Ji, Bobby Seale had fled the Panthers in fear of Huey Newton, and Tom Hayden, married to Jane Fonda, was trying his luck in the Democratic Party. As the weary rank-and-file New Leftists tried to pick up the pieces of their fractured lives, some turned to environmental issues or returned to academia; a number of women reinvented themselves as socialist-feminists, lesbian Marxists, or lesbian-feminists with a third-world perspective. A handful of political fugitives who had gone too far out to come back drifted aimlessly "underground." Isolated clusters of aboveground radicals, unable to shut off their spigots of anger, rededicated themselves by forming minuscule, inconsequential revolutionary units.

The most hallucinatory manifestation of the far left's derangement erupted in San Francisco when a handful of whites led by an escaped black prisoner named themselves the Symbionese Liberation Army and kidnapped the heiress Patty Hearst, demanding a ransom of free food for poor people. As the bizarre drama played out for the public in crackling audiotapes, lurid headlines, and video footage, Patty metamorphosed into Tania the urban guerrilla, robbing a bank with her captors; in the next unbelievable installment, six of the terrorists perished in flames during a televised shoot-out. Hearst was recaptured nineteen months after the start of her strange odyssey. A very confused heiress asked from jail for some books on "the women's struggle."

The final act of another movement drama, this one dating back to the late sixties, the American left's most despairing and violent years, was played out when several of that era's radical fugitives resurfaced or were captured. In the absence of forward motion, the issue of noncooperation with the government was seized on by their dispirited sympathizers and friends. The subsequent fallout would reach into the women's movement, creating a fresh round of suspicions, divisions, and virulent paranoia.

Although the left had fallen apart, the women's movement was still vigorous and growing. A generation that had been in high school during the sixties was entering its ranks even as many of the original stalwarts vanished, needing to get on with their private lives or drawn to eastern religions, ashrams, gurus, the spiritual quest. I felt bereft and took it as a personal repudiation when Sally Kempton, a gifted writer and one of my closest feminist pals, disengaged from the temporal world to seek bliss on a spiritual path.

Inevitably and predictably, professional writers and media communicators had superseded the broad-spectrum radical theorists whose fiery speeches and mimeographed papers had driven the juggernaut of Women's Liberation. New issues, such as lesbian rights and rape, had exceeded the vision, and in many instances the understanding and sympathies, of some of the movement's key founders. Anger as well as anguish widened the conflicts over differences in direction.

This combustible mix—the male left's disintegration, the expanding popularity and growth of the women's movement, and the eclipse of some feminist founders who did not take their displacement lightly—imploded during the spring and summer of 1975, plunging the ranks of Women's Liberation into vicious internecine battles at the very moment of its greatest success. Rifts, accusations, and countercharges pitted woman against woman with an ugliness and intensity few of us had experienced before.

•   •   •

Jane Alpert, a fugitive since her appearance in a New York court in 1970, when she pled guilty to an antiwar bombing conspiracy with her lover Sam Melville, had undergone a change in her political thinking one year into her life underground. No longer a believer in revolutionary violence, the former Swarthmore honors student who had been willing to die for her cause moved from city to city under a series of assumed names, supporting herself by secretarial work and occasional aid from her loyal, distraught parents. Posing in San Diego as Ellen Davis, nicknamed Foxy, she walked into the Women's Center one evening when the need for companionship triumphed over her fear of exposure. A consciousness-raising group was in formation, and she decided to join it. It was there that she experienced her belated feminist conversion.

Sam Melville died at Attica in September 1971, when New York state troopers mounted a helicopter assault to quell the prison rebellion, killing three dozen inmates and three guards. Jane, spirited by the underground network into New York City to view his body, wrote a remembrance of their life together for a collection of his letters. Her mildly critical essay, written in haste, foreshadowed her changing perceptions. Robin Morgan, in secret visits, had become Alpert's mentor in feminism, having severed her own ties to the radical left. Migrating to Santa Fe, then Albuquerque, then to suburban Connecticut, Jane studied some classic feminist texts and tried to make sense of her derailed existence. An unsatisfactory rendezvous with the Weather Underground, not her first, confirmed her political alienation from the clandestine band. She moved on to Denver, found employment as Carla Weinstein in an Orthodox Jewish school, and started composing a statement of her new beliefs.

Alpert's vaguely spiritual, matriarchy-and-goddess-oriented essay bore the name "Mother Right," and held that reproductive biology was the revolutionary source of female power. As a piece of theoretical writing it suffered from the fugitive's intellectual isolation, but it nonetheless ignited a long fuse. The first part of the document, addressed to "Dear Sisters in the Weather Underground," delivered a scathing reappraisal of Melville and a harsh critique of sexism in the radical left, a movement she referred to with brutal honesty as "forgotten" and "dying." Angrily challenging the banner of Attica, she wrote, "I will mourn the loss of 42 male supremacists no longer." She would come to regret the rhetorical excess of that line.

A mailing of "Mother Right" to a handful of weekly alternative newspapers in the spring of 1973 brought no response. A second mailing, to reporters who had covered her 1970 case, drew a story in the *Times*, "Female Fugitive Bids Women Shun Leftist Units," and the publication of "Mother Right" in *off our backs*. Robin Morgan happily paved the way for *Ms.* to publish the full text in August with a compassionate introduction by Gloria Steinem.

Another year passed while Jane began the delicate process of turning herself in. She surfaced in November 1974, represented by an experienced Washington lawyer Gloria had suggested to Robin. Unwilling to reveal anyone's whereabouts in the underground network, Alpert walked a highwire in her meetings with the Justice Department and the FBI, minimizing her contacts with Weatherman and changing the cities of their rendezvous. As a government court document shows, she told the authorities she knew nothing of Pat Swinton, a second fugitive in the Melville case with whom she had traveled during her first year underground, until the stress of life on the run had splintered their friendship. Nonetheless, Jane had been sufficiently worried about Swinton's safety to visit her estranged friend in the Vermont town of Brattleboro before she surfaced, to suggest that Pat take cover or move since the faintest of inadvertent clues, an old address of Jane's or an alias, could conceivably lead to Pat's door. Swinton, renamed Shoshana, had found a tranquil refuge at Total Loss Farm, a renowned left-pacifist commune, and was working in pleasant surroundings at a health food co-op. She chose to stay put.

Alpert was sentenced to twenty-seven months for the bombing conspiracy and bail jumping, and was shipped off to prison in Muncy, Pennsylvania. Three months later, in March 1975, Swinton was arrested at the food co-op in Brattleboro. Grandstanding for the press in a classic move to gain sympathy for his client, Swinton's radical attorney placed the blame on Alpert. He disclosed that the two fugitives had traveled together, leaving Jane open to a perjury charge, and added that Pat had expected to be picked up after Jane's surrender. Elevated overnight to the iconic status of Shoshana, radical heroine in jeopardy, Swinton embarked on a series of speeches, arranged by her defense committee, in which she concurred that Jane's talks with the FBI must have led to her capture. Already predisposed to think the worst of Jane for her recantations in "Mother Right," the leftists around Swinton mounted a smear and innuendo campaign accusing Alpert of being an informer. I did not believe them, and watched in horror as the virus spread into feminist circles.

Ti-Grace Atkinson and Flo Kennedy led the relentless attack on Jane inside the women's movement, taking "We Are Attica" as their slogan. Flo, it is true, had always placed prisoners and prison issues near the top of her long list of causes, but a frontal assault on Jane was an irresponsible forum for these vital concerns. The kick-ass lawyer in the cowboy hat often wisecracked, "The women's movement is my hustle," to explain her theatrics on the lecture circuit. To her many fans the quip was a charming, outrageous Flo-ism; I was less forgiving.

Ti-Grace was bad news through and through. She had made a ridiculous spectacle of herself in 1971 at a "Women and Violence" panel in New York shortly after the shooting of the mobster Joe Colombo, with whom she was acquainted. Walking up the aisle barefoot in flowing white garments on that occcasion, she unveiled the Mafia leader's picture and intoned, "This is Sister Joe Colombo." Then she had vilified everyone present, and some of those not present (including me), concluding with the incantation, "I, Ti-Grace Atkinson, divorce you." Next she popped up in a bitter dispute between Philadelphia and Chicago feminists over an abortion clinic and its methods, to propose that she preside over a movement tribunal. The high court of movement justice à la *Alice in Wonderland* and "Off with her head" seemed to be the direction in which she was going.

Why anyone was still listening to Ti-Grace was a mystery to me, but inflammatory rhetoric never fails to capture some of the people some of the time. Atkinson was a master at it. Employing the epithet coined by the Panthers, she called Jane "a high-level pig."

I had no trouble figuring out which side I was on, and neither did most of my friends when Robin Morgan summoned us to an emergency meeting. I named our committee the Circle of Support for Jane Alpert. Florence Rush, at work on her history of the sexual abuse of children, and Barbara Mehrhof, of the old FEMINISTS, were the mainstays in New York. On the West Coast Susan Rennie and Kirsten Grimstad, editors of the *New Woman's Survival Catalog*, and Susan Griffin, the poet and writer, pulled their connections to present Jane's side of the story in the feminist press.

Statements were drawn up and circulated on both sides of the division. Some people straddled the fence, hoping Pat Swinton could avoid going to jail for whatever it was she had done, while remaining unconvinced that Jane's actions had led to her capture. Grace Paley and Barbara Deming, the leading peace-movement feminists, signed both sets of statements. Women's newspapers around the country lavishly reported the controversy. *Big Mama Rag* in Denver, *her-self* in Ann Arbor, and *Plexus* in San Francisco were sympathetic to Jane. *Off our backs* wavered. *Lavender Woman*, Chicago's lesbian-feminist newspaper, wound up in Jane's corner while extending compassion to everyone. The Weatherwomen issued a statement from the underground maintaining that Alpert had jeopardized their safety. In an ugly bit of business, *Midnight Special*, a leftist newsletter distributed in Muncy and other prisons, called Jane a traitor and warned people to watch out for her. With good reason, she feared for her life.

As it turned out, Pat Swinton was aquitted of all charges in connection with the Melville bombings, and Jane Alpert got an extra four months tacked on to her sentence for refusing to testify in court against her. In all, Jane served two full years before getting time off for good behavior. By then it should have been clear to her attackers, as it was to the Department of Justice, that she hadn't informed on Swinton or the Weather people, yet only one person involved in the smears was decent enough to send her an apology, the fellow who called her a traitor in *Midnight Special.* Jane and I became close friends after her release from jail and she even joined the antipornography campaign for a while, but her heart wasn't in movement politics any longer. She'd had more than enough for one lifetime.

• • •

Susan Saxe and Katherine Ann Power, two former students at Brandeis, were on the FBI's Ten Most Wanted list for a 1970 bank robbery in Boston meant to finance their revolutionary operations. During their getaway, a much decorated member of the Boston police force who happened to be the father of nine children was murdered. The FBI easily captured three men involved in the bank heist, including the shooter (they were white ex-convicts enrolled in a special program at Brandeis), but the women eluded their net.

Saxe came out as a lesbian during her fugitive travels, finding shelter along with Power, as Lena Paley and May Kelly, in a scattering of college towns from Connecticut to Kentucky. At some point the two fugitives went their separate ways. Saxe was arrested in Philadelphia in March 1975, a week after Pat Swinton's capture. Refusing to talk about Power, she pleaded guilty to the Boston bank robbery, received a sentence of twelve years, and issued a statement scoffing at bourgeois feminism and Jane Alpert. She vowed, "I intend to fight on in every way as a lesbian, a feminist, an Amazon."

It has never been clear how many of the women who harbored Saxe as "Lena Paley" were aware of her real identity before the FBI, on a tip from Lexington, Kentucky, zeroed in on the lesbian network. Neither is it clear what clues to her whereabouts and to Power's those who had given her refuge may have possessed. Antigovernment sentiments in that era were such, however, that in the period prior to and after her capture, two young lesbians in New Haven, Ellen Grusse and Terri Turgeon, who called themselves revolutionary Marxists, spent seven months in prison for refusing to cooperate with a grand jury investigation. A lone holdout in Lexington, Jill Raymond, was jailed for more than a year for *her* refusal to cooperate with a grand jury.

The Saxe case with its long tentacles and excruciating side issues did not vitally engage some of us who were urgently enveloped in the Alpert-Swinton controversy. Alpert had disavowed violence and attempted to create new feminist theory, while Saxe was professing a continuing commitment to violence, and her lesbian identity seemed irrelevant to her plight. As Jill Johnston wrote in *The Village Voice*, it was highly improbable that Saxe's sexual identity figured in the 1970 Boston bank robbery, so why should it matter in 1975? Johnston called Saxe "an interesting liability" and deplored the case's romantic attraction for those lesbians who were rushing to glorify Saxe and the still-at-large Power as "Bonnies without Clydes."

Romance aside, the Saxe case resonated profoundly among many lesbians who believed "the Man" was hounding their community because of its sexual orientation. For more than a year, until interest in Saxe subsided, they debated such questions as cooperation with the state, the harboring of radical fugitives, and the implications of standing by a lesbian sister defiantly committed to armed struggle.

•   •   •

The Redstockings attack on Gloria Steinem for her former CIA connections broke out in the middle of the fugitives' storm, adding to the rampant paranoia over agents and informers. This painful internal schism burrowed deeply into the movement's psyche, pitting some of its most important founders against the popular leader whose ascendance had eclipsed them in the public's eye.

Few early theorists and stouthearted activists had been so instrumental to the birth of Women's Liberation as Kathie Amatniek Sarachild and Carol Hanisch. Hanisch had left New York in 1969 for a less stressful feminist life in Gainesville, Florida. Sarachild had hung in to become the acknowledged leader of Redstockings after its famous abortion speakout, and seemed unperturbed when its membership declined in favor of some of the newer groupings the following year. Obsessed with ideological purity, she stubbornly promoted "the pro-woman line," a theory that refused to blame women, whatever their circumstance, for their own oppression, and concentrated on a cluster of issues, chiefly equality in marriage and a strong pro-monogamy stance, that she considered crucial to the feminist revolution. When Redstockings finally disbanded, she founded and edited *Woman's World* with a small group of colleagues. In its pages she noted with favor the appearance of *Ms.*, a helpful addition, she thought, to the liberal pincer of the feminist struggle. Subsequently she saw fit to criticize *Ms.* for publishing a guideline to consciousness-raising that she believed had diluted her method while her contribution as the c.r. evangelist appeared in a footnote.

Shortly afterward she received a call from Letty Pogrebin, the editor at *Ms.* who often initiated media spin-offs like books and records. The call had been made at Ellen Willis's suggestion. Pogrebin wondered if Sarachild might like to write a book under the *Ms.* imprimatur that explained consciousness-raising and its techniques for a mainstream audience. Sarachild had several meetings up at the *Ms.* office. Toward the end of one session, she recalls, one of the *Ms.* editors dropped a bombshell. She said that Gloria Steinem would write the introduction.

A quarter century later Kathie Sarachild reports, "I said to myself, '*What*? Gloria Steinem will introduce *me*? If anything, I should be introducing *them*, the newcomers at *Ms.*'"

Eventually the project faltered. "I'd begun to feel we were adversaries," Sarachild says darkly. "It was during that time that we began to learn more about them."

During the late Eisenhower and early Kennedy era, before her career in journalism took off, Gloria had directed the Independent Research Service, a CIA front that recruited anti-Communist students to attend Communist-sponsored youth festivals in Europe to defend the United States and its values. In 1967, when *Ramparts* had done an exposé on CIA funding, Gloria had defended her Cold War actions as something a good political liberal would do, and the story had died. When Kathie Sarachild and others looked at the story again seven years later, the CIA's dirty tricks at home and abroad had become common knowledge, and anything, past or present, with a CIA taint was in bad odor. In the meantime Gloria's meteoric rise to celebrity had given fresh currency to any unusual detail from her past, especially to a secretly funded activity that was so out of keeping with her popular image. Kathie was a Red Diaper Baby. In my opinion, Kathie's interpretation of Gloria's behavior was influenced by the belief system she'd grown up with.

Sarachild persuaded Carol Hanisch to return to New York to put together a book, *Feminist Revolution*, in order to reclaim the movement and their prideful contributions to its birth. A full laundry list of political tendencies had emerged in the last few years that they and their colleagues felt were wrongheaded and needed to be demolished. They had no use for feminist spirituality, goddess worship, and the matriarchists who claimed that women had ruled in prehistory. Alarmed by lesbian separatism, they deplored same-sex relations as a political solution to women's oppression. And they did not understand how it had come about that the mainstreamers at *Ms.* were speaking for the entire movement while they, the founders, were shut out of the public discourse.

As they worked on their essays, trying to piece together what had gone wrong and what factors had led to their eclipse, all roads seemed to lead to Gloria Steinem. The amateur sleuths noticed discrepancies and ellipses in Gloria's bios, particularly the ones that minimized her association with the Independent Research Service in later editions of

Who's Who. They scoured the pages of *Ms.* for sinister signs of its liberal obfuscation, and collected stories from people whose work was rejected or vitiated severely in the editing process. They pondered the role of Warner Communications, a giant corporation, in funding the magazine; they tried to trace the money flow in and out of the Women's Action Alliance and the Ms. Foundation, Gloria's other enterprises. When they were unable to create a solid trail of facts, their conspiratorial reasoning filled in the blanks. The CIA liked to set up "parallel organizations" as an alternative to revolutionary ones; it followed, then, that similar forces were behind the co-option of feminism by Gloria Steinem.

They were in too great a state of anguish to wait until *Feminist Revolution* was ready for the printers. In May 1975, Sarachild, Hanisch, and some of their political allies reconstituted the defunct Redstockings and released a documents packet at a media convention sponsored by *MORE*, a journalists' magazine, and attended by representatives of the alternative press. Their statement began, "Gloria Steinem has a ten-year association with the CIA stretching from 1959 to 1969 which she has misrepresented and covered up. Further, we have become convinced that *Ms.* magazine, founded and edited by her, is hurting the women's liberation movement."

Establishment journalists were unimpressed by the Redstockings charges, but portions of the women's movement reacted with shock and dismay. The unpaid volunteers who staffed the movement's most ideological newspapers, women who had long labored in the shadow cast by *Ms.*, initially delayed publishing the broadside until they could do some independent fact-checking and get Gloria's side of the story. This was the first time some of the antiestablishment radicals had ever telephoned the switchboard of the glossy magazine; their suspicions hardened when Gloria was unavailable to take their calls.

Joanne Edgar, Gloria's loyal assistant, attempted to field their questions: Gloria was too upset to address the charges; Gloria had been a student when she'd gone to those youth festivals; Gloria was in Mexico City with Bella Abzug for International Women's Year meetings; Who were these Redstockings women and where were they coming from; and no, Gloria had not read their statement.

"Gloria and I had some long discussions," Edgar remembers. "We were convinced that we could handle it, keep it contained in the radical press. What we did not want was to dignify the charges and take them to another level of credibility. Plus, she didn't know what to say and I thought the whole thing was ridiculous." *Ms.* was beset by another damage-control problem that season, one the editors deemed more serious than the Redstockings charges. Elizabeth Forsling Harris, the departed and disgruntled founding publisher, was suing Gloria and Pat Carbine for stock fraud, claiming they had schemed to shut her out of the magazine's future profits. Feeling she had suddenly entered a twilight zone of paranoid suspicions, Edgar hand-lettered a sign, CIA, and taped it to the office door as a giddy joke.

Edgar was badly misreading the mood of the radical movement. So were Gloria and everyone else in the office, except for Ellen Willis, who chose this moment to exit the magazine with a long, angry blast. Willis, a founder of the original Redstockings, had not been happy in her two years at *Ms.* Taking the job because she needed the money, she had chafed from the outset under Steinem's accumulation of power, her ties to the Democratic Party, and the magazine's electoral-politics slant. In her accusatory farewell, later enlarged for *Feminist Revolution*, she charged that "a mushy, sentimental idea of sisterhood" and "a pervasive upper-middle-class bias" had led the others down an antileft path, as evidenced by Gloria's embrace of Jane Alpert and her refusal to deal with the CIA charge.

Joan Nixon, an enterprising reporter for *Lavender Woman*, Chicago's lesbian-feminist paper, caught up with Steinem in June at a fund-raising concert in Detroit for Inez Garcia and Joan Little. Pushing past photographers, elbowing Lily Tomlin and the Deadly Nightshade rock band aside, she approached her quarry with a determination made bold by her sympathies. As she related in print, "Redstockings has got Steinem by the ovaries and at the very least she should be yelling OUCH." Her story captured Gloria's beleaguerment with good will and humor.

"I'm defending you in this Redstockings thing," Nixon began. "Are you still not talking about it?"

"Everyone is advising me not to reply," Gloria answered, "but I will have to do something. It's very painful. Just because I went to a youth festival sixteen years ago, they are attacking me."

Nixon's heart sank at the naive bit of stonewalling, but she observed that Steinem seemed in genuine pain. She reckoned correctly that the women's newspapers, especially the stern, ideological ones that had no use for *Ms.*, would pounce on Gloria for not taking them seriously enough to address the charges, and here she was, offering her a friendly opportunity that was going unheeded. "Steinem looked vulnerable in her tailored blue jeans, even fey," she wrote in a small digression. "Skinnier than I imagined. And beautiful, like everyone said. I wonder if she's a dyke."

The concert organizers were ready to take Steinem out to dinner. Gloria took a moment to give her hotel room number to the Nightshade women and gently informed Nixon she was meeting with some lesbian mothers involved in a custody battle later that evening, so there would be no time to discuss "the Redstockings thing." A shy woman identifying herself as an American Indian approached with a "Free Yvonne" flyer. Gloria asked several questions about the Wanrow case, listened carefully, and took extra copies of the flyer as she ducked into a waiting car. Nixon's brief encounter was over.

"As long as Steinem won't answer Redstockings, she looks guilty," she wrote in a short note to Joanne Edgar.

By the end of the summer, *Majority Report* in New York and *off our backs* in Washington had printed the charges in full, declaring their editorial sympathy for the Redstockings position. *Big Mama Rag* in Denver, *Plexus* in San Francisco, *Lavender Woman* in Chicago, and *The Lesbian Tide* in L.A. covered the story in detail but came down on Gloria's side. "Many of us in the lesbian-feminist press knew each other," Nixon says. "We wanted to defend Gloria because we saw her as pro-lesbian. We sure knew the Redstockings women weren't."

From Mexico City, where she, too, was attending the International Women's Year meetings, Betty Friedan, at one of her low points in her relations with Gloria, fed the story of the CIA charges to a New York tabloid and found a receptive audience in some foreign reporters. Friedan had been trying ineffectually to ground Steinem's airship for years, first by insisting that Gloria was a media creation and not a leader, then by floating the ludicrous assertion that Gloria was an extremist who hated men. Betty's proscribed list of extremist man-haters encompassed the Redstockings, naturally, but suddenly she found herself aligned with their thinking. I think the youth festival episode from Gloria's past was so at odds with Friedan's political values during McCarthyism and the Cold War that she exaggerated its current importance in her pain at being overshadowed by the glamorous, appealing figure the media and masses of women adored.

Earlier that spring, Betty had telephoned to ask me a loaded question: Didn't I think the CIA charges, whatever their merit, "deserved a full airing"? Betty had called me only once before, to solicit my help in getting out a Women's Political Caucus mailing. This summons, most obviously, was not as straightforward. My blood pressure jumped.

I told her flatly that I could not be of use to her. Morally and ethically my position on Gloria was similar to the one I had taken on Jane Alpert. I'd done plenty of foolish things in my youth that I hoped would never come back to haunt me. Yes, I'd been taken aback by the extent of Gloria's energetic Cold War involvements, but it was amply evident that she had become a different person. Oh sure, on my bad days I had terrible twinges of resentment over Gloria's fame. How could I not, remembering how I had been mauled five years earlier merely for getting my name in the papers during the movement's "We don't need leaders" phase. But Gloria had had nothing to do with that. Besides, the Redstockings' assertion that the CIA was behind *Ms.* and its shortcomings was not only laughable, it was loony.

Still, I was bewildered that such a savvy political person as Gloria had chosen not to answer her accusers. All she needed to do to pull the rug out from under them, and disarm everyone else, was to say forthrightly, "Yes, once upon a time I did work wittingly for a CIA front and today I'm sorry. If I'd known then what I know now," et cetera. Instead, she was silent. In her silence more paranoia erupted. Before long it reached a fever pitch that would have unforeseen implications for a think tank pondering feminist issues that turbulent summer.

Sagaris, the mighty double-edged sword of Amazon legend, was the name given to a radical feminist institute that convened at a small college perched on a hilltop in rural Vermont during July and August of

1975. The experimental program was the brainchild of three women on the faculty at nearby Goddard College: Marilyn Webb, the founder of D.C. Women's Liberation and *off our backs* who had moved on to create Goddard's department of women's studies, one of the first in the nation; Joan Peters, a professor of literature; and Blanche McCrary Boyd, a proudly out lesbian from South Carolina whose first novel, *Nerves*, was with Daughters, Inc., the feminist press that had an underground best seller in Rita Mae Brown's *Rubyfruit Jungle*.

"We incorporated as the Sagaris Collective, got a couple of small grants, and tried to hire every important feminist thinker we'd ever heard of," Boyd recalls. "You can only do this sort of thing when you're twenty-seven and very naive."

Inviting a select handful of East Coasters, and ignoring the antirape movement in their unrepresentative mix, the Sagaris women leased part of the campus of Lyndon State College for their summer retreat. About two hundred students, drawn from ads in the women's press, signed up for the program, not enough to cover its costs. Session One in July went off with only the usual grumbles.

"Charlotte Bunch's lectures on lesbian-feminism were superb," recalls the novelist Bertha Harris, another Daughters, Inc., author. "Rita Mae, I think, had gotten up a series on eighteenth-century male political theorists. Harmony Hammond was teaching tai chi. And I was teaching creative writing; it was unbelievable to get paid. Sagaris was one of the high points of my life. Little Dorothy Allison from South Carolina was one of my students—she'd saved up her money and wanted to come. Dorothy was very quiet and studious, and she taped all my lectures. I'm immensely proud of her today."

A second crew arrived for the August session, and with them came trouble. A volcanic tension, some even said primitive and jungly, hung over the campus. Women danced bare-breasted on the rolling green lawns; the couplings at night were intense. Pat Swinton came by from Total Loss Farm to tell her story; "the Philadelphia women"—supporters of Susan Saxe—arrived to explain the details of her case. Sagaris from the inside looked like the revolution. That was the misty impression of novelist Alix Kates Shulman, caught up in the drama.

"We were broke, that's the truth of it. We began the August session about three thousand dollars short, and the *Ms.* Foundation had already given us five thousand," Blanche Boyd relates. "So I placed a call to Aileen Hernandez, who was on their board. It turned out they were meeting that week. 'What do you really need to feel comfortable?' she asked me. 'It would be a terrible shame if Sagaris went down the drain.' Aileen drove up to Vermont with a ten-thousand-dollar check in her pocketbook. 'Hey, good news!' I shouted. 'Glory be, we're solvent!'"

"The *Ms.* grant came in at the last minute," Marilyn Webb confirms. "Hand delivered. Blanche thought it was absolutely wonderful, but I did not think it was such a great idea at all. I mean, this was at the height of the Redstockings charges. It looked like they were buying us off. The least we could do, I thought, was to tell the entire faculty and the two hundred students."

When Blanche made the announcement in the school cafeteria, all hell broke loose at the hilltop retreat. Faculty member Ti-Grace Atkinson, fresh from her attacks on Jane Alpert, howled that the grant was "dirty money." Gloria's speaking partner, Jane Galvin-Lewis, hired to lecture on race, roared back, "Bullshit, all money is tainted. What's the big deal?" Poet Susan Sherman, an Atkinson ally, demanded that the grant be returned. Alix Kates Shulman, proud to have been an original Redstocking, proclaimed that she would rather forgo her Sagaris salary than take suspect funds. Joan Peters of the Collective laid out the facts: "We can't pay our phone bill; we owe Lyndon State." Blanche Boyd pleaded for trust and reason. Alix announced that she was withdrawing an essay she'd written for *Ms.* until Gloria produced some satisfactory answers.

The debates and discussions went on every night for a week. Barbara Seaman, hired to lecture on women's health, packed her bags and went home. She would maintain ever after that agents—government agents!—had somehow fomented the unholy chaos. In the upshot, twenty-nine women, about one-third of the remaining Sagaris faculty and students, marched down the hill behind Ti-Grace Atkinson to conduct a free school at the Bemis Church community center "with no stars and no bosses like those at *Ms.* magazine."

Gloria's long-awaited answer was delivered by another *Ms.* messenger at some point during the furor. The rambling six-page mimeo-graphed letter, single-spaced on legal-size paper with edit marks and cross-outs, bore the advise that it was a copyrighted exclusive to "Dear Sisters" of the feminist press. It looked like what it was, a document written under duress by a woman who had faced adversarial conflicts since childhood with external composure and tight inner control. "Control" was a conscious and unconscious leitmotif as she addressed the most serious of the Redstockings' charges.

"I took no orders at all from the U.S. government in any of its forms or agencies," she said of her work for the Independent Research Service. "For better or worse, I have always been my own person. I naively believed that the ultimate money source didn't matter, since no control or orders came with it. It's painfully clear with hindsight that even in-direct, control-free funding was a mistake but I didn't realize it then."

Although they would claim it as their triumph, the defensive con-fession they'd wrung from Steinem did not assuage the angry walkouts at the bottom of the hill. Their focus had switched from Gloria to the "elitist power structure" of Sagaris, Inc. Calling themselves the August 7th Survival Community, they marched to the campus only at meal-times and to retire to their dormitory rooms at night.

At this inauspicious moment, Lucinda Franks of *The New York Times*, a Pulitzer-prize-winning reporter of sunny good cheer, arrived at Sagaris to do a feature on feminist scholars in rural Vermont. A weary Blanche Boyd escorted her around the hilltop campus, then pointed her toward the August 7th Survival Community down below. Entering a meeting room, Franks distinctly heard a surly whisper, *"That's the reporter who wrote about Jane Alpert!"* Three women glaring in her direction abruptly got up and walked out. Franks had been gath-ering tidbits about the clash over Steinem, and she most certainly was the reporter who had written sympathetically about Alpert, but she had no idea that the movement's divisions had grown so venomous or were so flagrantly open.

"Lucinda was freaked," Blanche Boyd remembers. "Somebody down the hill chalked on a blackboard, 'A smiling face should be hit.' She thought it was about her, and it probably was."

Franks hung around Sagaris just long enough to pick up a few quotes before she fled to New York to call more sources. Her story, "Dissension among Feminists: The Rift Widens," occupied three-quarters of "Family/Style," the closely read women's page, and was syndicated widely. Gloria's containment policy during the long, hot summer had been blown sky-high by the Sagaris experiment and *The New York Times*.

In time the CIA contretemps was forgotten. The overheated militants had succeeded in giving Steinem an ugly black eye, but the attack launched by the Redstockings, with its strained link to the fugitives' cases, was not a simple matter of revolutionary feminists engaged in a mortal stuggle against mainstream reformers, as Ellen Willis tried to maintain at the time. It did write "The End" to the longest chapter in the movement's life, although in truth that chapter had been concluded a few years before. A second wave of theorists was forcing new break-throughs—in rape, in battery, in sexual harassment—but by 1975 most of the early all-purpose agitators, the sine qua non of Women's Liberation, had played out their historic role. Like most utopian visionaries at war with the world, they lacked the flexibility and the practical skills to triumph on the larger stage they had brought into creation.

Blanche Boyd and Marilyn Webb, on opposite sides of the great divide at Sagaris, never spoke to each other again, and both retreated for many years into political inaction. None of the Sagaris principals ever succeeded in writing its story, although several tried. (Twenty years later Boyd incorporated some of its crazy emotions in *Terminal Velocity*, a novel she published in 1997.) Robin Morgan replaced Ellen Willis as the house radical at *Ms.* Kathie Sarachild and Carol Hanisch had a reprise in 1978 when Random House, through Betty Friedan's intercession, published *Feminist Revolution* in paperback, but the material on Gloria was excised when she threatened to sue. The two stubborn Redstockings had their own falling-out a decade later over an arcane, unmemorable political dispute. Ti-Grace went on being Ti-Grace, in parlous financial straits, and Flo Kennedy went on being Flo. To her credit, she had declined to go up against Steinem, whom she deeply respected.

A profound sense of powerlessness and rage always drives revolutionary movements, often to the point of their destruction. The quake of 1975 inside the women's movement, admittedly high on the Richter scale, was hardly the last of its periodic convulsions. Those of us who were still trying to keep the movement going blinked hard, shook our heads, and carried on with our work, until one by one each of us arrived at our own pivotal moment when enough was enough.

Years later, in the context of another convulsion in which I'd become the main target, Gloria whispered something into my ear that I've never forgotten. "We're lucky this is the women's movement," she quipped in a low voice ending in a light laugh. "In other movements they shoot each other."

FEMINIST AUTHOR

WRITING *AGAINST OUR WILL* felt like shooting an arrow into a bull's-eye in very slow motion. Few people are lucky enough to be in on the creation of a new cause, and then to publish a book on the subject five years down the line, when a large, mainstream audience is ready to receive it.

October 1975 was a great moment for me. A powerful publisher was committed to turning a heavy, provocative treatise into a commercial best seller, feature writers and book reviewers were prepared to treat a feminist analysis of rape seriously, and public interest programming was getting good airtime on television and radio stations. Individual women, wherever they had a foothold, rose up to help the cause. Joni Evans, Simon and Schuster's director of subsidiary rights, alerted Lucy Rosenthal at the Book-of-the-Month Club, who took it upon herself to be my champion. The book became a main selection. All the general interest periodicals edited by men passed on prepublication excerpts, but *Mademoiselle*, *Glamour*, and *Family Circle* stepped into the breech, thanks to a determined feminist editor inside each house.

The first interview I did was totally a product of the movement's positive strength and spirit. Sandra Elkin, a feminist in Buffalo, originated and produced a weekly half-hour talk show, *Woman*, for WNED-TV, her local educational television station, which was carried by two hundred outlets on the PBS network. She invited me to Buffalo for a long, serious taping during the summer. PBS aired two successive programs on the book in October. The conversations with Sandy turned out to be the most substantive discussion of *Against Our Will* I ever had.

When I finished my telephone interview with reporter John Leo of *Time*, my first major brush with the real world, I staggered into the bathroom and retched. His story came out pretty well, even if he did claim I saw rape as "a conscious conspiracy among all men." Nearly every major newspaper and magazine treated the book with seriousness and respect.

Someone I'd worked with in television persuaded a reluctant Barbara Walters to take me for the *Today* show. The Walters line of questioning was followed by so many subsequent interviewers that I've got a permanent reel of tape embedded in my head. Press a button and I go into automatic:

Q: Why did you write this book?
A: I wrote this book because I'm a woman who changed her mind about rape.
Q: What do you mean?
A: Well, I used to believe all the myths and misconceptions, that no woman could be raped against her will, that a raped woman was asking for it . . .

As I was leaving the studio Walters confided that she'd worn a black dress with low décolletage that morning so one of us, at least, wouldn't appear anti-male.

Simon and Schuster sent me on a six-week tour of twenty-one cities. Like so many authors, after a while I got punchy. I thought I had written a treatise of tremendous complexity that was going to change world opinion, but the questions, with a few shining exceptions, were so narrow. *So, what happens when a rape victim arrives at the police station? And how does the hospital respond? Are the laws getting better?* In Houston, I remarked to the S & S sales rep that the lobby of a television station looked oddly familiar. "You've been here twice today already. This is a third program," he gently explained.

The sales reps were pleasant companions, but I was on my own when the hostility erupted. I walked out of one all-night radio show when the host got abusive, I was reduced to tears by another late-night show in Chicago, and I will never forget the *Denver Post* reporter. She barreled into my hotel room screaming, "You have no right to disturb my mind like this!" Her photographer, a sweet, thoughtful fellow, tried to calm her, to no avail. Who knows what experience in her past my book had tapped into? She got her revenge. Her story, "Author Says She Is Obsessed by Rape," disturbed my sleep for several nights running, as did the article by a journalist in another city who began her lead, "Susan Brownmiller is the kind of woman who doesn't hesitate to march into the men's room if the ladies' room is occupied."

By the time I returned to New York, *Against Our Will* was a national best seller. Breaking its "Man of the Year" tradition, *Time* celebrated twelve women for 1975; I was honored to be on the cover in a montage that included Billie Jean King and Governor Ella Grasso.

I'd done what I could, and now I wanted to let the book speak for itself. That isn't what happened. A professor in Athens, Ohio, invited me to speak at his university. Depleted and uncertain about what to do next, I'd become uncharacteristically dependent on others for my sense of direction. So I flew to Ohio and addressed my first live audience of college students. My tongue was thick from stage fright as I gripped the lectern and marched through rape's history. College kids are very generous with their approval. They bowled me over.

For the next two years I crisscrossed the country, often hitting three colleges a week, giving what evolved as my set speech on rape. After a while I found the life of the circuit rider more alienating than rewarding. Years later I learned that students at several universities organized rape crisis centers after my visits. But once I mastered the technical challenge, life on the road wasn't for me. I lost touch with my habitual rhythms and inner dialogues of the mind. I disliked the rustle of anticipation, the collective murmur I interpreted to mean "Now we'll get a good show," as I walked onto the stage. Plundering my own material, I felt fraudulent repeating the same speech over and over. Relief came only with the spontaneous question-and-answer period at the end. Serious information is communicated to serious listeners on the lecture circuit, but I was in danger of making rape my shtick.

Once at some airport on a snowy night as I plodded toward my gate, I bumped into Gloria Steinem hurrying toward her gate, looking so alone and solemn. We hugged and promised to get together and take in a movie sometime, as we usually promised but never managed to do. One thing that always puzzled me about Gloria is how she could keep going from airport to airport, from speech to speech, year in and year out. It's a kind of fortitude, a politician's skill, that is not in my makeup. I was sublimely happy when I was organizing and writing, and I did get a kick out of some of the media stuff, but my sense of mission began losing its urgency in repetitive public speaking. I did not extract nourishment from the ephemeral adulation of strangers, the only sure palliative that can make the routine indignities and outbreaks of hostility bearable on a long-term basis.

· · ·

Outraged criticism of *Against Our Will* started pouring in from the right and the left after the first positive wave of media attention. I should not have been surprised, since feminism overturns so many facets of conventional political wisdom, but I believed my arguments about male violence were so convincing, and my evidence for seeing the routine deployment of rape as a weapon of intimidation was so impressive, that thoughtful people would say "Aha!" and take it from there.

My first inkling that not everyone on the intellectual left was prepared to thank me for their enlightenment had come when an old acquaintance in publishing accosted me on the street. "You," he thundered, shaking involuntarily and wagging his finger, "have set back the cause of civil rights and civil liberties ten years."

New York's certified male intellectuals, the *New York Review of Books* and *Partisan Review* crowd, had been caught off guard by the tidal wave of feminist thinking. We upset their applecart, trampled with muddy

boots on their tight little island of political certainty. Most male intellectuals reacted badly to feminism throughout its explosion, trying to
ignore it and not give an inch. The two or three females in their midst,
the loopholes, didn't dare risk their standing by identifying too
openly—or identifying at all—with the feminist camp. They had
fought too hard to be honorary men.

The silliest response came from the nonconservative Michael No-
vak, who published a diatribe in *Commentary* that called my book "a
tract celebrating lesbianism and/or masturbation." *Commentary*'s readers bombarded the Letters column with fierce objections, bless their
hearts.

The people who challenged my ideas most deeply were the women
of the activist left. I must say I was unprepared for their concentrated
assault. Several women, black and white, accused me of being a racist,
a charge that still crops up from time to time. Nothing devastates me
more.

When I wrote chapter 7, "A Question of Race," in *Against Our Will*,
I knew I was challenging Old Left dogma. After describing the bitter
legacy of rape in slavery, mob lynching by whites, and the discriminatory application of the death penalty to black men convicted of rape, I
had explored the Communist Party's use of the interracial rape case,
beginning with Scottsboro, as a dramatic symbol of American injustice.
My point was that the left and those influenced by the left saw rape as
a political cause only when they believed a white woman was falsely accusing a black man. Going further, I reserved my toughest comments
for the story of Emmett Till, the fourteen-year-old youth lynched in
Money, Mississippi, in 1955 for whistling at a white woman. I said that
Till and the men who lynched him shared something in common: a
perception of the white woman as the white man's property. For leftists with inflexible minds, this observation amounted to heresy. Some
dogmatists willfully interpreted it to mean that I condoned the lynching.

Alison Edwards, a white attorney in Chicago with the National
Lawyers Guild, wrote a pamphlet titled *Rape, Racism, and the White
Women's Movement: An Answer to Susan Brownmiller* that called *Against
Our Will* a "dangerous law and order book which, unless repudiated,

will fan the fires of racism." A broadside repeating the charge issued from Louisville, anonymously. I subsequently learned it was the work of Ann Braden, cofounder of the Old Left's most venerable civil rights organization, the Southern Conference Education Fund. But it was Angela Davis who delivered the worst blow. She devoted her radio program on KPFA in Berkeley one evening to my purported racism. Warming to the task, she extended her damning charge to Diana Russell's *Politics of Rape* and Shulamith Firestone's *Dialectic of Sex* in a second program, and recycled her views in *Freedomways* and *The Black Scholar*.

Trapped by their intellectual dependence on Marx, Angela Davis and her colleagues wished to see rape as a sick manifestation of the deteriorating capitalist system that would vanish in a new socialist order. According to their theories, my view that economic exploitation did not explain the totality of male violence was deficient in "class analysis." They concluded that the scrutiny I gave to black-on-black rape and black-on-white rape was a racist scare tactic. Davis wondered aloud if red-baiting was part of my secret agenda, since I'd taken some knowing jabs at the moribund Communist Party. She hinted that the media had conspired with my publisher to foist my reactionary ideas on an unsuspecting public—why else, after all, had I gotten so much attention? Angela Davis was an untouchable icon, not a good enemy to have. Even today I am perplexed by the Old Left rigidity in this intelligent, charismatic woman.

Diana Russell, living in Berkeley, was hurt by her attacks more than I was. Although Davis herself never stooped that low, other Bay Area leftists pointed to Diana's South African birth as proof of her racism. Diana was hounded at conferences, shunned by some of her peers. The irony was that Diana's work for an underground anti-apartheid group in Capetown and my work with CORE and SNCC gave us better records in civil rights activism than many or most of our accusers.

In Louisville, while I was on the lecture circuit, a gray-haired woman, fifth row center, started heckling me during my speech. Scottsboro, Till, the death penalty—she wouldn't quit. Neither would the small group of people with her. The political strategy of planned disruption had come into flower during the Vietnam era as a desperate cry of the powerless who needed a dramatic means of getting their antiwar views across. We in the women's movement had borrowed the technique and made effective use of it on occasion. It never crossed my mind that one day I would experience planned disruption from the vantage point of the target.

Louisville, the unsigned broadside? Click!

"Pardon me, are you Ann Braden?"

Flustered, she allowed that she was. It's one thing to disrupt a speaker, and quite another to be recognized by name. I really was pleased to meet the legendary cofounder of SCEF, although a confrontation is not exactly a meeting. To my disappointment, Braden vanished right after my speech, along with her friends.

A couple of months later Angela Davis ducked a chance for us to meet live on radio KPFA when I was passing through Berkeley. When you demonize someone, I guess you need to stay at a safe distance.

I toughed out the racism charges publicly in my usual dukes-up manner, but I grieved inside knowing that *Against Our Will* would never be read by a substantial number of radicals whose opinions were formed by the harmful attacks. Anyone who thinks that the Index of the Catholic Church was unique as a censoring mechanism of political thought in these United States does not know much about radical history.

• • •

Far from operating as a conspiracy, the establishment media pursued their own agenda and interests when it came to rape. Even before my book was published, I had received calls from journalists asking if I could find them a victim or two willing to "go public." TV people led the chase. Unashamed rape victims were news; producers wanted them for their documentaries and talk shows. At first I was happy to comply, because every woman who spoke out in the early days added a fresh perspective and an additional clue to rape's dimensions. Later on the women started to feel exploited, and I began to feel like the number-to-call in Central Casting. The D.C. Rape Crisis Center also grew weary of the media's incessant demand for victims. An interesting paradox emerged. The feminist antirape movement was founded on the testimony of raped women, and its success in changing public opinion derived from their truths. Criminologists, psychologists, and law enforcers, proving to be quick learners, adjusted their theories to reflect the new thinking. As the seventies turned into the eighties, however, and self-disclosure became the stock-in-trade of the proliferating talk shows, the rape victim became indistinguishable from the typical fodder of daily TV, yet another person with a gruesome story. By then the issues of battery, sexual harassment, and date rape had been added to the mix, and critics of feminism began blaming us for portraying all women as victims. I think the criticism was simplistic. Our goal in politicizing rape had been to illuminate the role of the male aggressor, not to train a perpetual spotlight on women as victims. Of course, the political explication of male violence proved infinitely harder to keep in the public eye than the victimization of women, but the failure to do so wasn't the movement's fault.

* * *

I have to admit that my abilities as a media communicator were imperfect. I lacked a certain humility and betrayed too much impatience, interpreted as arrogance, before a live studio audience. The person who brought me down on *The Phil Donahue Show* was Eldridge Cleaver, a very adept communicator indeed. Cleaver's unabashed confession in *Soul on Ice* that he had vented his rage against white men by raping white women, practicing first on black women to develop his confidence, had made him an obvious feminist target. Naturally I had given him what-for in *Against Our Will*. Even Angela Davis in her radio program was not about to defend Eldridge Cleaver, who had become anathema to black radicals during his exile for many acts having nothing to do with rape. Cleaver had undergone a strange transformation in Algiers and Paris after he'd been thrown out of the Black Panther Party by the Huey Newton faction. In place of "Power to the People," he began promoting codpiece trousers of his own design as a masculine identity statement. (Cleaver's spiritual conversion took root and flowered after his unsuccessful foray into men's fashion.) Returning to the States to square away some earlier criminal charges, the former Panther volunteered to reporters that he had been tremendously affected by *Against Our Will*. Quick as a flash, the Donahue producers arranged a two-part program for Cleaver and me, inviting the La Leche League of Green Bay, Wisconsin, to fill the studio seats.

"Uh-oh, white women in polyester, they're your people," Cleaver muttered as we took our places on the *Donahue* set. Neither of us figured that the militant breast-feeders might be more suspicious of a radical feminist than of a former Black Panther wanting to recant about rape. Things started off well enough. I asked Cleaver to apologize to black women. He did. Then I asked him to apologize to white women. He did that as well. Penitence was an unaccustomed role for the irrepressible showman. Midway through the program the old Eldridge of the street smarts reasserted himself. He started playing to the crowd.

"Aww, you know what those young girls are like," he teased with a big grin. "There's a word for it—I can't say it here but I know you all know it. C., uh, T." The audience tittered. I tried to bring them back. Sensing his advantage, Cleaver leaped from his chair. "Damn, woman, you won't let a man speak!"

Cheers and applause. It was all over for me. The La Lechers went for the kill. "Have *you* been raped? What makes *you* an expert?" one of them taunted.

We had a postmortem after the show. Donahue was devastated. His producers were devastated. I was devastated. So, curiously enough, was Eldridge Cleaver. As he packed his suit into a garment bag for his next public appearance, he looked at me gravely and said, "Don't make the mistake I made. Don't get too far ahead of the people."

By late 1976, a moment in time when *Against Our Will* was reaching bookstores in its paperback edition and I was meeting Cleaver on *Donahue*, four hundred rape crisis centers were in place around the country. Few of the centers, however, bore more than a faint resemblance to the original radical feminist model run by a volunteer collective of movement women. Professional social workers and psychologists had moved into the field, and even in cities where they hadn't, most of the centers had applied for and received federal funding, either through the LEAA (Law Enforcement Assistance Administration) or the NIMH (National Institute of Mental Health). The newly available public monies, a tribute to the antirape movement's success, acted to turn the centers into pure service and counseling organizations with paid staffs and conventional structures. With amazing speed, the rape crisis centers became *part* of the system, not a radical political force in opposition to the system. I witnessed the evolution firsthand while I was on the road with my book.

Changes in the law took place just as swiftly. In one year, 1975, thirty states overhauled their rape laws to make them more equitable to victims. Between 1970, when the feminist movement first started to talk about rape, and 1979, when the militance had receded, every state in the union went through a serious reevaluation of its rape codes and made significant adjustments. Hospital procedures and police attitudes were transformed as well. The revolution in thinking about rape was profound. I am very proud to have been part of it, along with thousands of others who did not write best-selling books.

• • •

My tenure in the public eye was brief. Readers yearned to hear strong women's voices in those consciousness-raising times, and the women had plenty to say. Shortly after *Against Our Will* was published, Shere Hite reached the top of the national best seller lists with the eponymously named *Hite Report* on female sexuality.

Everybody knew Shere Hite in the New York movement, at least by sight. You couldn't help but notice the willowy NOW person with the bulging briefcase, porcelain skin, and reddish-blond hair who stood up at meetings and pleaded with people to take home her questionnaire. I filled one out, more or less as a favor to her, but I was so absorbed with my own piece of the puzzle that I rarely saw the significance in what others were doing.

Shere was one of the movement's great originals, a graduate student at Columbia who'd done some modeling and liked to dress in silky blouses with dark red lipstick and platform shoes. She pronounced her name "Sherry" then. "Sheer," as in stockings, or "Cher," like the singer, came later, when the broadcast media put their own spin on the offbeat spelling and she decided she liked the authoritative ring.

In 1974, Shere had come out with a little paperback, *Sexual Honesty*, an interim study based on her first forty-five samples, which did not make any ripples. Another researcher might have quit then and there, but Hite doggedly continued her investigations, determined to acquire at least one completed response from every state in the union. Ultimately she collected three thousand responses. Her luck turned when Barbara Seaman introduced her to Regina Ryan, then a junior editor at Knopf. Barbara, who had followed *The Doctors' Case Against the Pill* with *Free and Female*, was one of those rare and generous feminist authors who always seemed to know what everyone else was doing.

Regina Ryan was intrigued enough by Hite's questionnaire project to set up a lunch. "Shere arrived in something flowing and lacy and started talking about orgasms and clitoral stimulation," she recalls. "Everyone in the restaurant kept staring at us. I was amazed at what she was up to. This was the first time anyone had asked women directly what they liked and what they didn't like about sex. I knew it could be a major book."

The Hite Report was published by Macmillan after Regina Ryan moved there as editor in chief, the first woman in publishing to reach the top spot. Her all-male sales department hated the book so much that Ryan agreed to a small first printing. *The Hite Report* became a true reader phenomenon. The book ended up selling hundreds of thousands of copies, but Shere had to go to court to free up her royalties because in her naivete she had asked for a contract limiting her pay-out to twenty thousand dollars a year.

The Hite Report was tremendously liberating for its day—all those women's voices talking frankly in minute detail about their orgasmic satisfactions, or lack of satisfactions, and reporting on their infinite varieties of masturbation, with Shere weaving in and out of the text in an encouraging manner. In a blow to male vanity, 70 percent of Hite's voluble respondents admitted that conventional intercourse was just another, and not very reliable, way to reach orgasm. Shere's statistics and methodology were always under fire, and never more so than in the next decade, when she became a lightning rod for the "profamily" backlash, but her powerful case for the intrinsic differences between male and female sexual pleasure freed a lot of women from the fear that their likes and needs were a personal problem. Men learned a lot from Shere Hite, too.

The next feminist best seller was *The Women's Room*. None of us in the movement knew its forty-seven-year-old author, Marilyn French. She wasn't a joiner. Even at the height of late-sixties radicalism, when she was living in Cambridge as a teaching fellow at Harvard, writing her dissertation on James Joyce, what she learned of the new stirrings she absorbed only by observation. But she had always known, ever since she was a rebellious little Polish Catholic girl in Ozone Park, Queens, that one day she was going to be a writer. Her circuitous path toward that goal reflected the compromises and choices taken by nearly all young middle-class women in the post–World War II era who came of age vaguely wanting to do something important. Marilyn got married while she was still in college, supported her husband through law school, and settled in a tract house in Levittown, where she raised two children. If at first the domestic contract seemed like a fair exchange for the few hours she was able to carve out of her day for her true ambition, the reality drowned her in misery.

Emboldened by her reading of Beauvoir and Lessing, the house-wife-who-wrote observed the lives of her Levittown set as if she were an anthropologist in a foreign country. Typing at night when the house was quiet, she mailed her short stories to the women's magazines, but the bitter tales always came back rejected. Undaunted, she retyped the pages and mailed them out again and again while she pecked away at drafts of unfinished novels. She had hopes for something she was call-ing then "Myersville," a panoramic account of the choking despair of suburban housewives as reported through vignettes of their daily exis-tence.

In a visible cause-and-effect process, one of many during the Vietnam War, the Selective Service Act of 1967 that eliminated draft deferments for male graduate-school students opened unexpected opportunities for women. Marilyn applied to Harvard the following year and was accepted into its English literature graduate program. Leaving her husband behind, she moved to Cambridge with her two children to begin a new life, a generation older than nearly all the other graduate students she met on campus.

Six years later Marilyn's own kids were in college and their mother was teaching Shakespeare at Holy Cross. During her summer vacation she finally solved a technical problem, a matter of voice and distance, that allowed her to graft long sections of the Myersville novel onto a new piece of fiction about Harvard in the late sixties. The result was a tale of two cultures, more than eight hundred typed pages long, that contrasted the unfulfilled lives of the women of her generation— housewives drowning in "shit and stringbeans," in her unforgettable metaphor—with the kids coming up who believed they could change the world. "This sounds egotistical but I can't help it," she says with solemn pride. "When I finished the last page, I knew I had done something great."

A struggling agent named Charlotte Sheedy received the bulky manuscript from another agent, who thought it a tough sell. "It took me three days around the clock to read it," Sheedy remembers. "For three days I never put it down. I hadn't lived in the suburbs and I'd always been politically active, but I'd raised three children while I'd worked as a secretary and book scout, and I'd been one of the older women returning to school in the early seventies. So in many respects I felt *The Women's Room* encompassed my life."

Five years younger than French, Sheedy had marched with Women Strike for Peace and worked as a draft counselor for the antiwar movement before leaping into Women's Liberation at Columbia in 1970, where she met Kate Millett and filled out one of Shere Hite's questionnaires. On July 4, 1974, an infamous day in the Sheedy family history, she was waiting her turn at the cheese counter of Zabar's with her daughter Ally when a customer goosed her. Grabbing the molester by the wrist, she yelled in vain for someone to call the police. "Even at the lox counter, where they knew me," she reports with injured pride, "they said, 'Mrs. Sheedy, why are you making such a fuss?'" The molester broke free and escaped in a taxi, but the fuss for Zabar's was just beginning. Taking her story to the newspapers, Sheedy won a settlement against the landmark appetizing store with the help of my lawyer friend Jan Goodman.

As soon as Sheedy finished reading the manuscript, she called Marilyn French to say she'd represent her. A few months later *The Women's Room* was sold for ten thousand dollars, the typical feminist's advance, to Jim Silberman, a respected publisher who was starting a new imprint at Simon and Schuster.

"*The Women's Room* came at a time when the mass consciousness was changing," Sheedy assesses. "It wasn't for those of us who had been in the movement, it was for *them*, the ones who were just beginning to understand about consciousness-raising and the politics of housework. People started debating it in their living rooms. You could actually track its course for the first three months as it picked up steam across the country."

• • •

Beauvoir's *The Second Sex*, Friedan's *The Feminine Mystique*, and Doris Lessing's *The Golden Notebook* had preceded the women's movement and helped lay the intellectual groundwork for it. In the seventies an entire industry of feminist theoretical works, novels, biographies, literary criticism, art criticism, and movie criticism flowered. Women suddenly, and in many instances defiantly, had developed an urgent need to read women authors who were shedding new light on women's lives, sexualities, and dissatisfactions. Publishing houses that initially predicted a six-month boom for the unexpected women's phenomenon began signing up writers, good, bad, and indifferent, while bookstores carved out new sections labeled "Women" or "Women's Studies." Nancy Milford's *Zelda* set the benchmark for the treatment of a woman in biography when it came out in August 1970, the month, coincidentally, of the first Women's March for Equality and the publication of *Sexual Politics* by Kate Millett. A couple of years later biographies of forgotten or overlooked women had become a publishing staple. The coming-of-age novel, a reliably popular genre mined almost exclusively by men, was enlarged by the success of Toni Morrison's *The*

Bluest Eye and Alix Kates Shulman's *Memoirs of an Ex-Prom Queen*. A half decade later there was a mass audience for ethnic women's coming-of-age memoirs, novels, and plays: among them, Ntozake Shange's brilliant stage play *For Colored Girls Who Have Considered Suicide When the Rainbow Is Enuf* and Maxine Hong Kingston's *The Woman Warrior*, and women were also devouring lesbian coming-of-age books, like Lisa Alther's *Kinflicks* and Rita Mae Brown's *Rubyfruit Jungle*. Ursula LeGuinn's *The Left Hand of Darkness* had stood alone in the male-dominated science fiction genre for years, until the new feminism spawned Joanna Russ, Marge Piercy, and others. The mainstream welcome accorded to so many of these books in the seventies (and into the early eighties, with the triumph of Alice Walker's *The Color Purple*) was akin to the excitement that greeted the movement's mimeographed papers during the late sixties, but a wider audience carried bankable rewards, at least for some of us. I was very grateful.

The term "feminist author" largely replaced the odious "woman writer," or worse, "lady writer." Lumped together as a group, the novelists and nonfiction authors mining the new feminist themes, or benefiting from the sudden interest in all things female, were not a cohesive entity in any sense, but the New York writers bumped into one another regularly at publication parties. Two or three wine-and-cheese receptions a week were not unusual in those years. It was remarkable how few male authors, if any, showed up for the festivities. A sprinkling of proud husbands and tweedy, pipe-smoking editors was about the extent of male representation. The novelists in our midst felt the snubs from their male peers most keenly. Whatever entry into the literary world meant to them, their dreams of "arriving" did not anticipate ghettoization.

Those of us whose writing careers were enlarged or made possible by feminism occupied a special niche inside the movement. Our appearance between hard covers elevated us to the status of Famous Feminists—"FFs" in movement shorthand—a little aristocracy imbued with the self-congratulatory importance that afflicts all little aristocracies that emerge from within outsider societies.

Ever the realist, I tried to retain some perspective on my changed fortune.

"NO MAN IS WORTH DYING FOR"

MOST OF THE GREAT feminist issues of the 1970s were Made in America exports, but the campaign against domestic violence began in England, when Erin Pizzey founded the first shelter for battered women in the London suburb of Chiswick. *Scream Quietly or the Neighbours Will Hear*, Pizzey's pioneering book on battery and the shelter concept, was never published in the United States, but many of us managed to acquire copies at feminist bookstores or conferences.

Capacious in size, by turns generous and truculent in nature, Erin Pizzey was an opinionated housewife with a BBC reporter husband, two small children, and a dream of becoming a writer when she volunteered to do office work for the Women's Liberation Workshop in London. Fairly quickly she ran afoul of the group's radical-left orientation. In fact, Pizzey won the distinction of being the first and only woman officially thrown out of the London movement, by formal letter, after she called the cops on The Angry Brigade, a violent faction. That was Erin; she was always battling some force or other. Born in China on the eve of World War II, the daughter of an Irish career officer in the British foreign service, she had experienced a peripatetic childhood that had been emotionally deprived and fitfully violent.

After her banishment from the London group, Pizzey and a handful of her supporters persuaded the borough of Hounslow to give them a dilapidated, condemned house in Chiswick to use as a daytime women's center. Fixed up by volunteer labor, No. 2, Belmont Terrace opened in November 1971. It consisted of "two rooms up, two rooms down, with the lavatory outside," in Pizzey's words, and its interior was painted bright orange. It had a children's playroom, the first priority in the rehab process. After much discussion, a sign bearing the rather old-fashioned name "Chiswick Women's Aid" was tacked on the front door. The friendly gathering place where neighborhood mothers were encouraged to bring their kids would prove to be only the beginning of a much larger, astonishingly inventive project.

"A year later there were thirty-four women and children living in the community," Pizzey relates in *Scream Quietly*. "If we'd known what was to happen I wonder whether we might not have put down our paint brushes and run."

The first battered woman to seek shelter at Chiswick Women's Aid is called Jenny in *Scream Quietly*. Her real name was Kathy. "Kathy didn't say anything when she walked in," Pizzey remembers. "She just took off her wool jersey and she was covered with these liver-blue bruises. I snapped. I mean, I suddenly regressed into my own past, when I'd looked like that as a child. Kathy was our first overnight guest. Naturally I couldn't leave her alone in Belmont Terrace, so I took her home with me. When my husband came in, I said 'Jack, be quiet, there is a very badly beaten woman upstairs and she's sleeping.' He asked, 'Has her husband come around?' 'Of course not,' I replied. "He doesn't know where she is.' With that, there was a *bang, bang, bang* on the door and there was Wally, her husband, and he's bellowing '*I am a very violent man.*' You should have seen Jack run! So I held Wally back and said 'No, Wally, you can't come in, this is my private house. I'll come round and see you tomorrow.' Well, after that it was like a flood."

Within a year Pizzey was being excoriated from the local pulpits as a home wrecker and marriage breaker. On the brighter side, No. 2, Belmont Terrace had been joined by No. 369, Chiswick High Road, a substantial old house with three indoor toilets and a large rear garden. Pizzey had found a benefactor in one of the British Astors, who contributed sixty thousand pounds toward the new shelter's rehabilitation and upkeep. Another prominent backer walked in one day, plunked himself down on a mattress, and asked, "What do you need?" He turned out to be the managing director of Bovis, the huge construction firm. "I was very good at hustling money," she reminisces. "Of course we had our jumble sales as well."

Pizzey ran her battered women's shelter on a principle she called "therapeutic chaos," a style that was enjoying a vogue at that time through the work of R.D. Laing and others. "Oh, I loved Laing," she says. "We were happening at the same time. But I was influenced by the therapeutic community ideas of Maxwell Jones, who wrote fascinating papers on his social rehabilitation unit at a psychiatric hospital in Surrey."

She provided a lively, crowded, and noisy environment for her emotionally strung-out charges. The television set blared, the air was thick with cigarette smoke, and the women, who came and went at will, danced, sang, chased about, and slept on mattresses arranged on the wood floor. Anne Ashby was her chief associate. A male helper, Mike Dunne, was hired to make the point to the women and kids that not all men were violent.

"Most of these mothers had never played when they were kids," Pizzey explains. "They were sitting on their rage. We would take up their energy level with our energy level. I had enormous energy levels—I'd exhaust everybody. Some of the women were half my age and I'd still be dancing around while they were crawling off to bed. One woman was so angry yet so totally passive that I knew she was using every ounce of her energy to hold herself in. I told her, 'It's okay to explode.' So she got drunk, exploded, and attacked *me*. I weighed 250 pounds then, so I just very gently put her on the floor and held her in my arms and sang 'Baa, Baa, Black Sheep' to her until she got calm. A lot of Chiswick was about letting people cry, especially the young, violent boys, because they didn't know how."

Empowerment was another of Erin's principles. House meetings were held every morning—attendance was optional but everyone came—and the residents voted on their own rules. Women seeking refuge could come, go, or stay at the shelter for as long as they wished. (For some women, Pizzey discovered, the shelter would always be a revolving door.) When a filmmaker arrived to do a documentary, Pizzey stayed in the back room and let the residents run the show. When the borough of Hounslow tried to close down No. 2, Belmont Terrace as a health hazard because of overcrowding, the residents led marches on the council.

Pizzey's shelter concept spread rapidly to Leeds, Liverpool, Acton. A wife-and-husband team, Rebecca and Russell Dobash, pioneered the refuge idea in Scotland and began to write extensively about domestic violence. *Time's* London bureau did a story on Chiswick, but the piece ran only in the international edition. The magazine's New York editors had pigeonholed battery as a British problem, just as a London newspaper was to pigeonhole rape as an American problem a few years later.

Scream Quietly—its title came from one of Pizzey's battered women—was published by British Penguin in 1974. By then, news of the shelter movement had filtered into the States. On a visit to London in 1973, Karen Durbin reported on Chiswick for *The Village Voice*, but the editors stalled for a year before running her story. "The subject was strange and upsetting back then, shrouded in a dozen kinds of denial," Durbin recalls. *Ms.* ran a short piece based on Durbin's reporting, and the *Ladies' Home Journal* printed her anecdotal account of wife beating in America. Marjorie Fields, director of Legal Aid Service in Brooklyn, analyzed five hundred divorce cases and found that more than half of the female litigants had been physically assaulted by their husbands. The sociologists Richard Gelles, Murray Straus, and Susan Steinmetz undertook an epidemiological study, reporting that a physical assault occurred in 28 percent of all American households in a given year. In the meantime, rudimentary shelters were popping up in activists' homes across the country.

Wiry, energetic Sandy Ramos believes she started the first shelter in North America, almost by accident, in her purple-painted, three-bedroom house at 133 Cedar Avenue in Hackensack, New Jersey. A Jewish runaway from Brooklyn, Ramos had spent three years in an upstate New York reformatory before she married at eighteen. In 1970 she was pregnant with her third child, enthralled by the Black Panthers, and going through a divorce. "I didn't know what I was doing," she says, "but I knew I wanted to share my house with other single mothers. It turned out that a lot of them had been battered. Helga, my first resident, came in the middle of the night with her three children and three cats."

Seven years later Ramos had twenty-three people living with her. A church in Paterson was sending over meal cans. She named her refuge Save Our Sisters, made T-shirts with the slogan "Never Another Battered Woman," and fought to start more shelters in New Jersey. "People would say, 'We don't want battered women in our neighborhood,' and I'd say 'You have them already, behind closed doors.' I'm five feet four and I was fighting the whole establishment," she exclaims. "In those days the courts didn't even have restraining orders. When we heard that the Bergen County freeholders had allocated a million dollars for a dog shelter and nothing for battered women, we brought poodles to their next meeting. The press grabbed ahold of it. Confrontational politics worked."

Like most of the early shelters, Woman's Advocates in St. Paul, Minnesota, evolved in an unpremeditated fashion. It grew out of the political work of a Twin Cities collective led by Sharon Rice Vaughan, a St. Paul native and activist in the Catholic left, and Susan Ryan, an idealistic VISTA volunteer from New York.

Divorced in 1970 and raising three small children, Sharon Vaughan was a mainstay of the Honeywell Project, dedicated to stopping the Minneapolis company from making the antipersonnel cluster bombs that were dropped on Vietnam. Her antiwar activism had led to an arrest in Harrisburg, Pennsylvania, during the trial of the Berrigan brothers and Sister Elizabeth McAlister. "Oh, I was arrested several times," she recounts. "That time I spent a week in jail."

Ryan was five years younger than Vaughan and more inclined toward the counterculture. She, too, was active in the Honeywell Project, as well as in a consciousness-raising group that hoped to start a women's center and food co-op. She recruited Vaughan for a new VISTA program, a phone service offering information on legal rights in separations and divorce. "The women called about everything," Vaughan remembers. "We learned that you can't isolate and fragment women's issues. A lot of the women were battered, and trapped in their homes for lack of options. There were thirty-seven places in Minneapolis–St. Paul for a man to stay, and one place for a woman—a welfare hotel."

In 1972, Susan Ryan began sheltering women in her spartan one-bedroom apartment. When Ryan's landlord started eviction proceedings, Sharon Vaughan moved the informal shelter to her home.

"I was living on child support and two hundred dollars a month from VISTA," Vaughan relates, "but I filled the house for two years, especially in the summer, when my kids went away with their father. The women slept on the floor, next to the green plastic garbage bags that held their belongings."

"We had volunteers answering the phone day and night," Ryan adds. "Bernice Sisson would pick the women up in her car. We bought the food, and the women helped with the cooking. There was a sign-up sheet for chores. Some women got food stamps—it was easier in those days to qualify for food stamps."

"My five-year-old came home from her private school one day and asked, 'Mother, are we rich or are we poor?'" Vaughan remembers. Ultimately 118 women and kids passed through her doors. "A few of them robbed me," she admits. "The Tiffany wedding silver went. They didn't take the knives, for some reason. Then my jeans got stolen from the clothesline in the basement—that made me madder than anything."

"Sharon's house started to be overcrowded," Ryan continues, "so we stepped up our plans to buy a real shelter. On behalf of Woman's Advocates we sent a letter to five hundred people and got about six hundred dollars a month in pledges." The two women found a ramshackle six-bedroom frame house with two fireplaces and a huge attic on Grand Avenue, ten minutes by bus from downtown St. Paul.

"We thought we could start this house without going for what we were then calling 'dirty money,'" Vaughan says, "but we couldn't." Woman's Advocates applied for and received grants from two private foundations and the Ramsey County mental health division. The financial aid came with procedural stipulations, review policies, plans for a second facility, and the requirement that the women's nonhierarchical collective be replaced by an overseeing board and a staff director.

Susan Ryan walked out in the middle of a foundation meeting. "I hated the professionalization of our shelter," she says. "My vision was a small place the women would run themselves. Who were these people to tell us to put our energy into writing proposals? We'd been doing the job for two years! My leaving hurt Sharon very badly, but it was a two-way thing. We put our lives on the back burner to create that shelter. I sacrificed my marriage to that shelter, I had a traumatic childbirth, an emergency cesarean on my lunch hour, because of that shelter."

Vaughan flew to London to take a look at Chiswick Women's Aid. (Too chaotic, she thought.) Upon her return, she assumed the directorship of Woman's Advocates and then stubbornly turned it back into a collective. She stayed with it through all its Sturm und Drang until 1978, when she moved to the newly created Harriet Tubman Shelter across the river in Minneapolis. That year she helped write a comprehensive Domestic Abuse Act for Minnesota. "We had a legislator who would sponsor anything we wanted," she recalls. She also helped found the National Coalition Against Domestic Violence, an ambitious attempt by movement activists to develop a national network of shelters that shared their radical political values.

The first American book on domestic violence, *Battered Wives* by Del Martin, came out in 1976. Martin's editor at Glide Publications, an offshoot of San Francisco's progressive Glide Memorial Church, had suggested the project after encountering the British shelter movement and Pizzey's book on a visit to London. Battery was a fresh field of inquiry for Martin, a pioneer in lesbian rights.

Martin had joined NOW in 1967 with Phyllis Lyon, her lifetime partner and cofounder of Daughters of Bilitis, the nation's first lesbian organization. "Gay men were just as sexist as heterosexual men," she relates. "Phyllis and I knew that. We also knew that the feminists needed our input." Hearing that NOW offered a reduced membership rate for couples, she and Phyllis applied together. "Ho, I think they dropped the couples membership plan after we sent in our application." Martin and Lyon were received warmly by NOW's San Francisco chapter, however, and in 1973 Martin was elected as the first open lesbian to NOW's National Board. "And then I found three other lesbians, but they were closeted," she laughs. "They avoided me like the plague."

Martin began her battery research by putting out the word to the feminist movement. "My editor and I knew," she says, "that it was not just a British problem." Betsy Warrior, one of the original Cell 16 theorists in Boston, had turned to battered women's advocacy and was able to put her in touch with several shelters in the planning stages in Massachusetts. Sharon Vaughan used her quiet time on overnight duty at Woman's Advocates in St. Paul to answer Martin's inquiries in long, detailed letters. Martin learned about La Casa de las Madres, just getting started in San Francisco by Marta Segovia Ashley and Marya Grambs. She corresponded as well with Dorothy Jackson of Bradley/Angle House in Portland, named for two women who had died violently in that city. *Battered Wives*, highly regarded in the movement for its straightforward treatment of shelter organizing and funding, was updated and republished in 1981. By then several other books on the subject were on the shelves.

Lenore Walker, an empathic young psychologist on the faculty of Rutgers, had begun to collect data on battered women in 1975, inspired by the report in *Ms.* on Pizzey's shelter. In the throes of a divorce, she packed up her two kids and moved to Denver, taking an appointment at Colorado Women's College to be near the man who eventually became her second husband. "I took my research with me," she says. A field trip to Florida produced a set of interviews with elderly women, "and it was like wow, this thing doesn't stop! At the time we still believed that criminally violent behavior decreases significantly after the age of forty." The following year she visited Erin Pizzey's shelters in England and observed the daily routines at a couple of safe houses run by Women's Aid Federation, a rival feminist group that was deeply antagonistic to Pizzey's anarchic, flamboyant style.

Walker also studied some intriguing animal behavior theories based on laboratory research. She began to see startling connections between the coping mechanisms of battered women and the behavior of caged dogs subjected to random and variable electric shocks. "Learned helplessness" became one of the linchpins of *The Battered Woman*, published by Harper and Row in 1979. Coining the phrase "battered women's syndrome," Walker delineated a common cycle of violence: a honeymoon period followed by a buildup of tension, followed by an explosion and battery, followed by regrets and apologies, followed by another honeymoon period, etc. By featuring the stories of several professional women who had endured physical abuse in marriage, Walker put to rest the myth that battery was strictly a lower-class problem. Indeed, she showed that battery cut across all class lines without regard to income or professional status.

I heard Lenore Walker discuss her findings in May 1977, at a conference on violence at the University of Washington in Seattle. Women in the audience, evidently victims of battery, were nodding their heads and exchanging glances, as if to say *Yes, that's how it was! She knows!* The electricity in the air reminded me of the early speak-outs on abortion and rape. Once again feminism was exposing hidden truths and offering fresh insights.

As it happened, the Seattle conference nudged the articulate psychologist in an unexpected direction. Pleading for a national campaign to change social attitudes, she declared, "We should have billboards across the country with John Wayne shaking his finger, saying, YOU'RE A SISSY IF YOU BEAT YOUR WIFE."

"Women are being killed every day!" shouted a voice from the audience. "Can your words and theories help them?"

"Yes," Walker replied, caught up in the fervor. "If they're in danger of being killed and they fight back and kill the man, I'll provide a defense for them!"

A wire service reporter quoted her stirring words, and a few days later she received a phone call from a lawyer in Billings, Montana, who was representing a battered woman who had killed her husband. He invited Walker to testify about battery cycles and learned helplessness for his jury. Nervously she agreed, and the trial ended in a not-guilty verdict by reason of self-defense. Walker got more requests to testify in court. She discovered that she never got rattled or lost her temper on the witness stand. Twelve years later, after appearing as an expert witness in more than 150 murder trials across the United States, the personable psychologist with a clear, forthright manner calculated that 25 percent of the women she'd testified for had been fully acquitted, and two-thirds had not served any jail time.

The legal evolution of the "battered women's defense," as it came to be known, was built on the "rape defense" successfully argued by lawyer Susan Jordan in the second trial of Inez Garcia, and the successful appeal filed by Jordan, Nancy Stearns, and Liz Schneider for Yvonne Wanrow, the Spokane woman hobbling on crutches who killed a man for molesting her son. In 1977 the Washington State supreme court held in *Wanrow* that not only does the size and strength differential between men and women need to be considered, but also "women suffer from a conspicuous lack of access to training in and the means of developing those skills necessary to effectively repel a male assailant without resorting to the use of deadly weapons."

I had used similar arguments in *Against Our Will* to explain the nature of rape, but I had not anticipated that they would become an aid to defense lawyers representing desperate, half-crazed battered women who had seen no way out other than to kill their tormentors. Lawyers do what they must to win acquittals. Armed with the new, and newsworthy, feminist concepts—"battered women's syndrome," "unequal combat," and "imminent danger," their defense strategies helped focus a spotlight on domestic violence. One such case, the horrendous story of Francine Hughes, a battered woman who set fire to her husband's bed as he lay in a stupor, ended in acquittal on temporary insanity. Hughes had managed to save herself and her children before her house went up in flames. Her story became *The Burning Bed*, a book by Faith McNulty that was made into a prime-time television drama, starring Farrah Fawcett, in 1984.

Battered women who killed their tormentors were a very small part of the national picture, but every case that was publicized made the point that batterers needed to be stopped in their tracks by a responsive criminal justice system, beginning at the local precinct level, where too often a woman's calls for help went unheeded.

Every aspect of the battered women's movement—the shelters with their paid and unpaid staffs, the defense committees and legal strategies for women who killed their tormentors, the legislative initiatives on local, state, and federal levels, the advocates who helped their unfortunate clients thread their way through a confusing maze of social services, the writers who produced a steady stream of books and articles—played a role in uncovering the heretofore hidden phenomenon of domestic violence. As in all the causes unearthed and promoted by feminist activists and theoreticians, the earliest pioneers were dedicated utopians on a mission, but this time, with this issue, they really had a tiger by the tail. By tackling spouse abuse, they were challenging male supremacy and patriarchal rule inside the family, where for centuries, aided by tradition and papered over by the conservative tenets of religion and an indifferent criminal justice system, any outside interference had been kept at bay. Once the battered women's movement made its voice heard, a man's home was no longer his castle.

Replicating the experience of the stop-rape movement, the battered women's movement sought out and received government funds. The LEAA (Law Enforcement Assistance Administration) and the NIMH (National Institute of Mental Health), had allocated grants to antirape projects two years after the first rape crisis center was founded. Once again responding to a feminist initiative, the agencies began earmarking a portion of their budgets for the new campaign against domestic violence. After VISTA, a Nixon administration program, was phased out, CETA (the Comprehensive Employment and Training Act), a Carter administration program, took up the slack. Coveted CETA contracts enabled shelters to pay minimal salaries to a small number of staff workers.

The fierce scramble for government funds among competing groups exacerbated the differences in philosophy that inevitably arose among shelter programs. Some points of contention: how overtly feminist (or anticapitalist, or antihierarchical) should a shelter be? should advocates cooperate with the legal prosecution of a batterer when the victim doesn't want to see her husband jailed? how closely should the shelter movement work with child abuse interventions? how useful are group therapy programs for batterers, or for batterers and spouses? Many of the original shelter workers reacted with dismay when professional psychologists and social workers converged on the field in which they'd done the crucial spadework. Fearing that their movement's mainstream acceptance signaled that it was being taken away

from them—a common fate for radical activists who launch new issues—some intense ideologues seized on the imagined perfidy of others, bruiting about charges of racism, homophobia, class privilege. One
issue proved too close to home to be addressed at all at this time: physical violence and partner abuse in the lesbian community did not
emerge as a movement issue until the mid-1980s.

●　　●　　●

After the first, intense flush of excitement, the battered women's
movement was a tough venue to work in, perhaps the most difficult
of all the feminist causes. It suffered from burnout and divisive internal struggles stemming from the usual problems endemic to all
movements for social change—theoretical disputes, personality differences, ego trips, and power plays. Additionally, the women's prox-
imity to irrational violence, and to great fear and suffering, heightened their tensions. Shelter founders who started off as sisterly
comrades and fast friends were often at each other's throat a few years
down the line.

In San Francisco, Marya Grambs and Marta Segovia Ashley of La
Casa de las Madres had been a great team at the beginning, partly because they were such an unlikely combination. Marta was a Chicana
from a poor, working-class family who was drawn to social activism and
who also wanted to make films. Marya was a recently divorced young
mother seeking to put her master's degree in clinical psychology to
good use. Her mother taught at a university and wrote sociology textbooks, and her father worked in the federal government. But beneath
their class differences, the two young women shared a bond of terrible
family violence. Marta's stepfather had murdered her mother. Marya's
childhood home in a Washington suburb had been haunted by the
sounds of her unstable, alcoholic father beating her mother, who never
gathered the courage to leave him.

The founding of La Casa was a wonderful movement story. Marta
Segovia Ashley was housing battered women in sleeping bags in her
house when Marya Grambs, a volunteer at A Woman's Place bookstore, heard of her work and sought her out. Grambs had the skills that
Ashley needed to turn her dream of a full-service shelter into a reality.

"Joining up with Marta was my epiphany," Marya Grambs relates. "The violence in my childhood had derailed me for years. I'd had a breakdown at college, and it had taken me nine years to get my degree. Okay, it was too late for my mother, too late for me and my brother and sister and my father, but here was a chance to do something for others, a powerful, extraordinary, meaningful opportunity."

The two women had barely begun to work together when they were featured on a San Francisco television program, for such was the media's interest, in those days, in what feminists were doing. Marta and Marya were perfect in tandem. "Just fabulous," Marya recalls. Marta, flamboyant and charismatic, spoke of the macho resistance to dealing with battery in the Latino community. Marya, calm on the outside but inwardly quaking, offered a few select details from her childhood to make the point that battery was a form of male violence that cut across class lines. After the TV program their phones started ringing off the hook, and Marya sat down and wrote some grant proposals. In short order, La Casa de las Madres acquired a decrepit four-story Victorian house on a dead-end street in the Duboce Triangle, which the women furnished with twenty-five beds. Later the shelter moved into a vacated convent. As one of the first shelters in the nation, La Casa became the model for ten spin-offs in the Bay Area alone.

"People flocked to us to learn how to do it," Marya Grambs reminisces, "and we were so naive about everything. I mean, we were just going out of our hearts. I thought I'd spend my time doing counseling—that's what I'd been trained for—but instead I did administrative work and raised money. As a collective, we needed to make so many policy decisions. We decided not to take substance-abusing women, or women who were not honorable and honest. I think we debated and decided not to take in the sons of battered women if they were over sixteen. Whether or not to make the address of the shelter public was always an issue. A lot of our white women had been beaten in interracial relationships, but we decided not to make that public because it was too incendiary. And we always denied that there was a greater incidence of battery among low-income families, although the studies today show that it's true. There was always too much political correctness in the battered women's movement."

The battered women's movement dearly wished to be a model of harmony that cut across the divides of race, class, and culture, but negotiating the shoals of political correctness proved particularly sticky in one regard at La Casa. In her enthusiasm, Marya Grambs had involved many of her white, middle-class, college-educated lesbian friends in the shelter. Their lifestyles were at a great remove from the battered women of color on the La Casa staff, who were mainly heterosexual and working class, and had not had the benefits of a college education. It cut no ice with the battered women of color when the white lesbians maintained that they too were oppressed, marginalized pariahs in the outside world. Two and a half years after La Casa's inception, Marta Segovia Ashley and the battered women of color routed the middle-class white lesbians from their posts. "After an unsuccessful attempt at mediation, we capitulated," Grambs says. She departed for another shelter in Contra Costa. Ironically, Marta Segovia Ashley also departed La Casa soon after her victory, to pursue her interest in filmmaking. "La Casa was a mess for a long time," Grambs sighs.

Yolanda Bako, a founder of Women's Survival Space in Brooklyn, calls her years as a battered women's organizer "the best time in my life until I got demoralized and burnt out." The Bronx-born daughter of Hungarian immigrants had grown up in an abusive family. After high school she earned her living as a secretary and joined New York NOW, where she was soon heading a rape prevention project. ERA lobbying, NOW's priority that season, was too namby-pamby for her, but battered women's organizing was just beginning to take off. When some state funding finally came through, Bako and Jan Peterson set up their shelter in an obsolete maternity hospital in Brooklyn that was offered to them by the city. Barbara Omolade, an African nationalist and community organizer, was one of their first hires.

At Women's Survival Space, Bako mediated disputes between smokers and nonsmokers, women who cooked pork and those to whom it was an abomination, women who kept their quarters clean and women who didn't, and she worked double shifts when no one came to relieve her. She tried to be understanding when her purse got stolen, and tried to be equally accomodating to the funding organizations on whom they were dependent. I "bent myself into a pretzel," she sighs, "to fit the terms of the grants," traveling alone to San Juan one year to jump-start a battered women's project when she did not speak any Spanish. All these things were bearable, and often exciting.

July 20, 1977, ranked as one of the high points. Bako and a score of her counterparts from shelters around the country assembled in the Roosevelt Room of the White House with government staffers to discuss family violence and to offer their input on national legislation. The meeting, which had been Jan Peterson's idea, was arranged by Midge Costanza during her brief, lively tenure as President Carter's liaison to grassroots organizations and "special interest groups" such as theirs. Bako carefully preserved the paper napkin with the gold seal of the United States that came with her cup of coffee.

But other aspects of Bako's work were not bearable. She reflects, "At the Brooklyn shelter we saw stuff way above our abilities to handle. We took in substance-abusing battered women, schizophrenic battered women, battered women who were working as prostitutes, battered women who were hitting their kids. If you'd ask them about *that*, they'd say, 'How do you expect me to get my kids to behave?' At the shelter I had women with lifetime careers of being abused by many people and who were also abusing their own children. I remember one woman who had five children, each one with a different abusive spouse, and she was pregnant with her sixth. I had to strangle myself not to say anything negative. The way you get funding and church donations is to talk about pure victims. If you talk about the impurity of the victim, the sympathy vanishes. At this time I was still thinking I could change the world, but the truth is the shelter was not this collective sisterhood that we had hoped."

Betsy Warrior's hopes for collective sisterhood had been rudely shaken years earlier by the quarrels and dissolution of Boston's Cell 16, but the self-educated working-class theoretician persevered once again in the new movement for battered women. Betsy, who had not finished high school, was quick to say that she knew about battery firsthand from her seven-year marriage. She helped out at Transition House, a shelter in Cambridge founded by Chris Mendez and Cheri Jimenez, two women on welfare who had left their abusive husbands but kept their names—although Chris Mendez altered hers to Womendez, as a feminist statement.

Betsy's go-to-meeting days were behind her. She viewed the National Coalition Against Domestic Violence, the strategizing and networking effort that had drawn in Yolando Bako of Brooklyn and Sharon Vaughan of St. Paul, with the weariness of a battle-scarred veteran. The National Coalition people were sincere, she felt, but too many of them "wanted to meet, meet, meet all the time," and she was beyond that. Plus, she could see the handwriting on the wall. Careerists, social workers, professionals of all stripes were jumping onto the battery bandwagon, and she had never gotten on with those types. In all her years as a radical activist she hadn't earned a penny from the movement, and that wasn't about to change. So she never went to the conferences, the steering committees, the regional sessions. Instead she turned her apartment into an international clearinghouse for shelter information. Using index cards and an IBM Selectric, she compiled a Battered Women's Directory of shelters, hot lines, and legal services in all fifty states. When the information on shelters started flooding in from abroad, she added those listings, too. "I was not a good typist," she sighs, "but I got volunteers to help me."

The Directory was not just a directory. Betsy included news clips and articles that interested her, and printed some of her own essays, too. She did the layout herself and put in pictures that she and Cheri Jimenez drew to break up the columns of type. Betsy Warrior's directory was an invaluable service at a time when shelters were popping up nationwide and people were eager to make connections. The work wasn't easy. Shelter addresses changed constantly, and there were always new listings to be added. Getting out each new, revised edition and scrounging up the money to pay the printer was a full-time job, but Betsy somehow managed it while working part-time as a janitor, a library clerk, a gas station attendant, even going on welfare when she had to.

When technology changed, Betsy acquired a computer and taught herself WordStar. That speeded up the process. And then one day she received a call from someone in Washington who said that her group had gotten a grant to produce a directory of services for battered women, and could Betsy please send along her lists to help them compile theirs? "I couldn't believe it," she says. "I'd been *doing* the work for years while *they'd* been out looking for *grants*." The ninth and final edition of Betsy Warrior's self-published Battered Women's Directory, 283 pages, appeared in 1985.

I watched the battered women's movement from a sisterly distance, and was deeply impressed even as I developed philosophic differences with some of its tenets. The larger women's movement had begun to lump rape and battery together under the general rubric of "violence against women," and I thought that was sloppy thinking. Rape was a one-time event, whether it happened in the context of a date or was committed by a stranger, or strangers, unknown to the victim. Battery was systemic violence within an intimate, ongoing, emotionally complex relationship. Any woman could become a victim of rape, but a pattern of physical abuse in a long-standing relationship begged for further interpretation.

The battered women's movement seemed off to a good start in its early years. Lenore Walker's first book offered interesting observations about the pervasive sense of guilt and the low self-worth of the battered women she studied, their denials, manipulations, chronic depressions, and uncanny ability to withstand enormous amounts of pain during a violent episode, their secret fears of not being conventionally feminine, their agonizing dread of failing at the supreme test of keeping a man. I hoped that Walker and other theorists would pursue these important lines of inquiry. Instead, movement theory went into stasis, to avoid the trap of "blaming the victim."

It seemed to me that many of the battered women's advocates developed a bunker mentality marked by rigid and fixed positions partly because of the enormity of the violence they were confronting, immersed as they were in what amounted to a war zone. Shelter volunteers and staff workers heard war stories every day; they saw the bruises, the black eyes, the effects of the broken ribs. Identifying with the guarded, fearful personalities of the women they were championing, they oversimplified the complexities of male-female relations and publicly characterized batterers as all-powerful brutes, and the women in their sway as pure victims, even when they had reason to know better.

The battered women's movement developed a serious blind spot in its refusal to take a hard look at the women who stayed in battering relationships or who returned to their deadly batterers again and again. "Fear," "economic dependence," and "society's lack of options" became the only permissible answers to the nagging question "Why doesn't she leave?" The question became the movement's bugaboo, and still is today.

In England, Erin Pizzey tackled the question head-on in her 1982 book, *Prone to Violence*. Pizzey's refuges were famous for taking the most difficult cases; in ten years of work she had seen too many of her women go back to their abusers, only to be killed at their hands. After one such tragedy, she invented a powerful new slogan: "No Man Is Worth Dying For." Reluctantly but inexorably, Pizzey arrived at the conclusion that some women sought out abusive relationships, at least subconsciously. For years she hesitated to discuss her findings, afraid the vast majority of nonrepeaters would be lumped with the violence-prone in the public's mind, but the time had become ripe, she felt, for a more sophisticated analysis of the hard-core cases. In her analysis, some women, subjected to violent abuse since childhood, had become "cross-wired" for pleasure and pain. Others, she theorized, were addicted to the rush of adrenaline that accompanied the drama of a big battle. Pizzey's findings were anecdotal and speculative, but, never one to shrink from controversy, she did not mince her words.

Neither did her infuriated opponents in Women's Aid Federation, the wing of the British battered women's movement that had long wished she'd disappear. "I was picketed at a lovely luncheon at the Savoy," she laughs bitterly. "The banners read ALL MEN ARE RAPISTS/ALL MEN ARE BATTERERS/ERIN PIZZEY IS THE ENEMY! It happened again when I spoke at St. Andrews University in Scotland. Scottish Women's Aid handed out leaflets with the charming words 'Erin Pizzey says women like to be beaten!'"

Pizzey became a prophet without honor in her home country and in the United States. Scorned by the movement she founded, she turned to writing novels, lush historical romances, to keep body and soul together. When I interviewed her for this book, she was living in Tuscany, divorced from her second husband, tending to her dogs, cats, and manuscripts, and waiting tables at a cafe while organizing a women's group in town. She has since returned to England, where she continues to write and publish.

After nearly a decade of feminist agitation in concert with legislative initiatives pioneered by Representative Lindy Boggs and Senator Barbara Mikulski, Congress passed the Family Violence Prevention and Services Act in 1984. Today, approximately eighteen hundred battered women's shelters, hot lines, and advocacy programs around the country are funded by the federal program.

My public quarrel with the battered women's movement did not take place until 1989 during one of the most avidly watched trials of the decade. I wish I had known then of Pizzey's *Prone to Violence*. I would have felt less alone.

I was watching the local TV news on the night in November 1987 when the Steinberg-Nussbaum case broke. Three days later I opened a new file in my computer and wrote the first page of a novel. Usually I tamped down my intermittent impulses to write fiction, but I was driven to imagine my way inside the world of my Greenwich Village neighbors Joel Steinberg, a lawyer, and his battered common-law wife Hedda Nussbaum, a children's book author and editor. I needed to understand the *folie à deux* that led to the death by Joel's hands of the six-year-old, Lisa, they called their adopted daughter. Crack cocaine played a crucial role in my novel, as I learned it had in the true story. I believed the delusions induced by freebasing, as much as Joel's disfiguring beatings, lay behind Hedda's profound disintegration and her failure to summon medical help for fourteen hours while Lisa lay dying.

Waverly Place, my roman à clef of a classic batterer and the narcissistic woman who fell under his sway, was published one year after I saw that first news report, during Joel Steinberg's trial but before his sentencing for second-degree murder. A new team at *Ms.* led by the Australian writer Anne Summers urged me to write an article about the case, feeling as I did that Hedda bore a serious share of responsibility for Lisa's death. We agreed it was time to stop excusing the behavior of all battered women by claiming each one was a helpless victim, a polit-ically correct but, to our minds, a psychologically and morally unten-able stance that damaged the movement's credibility. Furthermore, it was sending the wrong message to women in abusive relationships who needed to break free. Nussbaum's evasive testimony for the prosecu-tion, which she gave in exchange for immunity, served only to strengthen my views, so when *The New York Times* asked me to write a short essay defining her moral and criminal accountability, I was glad to comply in that venue as well.

Enraged battered-women's advocates saw my opinions in *The Times* and *Ms.* as a stab in the back to the movement. A pro-Hedda petition was circulated, and an acrimonious dialogue, feminist against feminist, was played out on *Nightline* and *Oprah*. Gloria Steinem addressed a pro-Hedda rally on the steps of the criminal court building, and the new team at *Ms.* capitulated, adding their names to the Hedda petition and printing a few self-serving words from Nussbaum in a subsequent issue.

The Hedda controversy seems very long ago to me now, but some of my movement friendships never recovered from the debate.

ITS NAME IS
SEXUAL HARASSMENT

As THE SILENCE on rape and battery gave way to a new awareness, sexual harassment in the workplace was named and launched as yet another urgent feminist cause. Narratives explaining how we got here from there are seldom tidy, for new ideas usually reach for the light simultaneously in many places, but the origins of this particular breakthrough are ineluctably precise. Its opening salvos were sounded in Ithaca, New York, in 1975, on Cornell University's hilly, tree-lined campus.

In one of many responses to a militant decade, Cornell had created a program called Human Affairs to bridge the gap between the privileged Ivy League school and the surrounding community. Teachers from nonacademic backgrounds were hired to initiate fieldwork and conduct seminars in such gritty problems as prison reform and urban redevelopment. The women's section was a late addition, an afterthought really, and the three friends who got it moving were lesbian feminists with a strong labor orientation. "We saw ourselves as Saul Alinsky–style community organizers," says Karen Sauvigne, who had trained with the Quakers and worked for the ACLU.

Lin Farley established the feminist beachhead at Human Affairs with a seminar on "women and work" in 1974. She was able to bring in Karen Sauvigne and Susan Meyer the following January when the two recruits, then lovers and partners, agreed to share one job line.

Meyer, an antiwar activist with SDS in Ann Arbor during her student days, had been in the *Rat* collective. Farley, who'd worked for a while as an Associated Press reporter, had testified at the 1971 New York Radical Feminist Conference on Rape. Her account had been so vivid that I'd included an excerpt in *Against Our Will*: "Did you ever see a rabbit stuck in the glare of your headlights when you were going down a road at night? Transfixed, like it knew it was going to get it— that's what happened." Sauvigne was in a NYRF consciousness-raising group during the hectic time when she, Meyer, and Farley were organizing for Lesbian Feminist Liberation in its break from the Gay Activist Alliance. At Cornell all the strands of the friends' political work were to come together.

One afternoon a former university employee sought out Lin Farley to ask for her help. Carmita Wood, age forty-four, born and raised in the apple orchard region of Lake Cayuga, and the sole support of two of her children, had worked for eight years in Cornell's department of nuclear physics, advancing from lab assistant to a desk job handling administrative chores. Wood did not know why she had been singled out, or indeed if she had been singled out, but a distinguished professor seemed unable to keep his hands off her.

As Wood told the story, the eminent man would jiggle his crotch when he stood near her desk and looked at his mail, or he'd deliberately brush against her breasts while reaching for some papers. One night as the lab workers were leaving their annual Christmas party, he cornered her in the elevator and planted some unwanted kisses on her mouth. After the Christmas party incident, Carmita Wood went out of her way to use the stairs in the lab building in order to avoid a repeat encounter, but the stress of the furtive molestations and her efforts to keep the scientist at a distance while maintaining cordial relations with his wife, whom she liked, brought on a host of physical symptoms. Wood developed chronic back and neck pains. Her right thumb tingled and grew numb. She requested a transfer to another department, and when it didn't come through, she quit. She walked out the door and went to Florida for some rest and recuperation. Upon her return she applied for unemployment insurance. When the claims investigator asked why she had left her job after eight years, Wood was at a loss to describe the hateful episodes. She was ashamed and embarrassed. Under prodding—the blank on the form needed to be filled in—she answered that her reasons had been personal. Her claim for unemployment benefits was denied.

"Lin's students had been talking in her seminar about the unwanted sexual advances they'd encountered on their summer jobs," Sauvigne relates. "And then Carmita Wood comes in and tells Lin *her* story. We realized that to a person, every one of us—the women on staff, Carmita, the students—had had an experience like this at some point, you know? And none of us had ever told anyone before. It was one of those *click, aha!* moments, a profound revelation."

The women had their issue. Meyer located two feminist lawyers in Syracuse, Susan Horn and Maurie Heins, to take on Carmita Wood's unemployment insurance appeal. "And then, because we were Alinsky-style labor organizers who had come out of Radical Feminists," Sauvigne reports, "we decided that we also had to hold a speak-out in order to break the silence about this."

The "this" they were going to break the silence about had no name. "Eight of us were sitting in an office of Human Affairs," Sauvigne remembers, "brainstorming about what we were going to write on the posters for our speak-out. We were referring to it as 'sexual intimidation,' 'sexual coercion,' 'sexual exploitation on the job.' None of those names seemed quite right. We wanted something that embraced a whole range of subtle and unsubtle persistent behaviors. Somebody came up with 'harassment.' *Sexual harassment!* Instantly we agreed. That's what it was."

In line with their mission at Human Affairs, the leaders did not want the speak-out to be "just a Cornell event" dominated by students. Calling themselves Working Women United, they reached out to nearby Ithaca College, set their alarms at 5:30 A.M. to leaflet at the town's two big factories, Ithaca Gun and Morse Chain, and surreptitiously deposited stacks of flyers at the town's banks. Letters announcing their campaign were mailed to eighty women lawyers and law students on one of Sauvigne's national lists. The *Ithaca Journal* and two local radio stations ran stories about Carmita Wood's unemployment insurance appeal and the upcoming speak-out on sexual harassment. Because of the sensitive nature of the accusations, no one dared utter the name of the professor, but that didn't matter. The pioneer work in naming sexual harassment already had surpassed the details of one case.

Saturday afternoon, May 4, 1975, was a typically rainy spring day in Tompkins County. The organizers were ecstatic as nearly three hundred women carrying ponchos and umbrellas crowded into the downtown Greater Ithaca Activities Center for the first speak-out in the world on sexual harassment. Carmita Wood was sitting up front with her adult daughter Angela, who'd come down from Buffalo to support her mother and to testify about her own experiences with sexual harassment on the job. Connie Korbel, who worked in Cornell's department of personnel, was there for her friend Carm, and to tell of work-related harassment she, too, had suffered. "There's lots of things that have happened on my jobs that I've never told anyone," Korbel said at the microphone. "Each single individual piece maybe didn't seem that important, but when you start thinking about them over your lifetime of work, you begin to wonder, why did this have to happen to me?"

Three waitresses spoke of their harassment by customers and bosses. "What are the statistics for waitresses?" one asked. "I'd say one hundred percent." A mailroom clerk, a factory shop steward, a secretary, an assistant professor, and an apprentice filmmaker took the microphone to add their stories. The inappropriate male behavior in the workplace revealed at the speak-out ran the gamut: crude propositions to barter sex for employment, physical overtures and masturbatory displays, verbal abuse and hostile threats that appeared patently designed to intimidate a woman and drive her out of her job.

Before everyone left to go home, Susan Meyer handed out Working Women United questionnaires. A striking 70 percent of the respondents, admittedly self-selected, had experienced some form of sexual harassment at work. Unsurprisingly, most of the women had not reported the incidents. They didn't want to make waves and lose their jobs; they feared their complaints would be dismissed as trivial; they'd agonized that the leering, pinching, and behind-patting, the sneaky feels and verbal propositions, were things a mature, "together" person should be able to handle.

Thanks to events that had been set in motion a month before the

Ithaca speak-out, the women's testimony that day would receive national attention. Lin Farley had learned that Eleanor Holmes Norton, New York City's Commissioner on Human Rights, was conducting hearings on patterns of discrimination faced by women in blue-collar and service-industry jobs. Seizing her opportunity, Farley had written to Norton brandishing her Cornell credentials and asking for a chance to testify. When her moment came, she half expected to be laughed out of the hearing room.

"The titillation value of sexual harassment always was obvious to us," Farley recalls. "When we leafleted outside the Ithaca factories, we were greeted by smirks and jokes. But Eleanor Holmes Norton treated the issue with dignity and great seriousness." Norton, who had monitored protest demonstrations and arrests in the South for the civil rights movement while studying law at Yale, was an instinctive, gut feminist, particularly when the cause was work-related. She had taken the *Newsweek* women's discrimination complaint back in 1969, pushing the researchers to the next level of militancy with her exhortation "Take off your gloves, ladies, take off your white gloves." So when Farley, her voice high and quaking, outlined the dimensions of sexual harassment and its effect on the physical health and ambitions of women in the workforce, Eleanor Holmes Norton asked the right, approving questions.

Reporter Enid Nemy, who usually strolled the trendy beat of society and fashion, was covering the hearings for the Family/Style page of *The New York Times*, an odd assignment for her, but evidently someone higher up had decided that Commissioner Norton's investigations were too "soft" for a business or labor reporter. Although she was not one of the paper's vocal feminists, Nemy had no trouble spotting an original news story in sexual harassment. She persuaded her editor to send her to Ithaca for the May 4 speak-out, and did follow-up interviews between other assignments. The story took a long time to piece together. But when it finally appeared in August 1975, "Women Begin to Speak Out Against Sexual Harassment at Work" sprawled across the Family/Style page and got national syndication. Lin Farley's list of intimidating behaviors appeared in the third paragraph: constant leering and ogling, pinching and squeezing, verbal sexual abuse, persistent brushing against a woman's body, catching a woman alone for forced sexual intimacies, outright sexual propositions backed by threat of losing a job, forced sexual relations.

"Nemy's story put sexual harassment on the map," Karen Sauvigne affirms. "Suddenly we had the authority of the *Times* behind us. We could point to it and say, Look, the *Times* says. . . . This may sound hard to believe, but we were still encountering resistance among some feminists. The first time we approached the Ms. Foundation for money, they turned us down. Later, of course, they were very helpful, but at the time, they told us that sexual harassment wasn't a bread-and-butter issue because it was not about equal pay for equal work. We utterly failed to persuade them that women were losing their jobs over this, that sexual harassment contributed to the discouragement and dead-end nature of women's careers."

"Career Women Decry Sexual Harassment by Bosses and Clients" was *The Wall Street Journal*'s special angle for its readers in a front-page feature in January 1976. The problem was murky and few corporations were taking it seriously, the *Journal* reported, but the EEOC was saying that sexual harassment was unlawful sex discrimination. *Redbook*, "the magazine for young mothers," did the first national survey that year. Eighty-eight percent of the magazine's nine thousand respondents had an incident to report. In June 1977, Letty Cottin Pogrebin used her column in the *Ladies' Home Journal* to ask, "Why haven't we heard more about this problem?"

That November, *Ms.* finally got its act together and ran freelancer Karen Lindsey's cover story. Mary Thom remembers the excitement as the editors readied their package, which noted the epidemic proportions of harassment on Capitol Hill and at the United Nations. The *Ms.* women held a speak-out-style press conference, which garnered a second *Times* headline, "Women Tell of Sexual Harassment at Work." Susan Meyer of Working Women United succinctly described the campaign's status: "It's where rape was five years ago." By the end of the decade every women's magazine had weighed in on the new issue.

Carmita Wood, whose case began everything, did not win her unemployment insurance appeal, but Cornell University found her a job in another department. Karen Sauvigne and Susan Meyer had an unfortunate falling-out with Lin Farley, an escalation of their long-run-ning quarrel over who actually named sexual harassment. Farley in-sisted that she had come up with the magic defining phrase. Sauvigne and Meyer argued that if eight people were tossing around words in one room, the eureka moment belonged to the group. It was a typical, destructive movement squabbling, the kind that dedicated activists of-ten fell prey to in the absence of sufficient recognition for their work.

The members of the Cornell team went their separate ways. Lin Farley started a book, *Sexual Shakedown: The Sexual Harassment of Women on the Job*. After twenty-seven rejections it was finally published in 1978. "I thought my book would change the workplace," she told me years later when it was no longer in print and few people remembered her name or her contribution. Karen Sauvigne and Susan Meyer moved Working Women United to Manhattan, where it became a clearinghouse and data bank for sexual harassment cases that were springing up at random around the country. Aggrieved complainants were filing for unemployment insurance, like Carmita Wood, or trying for workers' compensation. Some were going into court to sue their employers or bringing complaints to their local human rights commis-sions. Working with a large map and color-coded pushpins, Sauvigne and Meyer tried to match up unrepresented litigants with volunteer lawyers.

These were the years of the first landmark litigations. Across the river in New Jersey, Adrienne Tomkins, an office worker recently pro-moted to secretary at the Public Service Electric and Gas Company, had innocently gone out for drinks with her new boss to discuss her up-coming work evaluation. The atmosphere turned ugly when Tomkins refused to go along with her boss's plans for the rest of the evening. As a result her fortunes at the company took a sudden nosedive, and even-tually she was fired. Tomkins complained to the Newark office of the EEOC, where an investigator issued her a "right to sue" letter. Nadine Taub, director of the women's rights litigation clinic at Rutgers, was appointed by the court to represent her. "The judge said my students would find the case interesting," Taub remembers. "I'm still not sure exactly what he meant." When Tomkins and Taub won the first round, the utilities company appealed.

"We packed the courtroom with students," Taub recalls. "An EEOC lawyer from Washington joined the case, and an Associated Press stringer put the details on the wire. I'm no Perry Mason but I like to think that it was the way I argued that won the day." Public Service Electric and Gas gave Tomkins a cash settlement and agreed to set up procedures for sexual harassment complaints, and to put a notice announcing the new policy in every worker's pay envelope. "A few women like Adrienne stuck their necks out," says Taub. "That's how the case law developed."

By 1977 three pioneer cases argued at the appellate level had confirmed a harassed woman's right to sue her corporate employer under Title VII of the 1964 Civil Rights Act. From that point forward the EEOC became the most important means of redress, and company responsibility for the errant actions of department heads and supervisors became the key to a lawsuit.

Adrienne Tomkins happened to be white, but most of the aggrieved women seeking justice in these and other pioneer cases were working class and black. Paulette Barnes was a payroll clerk who sued her employer, the Environmental Protection Agency, after losing her job because she had fended off her white supervisor. Margaret Miller was an equipment operator who had been fired by her white supervisor after a similar hassle. Diane Williams was an African-American public information clerk at the Department of Justice who was hit on by her black supervisor and given a poor job performance rating that led to her dismissal when she refused to comply. Rebekah Barnett, another African-American complainant, was a shop clerk. The phenomenon of black women under sexual siege did not go away after this early flurry of cases. The case of Mechelle Vinson, a bank trainee, would become the subject of a Supreme Court ruling in 1986. Black women were significant at every stage in sexual harassment law.

It's interesting to speculate why so many of the courageous litigants were women of color, just as it's interesting to ponder the significance of lesbian feminist leadership in the naming and launching of sexual harassment. I'm inclined to believe that neither phenomenon was totally accidental. I believe lesbian feminists, the angriest of the angry, initially saw unwanted sexual attention by men with greater clarity than their heterosexual sisters and were less of a mind to be persuaded that it was vaguely complimentary or basically trivial. And black women, emerging from a history of slavery, segregation, job discrimination, and sexual abuse, were fighting mad. Doors were beginning to open for them, and then, *bam*, the same old story, opportunity turning to ashes. The success of race discrimination complaints during this time may have encouraged women of color to pursue their rights in cases of sexual harassment.

The first cases to get a sympathetic hearing by the courts were basically "boss fires worker after she rejects his demand for sex," and the first Hollywood movie to deal with sexual harassment mined the same territory. Produced by Jane Fonda's IPC films, the broadly comedic *Nine to Five* starred Fonda, Lily Tomlin, and Dolly Parton, with Parton playing the plucky secretary who fends off her lecherous boss. The movie's inspiration had come straight from the unionizing efforts of Karen Nussbaum, a clerk-typist in Cleveland and an old buddy of Fonda's from the antiwar movement, who was attempting to organize women office workers through a national network called Nine to Five. Released in 1980, the loopy comedy was a commercial success.

The boss/underling relationship with its obvious hammer of unequal power was only part of the workplace problem. The next logical step in understanding sexual harassment was for the general public, and the courts, to appreciate its lateral dimensions. It didn't require a lecherous boss to make a woman's work life intolerable. Often the harassing culprits were her coworkers, whose forms of hazing—taunts, catcalls, practical jokes, plastering her work space with pornography, sabotaging her projects, etc.—seemed less driven by libido than by the desire to drive her out of a male preserve.

Two key developments took place in the waning days of the Carter administration. In September 1980, the Merit Systems Protections Board, a regulatory agency seldom in the news, released the findings of a questionnaire distributed randomly to 23,000 male and female federal employees. Of the 21,000 who replied, Merit Board chair Ruth Prokop told Congress, 42 percent of the women and 15 percent of the men reported at least one incident of sexual harassment. Ninety-five percent of the harassers were men, whose actions ranged from outright sexual assault to garden-variety offenses: sexual jokes and pressure for dates, touching, pinching, disturbing letters and phone calls. To the surprise of those who had created the survey, a majority of the harassers, 60 percent, were roughly on the same job level as their targets. Unsurprisingly, only 2 percent of the victims had made a formal complaint. "This was the first decent methodological study," says Freada Klein, an adviser to the project who had pioneered work on sexual harassment in Boston.

One happy thrust of the Carter presidency had been the appointment of Eleanor Holmes Norton to direct the Equal Employment Opportunity Commission. The civil rights lawyer took her understanding of sexual harassment with her. "When I came to the Commission, there were a few good court cases but everything was tentative," Norton remembers. "Frankly, the floodgates never opened, and I thought I knew why. In sexual harassment there is so much risk in stepping forward, plus most women did not understand it to be a violation of federal law. I became convinced that the best way to get rid of it was to make employers proactive. That meant more EEOC guidelines. So here comes Norton with some more guidelines."

Two weeks after Ronald Reagan's landslide in the November 1980 elections, Norton seized the initiative and issued her new guidelines. Released as her EEOC tenure was about to expire, her terse one-page memorandum stated that sexual activity as a condition of employment or promotion was a violation of Title VII, as was the creation of an offensive, intimidating, hostile working environment. Verbal abuse alone might be sufficient proof of damage.

"Prevention is the best tool for the elimination of sexual harassment," the EEOC memo advised. Employers were urged to develop their own guidelines, complaint channels, and sanctions, inform employees of their rights, and take steps "to sensitize all concerned." With the wind at their backs and the responsibility resting squarely on their shoulders, major corporations began summoning experts like Freada Klein to set up sensitivity-training programs and harassment guidelines.

While a law student at Yale, Catharine MacKinnon had learned of the Cornellians' work on behalf of Carmita Wood. She also had a family connection to one of the pioneer Title VII harassment cases through her father, who was one of three judges on the panel deciding the case of Paulette Barnes (although Judge MacKinnon's concurrence attempted to narrow its scope). The young lawyer went to work on a book, *Sexual Harassment of Working Women*, which was published in 1979 by Yale University Press. Its timing was premature for a full-dress treatment of "hostile work environment," but the academic volume made effective use of the early quid pro quo cases to weave some impassioned theories that ventured far beyond questions of job discrimination.

MacKinnon seemed to suggest that sexual harassment was a paradigm for the power imbalance of the male-female sex act, or perhaps the sex act was a paradigm for the inequality of male-female relations. She was oddly dismissive of government attempts to regulate workplace harassment, because, she wrote, regulation smacked of "repressive impositions of state morality." In her words, "Inventing special rules of morality for the workplace would institutionalize new taboos rather than confront the fact that it is *women* who are systematically disadvantaged by the old ones." I found the book obfuscatory and dense; its author was more impressive as a speaker. In 1986, when the Supreme Court heard its first sexual harassment appeal, *Meritor Savings Bank v. Vinson*, and ruled in Mechelle Vinson's favor, MacKinnon was on Vinson's team under lead counsel Patricia Barry. Possessed of aristocratic features and a magnetic personality that conveyed urgency and earnestness with lithe, physically expressive charm, Kitty MacKinnon won many admirers in the press. Over the years they would convey the impression that she had single-handedly invented, if not quite named, sexual harassment law. Her identification with the issue was to cut both ways. MacKinnon would acquire devotees claiming her as the leading theoretical thinker on the frontier of sexual justice, and she would gain detractors who perceived her as the avenging angel giving birth, in the 1990s, to Monica Lewinsky and Paula Corbin Jones. Both views were exaggerated, in my opinion.

Sexual harassment simmered on a back burner for fifteen years as one of those "yes, that too" feminist struggles. Then came that memorable Friday, October 11, 1991, when Anita Hill's testimony before the Senate Judiciary Committee erupted on national TV and made front-page news the next morning throughout the country. No one was prepared for the force of the explosion. Demure, poised, and achingly refined in a blue linen suit, Hill had been a last-ditch witness, a card that few wanted to play, in the desperate effort by frustrated liberals to scuttle the nomination of Clarence Thomas, a conservative Republican and an exceedingly weak jurist, to the Supreme Court.

The thirty-five-year-old law professor from the University of Oklahoma, the youngest of thirteen children in a devout Baptist family, had a story to tell, but it was unlike any story that had ever come to light before at a Senate confirmation hearing. A month of exploratory phone calls to her home in Norman, Oklahoma, from various Democratic senatorial aides had preceded her appearance. In the initial overtures from Washington, Hill was assured that a signed statement would suffice and that her name could be kept confidential, but either the aides were playing cat and mouse with her or they were woefully ill advised. As Thomas's confirmation loomed as a near certainty, Hill grew stronger in her resolve to step forward. She signed a "personal statement" that was shown to a few committee members, and then to Clarence Thomas, who filed a sworn denial. Next, Hill's name and a portion of her allegations were leaked to *Newsday* and National Public Radio. Perhaps she still could have backed off, gone into hiding, but Anita Hill did not think that Clarence Thomas possessed the judicial temperament to be a Supreme Court justice. So she pushed aside her natural reticence to face the klieg lights and relive events from the first term of the Reagan administration, from 1981 to 1983, when she worked for Thomas, first at the Department of Education and next at the EEOC after Thomas, ironically, was appointed director.

For eight hours Anita Hill kept much of the nation spellbound as she recounted her troubling time in government service under the man President Bush intended to place on the highest court in the land: Over a period of three years, Thomas had subverted their professional relationship by pestering her for dates and assailing her with an intermittent stream of crude banter. He had mortified his young assistant with descriptions of big-breasted women having sex with dogs in bestiality movies, suggesting she might benefit from watching the films, and had referred to his penis as Long Dong Silver in a braggadocio claim for his sexual prowess. Unable to discourage his sexual importuning, Hill was hospitalized for five days with acute stomach pain that she attributed to the stress. In her version of the story, it appeared that Thomas seldom missed an opportunity to steer the office conversation toward sex. Once, reaching for a can of soda, he exclaimed, "Who put the pubic hair on my Coke?"

Thomas's aggressively raunchy behavior, so obviously hurtful to Hill's sensibilities, hardly befitted the image of a solemn deliberator on the Supreme Court. Wrinkling her nose during her testimony, Hill labeled it "disgusting." As I watched and listened on my home TV, I thought "puerile" was a better label. The harassment Hill had sustained was particularly bizzare for having taken place at the EEOC, the federal agency empowered to protect people from job discrimination, but as harassment went, it was relatively mild. I'd seen and heard far worse and so had many women, particularly those making inroads in skilled labor and other "nontraditional" occupations, from brokerage houses to firehouses and points in between. On the other hand, their harassers weren't up for jobs on the highest court in the land.

That same year, 1991, a shipyard welder named Lois Robinson, one of a small handful of skilled females among several hundred men, aired a horrendous case of a hostile, intimidating work environment before a Florida court. Spread-eagle labia shots from porn magazines had festooned the locker room and dry-dock area of the Jacksonville shipyard where she worked. "Lick me you whore dog bitch" was scrawled on the wall where Robinson hung her jacket. "Pussy" and "Eat me" were spray-painted over her work station during a break when she went to get a drink of water. Male co-workers hooted in her presence, "Hey, pussycat, give me a whiff"; "I'd like some of that"; "The more you lick the harder it gets"; "Women taste like sardines." The court ruled in Robinson's case that a reasonable woman had a right to find such a working environment abusive, and that its corrosive impact would damage her job performance.

Anita Hill was a very proper, sheltered young woman who had been out of school for only three years when Clarence Thomas humiliated her with his sexual insinuations, while I was a sophisticated, politically

active New Yorker from a generation that had learned to survive by developing a hard shell. I had to admit that Hill was raising fresh questions for me. How much discomfort should a woman have to tolerate
at work? To what lengths need she go to toughen herself in order to
stay on a job and perhaps to advance and prosper? I doubted that Hill
would have had a clear-cut, winnable case if she'd pursued her grievances in court. Her career had not been adversely affected; she had
segued nicely from her government job into academia, helped by a rec-
ommendation from Thomas. Despite the humiliation she had endured,
she would have been hard put to prove harm in a legal sense. But, like
most women who suffer in offensive work conditions, Anita Hill had
not tried to make a case of it. "Perhaps I should have taken angry or
even militant steps," she said in her prepared remarks. "I took no initiative to inform anyone. But when I was asked by a representative of
this committee to report my experience, I felt that I had to tell the
truth. I could not keep silent."

Thus was the battle drawn between a judge and a professor, between
a black man and a black woman, between the loyal teammates of President Bush, who had seen two earlier nominees for the high court go
down in flames, and the flustered liberal Democrats whose list of serious objections to this nominee had not included, until that fateful Friday, his sexual behavior toward women at work. Clarence Thomas held
a press conference to deny every piece of Anita Hill's story and to call
the hearings "a high-tech lynching." Rallying after their momentary
confusion, his Republican supporters regrouped to attack Hill's credibility like criminal defense lawyers hammering away at a victim of rape.
Through innuendo, conjecture, and ugly misstatement, Senators Orrin
Hatch, Alan Simpson, and Arlen Specter led the charge to destroy her.
Anita Hill was accused of seeking revenge because Thomas had
spurned her romantic interest, of concocting bizarre fantasies gleaned
from *The Exorcist*, of suffering from a delusional state of "erotomania,"
and finally, of committing perjury. I'd never seen such hypocritical
slander.

Hill's accusations, Thomas's denials, and the squalid, specious attacks on Hill's mental stability played in the news as a "She Said, He
Said" story. The reportage stoked the resentment of many African-

Americans, who noted that no white man of Judge Thomas's stature had ever had his penis discussed in public (though that time would come soon enough, and on that occasion the man would be the president of the United States). Neither did the stories assuage the agitation of women who learned the steep price, if they hadn't already known, of bearing witness in sexual matters. Pollsters reported that the majority of Americans felt the embarrassing spectacle had gone too far and accomplished little. (However, the hearings, which extended through the weekend, outstripped live television coverage of the baseball play-offs.)

But for all the hand-wringing about what the country was coming to, the Hill/Thomas face-off demonstrated, as had no other public forum before it, the vast gulf in perception between the two sexes—of behavior enacted by men as ribald fun, and behavior experienced by women as distressing, intimidating, humiliating, and degrading. Through an accidental chain of political events, Anita Hill had stepped unexpectedly into a glaring spotlight to stand in for every woman who had ever put up with a sexually toxic workplace. What the nation witnessed as she was pilloried by the Senate Judiciary Committee may not have matched the legal definition of sexual harassment, but it was close enough to be instructive. In the wake of Anita Hill, harassment complaints filed with the EEOC doubled; damages awarded in court cases soared dramatically, enabled by the Civil Rights Act of 1991; companies that previously had not addressed the problem hauled in employees for mandatory educative seminars and sensitivity training; and voters turning out for the 1992 elections doubled the number of women in the U.S. Senate.

Supreme Court Justice Clarence Thomas squeaked through his confirmation by a narrow margin; his subsequent record on the Court has been lackluster at best. Professor Anita Hill maintained her dignity, to emerge from her ordeal as a respected symbol of women's rights.

•   •   •

Giving a name to sexual harassment, as the women in Ithaca did when they took up the case of Carmita Wood in 1975, put into bold relief a pernicious form of job discrimination that previously had been laughed at, trivialized, and ignored. In the process, the women set in motion a new understanding in business corporations, in the halls of Congress, in the military, in the school systems, and in courts of law. The discourse surrounding this issue remains vigorous and expansive, if occasionally confused and contradictory. (I'm mindful that some people fear"sexual harassment" has become so broad a concept that it could encompass all sorts of innocent behavior, but I don't think we need worry about a Jacobin terror just yet.)

Sexual harassment was conceptualized by the women's movement as discriminatory behavior directed by men against women, and the law, in its reflection of popular thinking, followed that path for twenty years. In a major but salutary departure in 1998, the Supreme Court recognized same-sex harassment on the job as unlawful, too, when Joseph Oncale, hired as an oil rigger on an offshore platform, won the right to sue his Louisiana employer and three crewmates for singling him out for crude sex play and threats of rape that intimidated him into quitting the job after four months. (Oncale's slight build and sensitive disposition apparently led his tormentors to mistakenly assume he was gay.) Perhaps male-on-male harassment was not "a principal evil" in workplace discrimination, the Court remarked, and perhaps this particular form of harm had not been envisioned by the framers of Title VII in 1964, but it was discrimination nonetheless.

The 1998 ruling was long overdue.

THE PORNOGRAPHY WARS

THE RADICAL WOMEN'S MOVEMENT was already flagging when feminists started fighting feminists in the terrible pornography wars. Our internecine struggles not only expressed deepseated philosophical differences, they hastened the movement's decline. In retrospect, I don't think the sororal collision could have been avoided. But I resent the view that antiporn feminists reflected a prudish strain of right-wing thinking while pro-porn feminists and their pornographer allies were an embattled vanguard holding the line against sexual repression and incursions on free speech. The pieces don't fit.

By a miserable coincidence of historic timing, an aboveground, billion-dollar industry of hard- and soft-core porn began to flourish during the seventies simultaneously with the rise of Women's Liberation. The door through which the purveyors of pornography raced was opened by a 1970 presidential commission report declaring the effects of porn to be harmless and inconsequential; the subsequent avalanche derived its legality from a 1973 Supreme Court ruling, *Miller v. California*, which replaced existing obscenity guidelines with a vague and selective approach called "community standards." Did the men of the high court understand what their ruling was about to unleash? Interpreters in the press certainly didn't, but unpredictable outcomes are typical in times of vast and swift social change.

The staggering rise in the production and consumption of over-the-

counter pornography in the wake of *Miller* was cheerfully analyzed by
the pornographers themselves as a male counterreaction to Women's
Liberation. They had a good point. A significant part of porn's appeal
was its promise to reveal the ancient mysteries of sex, and its newer up-
dates, to a threatened, confused audience at a moment when traditional
masculinity was undergoing its most serious challenge. America's war
in Vietnam had collapsed in defeat, longhaired rock stars and flower
children had capsized parental values by celebrating sensual freedoms,
and women were demanding equality in the workplace as well as in
bed. As a result, porn grew as feminism grew, and many of us believed
that porn was acting to undo much that feminism was accomplishing.

Homemade porn in the left counterculture press had been one of
many provocations helping to fuel the rise of Women's Liberation. A
special porn edition put out in New York by their male comrades precipitated the women's takeover of *Rat*. The founders of *Tooth and Nail*
in San Francisco hijacked and dumped a set of printer's plates intended
for a porn issue of *Dock of the Bay*. Robin Morgan's invasion of Grove
Press, and a flurry of zaps against *Penthouse*, *Playboy*, and Playboy Clubs
in Boston, Chicago, San Francisco, New York, and Rochester, were
significant early protests against the commercial exploitation of
women's bodies.

I witnessed the post-*Miller* explosion of porn more closely than I
cared to while I worked on *Against Our Will*. The four-block walk from
Forty-second Street and Eighth Avenue, my subway exit, to the New
York Public Library on Fifth, where I did my writing, transmogrified
during those years from a familiar landscape of tacky souvenir shops,
fast-food joints, and kung fu movie houses into a hostile gauntlet of
Girls! Live Girls!, XXX, Hot Nude Combos, and illegal massage parlors one flight above the twenty-five-cent peeps. It wasn't just the visual assault that was inimical to my dignity and peace of mind. The new
grunge seemed to embolden a surly army of thugs, pimps, handbag
snatchers, pickpockets, drug sellers, and brazen loiterers whose murmured propositions could not be construed as friendly.

Running the gauntlet was too agitating a way to start the morning
and too dangerous a way to go home at night. I coped by taking another route to the library that entailed a change of trains and a differ-

ent exit, an avoidance strategy that put the visual assault out of sight, if not out of mind. In fact, it was so much on my mind that it made its way into my book. In "Women Fight Back," the final chapter, I defined pornography as one of the forces contributing to a cultural climate in which men felt free to rape. I called hard-core porn the undiluted essence of antifemale propaganda, said there could never be any equality in it for women, and challenged the liberal establishment, most specifically the ACLU, to pull off its blinders and acknowledge the danger in a virulent ideology that portrayed females as dehumanized objects to be used, abused, broken, and discarded.

A NOW chapter in Connecticut printed my pornography analysis in pamphlet form. Unfortunately, the retaliation from *Hustler* and *Screw* reached a far wider audience. *Hustler*, then a newcomer to the nation's magazine racks, printed a smarmy fantasy that began "My palm massaged authoress Susan Brownmiller's naked breasts," and went on from there. *Screw*, a New York guide to massage parlors and X-rated films, superimposed my head on a toilet bowl, said something choice about my mother, declared that I made porno movies, and printed my home address.

A newsstand pornographic assault was not among the responses I'd expected to receive for publishing a book, but luckily for my emotional balance I wasn't an isolated target. The smearing of outspoken feminists and serious, achieving women in all walks of life became a standard practice for the new porn moguls riding high on their free-speech protections. Gloria Steinem, Shere Hite, Betty Ford, Rosalynn Carter, Barbara Walters, and the actress Valerie Harper were among the popular celebrities selected for sexual humiliation by Larry Flynt and Al Goldstein, who gleefully distributed free copies of the smears to the national media, and of course to the targets. When Rosalynn Carter, the president's wife, and nine other prominent women, including Steinem and Walters, were offered a million dollars by Flynt "to pose in the *Hustler* tradition," it became a news story.

In February 1976 a movie named *Snuff*—"Made in Latin America Where Life Is Cheap" the ads proclaimed—opened at a Times Square theater amid persistent rumors, fanned by the *New York Post*, that a real woman had been dismembered to achieve its effects. The rumors evap-

orated under investigation, but the film's eroticized torture was horri-
fying enough to ignite Andrea Dworkin, a long-time activist in the left,
who mobilized her old friends and mentors in the pacifist movement to
picket the theater in a nightly vigil. Andrea had been imprisoned a
decade earlier for a Vietnam War sit-in with the pacifist War Resisters
League. During the early seventies she lived among the radical Dutch
provos in Amsterdam, in a nightmare of drugs and prostitution, until
she fled from her battering husband and returned to the States, where
she published *Woman Hating*, her first book. The *Snuff* protest was her
first feminist action; it sparked similar protests in other cities where the
movie was shown.

During the fall of that year, I met with Julia London and six members of WAVAW (Women Against Violence Against Women) in Los
Angeles. London's group, formed to combat the snuff film genre, was
zeroing in on another unsettling trend, the sadomasochistic imagery
creeping onto the covers of rock music albums. London's politics had
been honed as an organizer for the United Farm Workers in their national boycotts of grapes and lettuce. She wanted to use the same techniques she'd mastered during that struggle—direct action, boycotts, and
moral suasion—to get the music industry to see the error of its ways.
Several WAVAW members had taken spirited action in June when a
billboard for *Black and Blue* by the Rolling Stones appeared on Sunset
Boulevard. Depicting a grinning woman bound in a restraining harness,
it bore the line "I'm 'Black and Blue' from The Rolling Stones—and I
love it!" WAVAW spray-painted "This is a crime against women!"
across the billboard and summoned the press to protest "the perpetuation of the myth that women like to be brutalized." Days later the West
Coast manager of Atlantic Records ordered the billboard whitewashed
and offered his personal apology on behalf of Mick and the Stones.

After I met with her in L.A., Julia London came to New York to
present her slide show of soft-porn album covers for a group of feminist writers and activists I assembled in my apartment. She inspired us
to continue meeting, but we felt that record albums were too narrow a
focus. We wanted to tackle the mainstreaming of violent hard-core
porn. A number of impressive people floated into the New York
group—Adrienne Rich, Grace Paley, Gloria Steinem, Shere Hite, Lois

Gould, Barbara Deming, Karla Jay, Andrea Dworkin, Letty Pogrebin, Robin Morgan. Pondering what to name ourselves, the Women's Anti-Defamation League or Women for the Abolition of Pornography, we dreamed up plans for speak-outs and teach-ins, but no one had the energy to start organizing. I think in our arrogance we hoped we could skip that crucial step. Instead, we tried to compose a paid advertisement for the *Times*, to be signed by hundreds, that distinguished our feminist opposition to porn from the traditional conservative view. Conservatives believed that porn's danger lay in its exposure to innocent young girls. We believed that its exposure to and effects on young boys and men were the problem.

Our meetings to refine our thoughts, and to quibble over language, went on interminably through the spring and summer of 1977. Andrea, Adrienne, and Gloria worked up a draft: "What, after all, does our work against rape and wife-beating amount to when one of their pictures is worth a thousand words. . . ." Lois Gould, Barbara Mehrhof, and I preferred something calmer: "We would draw the line wherever violence or hostility toward women is equated with sexual pleasure, we would draw the line wherever children are sexually exploited. We do not oppose sex education, erotic literature, or erotic art. . . ." Barbara Deming put in: "The First Amendment was never designed to defend sexual terrorism . . ." Adrienne Rich supplied an urgent coda: "We affirm each woman's right to control her own body—the freedom of sexual preference, the freedom to choose or reject motherhood. . . ." Bella Abzug's office sent us a copy of her antipornography statement. Leah Fritz got nervous that our group was all white. I kept a thick file of everyone's copy and caveats, and then the group petered out from exhaustion.

While we were still meeting and amending, the antipornography front shifted to Berkeley, where Diana Russell, Kathleen Barry, and Laura Lederer started WAVPAM, an acronym for Women Against Violence in Pornography and Media. Russell and Barry were respected authors and activists known for their work against rape and prostitution. Lederer at twenty-six, a magna cum laude graduate of the University of Michigan, represented the bright hopes of a younger generation. "We did not spend our time discussing how do we define pornography," Russell recalls. "We became activists very quickly."

So quickly, Lederer recalls, that they rashly accepted free office space from COYOTE, a mismatch of intentions that nearly scuttled the antiporn activists before they got off the ground. COYOTE, an acronym for Call Off Your Old Tired Ethics, was a prostitutes' rights group run by Margo St. James, a colorful and media-savvy figure on the San Francisco scene.

WAVPAM chose International Women's Day, March 8, 1977, to confront the Mitchell brothers, San Francisco's leading porn entrepreneurs, at their live sex theater on Kearny Street. About two months later, on May Day, the group mobilized four hundred Bay Area women for an afternoon march down Broadway, the city's major porn thorough-fare. Demonstrators chanted, "Women Say No to Violence Against Women," "Pornography Is Anti-Woman Propaganda," "Pornography Is a Lie about Women," while they plastered THIS IS A CRIME AGAINST WOMEN stickers on sex shops along the route.

For one hundred dollars a week, which often went unpaid, Laura Lederer became WAVPAM's fulltime coordinator and editor of *Newspage*, its monthly bulletin of antiporn essays and actions. "I knew it wasn't enough to keep passing the hat at meetings," she recalls. "We had to raise money. Dianne Feinstein was mayor then, and she was speaking out about the Kearny Street blight, how it was bad for San Francisco's image, so I went to see her. She gave me five hundred dollars out of her own pocket and said, 'Keep going!'" Marya Grambs from the battered women's movement suggested that Lederer write a funding proposal. Two wealthy Bay Area feminists read the first draft and contributed five thousand dollars.

In June 1978, *Hustler* ran its notorious cover of a naked woman being fed into a meat grinder, a newsstand shocker even for the blasé. The cover, which bore the line "We will no longer treat women like pieces of meat," was the inspiration of Larry Flynt and his new hire, Paul Krassner of *The Realist*, a libertarian leftist whose specialty in print was gross excess. Called upon to defend the meat grinder cover, Krassner fell back on the classic "Feminists have no sense of humor."

The *Hustler* cover brought a flood of new recruits into the movement. Seizing the moment, WAVPAM initiated plans for a national "Feminist Perspectives on Pornography" conference. Diana Russell, the Mills College professor and rape researcher, advanced the group two thousand dollars from her personal savings. Twenty-two-year-old Lynn Campbell, a boycott organizer for the United Farm Workers, was brought in to work full-time with Lederer on the conference planning.

The first national feminist antipornography conference, at Galileo High School in downtown San Francisco, was called for the weekend of November 4–5, 1978. When hoped-for foundation grants didn't come through, the organizers plunged nine thousand dollars in debt to launch their event on a professional footing. Guests speakers received round-trip tickets and a one-hundred-dollar honorarium; out of respect for their talents, comparable payments went to a group of local artists and the singer Holly Near.

Activists Marg Hall and Martha Gever flew in from Rochester to conduct a workshop on a form of direct action they obliquely called "browsing." While pretending to peruse the porno racks in convenience stores, they'd drip glue on the magazine pages and insert messages such as "Pornography Hurts Women." Crystal Arp and Lori Bradford of the Colorado Bluebird Five in Boulder came to speak on "How to Get Attention Without Getting Arrested (We Hope)." I was part of a contingent of New York writers that included Florence Rush, Andrea Dworkin, Adrienne Rich, and Audre Lorde. Adrienne, invited to read poetry with Susan Griffin at the Friday night session, was one of the few movement celebrities to sense the group's financial straits and decline a fee.

Kathy Barry's opening address conjured a beautiful vision of a world without porn and called for imaginative new strategies to wage a battle against the ideology of sexual violence. To those who cautioned that any action against pornography infringed on the right of free speech, she retorted, "We must recognize this patriarchal tactic to keep us on the defensive, in our homes, and silent. There are no easy roads to liberation."

Saturday evening culminated in a candlelit "Take Back the Night" march (the first of its kind) through the porn district, kicked off by an exhortation by Andrea Dworkin. I'd seen Andrea in my living room, but this was the first time I'd seen Andrea in action. On the spot I dubbed her Rolling Thunder. Perspiring in her trademark denim coveralls, she employed the rhetorical cadences that would make her both a cult idol and an object of ridicule a few years later. Dworkin's dramatized martyrdom and revival-tent theatrics never sat well with me, but I retained my respect for her courage long after I absented myself from the pornography wars. Her call to action accomplished, three thousand demonstrators took to the streets, snaking past Broadway's neon peeps, "adult" book stores, and garish massage parlors while Holly Near sang from an amplified truck and local artists weaved through the line bobbing surreal effigies of madonnas and whores. The visual effect was very San Francisco. As I watched some onlookers gaily waving from the sidewalk, I sensed they mistook us for a lost tribe of Halloween revelers.

I stayed for the Sunday postmortem. By then we knew that the city's newspapers had blanked out the nation's first feminist antipornography conference and march, except for a feature on Margo St. James of COYOTE, who told reporters that *she* had organized "Take Back the Night" to show that feminists weren't opposed to the selling of sex, just the packaging of it. Taking advantage of the local media's political naïveté, the wily publicity hound had flummoxed WAVPAM and four months of work.

That afternoon I approached Laura Lederer and Lynn Campbell, the twenty-something organizers, and offered them a proposition that was rash, spontaneous, and eminently pragmatic. The weekend's disappointing outreach had convinced me that New York, the home of both Times Square *and* the national media, was the only place to launch a national feminist antipornography campaign. Laura and Lynn had the energy and vision; my battle-fatigued colleagues had the practical know-how and media savvy. If the two women cared to uproot their lives and organize in New York, we might be able to get somewhere.

The two women came east to take their political soundings. Laura decided she would be more effective if she stayed put and edited an anthology based on the San Francisco conference. (*Take Back the Night: Women on Pornography* appeared in 1980, with an afterword by Adrienne Rich.) Lynn was eager to relocate and start organizing. We set our sights on a huge East Coast conference, to be held in the fall, and a plan to follow up the conference at a later date with a march on Times Square.

Lynn Campbell arrived in New York in April 1979. A group of us met her at the airport with flowers. Adrienne Rich, Frances Whyatt, the poet and novelist, and I each put in one thousand dollars to open a bank account for her living expenses. Maggie Smith, the hip owner of Tin Pan Alley, a bar and restaurant on West Forty-ninth Street, had lined up a cheap apartment. Everyone was captivated by our slight, angelic blond cheerleader, so earnest that she had dropped out of Stanford to organize for the Farm Workers, so ascetic that her idea of a dinner treat was a small container of coffee yogurt. Lynn's time on earth was very short. Two weeks after her arrival, she learned that she had a malignant melanoma. Still she decided to stay with the job she'd been summoned for.

The group that became Women Against Pornography was livelier and more disparate than any I'd ever worked with in the movement. Maggie Smith's bar, with "I Will Survive" blaring on the jukebox, was a pit stop for the neighborhood prostitutes she was trying to keep off junk. Amina Abdur Rahman, education director for the New York Urban League, had been with Malcolm X in the Audubon Ballroom on the night he was murdered. Dianne Levitt was the student organizer of an anti-*Playboy* protest at Barnard, Dorchen Leidholdt had founded New York WAVAW, Frances Patai was a former actress and model, Marilyn Kaskel was a TV production assistant, Angela Bonovoglio did freelance magazine writing, Jessica James was starring off Broadway, Janet Lawson was a jazz singer, Alexandra Matusinka's family ran a nearby plumbing supply store, Sheila Roher was a playwright, Ann Jones was writing *Women Who Kill*, Anne Bowen had played guitar with the Deadly Nightshade, and Myra Terry was an interior decorator and a NOW chapter president in New Jersey.

A month or so into our work, two veteran feminists joined Lynn Campbell as full-time staff organizers. I told Dolores Alexander, NOW's first executive director and co-owner of Mother Courage restaurant, she could have a job for one hundred dollars a week, what we were paying Lynn, if she could raise her own money. Dolores was so successful in getting donations from some of the smaller progressive foundations and her personal friends that we were able to bring in Barbara Mehrhof, a founding member of Redstockings and THE FEMINISTS. Barbara offered ideological continuity that extended back to the early days of New York Radical Women.

Our decision to target Times Square was only one of WAP's strategies, but it turned out that a campaign in the belly of the beast brought us unexpected allies. The legitimate Broadway theater owners, their business hurting from neighborhood crime, were crying for someone to "do something" about the blight. I suspect that *The New York Times* paid us close attention at least partly because its stone bulwark on West Forty-third Street was under siege on all sides by the sex industry's weedy growth.

After I wrote him a testy letter, we met with Carl Weisbrod, head of the Mayor's Midtown Enforcement Project, who was charged with the thankless task of trying to close down the illegal brothels that hid behind the porn bookstores' facades. He worked with Fred Papert, whose Forty-second Street Redevelopment Corporation was experiencing little luck in luring legitimate businesses into the swamp of Times Square. Carl Weisbrod turned out to be an imaginative and ethical young lawyer open to new ideas. When he asked what we needed, Lynn Campbell piped up, "Office space." A few days later Weisbrod called to say there was an empty bar and restaurant on Ninth Avenue and Forty-second Street that we could use, rent-free, until Papert's corporation found a buyer. Women Against Pornography was to occupy the funky little storefront on the edge of Times Square for more than two years, until two adjacent buildings collapsed during a renovation. The only prospective buyer to appear during our tenure was Bob Guccione of *Penthouse*, wanting to open an establishment called the Meat Rack. Alerted by WAP, neighborhood folk rallied to scotch the plan.

The neighborhood's response was affirming from the minute we opened our doors. St. Malachy's, an actors' chapel on West Forty-seventh Street, sent over four desks they'd been keeping in storage. We placed them across from the massive oak bar, our literature table, and ordered some phone lines. Four desks, three paid organizers. I had not intended this to happen—I'd warned everybody not to think it might happen—but I put aside the book I was working on (*Femininity*, already past its deadline) and took the fourth desk as an unpaid organizer. Things were moving so rapidly that I couldn't stay away.

We put together an educational slide show of hard- and soft-core porn that was accompanied by our critical commentary, and trundled the carousel to people's homes for consciousness-raising evenings. Then Lynn suggested that we run actual tours through Times Square. Exploratory forays into the raw netherworld of the twenty-five-cent peeps and the glitzy, multifloored sexploitation arcades like Show World, one block from our office, had convinced her and Dolores that people who were not porn consumers had no idea what went on behind the facades of Girls! Live Girls! and were afraid to find out. Women went out of their way to avoid the area, reluctant to subject themselves to its visual assaults and physical hassles.

In what became our most popular tactic, Women Against Pornography opened up the hidden life of Times Square for a suggested five-dollar donation. I plotted the itinerary and wrote a script based on information, supplied by Carl Weisbrod and Maggie Smith, about which mobster reputedly owned what X-rated theater or coin arcade, and what sort of wages the employees at Show World, the Dating Room, the Mardi Gras, or the Pussycat received of an evening. A WAP tour was never without spontaneous encounters—getting tossed out bodily by hysterical managers; watching the customers, often white men in business suits, slink away in confusion; engaging in short, frank dialogues with the amused, blasé, embarrassed, or furious Live! Nude! Topless! Bottomless! performers when they emerged from their circular cages to take their hourly breaks. The unexpected appearance of women in clothes, to observe men in clothes watching naked women writhe in mock sexual pleasure for the men's entertainment, dramatically altered the atmosphere of the live sex shows' self-contained world. We had not thought this out very clearly beforehand, but our intrusion was shattering to the careful construct of denial the performers relied on to get them through the night.

Georgia Dullea took one of the first tours and wrote a big feature for the Style section of the *Times*, which in turn precipitated a media avalanche: stories in *People, Time*, the *Philadelphia Inquirer*, several European papers; features on the city's local TV news programs and talk shows; a coveted summons from *The Phil Donahue Show* in Chicago. Alerted by the news coverage, whole classes of high school and college students, accompanied by their teachers, signed up for the tours. We escorted, most memorably, two intrepid Benedictine nuns from Erie, Pennsylvania, a delegation from the Jewish War Veterans and the Anti-Defamation League, livid with rage when we showed them the Nazi porn genre, a study group of Chinese-American women wanting to see how they were portrayed in *Cherry Blossoms* and similar magazines. Someone in the group calculated that more than 2,500 people took the walking tours that first year, including whole groups of foreign tourists who'd heard on the grapevine that we offered the best sightseeing bargain in town. There was no time to stop and consider the emotional drain on our psyches as we kept hurling ourselves into the twice-weekly confrontations.

One day two university psychologists in town for an academic convention sought us out. Ed Donnerstein from the University of Wisconsin and Neal Malamuth from UCLA were investigating the effects of violent pornography on attitudes toward rape, and their initial research was confirming the "hypothesis," as Ed called it, that I'd advanced in the final chapter of *Against Our Will*. Cooperation materialized from other sources, too. The League of New York Theater Owners wrote us a check for ten thousand dollars, although Gerry Schoenfeld of the Shubert Organization, the czar behind the generous gift, threw a fit when he saw that our mission was somewhat broader than "clean up Times Square."

"*Playboy?*" he yelled one day, barging into the office. "You're against *Playboy*? Where's Gloria Steinem? Does she know what you're doing?"

With some trepidation we paid a courtesy visit to Father Morton A. Hill, S.J., the aging director of Morality in Media, up at the interfaith office building jokingly called "the God Box" on Riverside Drive. Hill had written the minority report for the Presidential Commission on Obscenity and Pornography in 1970, the report that articulated pornography's dangers. In our terror at being lumped with religious conservatives, "abortion" and "gay rights" were the first words out of

our mouths. Father Hill was a good, kindly man, and very knowledge-
able about our mutual interest. The meeting was a poignant study in
contrasts. We honestly believed that radical feminists, with our deeper
understanding of porn and our sophisticated knowledge of sexuality,
would succeed in turning around public opinion where the old-fashioned moralists had not.

When we weren't coping with the ringing phones, the media, the
slide shows and tours, the neighborhood people bursting through the
door to tell us "It's about time!" (we decided to make "It's about Time"
our official slogan), we concentrated on putting together the intricate
pieces of our September conference and October march. Tempers
flared among the four full-time organizers, partly from the dizzying
speed at which we were working, partly from the stress of our daily exposure to porn. Twice I turned into a screaming banshee—shooing
away a photographer and model as they set up a porn shoot in front of
our storefront, ejecting a drunken fellow, claiming to be a Vietnam vet,
who offered to blow up any target on Forty-second Street we wanted.
And I have to confess that I spoke intemperately on the *Donahue Show*
when Phil asked me about Larry Flynt, recently paralyzed by a gun-
man's bullet.

"Well, Phil," I quipped, as I might have in my living room, "that
may have been the best thing that ever happened to Flynt."

Donahue's studio wasn't my living room. He read me the riot act
and called me an Ayatollah Khomeini. Although I maintain to this day
that he overreacted, the deeper truth is that I still feel ashamed that my
hard-boiled wisecrack let my colleagues down.

We already had an inkling that some feminists were not happy
about what we were doing, although the opposition hadn't yet solidi-
fied into an organized campaign. The slide show was hitting raw
nerves. Dolores Alexander, a whiz at raising money through the lesbian
social network, had encountered a negative reaction at one of her pre-
sentations. When she projected a slide of women in bondage, a guest
screamed, "You're attacking my sexuality! I find that picture very sexy!"
We began to get agitated responses from straight women as well.
Sometimes they were emotional defenses of free speech, but to our bewilderment, we also saw that some women identified their sexuality

with the s/m pictures we found degrading. Porn turned them on, and they didn't want to hear any political raps about how women were conditioned to find their sexual pleasure within the mysogynistic scenarios created by men. They claimed we were condemning their minds and behavior, and I guess we were.

Seven hundred women attended the East Coast Feminist Conference on Pornography at Martin Luther King, Jr., High School, near Lincoln Center, on the weekend of September 15–16, 1979. The blood on the floor at the end of the weekend was all mine.

Nearly every feminist star—Abzug, Steinem, Robin Morgan, Shere Hite, Phyllis Chesler, etc.—and a host of distinguished feminist artists and writers came out for Women Against Pornography's intensive conference. Among the weekend's highlights were Daphne Ayallah's slide show on breasts and breast fetishes and the redoubtable Fran Hosken's research on clitoridectomy, billed for our conference as "the *reality* of sexual mutilation." Hosken made genital excision a feminist issue twenty years before it became an international concern. We had panel discussions on erotic art, pornography and incest, pornography and sexuality, pornography and the older woman, sadomasochistic images in fashion photography, the use of animals in pornography and sex. Wendy Kaminer from the Mayor's Midtown Enforcement Project, and the author of WAP's First Amendment position paper, conducted a workshop on antiporn activism, the legal concept of prior restraint, and free speech. In the spirit of open dialogue, we handed over two panels to feminist critics of the antiporn movement whose views we respected. Ellen Willis and Alix Kates Shulman led a discussion titled "Prudery, an Infantile Disorder," and Joan Nestle and Deborah Edel of the Lesbian Herstory Archives presented the case for lesbian erotic art.

I chaired the concluding open-mike session, "Strategies for the Future," on Sunday afternoon. There is no way to explain what happened, except to note that the concentrated exposure to graphic images combined with intimate consciousness-raising on rape, battery, and incest in close quarters for two full days had brought many raw emotions roiling to the surface. The session had barely begun when a heckler started badgering me from the front row.

"Why isn't your literature in Spanish?" she razzed.

I tried to ignore the disruption.

"You're a bunch of fucking middle-class white elitists. *Why isn't your literature in Spanish?*"

If there is a cool, effective way to handle hecklers, I never found it. Neither did I ever learn how not to rise to the bait.

"We'd love to have our literature in Spanish," I shot back. "We want it in Braille and in every language. At this point we're still struggling to put it in English."

The heckler made her way to the stage. She had on a cheap man's suit, a stiff-collared white shirt, and a dark tie. Later I learned she called herself Frog, and identified herself as an incest victim. Frog grabbed the open microphone and jerked her thumb in my direction.

"I'm sick of this elitist bullshit. *We* do all the work in this movement, and *you* go home and suck cock."

Wrong, Frog, wrong. I was going home every night to an empty apartment. I had been living alone for five years.

Her charge delivered, Frog sauntered back to her seat. I waited, hoping that one of my colleagues would rise to my rescue. Nada. Did they not think I required rescue? An air of expectancy hung over the auditorium. Blood boiling, I stood up and walked the few steps to the open mike.

"I'd like to ask you something. If you hate men so much, why are you wearing men's clothes?"

The gasp was audible. So much for "Strategies for the Future." The next two hours went by in a blur of tearful statements and harsh accusations, mostly (I think) about the invested power of men's suits in a patriarchal society, and the pros and cons of my right, as a heterosexual woman in pants, to challenge the attire of a lesbian in drag.

On Monday morning a very positive report by Leslie Bennetts, "Conference Examines Pornography as a Feminist Issue," was splashed across our familiar venue, the Style section of the *Times*. Bennetts had not hung around for the Sunday afternoon disruptions, but some people who had, or who had not been there but had received sketchy accounts, could not let it go. Adrienne Rich had begged off from the weekend, pleading an overload of work and public commitments. Days later she resigned from WAP by letter, citing my "homophobic attack on a lesbian wearing pants" (I'm paraphrasing from memory but I believe that's close). When I called her at her home in western Massachusetts, she would not hear me out. Adrienne and I had been political allies for nearly a decade; I treasured the company of this brilliant, internationally recognized poet who bore up so stoically under physical disability and personal trauma, whose twin worlds of intellectual achievement and radical activism were an unending search for perfection. We never spoke again. I think Adrienne was already in tremendous conflict over the implications of an antiporn movement, although her break from it did not come for another five years.

With slightly more than a month left to go, WAP put its painful emotions on hold and hunkered down for the October 20 March on Times Square. Lynn Campbell, Marilyn Hayes, Renee Mittler, and Dana Lobell firmed up the out-of-town contingents, who were arriving on chartered buses from U. Mass., Amherst, Hampshire, and Brown. We had solid commitments from many of the actors of Forty-second Street's Theater Row, who had to make their way day and night past the sex-shop grunge, as well as from the residents of Manhattan Plaza, a high-rise apartment building in the neighborhood populated mainly by senior citizens and theater people. The Coalition of Labor Union Women and a women's caucus of post office workers were eager to join the march.

Lynn optimistically projected a turnout of twenty thousand. I redid the numbers and came up with five thousand, tops. Anything under that magic figure, the man in charge of police permits had warned, and we'd be trotting along the sidewalk, not coursing through the streets. Dolores Alexander juggled the list of speakers for the postmarch rally in Bryant Park. No problem there. We had Abzug, Steinem, Robin Morgan, Andrea Dworkin, and Charlotte Bunch, the former lesbian separatist, who had agreed to come up from Washington to add her voice. While Dolores lined up the speakers, I negotiated endlessly with the NYPD commanders of Midtown North and South, who were not thrilled about diverting a twenty-block stretch of traffic along Broadway from Columbus Circle to Forty-second Street on a busy Saturday afternoon. Neither, I think, were they convinced of our peaceful intentions.

Two gum-chewing babes in leather jackets sashayed into the storefront one evening, looking impossibly conspiratorial and tough. "Where's the *heavy stuff* gonna happen?" they whispered.

"Say what?"

"You know, the *heavy stuff*."

I giggled. They had to be undercover cops.

The storefront became a nightly beehive of Day-Glo paint and thick brushes, staple guns thwacking on plywood poles. Off in one corner, Yolanda Mancilla presided over the cutting and stitching of the largest banner I'd ever seen. A high school student recently accepted to Harvard, Yolanda had walked into the office after the conference with a tearful pledge to translate anything we had into Spanish. It turned out she had a talent for artwork as well.

Harold Prince had given me some useful pointers when I'd solicited his advice after seeing *Evita*, marveling at how he had staged a rousing street demonstration with a handful of actors and picket signs that somehow conveyed the impression of great multitudes.

"How many folks you expecting?" the director inquired.

"Five thousand."

"How many posters?"

"We're making five hundred."

"Verticals and horizontals? Mix of colors and slogans?"

"Of course!"

"Okay, here's what you do. You place your five hundred posters among your first thousand marchers."

"But, Mr. Prince, the other four thousand marchers will want to carry some posters."

"You did your organizing, now you're going for the picture," said the genius of spectacles. "A sea of waving posters from the front of the line."

The Women Against Pornography March on Times Square got between five and seven thousand demonstrators, and nearly every second marcher seemed to have brought her own homemade sign. The sea of waving posters at the front of the line looked glorious that night on the CBS network news and in the morning papers. Most certainly we would not have gotten such extensive coverage without our great visuals. The guy from 1010 WINS News Radio hugged me. The *Times* actually used the phrase "sea of waving placards." Harold Prince phoned in his congratulations.

Lynn Campbell resigned as a paid organizer for Women Against Pornography the week after the march. She needed less stressful work to preserve her dwindling health. (This wonderful person hung on to her life for another five years.) With Lynn gone, I resigned from WAP as an unpaid organizer, to return to the task of earning a living by completing my book on femininity. We had fulfilled the promise we'd made to each other in San Francisco the year before, when I'd said "Organize in New York and we'll make pornography a national feminist issue." Others were ready to carry it forward. I hadn't intended to be a full-time antipornography worker, nor did I want pornography to overshadow rape, a tail wagging the dog, but the campaign had been too exciting to walk away from—until the strain wore me down. Nothing in our women's movement was ever accomplished without severe emotional depletion and fractured personal relations. Dolores Alexander and I were barely speaking between the conference and the march. My long-standing friendship with Barbara Mehrhof was in tatters. Much of the bad feelings had to do with "elitism" and "personal publicity," the movement's names for recognition and credit. Four organizers had worked side by side at the WAP storefront for six frantic months, yet it was my name, usually bracketed by Steinem's and Abzug's, that most often appeared in the papers, and it didn't help that I'd begun to bark orders like a martinet. The people I needed to distance myself from were the women I'd brought together, and I believe that the feelings were mutual, at least for a while.

Through the outreach we'd done—the conference, the march, the slide shows, the tours—Women Against Pornography had attracted many new volunteers, most of them young enough to be my daughters. The newcomers had been in high school during the early seventies, yearning to be part of the feminist revolution. Dorchen Leidholdt, an editor of college textbooks at Random House, and a WAP founder, took on a leadership position, duly noted by *Hustler* in its usual scatological manner. The group continued to make news on a regular basis by initiating the WAP zaps, a series of awards and brickbats bestowed on the advertising industry, and by demonstrating sisterly support for Linda Marchiano, the former Linda Lovelace, when she exposed the brutal truth behind her life as the can't-get-enough star of *Deep Throat*. At this time, WAP's approach was still strictly educational, in line with the founders' vision. It kept up the Times Square tours, organized panel discussions, sent out speakers and slide shows, conducted the occasional protest demonstration, and did not advocate any new legal measures to curb the growing pornography menace.

I think the new conservatism of the Reagan era caught most feminists by surprise—I know the overwhelming sweep of the 1980 elections caught *me* by surprise—but it soon became transparently clear that the political and cultural climate of the nation was undergoing a change of tremendous proportions. We had entered the greedy Me Decade, with "Lighten up!" and "Family Values" as its conflicting mottoes. It was against this inauspicious backdrop that the internecine feminist pornography wars became a pitched battle.

In the summer of 1981 two significant books articulating the feminist opposition to porn, Susan Griffin's *Pornography and Silence* and Andrea Dworkin's *Pornography: Men Possessing Women*, were negatively assessed in *The New York Times Book Review* by Ellen Willis, whose weekly columns in *The Village Voice* had made her the de facto leader of the increasingly vocal feminist anti-anti-pornography forces. Granting the misognyny rife in porn, Willis argued that the larger demon was the sexually repressive family structure. She pondered whether the "peculiar confluence" of feminist antiporn activism and the antipornography stance of the fundamentalist New Right indicated a subconscious feminist shift toward the conservative cultural tide, and concluded that it did.

Later that year I received an urgent long-distance telephone call from Alice Schwarzer, the formidable editor of *Emma*, the German feminist magazine. Schwarzer's halting command of the English language made her speech come out in short bursts, but she seemed to be saying that someone named Pat Califia, a pornography writer in California, was launching an important new feminist movement. *Emma* was going to run one of her essays, and the magazine hoped I would write a response.

"What's the new movement?" I inquired with interest.

"Lesbian sadomasochism," Schwarzer replied. I thought I misheard her. *"Lesbian sadomasochism!"* she shouted into the receiver. "It is sweeping your movement. You do not *know*?"

I didn't know, and furthermore, I didn't believe her. I told her to send the essay to Dorchen Leidholdt, the new leader of WAP.

"I was horrified by the Califia article," Leidholdt remembers, "horrified that a German feminist magazine was going to publish statements like 'An s/m scene can be played out using the personae of guard and prisoner, cop and suspect, Nazi and Jew.' My name is German, my father is of German descent. I felt almost a sense of personal responsibility." Leidholdt wrote an agitated response for *Emma* and set out to learn more about Pat Califia's organization.

A rare "top" in a field of "bottoms," the San Francisco pornographer led an s/m group named Samois, for the house of torture in *The Story of O*, and was editing an anthology of lesbian s/m writings called *Coming to Power*. Califia's evangelistic promotion of lesbian sadomasochism as a new oppressed minority had first seen the light of day in *Heresies*, a New York–based feminist magazine of the arts, in a steamy "Sex Issue" extolling the pleasures of pornography, s/m, and butch-femme erotics. "I enjoy leathersex, bondage, various forms of erotic torture, flagellation (whipping), verbal humiliation, fistfucking, and water sports (playing with enemas and piss)," the author explained to her "vanilla friends." Joan Nestle, who'd given a presentation at our conference, contributed a personal narrative of her life as a femme drawn to working-class butches in the 1950s. There was also a racy younger-generation dialogue, "What We're Rollin' Around in Bed With," between Amber Hollibaugh and the Chicana poet Cherrie Moraga, which, like Nestle's piece, was an open challenge to lesbian feminism's proud assertion in the seventies that butch-femme roles were an outworn mimicry of the dominance/submission mode of heterosexual relations.

"Then," Dorchen recalls with a shudder, "came the Barnard conference."

The ninth annual "The Scholar and the Feminist" conference at Barnard College on Saturday, April 24, 1982, proclaimed "Towards a Politics of Sexuality" as its groundbreaking theme. Months of planning by Carole Vance, a Columbia anthropologist, and a team of advisers of her choosing had gone into the day's proceedings, intended to produce a joyful exploration of "politically incorrect" sexual behavior, to counter the "fascist" and "moralistic" tendencies of WAP. The bizarre result was a somewhat nervous, somewhat giddy, occasionally tearful exposition of the pleasures of s/m starring the *Heresies* contributors and augmented by Dorothy Allison, Esther Newton, and Gayle Rubin, the last a feminist scholar who had emerged as a leading member of Samois.

A dozen WAP women, their T-shirts emblazoned with "Against Sadomasochism" and "Feminists for a Feminist Sexuality," picketed outside with their protest leaflets. "From the response, you'd have thought we dropped an atomic bomb on Barnard," Dorchen Leidholdt remembers. Adding to the furor, alarmed college authorities had confiscated a "Conference Diary" intended for registrants, a pastiche of the planners' notes and scribbles interspersed with arty graphics of lipstick kisses, razor blades, safety pins, and chain collars, and an empty page reserved for phone numbers. Ellen Willis's scribble had hailed the planning sessions as "a radical act" embodying a political urgency she had not witnessed since the early days of Women's Liberation.

Not every speaker at Barnard that day addressed s/m or butch-femme roles. A few invitees read academic papers tracing the "social purity" ethic, cast as a strain of repressed sexuality, in nineteenth-century feminist movements, while the young historian Alice Echols brought matters up to date by accusing Adrienne Rich of taking the sex out of lesbianism by championing women's sexuality as more diffuse and spiritual than the sexuality of men.

On Sunday, the Lesbian Sex Mafia, Dorothy Allison's s/m support group and dangerous-games society, held an off-campus speak-out featuring dildos, nipple clamps, and a bondage slide show by Betty Dodson, a movement entrepreneur who made her living by conducting workshops on masturbation. "I love rough sex and I have many fetishes," Allison announced, "and if something's possible to do, I'll try it three times." (The novelist Bertha Harris, one of her early mentors, recalls that during this experimental period in Allison's life some of her friends were deeply concerned for the young writer's health and safety.)

Four reporters from Washington's feminist newspaper *off our backs* labored to make sense of the Barnard conference for their readers. "A travesty," concluded Fran Moira. "I was deeply disturbed," editorialized Carol Anne Douglas, who resisted the s/m speakers' claim that they were sexual radicals. "I think their positions were those of sexual conservatives," she countered, "to assume that attraction must be based on differences, polarities, or dominance." Guest columnist Claudette Charbonneau, incensed that the antiviolence movement had been excluded from the program, wrote that she felt she had entered "an Orwellian world." Tacie Dejanicus, upset by the name-calling, charges, and countercharges by the hardening factions, admitted that she did not know how the intense ideological split would shape feminism in the future, but concluded "it is certain to do so." The sexuality debate was to rage in *oob* and other feminist journals for several more years.

"I think most lesbian feminists were dismayed, and continued to be dismayed," Carol Anne Douglas reflects. "The s/m evangelists, or sexual libertarians, as I began to call them, emerged at a time when the American left wasn't going anywhere, and when lesbianism per se was no longer transgressive, to use one of their favorite words. But there was still a tendency to want to be the most militant and the most revolutionary. They were obviously suggesting that what *they* liked was the coolest, and that sex without those things was vanilla, or boring, which was pretty insulting to the rest of us." Douglas had further reason to feel insulted, when Susie Bright, an erotic writer in San Francisco, named her magazine ("for adventurous lesbians") *On Our Backs*, pointedly thumbing her nose at the earnest politics of America's oldest, continuously published feminist paper.

• • •

Andrea Dworkin, perceiving some ideological differences between her theories and the pragmatic approach of Women Against Pornography, had kept her distance from the storefront campaign, but she was happy to be included in WAP's solidarity press conference for Linda Marchiano, formerly known as Linda Lovelace, the star of *Deep Throat*. Dworkin invited her new friend Catharine MacKinnon, the author of *Sexual Harassment of Working Women*, to join her for the media event at which Marchiano was to go public with the horrors of her life as a porn star. Andrea was chewing on an idea. Even as the press corps was asking its questions and snapping its pictures, she was querying the feminist lawyer about whether Marchiano might have a legal basis to sue the pornographers, pimps, and johns in her past starting with Chuck Traynor, her husband and manager, and proceeding right along to Hugh Hefner. MacKinnon reeled off the civil rights statutes she thought might apply.

Two weeks later Dworkin and Mackinnon met with Marchiano, who was intrigued by the idea of a lawsuit. So was Gloria Steinem, who had been tremendously moved by Marchiano's story. In Dworkin's recollection, "Kitty and I researched the thing into the ground for a year and a half," before Gloria learned that the clock had run out under the statute of limitations, and Marchiano backed off. In the meantime the meeting of minds between Dworkin and MacKinnon had turned into an adhesive bond.

MacKinnon arranged for Dworkin to come to Minneapolis in the fall of 1983, for a one-semester appointment at the University of Minnesota. While Kitty lectured at the law school that autumn, and Andrea taught a class in literature to undergraduates in Women's Studies, the lawyer and the writer jointly conducted an interdepartmental course on pornography that was open to community activists and students. Entry requirements included a brief written biography and a statement of purpose, Sharon Vaughan remembers. Vaughan, cofounder of the first battered women's shelter in St. Paul, was one of sixty-six students admitted to the course, which unexpectedly gave way to a new form of activism within its first month.

"What happened," says Dworkin, "is that people started calling us from a neighborhood group in South Minneapolis, asking us to go to a zoning committee meeting at City Hall. They'd been trying for years to get the city council to strengthen its zoning laws and do something about the porn shops encroaching on their community. We told them we weren't for zoning, because zoning doesn't address woman-hating. We said we had developed a different approach, pornography as a violation of civil rights."

Charlee Hoyt, a liberal Republican and a frustrated zoner, per-

suaded her fellow members on the city council to hire MacKinnon and
Dworkin to draft legislation based on their civil rights angle. Ready by
December, the bill they prepared stated that pornography was "central
in maintaining and creating inequality" and was a form of sex discrimination. It defined injured persons as those coerced into performing for
pornographic pictures, those physically assaulted as a result of pornography, and those who had pornography "forced" on them in their
homes, jobs, or public places, and it offered them the remedy of suing
the makers, sellers, distributors, and exhibitors in civil court for damages, as well as for the "elimination of the products of the perfor-
mances from public view."

The Dworkin-MacKinnon ordinance was sponsored in the Minneapolis city council by Charlee Hoyt and Van White, a liberal black
Democrat, who promptly called a public hearing—not on the bill's
merits (few had read it), but on the need to take action. A city with a
can-do approach to governance, Minneapolis prided itself on its enlightened sexual-preference protections, its compassionate physical
disability codes, and its tough antismoking laws. Supporters of the ordinance hoped their bill would take its place as yet another pioneering
example of progressive social-policy legislation. Braving a snowstorm,
a score of local women filed into the chamber to tell how pornography
had harmed their lives. Linda Marchiano was flown in to testify as a national expert, along with Ed Donnerstein, the pornography researcher
from the University of Wisconsin, and Pauline Bart, a radical feminist
professor of sociology at the University of Chicago.

Andrea mailed me a copy of the ordinance on December 29, the day
before it passed by one vote in the city council. I hadn't even known
that she and MacKinnon were in Minneapolis and working on legislation, but on reading the bill I quickly concluded that it was unwork-
able—full of overblown rhetoric, overly broad and vague intentions,
tricky and convoluted legal locutions. Any court in the land, I believed,
would find it unconstitutional, an observation I offered in my usual
blunt manner when Andrea called a few days later to get my endorsement.

I assured her I would not go public with my negative opinion. I still
cared tremendously about the issue, and for all its flaws, I figured the

ordinance might be a valuable consciousness-raiser and organizing tool. In a bad lapse of political judgment, I failed to perceive how it would polarize an already divided feminist community by providing an even better organizing tool for the opposition. Not that what I thought mattered at that point. I had ceded leadership in antipornography work to those willing to carry it forward when I'd retreated to finish my book on femininity, just then reaching the bookstores after a very long haul.

Few people noticed my absence from the national list of ordinance supporters. Gloria Steinem, Robin Morgan, Phyllis Chesler, and the new leadership of Women Against Pornography had already sent Dworkin and MacKinnon their glowing commendations. "I thought it was fucking brilliant," Robin Morgan remembers, "just brilliant the way they circumvented the criminal statutes and obscenity codes identified with the right wing, and took a new path through the concept of harm and civil rights discrimination." Robin, coiner of the slogan "Pornography is the theory, rape is the practice," did not see any constitutional problem. "If I had," she concedes, "I doubt that it would have affected my position."

The ordinance was vetoed within days of its passage by Mayor Donald Fraser, who maintained that the city did not have the financial resources to defend the law's constitutionality in court. Seven months later it came up before the council again, with minor modifications. This time around, pornography was defined only as a "contributory factor," not "central" to the subordination of women. Dorchen Leidholdt flew to Minneapolis to help with a petition drive. Upon her return, she persuaded Women Against Pornography to contribute a few thousand dollars from its dwindling treasury to the effort.

The switch from a plucky, inventive campaign to educate the public about pornography's dangers to the promotion of new legislation was a huge change in direction for WAP, although given the times, it was probably inevitable. Mehrhof and Alexander, the last of WAP's original full-time organizers, had already resigned, needing a more reliable weekly paycheck than antipornography work could offer. Increasingly frustrated, the remaining activists had lost their faith in the powers of hand-cranked slide shows and hastily organized protest demonstrations to curb a phenomenal growth industry which was taking advantage of the latest technologies (pre-Internet) to create a multibillion-dollar X-rated home video market, Dial-a-Porn, and public-access television channels.

Although WAP backed the ordinance, other antiporn groups were not so sanguine about it. In Washington, political scientist Janet Gornick recalls, the ordinance split her group, Feminists Against Pornography, right down the middle, and ultimately she resigned. "We were black and white, lesbian and straight, and almost every one of us had been a victim of sexual violence," says Gornick, whose own activism had started six years earlier, after she was stabbed on the street, dragged twenty feet, and raped a block from the Harvard campus in a crime that was never solved. "FAP was doing very daring direct-action things in addition to the usual slide shows and Take Back the Nights," she relates. "We were waging a small war against the Fourteenth Street porn strip north of the White House. But the minute I heard about Minneapolis, I knew that it was a strategic catastrophe. It broke my heart. Before then we'd always maintained that we weren't for new legislation, that we weren't trying to ban anything. Some of our younger members just couldn't comprehend that very committed feminists— our elders, our leaders, who were pulling us along by their rhetoric— could make such a big mistake that would lead the movement astray."

For a second time the Minneapolis ordinance passed, and for a second time it was vetoed by the mayor. In between the emotional roller coaster of the two tries and vetoes, Dworkin and MacKinnon were invited to Indianapolis to work up a similar ordinance for that politically conservative city.

Indianapolis was a major tactical error for the two ambitious theorists intent on creating new law. Psychologist Ed Donnerstein, recalling how comfortable he felt when he testified in liberal Minneapolis, admits that he found the citizens' coalition behind the Indianapolis ordinance "scary." He says, "I remember thinking, *What am I doing here? What are Andrea and Catharine doing here?* One guy I spoke with, a prosecutor, told me he'd use the bill against *Our Bodies, Ourselves.* It was frightening to see the ordinance becoming an issue of explicit sex for the right wing, instead of a measure against violence."

Sponsored by a conservative Republican opposed to abortion rights and the ERA, the Dworkin-MacKinnon ordinance sailed through the Indianapolis city council by a wide margin and was signed into law on May 1, 1984, by William Hudnut, the Republican mayor, who was challenged in court that same day by the American Booksellers Association and a consortium of concerned interests, including *Playboy*. In a predictable chain of events, the ordinance was declared unconstitutional for its free-speech abridgments by the Indiana district court and the federal appeals court for the Seventh Circuit, the next rung up on the judicial ladder. The Supreme Court affirmed the lower courts' rulings without comment.

Anti-anti-porn feminists, caught off guard by the first go-round in Minnesota, had gotten their act together for Indiana. Nan Hunter, an ACLU attorney with movement credentials, filed an amicus brief for the Seventh Circuit on behalf of FACT, the Feminist Anti-Censorship Task Force, an ad hoc coalition of East and West Coast activists, writers, and sexual libertarians put together by Carole Vance, Ann Snitow, and Lisa Duggan, among others, that had emerged in the wake of the clumsy, chaotic drama of the Barnard conference.

Written by Nan Hunter and Sylvia Law, an NYU law school professor, the brief for FACT ranged over a wide spectrum of sentiments and worries, expressing alarm that Lina Wertmüller's movie *Swept Away* or Lois Gould's novel *A Sea Change* might be banned under the ordinance for their powerful images of rape and submission; voicing concern that explicit scenes of lesbian sex, or erotica for any unconventional sexual minority "in a generally hostile world," might be verboten. The brief articulated the right of all groups to express their sexual identities freely; affirmed the importance of a rich fantasy life and an untrammeled sexual imagination to artists and everyone else; and questioned the ability of censors to wield power wisely.

At the heart of the FACT brief lay the contention that violent sadomasochistic pornography could be a source of pleasure for some women, while its suppression "delegitimates and makes socially invisible women who find sexually explicit images of women in positions of display or penetrated by objects to be erotic, liberating, or educational.

"Women need the freedom and the socially recognized space to appropriate for themselves the robustness of what traditionally has been male language," the brief concluded. "Laws such as the one under challenge here could restrict that freedom."

Among the seventy-five signatories were Betty Friedan, Kate Millett, and Adrienne Rich. The decision to ally herself with FACT and against the ordinance had come only after some tortured soul-searching by Rich, whose previous expressions of faith in Andrea Dworkin had attributed to her leadership "the greatest depth and grasp." In a special statement for *off our backs*, optimistically titled "We Don't Have to Come Apart over Pornography," the activist poet wrote, "I am less sure than Dworkin and MacKinnon that this is a time when further powers of suppression should be turned over to the State." The lawyer and writer Wendy Kaminer, another early WAP member, went public with *her* opposition to the ordinance a year or so later.

People on both sides of the feminist pornography wars proved to be masters of harsh invective. Antiporn activists accused the FACT women of being pro-porn, as indeed many were. Conversely, the FACT women, taking a cue from the antiabortion movement's devilishly clever "pro-life" slogan, claimed that they were the "pro-sex feminists," thus implying that antiporn feminists were against sex per se, a difficult charge to refute if the rhetoric of Dworkin and MacKinnon was taken at face value.

I was glad to be out of the direct line of fire for once in my feminist career, although my duck-and-cover maneuvers were not entirely successful since I was not about to recant my antipornography beliefs. What I remember most about this unhappy time was the visceral recoil and emanations of pure hatred that accompanied chance meetings between pros and antis, and the stricken looks of those caught in the middle who still believed that pornography was not in women's interests but had lost the resolve to continue the fight, because all of a sudden it seemed so illiberal.

Donnerstein and Malamuth, the leading researchers on pornography's effects on aggression who'd sought me out so confidently in 1979, were caught in a similar crunch. Their laboratory studies were derided by one camp as proving nothing and put forward by the other side as incontrovertible proof of causative harm. The important distinction between violent porn and the explicit but nonviolent genre, about which their newest findings and those of their colleagues were equivocal at best, got lost in the shuffle. Tugged at on all sides, the academics were having agonizing second thoughts about the wisdom of lending their names to the advocacy of social policy by the time the Meese Commmision held its anticlimactic hearings on pornography in 1985. "Frankly, I was glad when the whole debate died down," Donnerstein admits.

So, I might add, was I.

Indianapolis signaled the downhill phase of the feminist antipornography struggle, but it was by no means the end. Insurgencies cropped up in other locales—in Bellingham, Washington, and in Cambridge, Massachusetts—that were led by young radical women barely out of college. Arriving on the scene a decade after the movement's groundbreaking work on rape, battery, incest, and sexual harassment, the young radicals had imbibed the classic texts of their elders in their Women's Studies courses. They were the first generation to grow up with the legal right to abortion, which they tended to take for granted, but they had never known a world that wasn't saturated with pornography. Amid radical feminism's general decline, which they bravely tried to resist, they searched for ways to make their own contributions to theory and practice.

Twenty-two-year-old Amy Elman was working at *Sojourner*, Boston's feminist newspaper, when Kathy Barry sent her a copy of the ordinance and a packet of information. "I found a lot of it overwhelming in terms of the legalities," she recalls, "but it made brilliant sense to me, to be able to sue pornographers for harm." The future political scientist and her friends Suzanne Melendy, Ellen Abdow, Eve Goodman, and Barbara Findlen already had organized against pornography in campus actions, bringing in Linda Marchiano to speak, staging a *Playboy* protest. "Barbara was still at Boston University, and Eve had just graduated," Elman reels off. "Ellen and Suzanne had been Mary Daly students at Boston College, and I had been a Kathy Barry student at Brandeis."

For their first foray into the real world, the friends borrowed a page from the Cambridge antinuclear movement, which had succeeded in placing a referendum for its cause on the city's electoral ballot. In the summer of 1985, Elman's group, the Women's Alliance Against Pornography, took the first steps to organize a voter referendum for the ordinance in Cambridge, setting up their headquarters in Suzanne Melendy's tiny apartment.

"Pornography attracted a lot of the radical minds of my generation," Elman reflects. "It seemed to be a synthesis of so many things we were interested in—all the violence-against-women issues; and poverty, because the women drawn into the industry had so few economic options; and racism, because black women, Asian women, and Jewish women were racially stereotyped in pornography magazines; and homophobia, because the porn images of lesbian sex were lesbian-hating; and capitalism, because here was a part of big corporate America grossing billions of dollars by selling what they said was sex. The FACT women's charge that we were part of the religious right just didn't make any sense to us. We didn't see the pornography industry as *challenging* conservatism, we saw it as *part* of conservatism. You had Larry Flynt out there calling himself a born-again Christian, *hello!*"

The Women's Alliance Against Pornography collected enough signatures to get the ordinance on the ballot. "For months it was basically the five of us and Betsy Warrior knocking on doors and sitting at tables with signs lettered by Magic Markers," Elman recalls. "A locally formed FACT chapter worked with the ACLU—they were our opposition." As Election Day drew near, Andrea and Kitty gave speeches at MIT and Harvard, Therese Stanton, their best Minneapolis organizer, arrived in Cambridge to oversee the campaign, and Dorchen Liedholdt and Norma Ramos of WAP doggedly took the train up from New York on weekends. In a light turnout on a rainy day, the referendum lost by a margin of 5 percent.

"We were in despair," Elman says. "It was hard enough to be fighting pornography, to see the posters—DON'T LET THE LEZZIE CUNT KIKES TELL YOU WHAT YOU CAN'T READ—that some crazy people put up around town, but it was devastating to realize that we'd been defeated by other women, by feminists who called us homophobic and who connected us with the right wing. Those were ludicrous charges, and they knew it. They knew damn well that our group was largely lesbian, largely radical, and largely Jewish. In Cambridge the pornographers learned that they didn't have to fight us themselves, they could find a woman to do it for them. We cried. We felt like, who do we trust now?"

•   •   •

There had been an innocent bravery to the anti-pornography campaign in the beginning, a quixotic tilting at windmills in the best radical feminist tradition. But the innocence was soon submerged in a tide of philosophical differences and name-calling. Movement women were waging a battle over who owned feminism, or who held the trademark to speak in its name, and plainly on this issue no trademark existed. Ironically, the anti-porn initiative constituted the last gasp of radical feminism. No issue of comparable passion has arisen to take its place.

EPILOGUE

MILITANCE EVAPORATES for a variety of reasons, and exhaustion is only a symptom, not a cause. I felt the feminist tide recede while I was writing *Femininity*. Less than fifteen years after the Miss America Protest consigned high heels and push-up bras to the dustbin of history, the cluster of trappings I called the feminine handicap had returned with a vengeance.

A more ominous sign of the decisive shift in social currents was the long, slow failure, from 1975 to 1982, of the Equal Rights Amendment to achieve ratification. Even as the opposition grew louder, the state-by-state lobbying effort, primarily a NOW initiative, never captured the imagination of movement radicals, who were less convinced of the ERA's revolutionary potential than its hysterical opponents. Whatever the wisdom of the pro-ERA strategy and NOW's decision to give it priority over other feminist goals, its failure was a huge repudiation and defeat for us all. In a similar vein, Walter Mondale's selection of Geraldine Ferraro, a pro-choice Catholic, as his running mate in the 1984 presidential elections created a bubble of euphoria that burst in two months as the reality of her doomed campaign set in. And what malevolent trickster in the government mint honored Susan B. Anthony and the suffrage struggle with a dollar coin that looked and felt like a quarter?

It is a happier task to chart a movement's explosive rise than to record the slow seepage, symbolic defeats, and petty divisions that attend its decline. At some indefinable point in the early eighties, the feminist discourse was declared passé, replaced and superseded in the barometer of media interest by inflationary Reaganomics, the fundamentalist backlash, and two-income, have-it-all yuppie couples weighing their affluent lifestyles against the countdown of their biological clocks. Although analysis and theory had moved from the joyous spontaneity of consciousness-raising in somebody's living room to the structured world of academic research and government grants, important work continued to emerge: Carol Gilligan's studies of female developmental psychology; the analysis of the sexual politics of touching and speech patterns by Barrie Thorne, Nancy Henley, and Robin Lakoff; the numerous (and ongoing) studies by anthropologists, zoologists, biologists, geneticists, and brain researchers to get to the tantalizing heart of intrinsic sex differences and their effect on aggression; the rich and fertile fields of historical research, literary criticism, and popular culture studies.

The drive for equality in the workplace marched forward, even as its beneficiaries, dressed for success and armed with a new sense of entitlement, sought to distance themselves from the rough-edged militants who had cleared the path. As the workplace underwent its transformation, thanks to an insistent barrage of Title VII class actions and the gradual enlightenment of men in power, female ambition was no longer suspect, the subject of dire psychoanalytic caveats and mocking portrayals. Women flooded into the nation's law schools, won acceptance at medical colleges, took graduate degrees in business administration, underwent rigorous training to pass stringent physical tests for the armed services and military academies, for firefighting jobs and police work, and stepped over the fallen barriers at construction sites and executive suites. Although many obstacles remained—entrenched pockets of male resistance, inadequate day care, the Glass Ceiling, inflexible working conditions that made it difficult to balance job and family life—the biggest barriers to equality had been toppled.

Tennis and figure skating were no longer the only female athletic pursuits to command an audience and popular participation. A rethinking of the role of sports in shaping the lives of young girls led to breakthroughs on the playing fields from the primary school to the university, effectively prompted by Title IX of the Education Amendments of 1972 that threatened withdrawal of federal funds from discriminatory programs. The following decades saw a passionate surge in women's gymnastics and soccer, and vastly increased opportunities for female swimmers, runners, skiers, speed skaters, and basketball players in college, professional, and Olympic competitions.

Feminism had found a voice in the Democratic Party early on in the life of the movement; within two decades it made significant inroads in Republican circles as well. The new thinking reached beyond the temporal discourse of electoral politics to have major impact in the sacral arena. Unanticipated by secular radicals, or by those devoted to goddesses, witches, and Eastern spirituality, a powerful movement to achieve equality emerged inside traditional Western religions, changing the rituals in many houses of worship, and enriching the theologies of the Catholic, Jewish, and Protestant faiths.

Yet for all these concrete manifestions of triumph, all the incontrovertible proof of the absolute rightness of the feminist vision, the radical movement whose brash confrontations had made the world larger for women was in retreat, and its first unifying issue appeared more controversial than ever, under constant assault from religious conservatives touting the slogan of family values. More than a quarter-century after *Roe v. Wade*, the battle to keep abortion safe, legal, and accessible had remained at the forefront of the fight for equality, in an unending war against rights-of-the-fetus lawsuits, Medicaid cuts, clinic blockades, and attempts to push through a ban by constitutional amendments. We live in an age where "pro-life" now embraces—although spokesmen for the cause publicly disavow—terrorist acts of murder against abortion providers.

As the movement waned in its organized forms, its heroic volunteers, never sufficiently honored and seldom financially rewarded, turned their belated attention to their private lives, renewing emotional relationships with men, forging life partnerships with women, seeking fresh purpose as single mothers. The years when a person could live well enough with a cheap apartment and a part-time job and have time for social activism were over. Financial security had become an urgent imperative, but by and large it was a younger generation just coming into its own that stood to benefit from the new career opportunities that feminism had wrought. Attempts to forge self-contained women's communities (that is, lesbian-feminist communities) fell apart, faring no better than most other utopian experiments in communal living. The devastation of AIDS prompted many lesbian feminists to redirect their priorities and reassert their political kinship and activist ties with gay men.

By the mid-eighties most of the feminist bookstores and coffeehouses had closed their doors and *off our backs* in Washington and *Sojourner* in Boston were the last remaining vestiges of the previous decade's lusty, indigenous feminist press. Weary of trying to keep *Ms.* afloat, Gloria Steinem sold the magazine to an Australian publisher in 1987. (She has since bought it back.)

My conflict with the battered-women's advocates over the culpability of Hedda Nussbaum came at the close of a decade that had begun with the debilitating pornography wars. It was the coda that marked my decision to retreat as a public spokesperson in the feminist cause. Radical movements that are past their peak often latch on to sectarian quarrels fought with the passion of earlier times, but the new social contract we had brought into being was awash in subtle complexities and unenvisioned ambiguities that required reasoned analysis, not passionate oratory. Gains had been won from which there could be no retreat, and the victories had been sufficient for the majority of women to desire a less confrontational, more peaceable time. We had moved into a holding pattern. Put simply, feminist theory had gone as far as it could go in the twentieth century.

Still, Women's Liberation outlived the two movements that spawned it, the civil rights and antiwar struggles. By questioning traditional sex roles, we opened the door, in turn, to Gay and Lesbian Liberation. Those academicians who cry in their beer about the destructive narrowness of "identity politics" have it all wrong. The sequence of black struggles to women's struggles to gay struggles that defined the latter half of the American twentieth century seems inevitable in retrospect, as it was while it was happening. It is worth remarking that the progression toward social justice on all these fronts required fresh insights, bold commitments, and new forms of organizing that rose to the surface outside the leadership of a white/male/heterosexist left.

Rarely in history have women been able to set aside their other concerns and political causes, their divisions of class, race, religion, ethnicity, their geographic boundaries and personal attachments, in order to wage a united struggle, so revolutionary in its implications, against their basic, common oppression. Indeed, a full century passed between the struggle for suffrage and what is often called the second wave. But when such a coming-together takes place, when the vision is clear and the sisterhood is powerful, mountains are moved and the human landscape is changed forever. Of course it is wildly unrealistic to speak in one voice for half the human race, yet that is what feminism always attempts to do, and must do, and that is what Women's Liberation did do, with astounding success, in our time.

Acknowledgments

Susan Kamil of the Dial Press suggested that I write this memoir, and never lost her enthusiasm for it during five years of labor. Frances Goldin of the Frances Goldin Literary Agency brought the accumulated wisdom of a lifetime in political activism to bear on the pages at every step. Lillian Lent, Joyce Johnson, Linda Steinman, and Beth Rashbaum applied their consummate skills to early and late drafts.

I owe a large debt to the hastily penciled notes, typed chronicles, diary fragments, and mimeographed broadsides in private archives as yet undeposited in a research library collection. Barbara Mehrhof, Marilyn Webb, Florence Rush, Jane Alpert, Becky Taber, Karen Sauvigne, Pat Lynden, and Dorchen Leidholdt hauled out their cardboard cartons from the top of the closet and generously allowed me to keep them on an extended loan. Anne Koedt provided an invaluable cache of early position papers and magazine clippings. Sharon Frost, Liz O'Sullivan, Betsy Warrior, Naomi Weisstein, Lilia Melani, Mary Ann Manhart, and Alison Owings sent me pertinent folders.

I tape-recorded more than two hundred leading activists across the country in order to capture their stories and voices. These interviews, ranging from one to three hours, were transcribed with care by Terese Brown, who additionally served as my cheerleader, sounding board, and reality check.

Several historians and biographers have examined related aspects of the women's movement. I benefitted from warm collegial exchanges with Karla Jay, Rosalyn Baxandall, Judith Hennessee, Carolyn Heilbrun, Sydney Ladensohn Stern, Mary Thom, Amy Kesselman, and Barbara Winslow.

A big thanks to the Saturday Night Women's Supper Club and the gang at echonyc.com for the very fine dinners and voluble laughter, the system upgrades and tech support, and the marathon poker games that gave me a new sobriquet, Queen of the Lows. Above all, I am grateful to the activists of Women's Liberation for giving me a life that makes me proud.

Source Notes

1. The Founders (pp. 11–34)

11   Origins of the Seneca Falls Convention: Eleanor Flexner, *Century of Struggle* (Cambridge, Mass.: Belknap Press of Harvard, 1959) Chapter 5.

12   History of SNCC: Clayborne Carson, *In Struggle: SNCC and the Black Awakening of the 1960s* (Cambridge: Harvard University Press, 1981).

13   Mary King and Casey Hayden in SNCC: Mary King, *Freedom Song* (New York: William Morrow, 1987).

13   Unsigned position paper: King, Appendix 2.

14   Carmichael, "What is the position": King, p. 452.

14   "A Kind of Memo": King, Appendix 3.

14   SDS, "Heather Booth and I": Author's interview with Marilyn Webb, New York, Oct. 23, 1994.

15   In *Liberation:* King, p. 468.

16   Women in the left were gathering: Sara Evans, *Personal Politics* (New York: Vintage, 1980).

16   Robin Morgan: Author's interview with Robin Morgan, New York, Sept. 22, 1994.

17   Women's liberation workshop in Ann Arbor, "Freedom Now" resolution: Kirkpatrick Sale, *SDS* (New York: Vintage, 1974) p. 362; Evans, p. 191.

17   National Conference for the New Politics: Evans, pp.196–199; author's interview with Jo Freeman, Brooklyn, Oct. 14, 1994.

18   Meeting at Jo Freeman's: Freeman.

18   "We talked incessantly": Naomi Weisstein transcript (mimeo), November 1987, for Peg Strobel, in author's possession.

19   *Voice of the Women's Liberation Movement:* Freeman.

19   Pam Allen, "I can organize . . .": Author's phone interview with Chude Pam Allen, San Francisco, Nov. 16, 1994.

19   "free space": Pamela Allen, *Free Space: A Perspective on the Small Group in Women's Liberation* (New York: Times Change Press, 1970).

19   Regional SDS meeting, Princeton: author's interview with Allen; author's interview with Bev Grant, New York, Dec. 24, 1998; author's interview with Anne Koedt, New York, Jan. 24, 1995.

19   "Nothing could have stopped me": Anne Koedt letter to author, Jan. 22, 1999.

19   Parents in Danish resistance: Author's interview with Koedt.

20   First meeting in New York: Author's interview with Allen.

20   Something called male chauvinism: Author's interview with Kathie Amatniek Sarachild, New York, Jan. 2, 1995.

21   "Kathie and I": Author's interview with Carol Hanisch, Port Ewen, N.Y., Nov. 29, 1994.

21   "I vaguely knew": Author's interview with Anne Forer, Tucson, Ariz., by phone, March 15, 1995.

21   "called it consciousness-raising . . .": Forer.

22   Action at Jeannette Rankin Brigade march on Washington: Amy Swerdlow, *Women Strike for Peace* (Chicago: Chicago University Press, 1993) pp. 135–41; *Notes from the First Year*, June 1968 (mimeo), in author's possession; Sarachild; Hanisch; author's interview with Koedt; author's interview with Rosalyn Baxandall, New York, Oct. 10, 1994.

22   On the train ride home: Sarachild; Koedt; author's interview with Gerda Lerner, Madison, Wis., by phone, April 13, 1996.

23   "So we met at my apartment . . .": Baxandall.

24   Chicago statement from left perspective: "Towards a Radical Movement," second draft (mimeo), April 1968, files of Barbara Mehrhof.

25   Naomi Weisstein wanted to storm . . . : Weisstein interview for Peg Strobel.

25   "The women in that early group . . .": Freeman.

25   Koedt speech at Free University: Anne Koedt, "Women in the Radical Movement," *Notes from the First Year.*

25   Firestone speech at abortion rally: Shulamith Firestone, "On Abortion," *Notes from the First Year.*

26   Landmark essay: Anne Koedt, "The Myth of the Vaginal Orgasm," *Notes from the First Year.* Expanded version in Koedt, Levine, Rapone, eds., *Radical Feminism* (New York: Quadrangle Books, 1973).

27   "into a tizzy . . .": Author's interview with Koedt.

27   "sent us a nice note . . .": Author's interview with Koedt.

27   SCUM Manifesto: Excerpted in Robin Morgan, ed., *Sisterhood Is Powerful* (New York: Vintage, 1970).

28   Ti-Grace Atkinson and NOW: Martha Weinman Lear, "The Second Feminist Wave," *The New York Times Magazine*, March 10, 1968; Marcia Cohen, *The Sisterhood* (New York: Simon & Schuster, 1988) pp. 155–167; author's interview with Dolores Alexander, New York, Oct. 18, 1994; author's interview with Jacqui Ceballos, New York, Dec. 7, 1994.

28   Roxanne Dunbar's story: Author's interview with Roxanne Dunbar, San Jose, Calif., by phone, Dec. 8, 1994. See also Roxanne Dunbar, "Outlaw Woman," in DuPlessis and Snitow, eds., *The Feminist Memoir Project* (New York: Three Rivers Press, 1998).

29   Dana Densmore's story: author's interview with Dana Densmore, Santa Fe, N.M., by phone, March 29, 1995. See also Dana Densmore, "A Year of Living Dangerously," in DuPlessis and Snitow.

29   Betsy Warrior's story: author's interview with Betsy Warrior, Cambridge, Mass., July 12, 1998.

30   Webb organizes for Sandy Springs: Webb.

30   "Hi all . . .": Undated letter (mimeo) in files of Marilyn Webb.

30   Two key SDS women: Files of Marilyn Webb.

31   Dohrn on women: Naomi Jaffe and Bernardine Dohrn, "The Look Is You" (mimeo) in files of Anne Koedt.

31   Brown and Jones, "Toward a Female Liberation Movement," (mimeo) 1968: in author's possession; reprinted in Leslie B. Tanner, ed., *Voices from Women's Liberation* (New York: Signet, 1970).

31   "us against the world . . .": Hanisch.

31   "I'd never heard of Valerie Solanas . . .": Webb.

32   Sunday's anguished session: Reel-to-reel tape and transcript in files of Marilyn Webb. See also Alice Echols, *Daring to Be Bad* (Minneapolis: University of Minnesota Press, 1989) Appendix A.

2. An Independent Movement (pp. 35–58)

35   "I'd always watched the contest": Author's interview with Carol Hanisch, Port Ewen, N.Y., Nov. 29, 1994.

36   "Atlantic City and Chicago": Author's interview with Robin Morgan, New York, Sept. 22, 1994.

36   "It said 'women reporters only' . . .": Author's interview with Lindsy Van Gelder, Miami by phone, Dec. 24, 1994.

37   "It was a gorgeous day": Author's interview with Jacqui Ceballos, New York, Dec. 7, 1994.

38   "I wrote those lyrics!": Author's interview with Bev Grant, New York, Dec. 24, 1998.

38   "Martin, my husband . . .": Author's interview with Alix Kates Shulman, New York, Oct. 11, 1994.

38   By one P.M. . . .: Charlotte Curtis, "Miss America Pageant Is Picketed by 100 Women," *The New York Times*, Sept. 8, 1968; video of Miss America Protest, Museum of Television & Radio, New York.

38   "I came up from D.C.": Charlotte Bunch, *Passionate Politics* (New York: St. Martin's Press, 1987) p. 6.

39   "They were alternating . . .": Leah Fritz, *Dreamers & Dealers* (Boston: Beacon Press, 1979), p. 24.

40   Amatniek and Hanisch unfurled their banner: Author's interview with Kathie Amatniek Sarachild, New York, Jan. 2, 1995; Hanisch.

40   Stink bombs: Grant; author's interview with Peggy Dobbins, Atlanta by phone, Dec. 4, 1998.

41   Carol Hanisch excoriated: Carol Hanisch, "A Critique of the Miss America Protest," Firestone and Koedt, eds., *Notes from the Second Year*, 1970.

44   "Oddball women, rebels!": Author's interview with Irene Peslikis, New York, Sept. 23, 1994.

44   Artist Pat Mainardi's paper: Pat Mainardi, "The Politics of Housework," *Notes from the Second Year.*

45   Paper on consciousness raising: Carol Hanisch, "The Personal Is Political," *Notes from the Second Year.*

45   Mehrhof and Cronan: Author's interview with Barbara Mehrhof, New York, Sept. 11, 1994; author's interview with Sheila Cronan, Washington by phone, March 12, 1995.

46   Pam Kearon's paper: Pamela Kearon, "Man-Hating," *Notes from the Second Year.*

48   Judy Gabree's paper: J. Thibeau, "Proposal for NY Radical Women Coordinating Structure" (mimeo), files of Barbara Mehrhof.

49   WITCH history: Author's interview with Rosalyn Baxandall, New York, Oct. 10, 1994; Morgan.

50   *No More Fun and Games*: Author's interview with Roxanne Dunbar, San Jose, Calif., by phone, Dec. 8, 1994; author's interview with Dana Densmore, Santa

Fe, N.M., by phone, March 29, 1995; Densmore, "On Celibacy," first issue (undated) in author's possession, and in Leslie B. Tanner, ed., *Voices from Women's Liberation* (New York: Signet, 1970).

51 Weisstein paper: Naomi Weisstein transcript (mimeo), Nov. 1987, for Peg Strobel, in author's possession; Weisstein, "Kinder, Kuche, Kirche As Scientific Law: Psychology Constructs the Female" in Morgan, ed., *Sisterhood Is Powerful* (New York: Vintage, 1970).

52 Marilyn Webb's plans: Author's interview with Marilyn Webb, New York, Oct. 23, 1994.

52 Helen Kritzler went to Boston: Author's interview with Helen Kritzler, New York, May 24, 1995.

52 "Abby had graduated": Dunbar.

52 Chicago conference: Webb; Koedt; Ceballos; Sarachild; Hanisch; Baxandall; Mehrhof; Peslikis; Densmore; author's interview with Charlotte Bunch, New York, March 16, 1997; author's interview with Nancy Hawley, Cambridge, Mass., by phone, May 19, 1995; author's interview with Jo Freeman, Brooklyn, Oct. 14, 1994; documents (mimeo) in files of Webb, Mehrhof, Koedt.

55 Counter-Inaugural in Washington: Webb; Mehrhof; Cronan; Morgan; author's interview with Margaret Polatnik, San Jose, Calif., by phone, Jan. 22, 1995; author's interview with Ellen Willis, New York, Oct. 24, 1994; Ellen Willis, "Up from Radicalism: A Feminist Journal" in *US*, 1969 (copy in author's possession).

3. Which Way Is Utopia? (pp. 59–80)

60 Jo Freeman was the odd woman out: Author's interview with Jo Freeman, Brooklyn, Oct. 14, 1994; Joreen, "The Tyranny of Structurelessness" in Koedt, Levine, Rapone, eds., *Radical Feminism* (New York: Quadrangle, 1973); Joreen, "Trashing" in *Ms.*, April 1976.

61 Naomi Weisstein believed: Author's interview with Naomi Weisstein, New York by phone, Sept. 16, 1996.

61 Chicago Women's Liberation Union: Margaret Strobel, "Organizational Learning in the Chicago Women's Liberation Union" in Ferree and Martin, eds., *Feminist Organizations* (Philadelphia: Temple University Press, 1995); Margaret Strobel, "Consciousness and Action: Historical Agency in the Chicago Women's Liberation Union" in Judith Kegan Gardiner, ed., *Provoking Agents: Theorizing Gender and Agency* (Urbana, Il.: University of Illinois Press, 1995).

61 Naomi conducted training sessions: documents (mimeo) in author's possession.

62 "The motivation was not to stop": Author's interview with Ellen DuBois, Los Angeles by phone, Sept. 18, 1996.

62 "We were all desperately ambitious": Weisstein.

62 Boston's Cell 16: Author's interview with Roxanne Dunbar, San Jose, Calif., by phone, Dec. 8, 1994; author's interview with Dana Densmore, Santa Fe, N.M., by phone, March 29, 1995.

62 Emmanuel College: Dunbar; author's interview with Nancy Hawley, Cambridge by phone, May 19, 1995.

63 First Congress, haircutting: Dunbar.

63 "People were sobbing": Author's interview with Ivy Bottini, Los Angeles by phone, April 1, 1997.

63   Diverted the crew's attention: Bottini; Rita Mae Brown, *Rita Will* (New York: Bantam, 1997) mentions incident on p. 236 but places it erroneously at the Second Congress.

63   "The theft": Marlene Sanders and Marcia Rock, *Waiting for Prime Time* (New York: Harper Perennial, 1990) p. 118.

64   "To her credit": Densmore.

64   Dogs and cats: Densmore.

64   Group was relieved: Author's interview with Betsy Warrior, Cambridge by phone, July 12, 1998.

65   Founding and naming of Redstockings: Author's interview with Barbara Mehrhof, New York, Sept. 11, 1994; Author's interview with Ellen Willis, New York, Oct. 24, 1994.

65   Redstockings abortion work: See Source Notes for Chapter 5.

65   Fights over equality: Mehrhof; author's interview with Sheila Cronan, Washington by phone, March 12, 1995; Mehrhof's history of Redstockings (typed) in files of Barbara Mehrhof.

65   "We got together": Cronan.

66   "Kathie was very nervous": Author's interview with Irene Peslikis, New York, Sept. 23, 1994.

66   "Shulie would never": Mehrhof.

66   Ellen Willis took off: Willis.

66   "Sending literature": Peslikis.

66   Cofounder Anne Koedt on FEMINISTS: Author's interview with Anne Koedt, New York, Jan. 24, 1995.

66   Class Workshop joins FEMINISTS: Mehrhof; Cronan.

66   "Ti-Grace's philosophy": Cronan.

67   Rules of THE FEMINISTS: Susan Brownmiller, "Sisterhood Is Powerful," *New York Times Magazine*, March 15, 1970.

67   One of their tasks: Mehrhof.

67   Feldman's performance: Mehrhof.

67.   Pam Kearon found a way: Cronan.

68   FEMINISTS' papers: files of Barbara Mehrhof.

68   Resolution directed at Ti-Grace: "Declaration of THE FEMINISTS" (mimeo), April 22, 1970, files of Barbara Mehrhof.

68   Truth squads: Author's interview with Rosalyn Baxandall, New York, Oct. 10, 1994; Author's interview with Robin Morgan, New York, Sept. 22, 1994; Peslikis.

69   Origins of anthology: Morgan.

70   Friedan's stormy marriage, Plaza sit-in, and "lesbian conspiracy": Author's interview with Dolores Alexander, New York, Oct. 18, 1994; Bottini; Marcia Cohen, *The Sisterhood* (New York: Simon & Schuster, 1988) pp. 266–269, pp. 271–272; Judith Hennessee, *Betty Friedan* (New York: Random House, 1999, pp. 121–134).

70   Rita Mae Brown: Brown, *Rita Will*; author's interview with Jacqui Ceballos, New York, Dec. 7, 1994; Alexander; Bottini.

71   "The Redstockings didn't think": Rita Mae Brown, "Reflections of a Lavender Menace," *Ms.*, July/Aug. 1995

71   "Yes, Rita Mae was with us": Author's interview with Kathie Amatniek Sarachild, Jan. 2, 1995.

71   "There was such an assumption": Willis.

72   Martha Shelley: Author's interview with Martha Shelley, Oakland by phone,
        Feb. 2, 1997.

72   Origins of D.O.B.: Author's interview with Del Martin, San Francisco by phone,
        March 2, 1998.

72   Stonewall: Donn Teal, *The Gay Militants* (New York: St. Martin's Press, 1995).

73   Lesbians in Gay Liberation Front: Shelley; author's interview with Artemis
        March, Boston by phone, March 30, 1997; author's interview with Ellen
        Shumsky, New York, March 24, 1997. See also Karla Jay, *Tales of the Lavender
        Menace* (New York: Basic Books, 1999).

74   Founding of *off our backs*: Author's interview with Marilyn Webb, New York, Oct.
        23, 1994. See also Carol Anne Douglas and Fran Moira, "off our backs: The First
        Decade" and Marilyn Webb, "off our backs and the Feminist Dream" in Ken
        Wachsberger, ed., *Voices from the Underground* (Tempe, Ariz.: Mica's Press, 1993).

75   Founding of *RAT*: Morgan; author's interview with Jane Alpert, New York, Oct. 12,
        1994; Jane Alpert, *Growing Up Underground* (New York: Morrow, 1981).

76   Contents of inaugural issue: *Rat*, Feb. 9–23, 1970.

76   Several other papers: Newspapers in author's possession. Author's interviews
        with Barbara Winslow; Ann Forfreedom; Laura X; Author's interview with
        Donna Allen, Washington by phone, May 21, 1995.

77   250 local feminist publications: Donna Allen.

78   Formation of New York Radical Feminists: see Anne Koedt, "Politics of the Ego: A
        Manifesto for N.Y. Radical Feminists" in *Notes from the Second Year*; also in Koedt,
        Levine, Rapone, eds., *Radical Feminism* (New York: Quadrangle, 1973).

78   At its height NYRF had 400 members: Membership lists in author's possession.

79   Spread of consciousness-raising: Mallory Rome, "Collective Wisdom and Col-
        lective Strength: Consciousness-Raising and Second-Wave Feminism" (un-
        published paper, 1996), in author's possession.

4. Confrontation (pp. 81–101)

82   Furor at the *New York Post*: Author's interview with Lindsy Van Gelder, Miami
        by phone, Dec. 24, 1994; author's interview with Bryna Taubman, New York,
        June 13, 1996.

82   "The guys may not have understood": Taubman.

84   Which magazine and what action: To tell the story of Media Women and the
        Ladies' Home Journal sit-in, I have relied on my files augmented by interviews
        with Signe Hammer, Karla Jay, Sally Kempton, Michela Griffo, and Rosalyn
        Baxandall.

84   Article suggestions: (mimeo) in author's possession.

85   *Journal* statistics: *Ladies' Home Journal* fact sheet prepared by Sandie North
        (mimeo) in author's possession.

85   "We demand": (mimeo) in author's possession.

89   Marlene thrust her microphone forward: sit-in film by Janet Gardiner (1970) in
        Gardiner's possession.

90   "Shulie, egged on by Ti-Grace": see *Newsweek*, March 30, 1970, p. 61; Karla Jay, *Tales
        of the Lavender Menace* (New York: Basic Books, 1999) p. 118.

91   Ros had seen us wave: Author's interview with Rosalyn Baxandall, New York,
        Oct. 10, 1994.

92 Grove Press sit-in: Author's interview with Robin Morgan, New York, Sept. 22, 1994; author's interview with Martha Shelley, Oakland, by phone, Feb. 2, 1997.
94 Confrontation with Hefner on Cavett: March 26, 1970.
94 "I was incensed": Author's interview with Michela Griffo, New York, Feb. 15, 1997.
95 "We didn't really distinguish": Author's interview with Ellen Shumsky, New York, March 24, 1997.
95 "We had this gay thing": Author's interview with Artemis March, Boston by phone, March 30, 1997.
97 "The Woman-Identified Woman": photocopy with signatures by March Hoffman, et al. in author's possession; published without names in Koedt, Levine, Rapone, eds., *Radical Feminism* (New York: Quadrangle, 1973).
97 Lavender Menace action: Griffo; Shumsky; March; Jay; Shelley; author's interview with Sidney Abbott, New York, Nov. 12, 1998; Woodul's observation in Alice Echols, *Daring to Be Bad* (Minneapolis: University of Minnesota Press, 1989) p. 215; "Women's Liberation Is a Lesbian Plot," *Rat*, May 8–21, 1970.
99 "Those of us who are writers": Verna Tomasson, *"Ladies' Home Journal,"* *Rat*, April 4–18, 1970; letter from Tomasson, April 9, 1970, in author's possession.
100 Short story: "Harrison Bergeron" (1961) in Kurt Vonnegut, *Welcome to the Monkey House* (New York: Dell, 1988).
100 Alpert jumped bail: Jane Alpert, *Growing Up Underground* (New York: Morrow, 1981).

5. "Abortion Is a Woman's Right" (pp. 102–135)

102 Pre-Roe history: See Lawrence Lader, *Abortion* (Boston: Beacon Press, 1966); Patricia G. Miller, *The Worst of Times* (New York: HarperCollins, 1993).
103 Jane O'Reilly's story: Author's interview with Jane O'Reilly, Middletown, Vt., by phone, May 5, 1995.
104 Sherri Finkbine: Lader.
105 Maginnis and Society for Humane Abortion: Susan Brownmiller, "Abortion Counseling: Service Beyond Sermons," *New York*, Aug. 4, 1969.
105 British law: Susan Brownmiller, "Prospect in Parliament: Abortions Will Be Legal," *The Village Voice*, June 15, 1967.
105 Reverend Moody's abortion referrals: Brownmiller, "Abortion Counseling."
106 Founding of NARAL: Lawrence Lader, *Abortion II: Making the Revolution* (Boston: Beacon Press, 1973).
106 NOW and abortion: Lader, *Abortion II*, pp. 36–37.
107 Redstockings disrupt hearing: Author's interviews with Kathie Amatniek Sarachild, Ellen Willis, Joyce Ravitz; contemporaneous news coverage, Feb. 14, 1969; Susan Brownmiller, "Sisterhood Is Powerful," *The New York Times Magazine*, March 15, 1970.
107 Redstockings public speak-out: Author's interview with Irene Peslikis, New York, Sept. 23, 1994; Susan Brownmiller, "Everywoman's Abortions: The Oppressor Is Man," *The Village Voice*, March 27, 1969; tape recordings of speak-out, Redstockings Women's Liberation Archives, in author's possession.
109 Another journalist in aviator glasses: Author's interview with Jane Everhart, New York by phone, Feb. 12, 1995.
109 Speak-out's effect on Gloria Steinem: Gloria Steinem, *Outrageous Acts and Everyday*

Rebellions (New York: Holt, Rinehart and Winston, 1983); Carolyn G. Heilbrun, *The Education of a Woman* (New York: Dial Press, 1995).

109   "Nobody wants to reform": Gloria Steinem, "The City Politic: After Black Power, Women's Liberation," *New York*, April 7, 1969.

110   Nancy Stearns: Author's interview with Nancy Stearns, New York, August 10, 1995.

110   *Belous* and *Vuitch*: Lader, *Abortion II.*

112   *Abramowicz v. Lefkowitz:* Diane Schulder and Florynce Kennedy, *Abortion Rap* (New York: McGraw-Hill, 1971).

112   Cook bill in Albany: Lader, *Abortion II.*

114   People to Abolish and WONAAC: Author's interview with Mary-Alice Waters, Socialist Workers Party, New York, March 1, 1996; Betsey Stone and Mary-Alice Waters, "The Abortion Struggle," *SWP Discussion Bulletin*, July 1973, in *Documents of the Socialist Workers Party, 1971–86* (New York: Pathfinder Press, July 1992).

114   George Michaels: Lader, *Abortion II.*

115   Washington state referendum: Barbara Winslow, "The Struggle for Abortion Reform in Washington State 1967–1970," unpublished paper in author's possession; author's interview with Barbara Winslow, New York, March 9, 1996; author's interview with Lee Mayfield, Seattle by phone, May 28, 1996; author's interview with Jill Severn, Olympia, Wash., by phone, May 28, 1996.

117   New Jersey suit: Author's interview with Nadine Taub, New York, July 23, 1998.

117   Connecticut suit: Amy Kesselman, "Women Versus Connecticut," Rickie Solinger, ed., *Abortion Wars* (Los Angeles, University of California Press, 1998).

118   Austin Women's Liberation and *Roe v. Wade*: Author's interview with Judy Smith, Missoula, Mont., by phone, June 4, 1995; author's interview with Sarah Weddington, Austin, Tex., by phone, May 28, 1996; author's interview with Linda Coffee, Dallas by phone, May 28, 1996; Sarah Weddington, *A Question of Choice* (New York: Putnam, 1992): Norma McCorvey with Andy Meisler, *I am Roe* (New York: HarperCollins, 1994); David J. Garrow, *Liberty and Sexuality* (New York: Macmillan, 1994).

121   Georgia suit: Garrow.

123   Chicago and Jane: Laura Kaplan, *The Story of Jane* (New York: Pantheon, 1995); *Jane: An Abortion Service*, film by Kate Kirtz and Nell Lundy, Juicy Productions, Chicago, 1995; author's interview with Madelyn Schwenk, New York, March 17, 1996; author's interview with Rev. Spencer Parsons, Chicago by phone, May 27, 1996. See also *Chicago Tribune*, May 4, 5, 6, 1972.

125   Los Angeles self-helpers: Rebecca Chalker and Carol Downer, *A Woman's Book of Choices* (New York: Four Walls Eight Windows, 1992); author's interview with Carol Downer, Los Angeles by phone, March 2, 1996.

127   Hirsches in Stamford: Chalker and Downer.

127   Mini-summit: Kaplan; Downer.

128   Roy Lucas: Garrow.

129   Weddington in New York: Weddington, *A Question of Choice.*

129   "He was really presumptuous": Coffee.

129   Supreme Court arguments: Bob Woodward and Scott Armstrong, *The Brethren* (New York: Simon & Schuster, 1979).

131   Onslaught of litigation: *Women's Rights Law Reporter*, No. 2, Spring 1972.

131   Hodgson and Wheeler: Garrow.
132   Democratic Convention: Nora Ephron, "Miami," *Crazy Salad* (New York: Knopf, 1975); Germaine Greer, "McGovern, The Big Tease," *Harper's Magazine*, Oct. 1972.
132   Nixon on abortion: Garrow.
133   Effect of Connecticut case: Woodward and Armstrong.
133   Reargument: Woodward and Armstrong.
134   Reactions: Weddington, *A Question of Choice*; McCorvey and Meisler; author's interviews with Downer, Stearns, Schwenk.

6. Enter the Media (pp. 136–166)

136   Susskind Show: Author's interviews with Jane Everhart, New York by phone, Feb. 12, 1995; Rosalyn Baxandall, New York, Oct. 10, 1994; Jacqui Ceballos, New York, Dec. 7, 1995.
137   Letters poured in: Ceballos; Mehrhof.
137   Vivian Gornick: Author's interview with Vivian Gornick, New York, May 30, 1996.
138   Dudar's ambivalence: In Helen Dudar, "Women in Revolt," *Newsweek*, March 23, 1970.
139   Baumgold: Julie Baumgold, "You've Come a Long Way, Baby," *New York*, June 9, 1969.
139   Kramer: Jane Kramer, "Founding Cadre," *The New Yorker*, Nov. 28, 1970.
139   Arbus photos: "Make War, Not Love," *Sunday Times Magazine* (London), Sept. 14, 1969.
139   Brandy and *Playboy*: *Newsweek*, May 18, 1970.
140   *Newsweek* women file EEOC complaint: *The New York Times*, March 17, 1970; *The Wall Street Journal*, March 17, 1970; author's interviews with Lucy Howard, New York by phone, June 18, 1996; Pat Lynden, New York by phone, June 20, 1996; Judy Ginggold, New York, June 29, 1996; Lynn Povich, Seattle by phone, Aug. 8, 1996; Diane Camper, New York by phone, Aug. 20, 1996; Leandra Abbott, New York by phone, Aug. 21, 1996.
144   "Which side am I": Katharine Graham, *Personal History* (New York: Knopf, 1997) p. 425.
144   "a newsmagazine tradition": *The Wall Street Journal*, March 17, 1970.
146   Women at Time, Inc.: Judith Hole and Ellen Levine, *Rebirth of Feminism* (New York: Quadrangle, 1971) pp. 260–262.
146   Women's Strike for Equality: Author's interview with Ivy Bottini, Los Angeles by phone, April 1, 1997.
147   Advance publicity for march: Judy Klemesrud, "Coming Wednesday: A Herstory-Making Event," *The New York Times Magazine*, Aug. 23, 1970; Anthony Mancini, "This Week, Women Lib It Up," *New York Post*, Aug. 24, 1970; Linda Charlton, "Women Seeking Equality March on 5th Ave. Today," *The New York Times*, Aug. 26, 1970.
147   Fifty thousand marchers: Newspaper estimates ranged from ten thousand to fifty thousand.
148   "A surprising examination": Kate Millett, *Sexual Politics* (New York: Doubleday, 1970).

148   Prashker's expectations: Author's interview with Betty Prashker, New York, July 7, 1996.
148   Lehmann-Haupt reviews: *The New York Times*, Aug. 5 and 6, 1970.
148   Millett on *Time* cover: Aug. 31, 1970.
148   Spinning out of control: See Kate Millett, *Flying* (New York: Knopf, 1974).
149   Feature in *Life*: Sept. 4, 1970.
149   Neatly typed page: photocopy in author's possession.
149   "Rita Mae Brown did this": Author's interview with Martha Shelley, Oakland, by phone, Feb. 2, 1997.
149   "I never placed or wrote": E-mail from Rita Mae Brown to author, July 23, 1999.
149   "Kate came in": Author's interview with Ellen Shumsky, New York, March 24, 1997.
150   "Kate looked like": Author's interview with Sidney Abbott, New York, Nov. 12, 1998.
150   Columbia panel: Shumsky; Abbott; Millett, *Flying*, pp. 14–17.
150   "bound to discredit her": *Time*, Dec. 14, 1970.
150   Press conference: *The New York Times*, Dec. 18, 1970, p. 47; author's interviews with Alexander, Bottini, March, Shumsky, Abbott.
150   "I was standing on a huge platform": As quoted in Sara Davidson, "Fore-mothers," *Esquire*, July 1973, p. 75.
151   Firestone and Morgan: Shulamith Firestone, *The Dialectic of Sex* (New York: Morrow, 1970); Robin Morgan, ed., *Sisterhood Is Powerful* (New York: Random House, 1970).
152   Leonard's group review: *The New York Times*, Oct. 29, 1970, p. 41; see also *NYT*, Nov. 6, 1970, p. 39.
152   Inner-movement disputes: Author's interview with Robin Morgan, New York, Sept. 22, 1994.
153   WRC case: Author's interview with Mary Catherine Kilday, Washington by phone, June 16, 1996; author's interview with Alison Owings, San Francisco by E-mail, 1996; files of Alison Owings in author's possession; author's interview with Nancy Stanley, Washington by phone, April 24, 1996; author's interview with Gladys Kessler, Washington by phone, Oct. 9, 1996.
155   NBC suit: Author's interview with Marilyn Schultz, New York, Nov. 7, 1996; Gwenda Blair, *Almost Golden* (New York: Avon, 1989) pp. 213–215; files of Alison Owings.
156   Greer: Anne Coombs, *Sex and Anarchy: The Life and Death of the Sydney Push* (Australia: Penguin, 1996); Jonathon Green, *Days in the Life* (London: Heinemann, 1988); Marcia Cohen, *The Sisterhood* (New York: Simon & Schuster, 1988); Tom Wolfe, *The Purple Decades* (New York: Farrar, Straus & Giroux, 1982); author's interview with Robert Stewart, New York, Oct. 22, 1996.
158   "Saucy Feminist": *Life*, May 7, 1971.
158   Lehmann-Haupt review: *The New York Times*, April 20, 1971.
159   "Betty!" she boomed: Author's interview with Joan Lader, New York, April 6, 1996.
159   Dreifus review: Claudia Dreifus, "The Selling of a Feminist," *The Nation*, June 7, 1971.
160   *Newsweek*'s "New Woman" cover story: *Newsweek*, Aug. 16, 1971.
161   A generational difference: see Judith Hennessee, *Betty Friedan: Her Life* (New York: Random House, 1999); Sydney Ladensohn Stern, *Gloria Steinem: Her Passions, Pol-*

itics, and Mystique (New York: Birch Lane, 1997); Carolyn G. Heilbrun: *The Education of a Woman: The Life of Gloria Steinem* (New York: Dial Press, 1995).

161 The Book: Betty Friedan, *The Feminine Mystique* (New York: Norton, 1963).
162 The Bunny story: Gloria Steinem, "A Bunny's Tale," *Show*, May and June, 1963.
165 Thought it best not to sit: Heilbrun, p. 191.

7. Full Moon Rising (pp. 167–193)

168 "The media tried": Judith Hennessee, *Betty Friedan: Her Life* (New York: Random House, 1999) p. 158.
169 "Jane" prospectus: In author's possession.
170 Depending on your perspective: For a partisan's view, see Mary Thom, *Inside Ms.* (New York: Holt, 1997).
173 Their voices got lost: See Anne Koedt, "Lesbianism and Feminism," in Koedt, Levine, and Rapone, eds., *Radical Feminism* (New York: Quadrangle, 1973).
174 *The Furies*: Author's interview with Charlotte Bunch, New York, March 16, 1997; author's interview with Joan E. Biren, Washington by phone, March 15, 1999; bound volumes of *The Furies* in files of Charlotte Bunch; see also Alice Echols, *Daring to Be Bad* (Minneapolis: University of Minnesota Press, 1989), pp. 220–241.
178 Jill Johnston in separatist camp: Author's interview with Jill Johnston, New York, Nov. 4, 1997.
180 *Our Bodies, Ourselves*: Author's interviews with Nancy Hawley, Paula Doress, Vilunya Diskin, Ruth Bell, Joan Ditzion, Wendy Sanford, Jane Pincus, Judy Norsigian, Norma Swenson, Pamela Berger, in Cambridge, Mass., or by phone, May 19–Oct. 16, 1995; author's interview with Alice Mayhew, New York by phone, Aug. 10, 1995; *Women and Their Bodies* (Boston: New England Free Press, 1970); Boston Women's Health Course Collective, *Our Bodies, Ourselves* (Boston: New England Free Press, 1971); Boston Women's Health Book Collective, *Our Bodies, Ourselves* (New York: Simon & Schuster, 1973, 1976, 1984, 1992).
186 *Plexus*: Author's interview with Becky Taber, Berkeley by phone, Feb. 5, 1998; Taber manuscript (undated) and copies of *Plexus* in files of Becky Taber; author's interview with Toni Mester, Berkeley by phone, Feb. 19, 1998; author's interview with Sandra Dasmann, Santa Cruz by phone, Feb. 23, 1998; author's interview with KDF Reynolds, Oakland, by phone, March 11, 1998; author's interview with Chris Orr, Berkeley by phone, March 14, 1998; author's interview with April McMahon, Albany, Calif., by phone, March 18, 1998; E-mail from Nancy Stockwell, San Diego, Feb. 17–22, 1998.
189 *Big Mama Rag*: Author's interview with Chocolate Waters, New York, March 11, 1998; author's interview with Carol Lease, Denver by phone, March 6, 1998; author's interview with Linda Fowler, Denver by phone, March 19, 1998; author's interview with Jackie St. Joan, Denver by phone, May 17, 1998.

8. "Rape Is a Political Crime Against Women" (pp. 194–224)

195 Cell Sixteen ahead of the curve: Dana Densmore and Roxanne Dunbar, "More Slain Girls," *No More Fun and Games*, No. 3, Nov. 1969.

195   Weapon of the patriarchy: Kate Millett, *Sexual Politics* (New York: Doubleday, 1970), p. 44.

196   Los Angeles feminists struck: *Everywoman*, Vol. 1, No. 7 (1970).

201   Sheehy's piece: Gail Sheehy, "Nice Girls Don't Get Into Trouble," *New York*, Feb. 15, 1971.

202   My story: Susan Brownmiller, "On Goosing," *The Village Voice*, April 15, 1971.

202   Wolcott's letter: *The Village Voice*, May 13, 1971.

202   Greer slipped into a workshop: Partial transcript of NYRF Conference on Rape (mimeo) in files of Lilia Melani.

202   A former Black Nationalist: Partial transcript in files of Lilia Melani.

203   "Once I started reading": Author's interview with Florence Rush, New York, June 20, 1997.

203   "The sexual abuse of children": Florence Rush, "The Sexual Abuse of Children: A Feminist Point of View," Noreen Connell and Cassandra Wilson, eds., *Rape: The First Sourcebook for Women* (New York: New American Library, 1974).

204   *San Francisco Chronicle* gave extensive coverage: Diana E. H. Russell, *The Politics of Rape: The Victim's Perspective* (New York: Stein and Day, 1975) pp. 11–12.

205   "My first impulse": Author's interview with Diana Russell, Berkeley by phone, June 23, 1997.

206   D.C. Rape Crisis Center: Author's interview with Elizabethann O'Sullivan, Raleigh, N.C., by phone, June 25, 1997 and subsequent E-mail; author's interview with Karen Kollias, Cleveland by phone, July 7, 1997.

207   Their script: "How to Start a Rape Crises Center" (unsigned mimeo, 1972) in author's files.

208   O'Sullivan compiled a list: "Participating Projects" (unsigned mimeo, May 1976), in author's files.

210   "Prostitution is a crime": Susan Brownmiller, "Speaking Out on Prostitution," Koedt, Levine, Rapone, eds., *Radical Feminism* (New York: Quadrangle, 1973).

210   Weekend conference: Robin Reisig, "Sisterhood and Prostitution," *The Village Voice*, Dec. 16, 1971, and subsequent replies; flyer and program in files of Barbara Mehrhof.

212   "If white groups do not realize": Frances M. Beal, "Double Jeopardy: To Be Black and Female," Robin Morgan, ed., *Sisterhood Is Powerful* (New York: Random House, 1970).

212   National Black Feminist Organization: Author's interview with Margaret Sloan, Oakland by phone, Oct. 18, 1997; author's interview with Jane Galvin-Lewis, New York by phone, Sept. 28, 1997; author's conversations by phone with Doris Wright, Deborah Singletary, Margo Jefferson.

215   NYRF-NBFO Joint Speak-out: Flyer in author's possession.

215   Wallace kept her distance: Michele Wallace, "On the National Black Feminist Organization," Kathie Sarachild, ed., *Feminist Revolution* (New York: Random House, 1978); see also Michele Wallace, *Black Macho and the Myth of the Superwoman* (New York: Dial, 1979).

217   Michigan Women's Task Force on Rape: Legislative proposals in author's files.

218   Joan Little: James Reston, Jr., "The Joan Little Case," *The New York Times Magazine*, April 6, 1975, and subsequent news coverage; Carol Lease, "Little Freed, Feminism Raped," *Big Mama Rag*, Sept. 1975. Little's first name was variously spelled Joan, Jo-ann, and Joanne in the feminist press.

218   Inez Garcia: Jim Wood, *The Rape of Inez Garcia* (New York: Putnam, 1976); au-

thor's interview with Shoshana (Susan) Rothaizer, New York, March 5, 1998; author's interview with Susan Jordan, Berkeley by phone, Feb. 22, 1998; "War Stories: The Feminist Defense," *The Recorder* (Berkeley), Dec. 1, 1997; *Plexus*, Sept. 1974, Nov. 1974, Dec. 1974.

222 Yvonne Wanrow: *Plexus*, July 1975; Jordan.

223 Storaska book: Frederic Storaska, "How to Say No to a Rapist and Survive" (New York: Random House, 1975).

223 Broyard review: *The New York Times*, Feb. 27, 1975.

223 hounded him off the circuit: see Hope MacLeod, "Rape Film Producer Hits Back," *New York Post*, Dec. 9, 1976.

223 Highest Neilsen ratings for NBC; Janet C. Gornick and David S. Meyer, "Changing Political Opportunity: The Anti-Rape Movement and Public Policy," *Journal of Policy History*, Vol. 10, No. 4, 1998.

9. Internal Combustion (pp. 225–243)

225 A new wave in fiction: *Newsweek*, May 5, 1975.

226 Patty Hearst: *Newsweek*, Sept. 29, 1975.

226 Issue of noncooperation: See Judith Coburn, "Pat Swinton: The Sixties Go on Trial in the Seventies," *The Village Voice*, Sept. 22, 1975, p. 32.

227 Evolution of Jane Alpert: "Profile of Sam Melville" in Sam Melville, *Letters from Attica* (New York: Morrow, 1972); Jane Alpert, *Growing Up Underground* (New York: Morrow, 1981); author's interview with Jane Alpert, New York, Oct. 13, 1994.

229 As government documents show, she said she knew nothing of Pat Swinton: *United States of America v. Patricia Elizabeth Swinton*, Government Memorandum in Support of Motion for Pre-Trial Hearing, submitted by Paul J. Curran, Attorney for the United States of America, May 12, 1975, in files of Barbara Mehrhof.

229 "We Are Attica": See "Alpert Controversy" (three petitions), *Majority Report*, March 8, 1975, p. 7.

230 "Women and Violence" panel: Florence Rush, narrative of Women and Violence panel (typed, 1971), in files of Florence Rush; Ti-Grace Atkinson, *Amazon Odyssey* (New York: Links Books, 1974) pp. 199–221.

230 Popped up in a bitter dispute: Sheryl Burt Ruzek, *The Women's Health Movement* (New York: Praeger, 1978) p. 202.

230 "high level pig": Edited transcript of interview with Ti-Grace Atkinson, Pat Swinton, and others, *off our backs*, July 1975, p. 2.

231 Weatherwomen statement: *Majority Report*, April 19, 1975, p. 6.

231 Apology from *Midnight Special* writer: Letter, Oct. 7, 1977, in files of Jane Alpert.

231 Saxe and Power: Richard Harris, "Annals of Law: The Fifth Amendment" (Parts I and III), *The New Yorker*, April 5, 1976, and April 19, 1976; *off our backs*, April–May 1975, May–June 1975, July 1975; Jill Johnston, "The Myth of Bonnies Without Clydes," *The Village Voice*, April 28, 1975.

233 Redstockings CIA charge: Author's interview with Carol Hanisch, Port Ewen, N.Y., Nov. 29, 1994; author's interview with Kathie Amatniek Sarachild, New York, Jan. 2, 1995. See also Sydney Ladensohn Stern, *Gloria Steinem: Her Passions, Politics, and Mystique* (New York: Birch Lane, 1997).

234 "Gloria Steinem has": Redstockings press release, May 9, 1975, in Redstockings, *Feminist Revolution*, 1975.

236 "Gloria and I had some long discussions": Author's interview with Joanne Edgar, New York by phone, Oct. 3, 1997.

236 Willis had not been happy: Author's interview with Ellen Willis, New York, Oct. 24, 1994.

236 "a mushy, sentimental idea of sisterhood": Ellen Willis, "The Conservatism of *Ms.*" in Redstockings, *Feminist Revolution*, 1975.

236 An enterprising reporter: Author's interview with Joan Nixon, New York, Oct. 1, 1997; Joan E. Nixon, "A Watergate . . . or a Feminist Soap Opera?" *Lavender Woman*, Aug. 1975, p. 5.

237 From Mexico City: Judith Hennessee, *Betty Friedan: Her Life* (New York: Random House, 1999) pp. 209–210.

238 Sagaris: Author's interviews with Marilyn Webb, New York, Oct. 8, 1997; Joan Peters, New Milford, CT., by phone, Oct. 26, 1997; Blanche Boyd, Guilford, CT., by phone, Oct. 20, 1997; Bertha Harris, Westport, MA., by phone, Oct. 27, 1997; Alix Kates Shulman, New York, Oct. 11, 1994; Jane Galvin-Lewis, Brooklyn by phone, Sept. 28, 1997; Barbara Seaman, New York, Oct. 3, 1995; Lucinda Franks, New York by phone, Oct. 9, 1997.

240 "with no stars and bosses": "An Analysis of Sagaris, Inc. by the August 7th Survival Community (mimeo), undated, in files of Marilyn Webb.

241 "I took no orders": Gloria Steinem, "Dear Sisters of the Feminist Press" (mimeo), Aug. 13, 1975, in files of Marilyn Webb.

242 "Dissension Among Feminists": *The New York Times*, Aug. 29, 1975, p. 32.

10. Feminist Author (pp. 244–258)

245 "a conscious conspiracy": *Time*, Oct. 13, 1975.

246 *Time* celebrated twelve women: *Time*, Jan. 5, 1976.

248 "a tract celebrating lesbianism": *Commentary*, Feb. 1976.

248 Readers bombarded: *Commentary*, May 1976.

249 Angela Davis delivered the worst blow: "Angela Speaks," broadcasts on KPFA, Berkeley, Jan. 15, 1976, and Jan. 22, 1976, tapes in author's possession. See also *Freedomways*, Vol. 16, No. 1, 1976.

249 Diana Russell was hurt: Author's interview with Diana Russell, Berkeley by phone, June 23, 1997.

251 Eldridge Cleaver on *Donahue*: The programs were broadcast in Oct. 1976.

252 Four hundred rape crisis centers: Janet C. Gornick and David S. Meyer, "Changing Political Opportunity: The Anti-Rape Movement and Public Policy," *Journal of Policy History*, Vol. 10, No. 4, 1998.

253 Changes in state laws: Gornick and Meyer.

254 "Shere arrived in something flowing": Author's interview with Regina Ryan, New York by phone, Oct. 1, 1997.

255 The next feminist bestseller: Author's interview with Marilyn French, New York, Nov. 18, 1997.

256 "It took me three days": Author's interview with Charlotte Sheedy, New York by phone, Nov. 10, 1997.

11. "No Man Is Worth Dying For" (pp. 259–278)

259   Pioneering book: Erin Pizzey, *Scream Quietly or the Neighbours Will Hear* (London: Penguin, 1974).

259   Housewife with a BBC reporter husband: Author's interview with Erin Pizzey, San Giovanni d'Asso, April 5, 1997.

259   Officially thrown out: Pizzey; author's interview with Sheila Rowbotham.

259   Born in China: Erin Pizzey, *Infernal Child* (London: Victor Gollancz, 1978).

260   "Kathy didn't say anything": Author's interview with Pizzey.

262   *Time*'s London bureau: Author's interview with Pizzey.

262   Karen Durbin reported: Karen Durbin, "A Simple Truth," *The Village Voice*, May 2, 1994, p. 22.

262   Editors stalled for a year: Author's interview with Karen Durbin, New York, April 3, 1998.

262   "The subject was strange": Karen Durbin letter to author, March 18, 1998.

262   Anecdotal account: Karen Durbin, "Wife-Beating," *Ladies' Home Journal*, June 1974.

262   Sandy Ramos believes: Author's interview with Sandy Ramos, Ringwood, N.J., by phone, May 4, 1998.

263   Woman's Advocates: Author's interview with Sharon Rice Vaughan, St. Paul by phone, March 16, 1998; author's interview with Susan Ryan, Minneapolis by phone, May 19, 1998.

265   "Gay men were just as sexist": Author's interview with Del Martin, San Francisco by phone, March 2, 1998.

266   Walker had begun to collect data: Author's interview with Lenore Walker, Denver by phone, March 13, 1998.

267   Expert witness: Lenore Walker, *Terrifying Love* (New York: Harper & Row, 1989)

269   Differences in philosophy: Author's interview with Esta Soler, San Francisco by phone, March 20, 1998; see also Del Martin, *Battered Wives* (San Francisco: Glide, 1976). Many of the disputes were played out in *Aegis*, a Washington, D.C., publication.

270   La Casa del Las Madres: Author's interview with Marya Grambs, Albany, Calif., by phone, July 7, 1998.

272   Women's Survival Space: Author's interview with Yolanda Bako, New York, March 9, 1998.

273   Betsy Warrior's hopes: Author's interview with Betsy Warrior, Cambridge by phone, July 12, 1998.

276   Pizzey tackled the question: Erin Pizzey and Jeff Shapiro, *Prone to Violence* (London: Hamlyn, 1982).

276   "I was picketed": Author's interview with Pizzey.

277   approximately 1800 shelters: Soler.

277   A novel: Susan Brownmiller, *Waverly Place* (New York: Grove Press, 1989).

277   My opinions: Susan Brownmiller, "Hedda Nussbaum, Hardly a Heroine," *The New York Times*, Feb. 2, 1989; Susan Brownmiller, "Madly in Love," *Ms.*, April 1989. The *Ms.* article was reprinted in the paperback edition of *Waverly Place* (New York: Signet, 1989).

278   Reaction from battered women's advocates: See Paula Span, "Women Protest 'Hedda-Bashing,' *The Washington Post*, March 13, 1989.

12. Its Name Is Sexual Harassment (pp. 279–294)

Note: Some of the material in this chapter is based on interviews conducted by Dolores Alexander and me for Susan Brownmiller and Dolores Alexander, "From Carmita Wood to Anita Hill," *Ms.*, January/February 1992 (interview notes in author's possession).

279   Cornell had created: Author's interview with Karen Sauvigne, New York, Feb. 13, 1998.

279   Lin Farley established: Brownmiller and Alexander.

280   Meyer, an antiwar activist: Author's interview with Susan Meyer, New York, Jan. 12, 1999.

280   Organizing for Lesbian Feminist Liberation: Sauvigne; Meyer.

280   Carmita Wood, 44: Brownmiller and Alexander; "Protest Sexploitation," *Ithaca New Times*, April 13, 1975; "Working Women Form Campaign To Expose Sexual Harassment," *Cornell Daily Sun*, April 18, 1975; "Ithacan Testifies on Job Sexual Harassment," *Ithaca Journal*, April 22, 1975.

280   Wood told the story: Sauvigne.

282   First speak-out: transcript of May 4, 1975, speak-out (mimeo) in files of Karen Sauvigne.

283   "The titillation value": Brownmiller and Alexander.

284   It finally appeared: Enid Nemy, "Women Begin to Speak Out Against Sexual Harassment at Work," *The New York Times*, Aug. 19, 1975, p. 38.

284   Front-page feature: Mary Bralove, "Career Women Decry," *The Wall Street Journal*, Jan. 29, 1976.

284   Mary Thom remembers: Mary Thom, *Inside Ms.* (New York: Holt, 1997) pp. 106–108.

284   Second *Times* headline: Ann Crittenden, "Women Tell of Sexual Harassment at Work," *The New York Times*, Oct. 25, 1977.

285   Farley started a book: Lin Farley, *Sexual Shakedown: The Sexual Harassment of Women on the Job* (New York: McGraw-Hill, 1978).

285   "I thought my book would change the workplace": Brownmiller and Alexander.

285   Adrienne Tomkins: Brownmiller and Alexander.

285   "The judge said": Author's interview with Nadine Taub, New York, July 23, 1998.

286   Most of the aggrieved women were black: "Digest of Leading Sexual Harassment Cases," prepared by Karen Sauvigne for Working Women's Institute (mimeo), Sept. 1981, in files of Karen Sauvigne; see also Catharine A. MacKinnon, *Sexual Harassment of Working Women* (New Haven: Yale University Press, 1979). Both documents identify race of complainants.

287   Unionizing efforts of Karen Nussbaum: Brownmiller and Alexander.

287   Merit Systems: Brownmiller and Alexander; "9,000 Women in U.S. Jobs Tell Sex Harassment," Chicago *Sun-Times*, Sept. 26, 1980, p. 32.

288   "First decent methodological study": Brownmiller and Alexander.

288   "When I came to the Commission": Brownmiller and Alexander; notes of 1991 interview with Eleanor Holmes Norton in author's possession.

288   Norton's 1980 EEOC guidelines: Facsimile of published guidelines in author's possession; excerpt appears in Laura W. Stein, *Sexual Harassment in America: A Documentary History* (Westport: Greenwood Press, 1999) p. 33.

288   Catharine MacKinnon had learned: Sauvigne.

289   "repressive impositions": MacKinnon, p. 173.
289   "Inventing special rules of morality": MacKinnon, p. 173.
289   Her identification with the issue: See Fred Strebeigh, "Defining Law on the Feminist Frontier," *The New York Times Magazine*, Oct. 6, 1991; Jeffrey Toobin, "The Trouble with Sex," *The New Yorker*, Feb. 9, 1998.
289   Anita Hill: Anita Hill, *Speaking Truth to Power* (New York: Doubleday, 1997); "Sex, Lies & Politics," *Time*, Oct. 21, 1991; *The New York Times*, Oct. 12, 14, 15, 1991.
291   Lois Robinson: Excerpt from district court opinion in *Robinson v. Jacksonville Shipyards, Inc.*, in J. Ralph Lindgren and Nadine Taub, *The Law of Sex Discrimination*, 2nd ed. (Minneapolis: West Publishing Co., 1993) pp. 220–221.
294   Oncale: Linda Greenhouse, "High Court Widens Workplace Claims in Sexual Harassment," *The New York Times*, March 5, 1998, p. 1.

13. The Pornography Wars (pp. 295–325)

295   1970 Presidential Commission report: *The Report of the Commission on Obscenity and Pornography* (Washington: U. S. Government Printing Office, Sept. 1970).
295   *Miller v. California*: Warren Weaver, "Supreme Court Tightens Rule Covering Obscenity, Gives States New Power," *The New York Times*, June 22, 1973.
297   Smears: *Hustler*, May 10, 1976; *Screw*, Aug. 27, 1973; Jan. 12, 1976; March 6, 1978; smears of other women in author's possession.
297   "to pose in the *Hustler* tradition": facsimile of Flynt's letter to Gloria Steinem, Feb. 27, 1976, in author's possession.
297   *Snuff*: Leah Fritz, "Why We Had To Picket *Snuff*," *The Village Voice*, April 12, 1976.
298   Fled from her battering husband: Author's interview with Andrea Dworkin, Brooklyn, Aug. 10, 1998.
298   Her first book: Andrea Dworkin, *Woman Hating* (New York: Dutton, 1974).
298   WAVAW spray-painted: WAVAW press release, June 22, 1976, in author's possession.
298   Manager offered his personal apology: *Rolling Stone*, July 1976.
299   Draft statements of Women for the Abolition: In author's files.
299   "We did not spend our time": Author's interview with Diana Russell, Berkeley by phone, June 23, 1997.
300   Rashly accepted free office space: Author's interview with Laura Lederer, Arlington, Va., by phone, Oct. 24, 1998.
300   WAVPAM actions: *Newspage* (WAVPAM newsletters) in author's files.
300   "Dianne Feinstein was mayor then": Lederer.
301   Plunged nine thousand dollars in debt: Russell.
301   The conference: Conference program (mimeo) and *Newspage* Special Issue: Conference Report in author's files.
301   Opening address: Kathleen Barry, "Beyond Pornography: From Defensive Politics to Creating a Vision" in Laura Lederer, ed., *Take Back the Night* (New York: Morrow, 1980) pp. 307–312.
305   Georgia Dullea took: Georgia Dullea, "In Feminists' Antipornography Drive, 42nd Street Is the Target," *The New York Times*, July 6, 1979, p. A12.
308   East Coast conference: program in author's files.
309   Leslie Bennetts: *The New York Times*, Sept. 17, 1979, p. B10.
311   "sea of waving placards": *The New York Times*, Oct. 21, 1979.

313 Willis review: *The New York Times Book Review*, July 12, 1981, p. 9.

314 "I was horrified": Author's interview with Dorchen Leidholdt, New York, Aug. 30, 1998.

314 "I enjoy leathersex": Pat Califia, "Feminism and Sadomasochism," *Heresies*, Vol. 3, No. 4, Issue 12, 1981.

314 Months of planning: See Carol Vance, *Pleasure and Danger* (Boston: Routledge & Kegan Paul, 1984).

315 A pastiche: "Diary of a Conference on Sexuality" (offset) in files of Dorchen Leidholdt.

315 Accusing Adrienne Rich: *off our backs*, June 1982.

315 Lesbian Sex Mafia: *off our backs*, June 1982.

315 Novelist Bertha Harris recalls: Author's interview with Bertha Harris, Westport, MA., by phone, Oct. 27, 1997.

316 Four reporters: *off our backs*, June 1982.

316 "I think most lesbian feminists were dismayed": Author's interview with Carol Anne Douglas, Washington by phone, Sept. 9, 1998. See also Carol Anne Douglas, *Love and Politics* (San Francisco: ism press, inc., 1990).

316 Dworkin invited her new friend: Dworkin.

317 At which Marchiano was to go public: See Linda Lovelace with Mike McGrady, *Ordeal* (Secaucus, NJ: Citadel, 1980).

318 Stated that pornography was "central": Copy of ordinance in author's possession.

318 A score of local women: Catharine A. MacKinnon and Andrea Dworkin, eds., *In Harm's Way: The Pornography Civil Rights Hearings* (Cambridge: Harvard University Press, 1997).

319 "I thought it was fucking brilliant": Author's interview with Robin Morgan, New York by phone, Sept. 25, 1998.

319 She persuaded Women Against Pornography to contribute: Leidholdt.

320 Split Feminists Against Pornography: Author's interview with Janet Gornick, New York, Nov. 4, 1998.

320 Donnerstein found Indianapolis coalition "scary": Author's interview with Ed Donnerstein, Santa Barbara by phone, Sept. 23, 1998.

321 At the heart of the FACT brief: Nan D. Hunter, Sylvia A. Law, "Brief Amici Curiae of Feminist Anti-Censorship Taskforce" in the United States Court of Appeals for the Seventh Circuit, April 8, 1985 (mimeo), in author's possession.

322 "greatest depth and grasp": Tribute by Rich on back cover of Andrea Dworkin, *Pornography: Men Possessing Women* (New York: Perigee, 1981).

322 "We Don't Have to Come Apart": *off our backs*, 1985, No. 7, p. 22, as quoted in Douglas, *Love and Politics*, p. 198.

322 Wendy Kaminer went public: See Wendy Kaminer, "Feminists Against the First Amendment," *Atlantic Monthly*, Nov. 1992.

323 "it made brilliant sense to me": Author's interview with Amy Elman, New York, Sept. 30, 1998; all Elman quotes from this interview.

Index